A MILLENNIUM GUIDE TO THE

D1044550

HOLY ROME

JAN - 7 2000

FODOR'S TRAVEL PUBLICATIONS, INC.
NEW YORK • TORONTO • LONDON • SYDNEY • AUCKLAND

WWW.FODORS.COM

CLEMENS XI
PONT·MAX·
FONTIS ET FORI
ORNAMENTO
ANNO SAL·
MDCCXI
PONTIF·XI

M·AGRIPPA·L·F

180.2034

Fodor's Holy Rome

Concept and design: Fabrizio La Rocca
Editorial development: Asterisco s.r.l. – Milano
Project editor: Luca Giannini

Editorial contributors: Emilio Del Gesso, "Rome of Saints and Martyrs"; Francesco Scoppola and Stella Diana Vordemann, "Rome's Jubilees: Origins and Chronology"; Carla Compostella, Holy Rome section; Donata Chiappori, Artists in Rome biographies.
Translation: Meg Shore
Copyediting: Ellen E. Browne

Photography: Luciano Romano* (with the exception of those listed on p. 180)
Layout: Tigist Getachew
Photo research: Ornella Marcolongo
Rome Atlas: Cartographic Service of the Touring Club Italiano
Prepress: Emmegi Multimedia – Milano

The section *Rome, the Year 2000, and the Christian Jubilee* was prepared by the Rome Agency for Jubilee Preparations.
Contributors: Francesco Bandarin, Caterina Cardona, Alberto Cortese, Maurizio d'Amore, Angela Stahl

Fodor's Travel Publications, Inc.
President: Bonnie Ammer
Publisher: Kris Kliemann
Editorial director: Karen Cure
Creative director: Fabrizio La Rocca

Touring Club Italiano
President: Giancarlo Lunati

Touring Editore
Chief executive officer and director general: Armando Peres
Vice presidents: Marco Ausenda and Radames Trotta
Editorial director: Michele D'Innella

Copyright © 1999 Touring Editore s.r.l. – Milano

Fodor's is a registered trademark of Random House, Inc.

All rights reserved under International and Pan-American Copyright Conventions. No maps, illustrations, or other portions of this book may be reproduced in any form without written permission from the publishers.

Published in the United States by Fodor's Travel Publications, Inc., a division of Random House, Inc., New York, and simultaneously in Canada by Random House of Canada, Limited, Toronto.
Published in Italy by Touring Editore s.r.l. – Milano
Distributed in the United States by Random House, Inc., New York.

ISBN 0–679–00454–8
First Edition

Acknowledgments
The Fondo Edifici di Culto (F.E.C.), which is controlled by the Department of Interior's Central Office for Religious Affairs, was established by Law N. 222 of May 20, 1985, following the February 18, 1984, agreement between the Italian State and the Holy See. It oversees over 600 sacred buildings in the country, as well as the works of art housed in these structures, an invaluable documentation of cultural developments in Italy over the course of centuries. The goal of the F.E.C. is to show off this patrimony to its greatest advantage, in terms of both preservation and protection and promotion.

Special Sales
Fodor's Travel Publications are available at special discounts for bulk purchases for sales promotions or premiums. Special editions, including personalized covers, excerpts of existing guides, and corporate imprints, can be created in large quantities for special needs. For more information, contact your local bookseller or write to Special Markets, Fodor's Travel Publications, 201 East 50th Street, New York, NY 10022. Inquiries from Canada should be directed to your local Canadian bookseller or sent to Random House of Canada, Ltd., Marketing Department, 2775 Matheson Boulevard East, Mississauga, Ontario L4W 4P7. Inquiries from the United Kingdom should be sent to Fodor's Travel Publications, 20 Vauxhall Bridge Road, London SW1V 2SA, England.

Printed in Italy by Amilcare Pizzi S.p.A., Italy

10 9 8 7 6 5 4 3 2 1

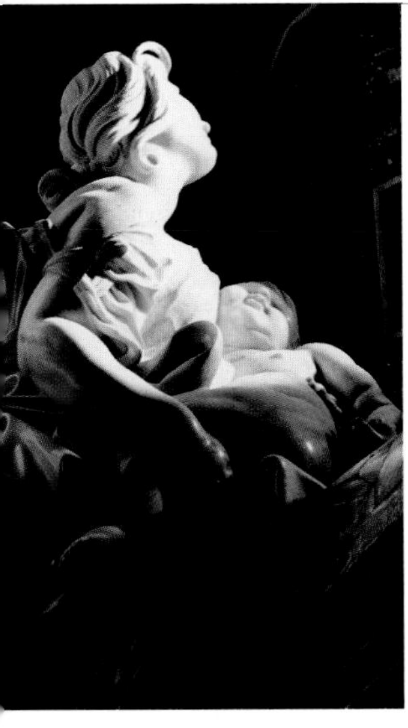

Gian Lorenzo Bernini and assistants, Tomb for Alexander VII Chigi, detail of the face of the Bambino della Carità (Infant Jesus of Charity).

Previous page: Piazza della Rotonda, with the fountain designed by Giacomo della Porta and, on the right, the Pantheon.

Contents

How to Use this Book

A GUIDE TO CHRISTIAN ROME

This book is organized in three sections. The first consists of two essays, dedicated respectively to Rome of the saints and martyrs and to the origins and history of the Jubilee. More than a historical-religious introduction, these essays are a key to the thematic interpretation of Christian Rome. Indeed, the dominant theme of the book is Christianity, experienced through churches, basilicas, tombs of saints and martyrs, catacombs, mausoleums, monasteries, and all the sites that have made Rome a Holy City as well as the Eternal City. Descriptions of these sites make up the entire second section of the book, Holy Rome. The third section contains information of a more practical nature. In 16 pages, the Roman Agency for Jubilee Preparations describes its preparations in the capital for the year 2000 and details the major religious and cultural events. The pages entitled Artists in Rome provide biographical summaries for Rome's most exemplary artists. Finally, the Rome Atlas contains 16 pages of information-filled maps.

Boxes complement the text and provide additional **biographical, historical,** and **artistic** information.

Flagellation
S. Prassede (☞126)
houses the relics of
and part of the
S. Maria Maggiore
(☞144)
In the apse of the middle
nave of the basilica, a
beautiful mosaic by
Jacopo Torriti depicts
the nine choirs of
2
3

Cross-references allow the reader to move from the essays to the Holy Rome section, where the monuments are described.

Small **maps** at the bottom of essay pages accompany the thematic itineraries, illustrating their stages and placing them within the urban context.

Thematic itineraries suggest sites that best illustrate the contents of the essays.

THE GEOGRAPHY OF A CAPITAL

The section Holy Rome consists of 12 chapters listing city monuments most closely linked to the history of Rome as the capital of Christianity. These chapters contain groupings of the 22 *rioni*, or districts, that make up the center of Rome, as defined by the 3rd-century Aurelian Walls that marked the outer limits of the city until the 19th century. The term *rioni* comes from the Latin word *regiones,* which referred to administrative subdivisions of ancient Rome. During the Augustan period there were 14 districts, but the number varied during the Middle Ages. When the municipality was reorganized in 1144, their number changed to 12, then 13 in the early 14th century, and 14 again in 1586. Their boundaries were confirmed in the administrative reorganization of 1743–1744, under Pope Benedict XIV. In 1874 the Monti *rione* was reduced in size and the Esquiline *rione* created. Finally, in 1921, 7 new *rioni* were carved out from the existing ones, raising the number from 16 to 22.

Each of the 12 chapters in the Holy Rome section is cross-referenced to an **area map** that illustrates the *rioni* discussed in the chapter and refers to the Rome Atlas for a more detailed view.

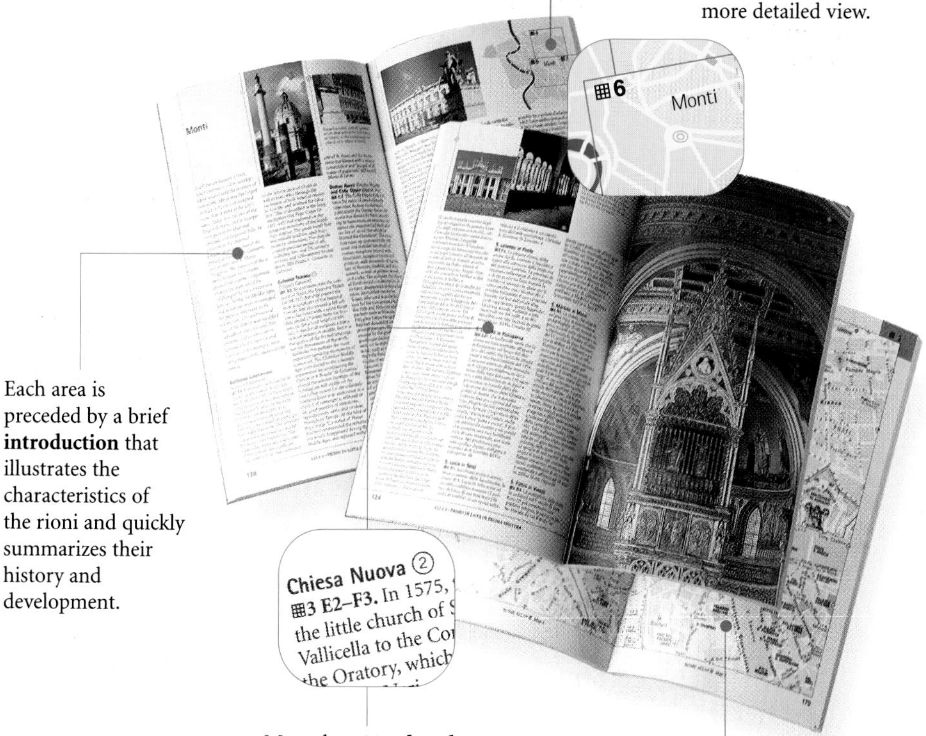

▦6
Monti
Chiesa Nuova ②
▦3 E2–F3. In 1575,
the little church of S
Vallicella to the Co
the Oratory, which

Each area is preceded by a brief **introduction** that illustrates the characteristics of the rioni and quickly summarizes their history and development.

More than 300 **churches, palazzi, streets, piazzas,** and **monuments**—all closely linked to the history of Christian Rome—are cross-referenced to individual maps marked by ▦ in the Rome Atlas (**▦3 E2-F3** indicates map 3, grid coordinates E2 and F3).

The **Rome Atlas**, on a 1:7500 scale, contains eight maps of the city with its most important monuments drawn in 3D. Readers can use this precise, essential tool to get their bearings in the center of the city.

Foreword

It is a great pleasure for me to introduce the Italian and international public to this guidebook. The entire publication is dedicated to Rome in the year 2000, when the city will celebrate the Jubilee that marks the passage from the second to the third millennium of the Christian era.

Promoted and developed by the Touring Club Italiano, by Fodor's Travel Publications, and by the Rome Agency for Jubilee Preparation, this guidebook focuses on the exceptional historical significance of the Jubilee, with an understanding that this is an occasion for spiritual reflection that can unite us. This book also conveys the city's pivotal position in a dialogue among peoples, an encounter between different cultures, in the support of peace.

Rome is a special city with unique characteristics. It is the capital of two states. It is also one of the few capital cities in the world that is the product of a millennial history still visible in its archaeological zones, in its streets and piazzas, in its monuments, both civil and religious. Rome is a complex city, and its celebrated beauty and destiny as a great center of international tourism must be compatible with the equally complex workings of a modern metropolis.

This is one of the reasons why, in recent years, Rome has made significant organizational efforts to prepare for this extraordinary event, which will draw millions of pilgrims and visitors. The face of the city has been renovated, new infrastructures have been put in place, and new services for pilgrims and tourists have been made available.

In the year 2000 Rome will be delighted and proud to welcome its guests, who will find a city that is renewed, thoughtful, and ready to receive them, with a yearlong series of events, as well as occasions for spiritual and cultural enrichment. Throughout the Holy Year, those who travel to Rome for religious reasons will be able to experience moments of intense emotion, and the cultural offerings will also be extraordinary. The importance of the passage of the millennium in our city is reflected in exhibitions, theaters, concerts, new installations in the city's great museums, and the renovation of spaces for culture and art.

Giulio Carlo Argan, a great man of culture and an unforgettable mayor of Rome in the 1970s, wrote, "from the 16th to the 18th century, Rome was for European art what Paris was in the 19th century and the first half of the 20th century." He added that "of all the European metropolises, Rome is without doubt the most visited, portrayed and described."

This book is not intended to be yet another guidebook to Rome. Rather it should be viewed as a precious traveling companion on the occasion of the Jubilee. Its originality and scope lie in its inspired mix of holy Rome, historic Rome, and everyday Rome, with all three taken into consideration and presented to the reader as a living and indivisible totality.

Without denying the ancient tradition of the Mirabilia Urbis, which, over the course of centuries, informed generations of travelers—pilgrims, scholars or those who were simply curious—about the legacy of the Eternal City, this book pursues new and different pathways that lead to a discovery of Rome in the year 2000. Thus, while it is accurate and exhaustive in every fact that pertains to historical Jubilee events, it also plays a secular role by presenting a wealth of cultural and tourism information. The coexistence of sacred and profane, which makes Rome such an interesting sociological phenomenon, has long prevailed along the banks of the Tiber.

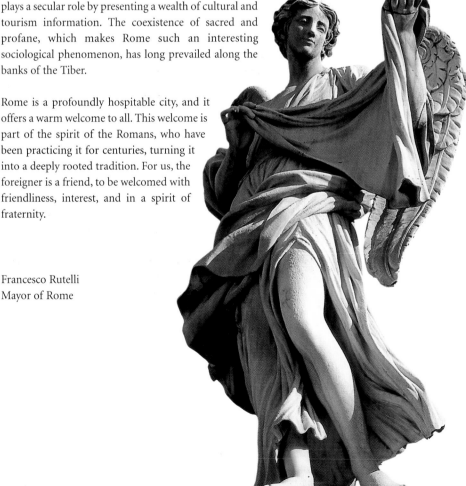

Rome is a profoundly hospitable city, and it offers a warm welcome to all. This welcome is part of the spirit of the Romans, who have been practicing it for centuries, turning it into a deeply rooted tradition. For us, the foreigner is a friend, to be welcomed with friendliness, interest, and in a spirit of fraternity.

Francesco Rutelli
Mayor of Rome

Opposite page:
St. Peter Presenting St. Cosma,
detail of the apse mosaic,
basilica of Ss. Cosma e Damiano.

ROME OF SAINTS AND MARTYRS

Rome's spiritual ties are deep, rooted in the early centuries of Christianity, and the city has always been known in Italian as "Roma Santa"—Holy Rome. This is in no small part because of the close ties it has had with its saints and martyrs and their relics through its entire history, up until the modern era.

Saints have been associated with Rome since St. Paul's letter to the Romans, which he addressed "to all God's beloved in Rome who are called to be saints" (Romans, 1:7, *Oxford Bible*). This use of the word "saint," applied to the Christian community's spiritual leaders at the time, had a much broader significance then than now. For the early Christians, "saint" ("devoted to worship," *sanctus* in Latin, *hagios* in Greek) was applied to those who played an important role in the community. According to another interpretation, which came to Christianity from the Jewish tradition, "saint" meant "separate" or "distinct." In the Christian religion all people could potentially become saints because Christ had sacrificed himself to redeem humanity from sin, but in the new Christian society, a category was created almost immediately for people who were "different," in that they were saints and officially recognized as such after death.

THE AGE OF PERSECUTIONS

When Paul arrived in Rome in AD 61, Christians were subject to no specific restrictions, nor did they endure threats from public institutions. But just three years later, during the summer of AD 64, when much of the city was devastated by fire, the emperor Nero, himself suspected of having caused the blaze, initiated the first persecution of the Christians. It was an isolated episode that took place only in Rome. Persecutions that involved all the empire's territories began in the 3rd century.

The idea of continuous persecutions sowed terror throughout the Roman world for 400 years after Jesus' death, but the systematic murder of hundreds of thousands of victims belongs more to the medieval imagination than to actual events. In the same way, the image of crowds of Christians hunted down

WHO DECIDES WHO IS A SAINT?

Today an individual achieves sainthood in the Catholic Church via canonization—that is, inclusion in a canon, a type of list. Canonization occurs only after a long inquiry by ecclesiastic authorities that involves the presentation of arguments for and against sainthood. One party provides proofs in favor of a candidate, while another party—the so-called devil's advocate—seeks to present counterproofs. If it is determined that the individual has accomplished at least two miracles after death, then he or she is beatified. Beatification, which confers the title of "Blessed," is the first step on the road to sainthood. Formal canonization, which may take decades, if not centuries, requires that other miracles be proved as well, and can be approved only by the pope. In the early centuries of Christianity becoming a saint was much simpler. A community could simply proclaim a person a saint by acclamation (*vindicatio* in Latin), as depicted in a scene in a panel on the wooden portal of S. Sabina (☞ 122).

The apostle Peter; detail of the mosaic in S. Maria Maggiore.

PETER AND PAUL IN ROME

Information about the martyrdom of these two saints is contradictory. Nevertheless, Rome is filled with sites that commemorate their presence and their suffering.

① **Basilica di S. Pietro** (☞ 52)
The largest sanctuary in Christendom is dedicated to the first apostle. The Crypt of St. Peter's contains the tomb of Peter, who suffered martyrdom a short distance away, in the Vatican circus.

A statue of the apostle in Piazza S. Pietro.

② **Carcere Mamertino** (☞ 110)
In this ancient water cistern transformed into a prison (opposite the Forum, on the slopes of the Campidoglio), Peter and Paul were held. Legend has it that they both baptized their jailers.

S. Francesca Romana's church and bell tower.

and hiding in the catacombs has it roots more in its portrayal in 19th-century paintings or novels such as *Quo Vadis?* and 1950s films such as *The Robe* and *Ben Hur*, than in historical sources. Although no one will never know how many early Christians were sent to their deaths for their beliefs, it is not impossible that, as historian K.T. Ware wrote in his *Orthodox Church*, more Christians died for their faith between 1918 and 1948 than in the 300 years following the crucifixion.

What inspired the persecutions is not clear. In the 1st century AD, far from looking upon Christians as a danger, Rome viewed them as a possible stabilizing political factor in the eastern Mediterranean, a means for pacifying a rebellious Judea. The messianic Christian "barbarians" could be more easily tamed, the reasoning went, than extremists such as the Zealots. After the death of Nero in AD 68, Christians enjoyed a period of tranquillity, and imperial authority seemed more concerned with protecting Christians than persecuting them; episodes of intolerance arose from the desire of certain provincial governors to display their power or to a specific emperor's politics and not from any deep-rooted policies held by the central government.

Nonetheless, Christians troubled the Roman world. Their belief in Jesus' sole authority set them apart from their fellow Romans and made them appear to be enemies of the state. Their belief in another God was disputed, although Rome had a policy of religious tolerance and even adopted the beliefs of conquered peoples on occasion. But the Christians' refusal to submit to imperial authority could not be supported, particularly in the provinces, which were perpetually under pressure to demonstrate their loyalty. In addition, Christians not only wanted to worship as they pleased, they also wanted to impose their new morality on the empire. To Romans, such proselytism was incomprehensible. Christians' ways were deemed subversive, but the line between lawful and unlawful behavior was blurred, and the decision to order a persecution often depended on a particular emperor's politics.

During this era, as emperors struggled to maintain the political balance or to distract impoverished classes from yet another social crisis, systematic persecutions alternated with restrictions

PLINY'S DOUBTS, TRAJAN'S RESPONSE

In AD 110 writer Pliny the Younger was governor of Bithynia and Pontica, and in his correspondence with Trajan about various political problems, he referred to the Christians. Pliny asked advice "about the great number of persons accused; in fact, without consideration of age, social class or sex, many are put on trial.... The contagion of this superstition now has become widespread, not only in the cities, but also in villages and in the countryside." Trajan responded in temperate fashion: "In general, one cannot establish a valid rule.... They should not be sought out; if they are denounced and are found guilty, they should be punished.... And as for anonymous denunciations, these mustn't be taken as valid in any trial, for they have the characteristics of the worst precedents and are not fitting for our times."

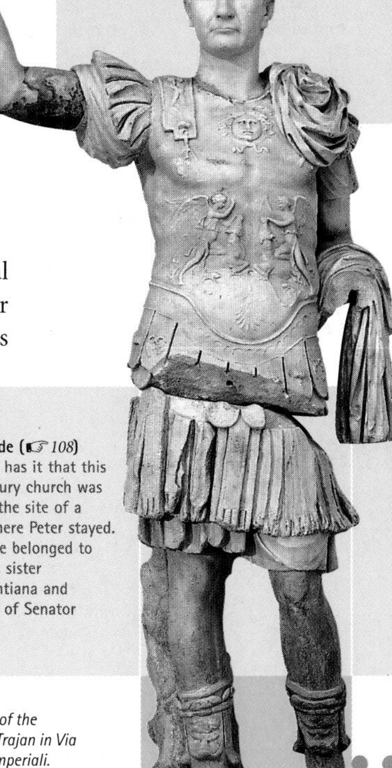

③ **S. Francesca Romana** (☞ *113*)
The church contains two stones said to bear the knee prints of the apostles, who knelt and prayed for the sorcery of Simon Magus to be revealed. In an attempt at flight the latter did indeed fall to his death.

④ **S. Pietro in Vincoli** (☞ *108*)
Housed in this church are the chains that bound Peter. For some time they were divided in two pieces, one in Rome, the other in Jerusalem. When they were placed next to each other, they miraculously fused.

⑤ **S. Prassede** (☞ *108*)
Tradition has it that this 5th-century church was built on the site of a house where Peter stayed. The house belonged to Praxedes, sister St. Pudentiana and daughter of Senator Pudente.

A bronze of the emperor Trajan in Via dei Fori Imperiali.

STRANGERS AMONG US

In Rome, the debut of a religion that arose from the Judaic world and that was expressed in Greek concepts and terms had more or less the same effect as the arrival of aliens in a spaceship. It is no wonder that great writers such as Svetonius or Tacitus described the Christians as a "race of men devoted to a new, strange and sorcerous cult" (*Vite dei Cesari*, Nero, XVI) and spoke of "ruinous superstitions" (*Annali*, XV, 44). To gain acceptance among the Roman cultural elite, the countercultural Christian community had to respond with traditional arts and letters. Such a task was left to intellectuals such as Minucius Felix, a lawyer who converted to Christianity. He used his oratorical talents in the *Octavius*, a three-way dialogue in which he lists and disproves, one by one, all the rumors about the Christians, including one about fried children.

A figure praying; a 4th-century fresco in the spaces beneath the basilica of Ss. Giovanni e Paolo.

and periods of tolerance. The worst persecutions were under emperors Decius (250), Valerian (258), and Diocletian (303–313).

"THERE IS NO RAIN, THE CHRISTIANS ARE TO BLAME"

Romans of all social levels accused the Christians of ignorance, atheism, immoral conduct, incest, and cannibalism. Intellectuals and higher social classes depicted the followers of the new religion as a sect of gullible dupes, because they refused to sacrifice to the gods. This was not because the accusers believed in the efficacy of their pagan cults, but because they remained deeply wary of the wrath of gods whose honor had been wounded. They could not comprehend the moral rigidity of the early Christians, who would not make sacrifices to the spirit of the emperor. Christians' refusal to observe pagan rites was tantamount to a rejection of the essence of being Roman.

Roman rancor was also rooted in misunderstandings. Imagine what might have happened if a Christian and a pagan—both members of the middle class, working as artisans, small merchants, or the like—decided to discuss Christianity. It shouldn't have been hard for them to communicate, because they probably had many things in common, including the same cultural background and even the same tastes. But when the Christian tried to enlighten a pagan about the principles of Christianity or the mystery of the Eucharist, the pagan would simply not have understood. The pagan might have thought that members of the strange sect practiced incest, since they all called each other "brother" and "sister," and that, since they claimed to eat the body and blood of their god, they also practiced cannibalism.

Soon Romans blamed Christians for all sorts of things. Today's Italians joke, "If it rains, the government is to blame," but during the mid-4th century people would say, "There is no rain, the Christians are to blame."

"MARTYRS FOR GOD" AND OTHER SAINTS

Until the 5th century, the victims of persecutions in the Christian community were recognized in two categories of martyrs of God: confessors of the faith and martyrs. Threatened with torture, confessors survived for various reasons. Martyrs

⑥
S. Giovanni in Laterano
(☞ 105)
This ancient basilica, erected immediately following the edict of Constantine, is the cathedral of Rome; above the high altar (*at right*), two silver cases enclose the remains of the heads of Peter and Paul.

⑦
Chiesa del Domine Quo Vadis
(☞ 129)
This church was built on the Via Appia, on the site where Peter, fleeing Rome, saw Jesus. "Quo vadis Domine?" ("Where are you going, Lord?") Peter asked. Jesus' response led Peter to return to the city to face his death.

⑧
Abbazia delle Tre Fontane
(☞ 128)
(Abbey of the Three Fountains)
This site on the Via Ostiense is where Paul was beheaded. Tradition has it that the saint's head fell and bounced on the ground three times, bringing forth three springs of water.

sacrificed their lives. ("Martyr," a word of Greek origin, means "witness," and these people are so-called because they gave witness to the truth of their beliefs with their death.) At first martyrs outnumbered confessors, but after the persecutions ceased the numbers switched. The term "saint" acquired widespread use only at the end of this period. To these two categories, the church soon added the worship of other saints, mainly those mentioned in the Bible: the Virgin Mary, John the Baptist, Joseph, the Magi, and Old Testament patriarchs, prophets, certain kings, and other figures. Angels, whose existence has been an article of faith since 325, were also venerated and considered saints in every respect. In 745, the Council of Rome sanctioned the worship of Michael, Raphael, and Gabriel, who served as messengers of God and defenders of men from evil.

A THOUSAND WAYS TO DIE

In the early centuries after Christ's death, martyrs automatically became saints in the eyes of the church. Their canonization was taken for granted, and the memory of their specific martyrdom was carefully preserved (and if the facts weren't well known, they were created). The attention the church paid to the sometimes macabre details, replayed in the accounts of the martyrs' sacrifices, arose partly out of a desire to present examples for the faithful, but was also a legacy of ancient Roman culture. Roman mythology assigned symbolic significance to different types of torture and execution.

The symbolism of a Christian's death often took second place to the Romans' desire to mount a spectacle, as seen in their circus games, and for this, the Greco-Latin literature offered a compendium of brutalities as sources of inspiration. During the games, mythological episodes of a tragic nature were staged, using Christians as stand-ins for the archetypal heroes: Hercules burning on the mountain, Marsyas flayed alive, Adonis torn to pieces by wild boars, Queen Dirce tied to the horns of a bull.

ICONOGRAPHY OF THE CRUCIFIXION

According to many historians, the oldest representation of the crucifixion, dating from the 2nd century and preserved in the Palatine Antiquarium, is a blasphemous graffito that depicts a crucified Christ with a donkey's head. A phrase, in Greek—"Alexamenos worshiping his God"—accompanies the pagan sneer. In this blasphemous graffito, as in the early Christian Eastern iconography, Christ's feet are apart. One of the oldest Christian representations of this kind of crucifixion is on S. Sabina's (☞ *122*) carved wooden door, which dates from the first half of the 5th century. In the churches of S. Maria Antiqua (☞ *113*) and Ss. Cosma e Damiano (☞ *116*), Jesus still appears with his feet apart and dressed in a short-sleeved tunic known as a *colobium*. After the 9th century, this image becomes rare and is replaced by what has become the traditional iconography: the Christ figure with feet together, dressed only in a loincloth.

⑨
S. Paolo Fuori le Mura (☞ *131*)
This large basilica marks the site of the tomb of Paul; inside the church, the Chapel of the Relics contains the chains of Paul's imprisonment.

Cloister of the basilica of S. Paolo Fuori le Mura.

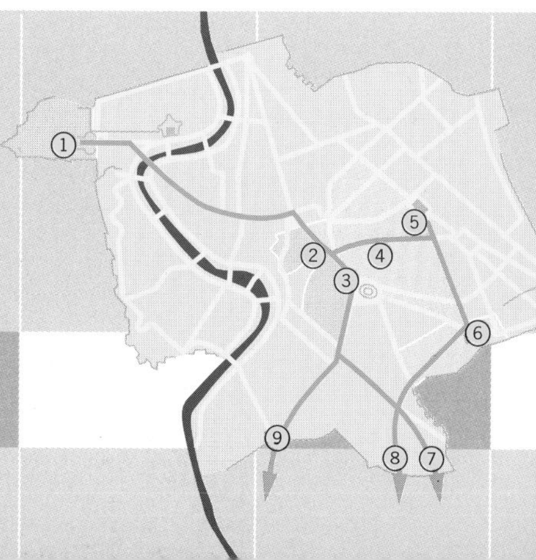

SOLDIERS OF CHRIST

In the military, many refused to sacrifice to the gods and went from being defenders of the empire to defenders of Christ. St. Sebastian is one of the most eminent "soldiers of Christ." He served in the emperor Diocletian's personal guard, a prestigious position in the Roman army. After declaring himself a Christian, he was tied to a stake and pierced by arrows aimed by his fellow soldiers. His body rests in the basilica dedicated to him on the Appian Way (☞ *132)*; his head lies in church of the Ss. Quattro Coronati *(☞ 117)*.

Crucifixion, the punishment for which the Romans were most famous, was traditionally inflicted on fugitive slaves and was a dishonorable way to die; it was used on a large scale during the slave revolts of the 1st century BC. Many Christians were crucified after Jesus, including the apostles Peter and Andrew.

The way martyrs died could also indicate legal status. Decapitation was reserved for Roman citizens, so many of the martyrs who were beheaded came from patrician Roman families. Pope Sixtus II, a patrician, was decapitated by order of the emperor Valerian in 258, and his Spanish deacon, Laurence, was crushed between two white-hot slabs and then roasted over a gridiron. Laurence is particularly venerated in Rome, and many churches are dedicated to him, in part because of his gestures toward the poor, to whom he donated the wealth of the church upon the orders of Sixtus II.

BREAKING DOWN THE SOCIAL BARRIERS

In martyrdom as in life, one of Christianity's disruptive effects, at least at the beginning, was the abolition of social barriers. Christian martyrs came from all walks of life: patricians, plebeians, soldiers, and even women and children, the "weak links" of Roman society. Many women—extremely young women, often little more than children—were raped and then martyred. Rape was a punishment in Rome because of the shame it entailed and because it forced the young girl to break the vow of chastity she had made with her God. Roman law, although more advanced than its Greek counterpart, failed to protect women and children, and the new religion wrought a cultural revolution. Women had a new central role that was founded in Christ's words. They were witnesses to his sacrifice and active participants in the new faith. Female saints greatly outnumber their male counterparts.

Christianity not only helped women embark on the long road to social liberation, but also encouraged its adherents to love children, a rare sentiment in a world

Guido Reni. St. Sebastian (detail), Musei Capitolini.

VIA DELLA GRATICOLA

Gridiron Road is the name given to the tour of churches dedicated to Laurence, patron saint of Rome, with a direct connection to the episodes of his martyrdom.

① **S. Lorenzo in Lucina** (☞ *99*)
This church (*at rigtht*), which has interesting subterranean vaults, houses the gridiron and chains used to imprison the saint. These are exhibited on his feast day, August 10.

② **S. Lorenzo in Miranda** (☞ *113*)
The Temple of Antoninus and Faustina, in the Roman Forum, was transformed to create this 7th- to 8th-century church, supposedly the site of the saint's trial (*at right*).

that viewed children as an economic burden. After Christ said, “Let the little children come to me,” (Matthew 19:14, *Oxford Bible*), children became a symbol of purity and were treated with increasing respect, if only symbolically. In the catacombs, tombs of thousands of children (most of whom died of natural causes) are inscribed with epithets such as Unsullied Lamb, Dove Without Gall, Sweeter Than Honey, Sweetest Son. These signs of sincere and profound grief are mitigated by the conviction that the children’s souls are making their way toward heaven.

THE SOURCES: PART HISTORY, PART FICTION

Everything that is widely known about the saints in the early centuries is based on the examination of two types of sources: archaeological evidence and texts, both liturgical and literary. In addition to the Bible, the writings of the church fathers, and imperial edicts, texts include the *Acta Martyrum* (Feats of the Martyrs), reports of the martyrs’ trials; the *Vite* (Lives) of the confessors; and sermons, discourses, and brief biographies, including tales of their good deeds and miracles.

For devotional purposes, the church immediately collected its martyrs’ names, death dates, and burial places, and recorded them in calendars. The Roman Calendar, one of these documents, dates from 313, and the *Depositio Martyrum* to 354. Martyrologies, in which saints’ names appear with some biographical data, were compiled on the basis of these calendars; the oldest of these date from the 5th century. Martyrologies compiled between the 5th and 9th centuries were used to draw up the *Martyrologium Romanum* (1584), which was adopted by the Catholic Church.

Starting between the 3rd and 4th centuries, the *Acta* were read in churches on the anniversary of a saint’s martyrdom, but the number of interpolations and apocryphal additions quickly expanded beyond the control of the church, so their liturgical use was eventually prohibited.

ABANDONED CHILDREN

In the Roman world, it was accepted practice to abandon newborns; infants were left out in the open, in the Holitorium Forum, at the foot of the Lactaria Column (the column of milk), whose name derived from this custom. Most of these children died, a few were adopted and were thereafter known as "pupils," and the rest were enslaved. The great number of children’s tombs in the catacombs seems to indicate that Christians took on the task of burying the abandoned children who died. In memory of their children, parents left inscriptions, many of which are now in the Vatican Museums or encased in cloister walls of basilicas outside the city. These are often embellished with simple designs such as a cross, the monogram of Christ, a dove (representing the soul), an anchor (symbolizing salvation), a tree (referring to Paradise), or a fish (because the Greek word for fish is an acronym for Christ’s name.

Above: inscription of Alessandra (4th century) praying, next to a dove. Museo Pio Cristiano.

③
S. Lorenzo in Panisperna
(☞ *106*)
According to tradition, this church was erected during the Constantinian era on the site of Laurence’s martyrdom; it was rebuilt in 1300 and again in 1574.

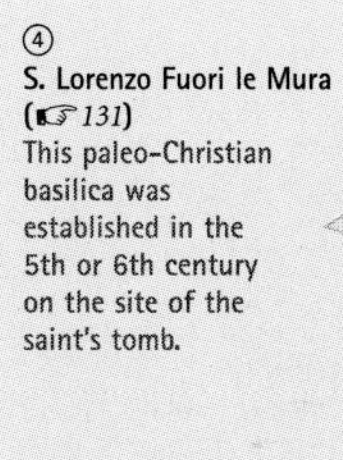
④
S. Lorenzo Fuori le Mura
(☞ *131*)
This paleo-Christian basilica was established in the 5th or 6th century on the site of the saint’s tomb.

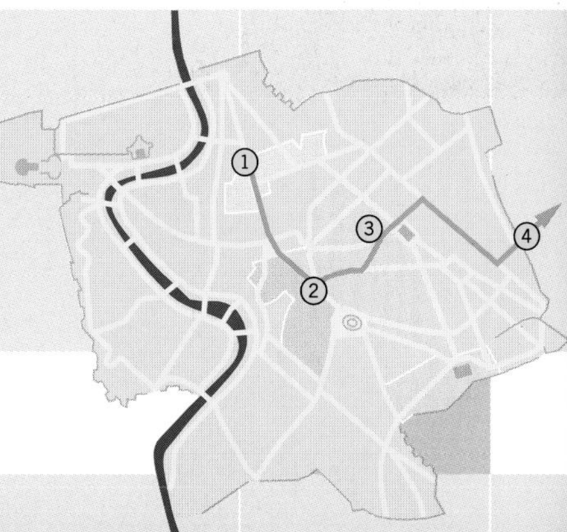

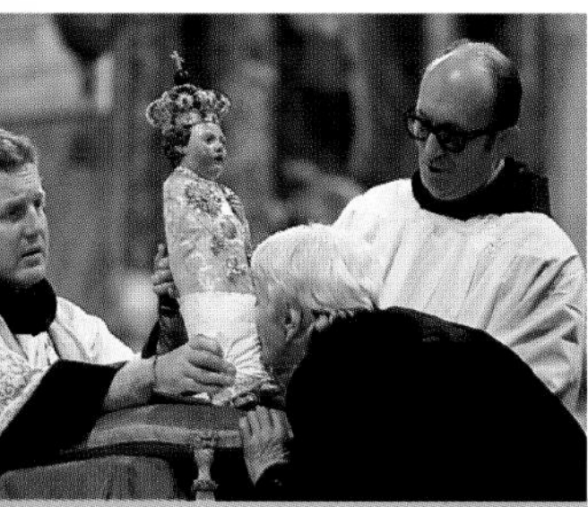

A VERY SPECIAL CHILD

The Christ child, widely worshiped in the Catholic world, is the cause and effect of the new emotional role children played among early Christians. The popularity of this figure has its origins in medieval times. St. Francis of Assisi constructed the first crèche with Jesus in a cradle. In 19th-century Rome, S. Maria d'Aracoeli's (☞ 115) image of the Christ child, which is thought to work miracles, was brought out to comfort the sick and dying. Now it is carried in a procession on January 6th *(above)*.

THE HISTORY OF A WORD

Both the *Acta* and the *Vite*, summarized and combined into various volumes, continued to be read, no longer as official texts but for instructional purposes, particularly in monasteries. These books, known as *comes* ("companions," because they were read during mealtime) or *legenda* ("things to read"), contained an incredible number of strange facts and popular elements that often borrowed from pre-Christian cults and symbology. The *legenda* enjoyed particular success beginning in the 13th century with the establishment of the Franciscans and Dominicans, monastic orders of preachers who used them in their homilies to illustrate the exemplary life. These collections were the source of the Middle Ages' major hagiographic texts, the most famous of which was the *Legenda Aurea* by the Dominican Jacopo da Varagine (ca. 1228–1298), who was also bishop of Genoa.

The transition from *legenda* to "legend" was anything but brief, and throughout the Middle Ages, the *legenda* were considered faithful accounts, to the extent that practically the entire iconography of saints is based on Jacopo da Varagine's work. If the word "legend" now implies an "altered, falsified account," it is because of Martin Luther, who rejected all the saints and all the literature about them, branding them as false. The Catholic Counter-Reformation (1545–1563), a movement of conservation and renewal that followed the Protestant Reformation, responded with a gigantic revision of its writings on the saints, culminating in the publication of the *Acta Sanctorum* (1643), edited by the Jesuit Jean de Bolland.

A NAME, A DESTINY

"*Nomen omen*" is a Latin saying that describes a belief still deeply rooted in the popular conscience: that a name has the capacity to indicate a person's destiny (in Latin, as in English, *omen* means "prediction"). This idea contributed in no small way to the development of many of the saints' legends. In the absence of other information, people looked to a saint's name for some clues about his or her life. Thus, St. Christopher (in Greek,"bearer of Christ") began to be depicted with the Christ child on his shoulders. St. Chistopher is patron saint of travelers, and his image is

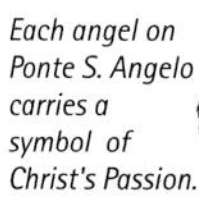

Each angel on Ponte S. Angelo carries a symbol of Christ's Passion.

GUARDIAN ANGELS

Deriving from Greek, *Anghelos* means messenger. Angels, in flight between man and God, are more spiritual than mortals, but are also endowed with free will. They are often pure voice, song, and idea. They listen and advise those who believe in them.

① **Cappella Sistina (☞ 55)**
In his immense depiction of *The Last Judgment*, Michelangelo assigns the human body a central role and nudity a value of primordial significance. In an indeterminate sky, wingless angels, also nude, rise upward, futilely supporting souls held by demons.

② **Ponte S. Angelo (☞ 61)**
The bridge, built by Hadrian during the imperial period, was embellished by Clement IX with the addition of 10 statues of angels bearing the symbols of the Passion. Bernini provided sketches and supervised students, who executed the sculptures.

③ **S. Maria della Pace (☞ 71)**
In the Chigi Chapel, created by Raphael, a bronze by Cosimo Fancelli depicts Christ transported by angels. To the right of the nave, at the sides of the arch, are prophets and angels by Vincenzo de Rossi.

extremely common along streets and in Alpine passes. Hippolytus's name derives from "divided by horses" (from the Greek *hippos*, "horse," and *lyo*, "undone, divided"), and hagiography has deduced that Hippolytus was quartered by horses. Other saints' characteristics can also likely be attributed to name interpretation. Agnes is represented with a lamb (*agnus* in Latin, symbol of purity); the distinctive features of Lucy of Syracuse are her eyes (in Latin *lux* means"light"), which are depicted resting on a plate. Legend has it that she was blinded during her martyrdom. She has become the patron saint of sight, and Rome's churches of S. Lucia del Gonfalone (☞ *72*) and S. Lucia in Selci (☞ *106*) are dedicated to her. Worshippers leave eyes made of wax as offerings in the former; in the latter, holy oil, considered soothing for the eyes, is distributed on her feast day, December 13.

A SAINT WHO COLLECTED BLOOD

St. Praxedes, sister of St. Pudentiana and daughter of Senator Pudens, was one of the few saints who did not suffer martyrdom during the centuries when Christianity was practiced in secrecy. Supposedly baptized by the apostle Peter himself, she is famous for having collected the blood of martyrs, after washing their remains and gathering them in a well. This is how she is depicted on the altar of the church dedicated to her (☞ *108*). A porphyry circle on the floor of the main nave indicates the site of the sacred well.

Below, the saint and St. Paul are portrayed in a detail of the church's mosaics.

ERRORS AND STEREOTYPES

Legends about the saints have also developed as a result of errors of interpretation. St. Caecilia, for instance, is the patron saint of music (her attribute is an organ) because of an error of translation of the word *organum,* which in Latin has several meanings, from the text about her martyrdom. In other cases, saints acquired unfounded military histories because the term "soldiers of Christ," occurring in eulogistic texts, was taken literally. Over the centuries, true soldier martyrs, such as Sergius and Bacchus, came to be depicted wearing a heavy chain because of erroneous interpretations of the gold collars they wore as members of the imperial guard.

Those who wanted to recount the lives of saints but had little or no information about them also resorted to stereotyping. If it was known that a certain martyr was brought to trial, then it could be supposed that more or less all martyrs must have stood before a judge. So trial scenes are inserted into practically every martyr's life story, especially for women. A well-known example is depicted in the iconography of St. Catherine of Alexandria, in particular in the frescoes of the chapel dedicated to her in S. Clemente (☞ *105*).

④
S. Maria della Vittoria (☞ *126*)
The frescoed vault of this church dedicated to St. Teresa, founder of the Carmelite order, is crowned by a circle of stuccowork angels that depict the *Assumption of the Virgin and the Fall of the Rebel Angels* by Giovanni Cerrini *(at left).*

ST. CAECILIA

Often depicted with an organ because of an error in the translation of the text that recounts her martyrdom, Caecilia is the patron saint of music. In 821, nearly six centuries after her death in 230, her remains were moved from the catacombs of St. Calixtus (☞ *129*) on the Via Appia to the church in Trastevere that is dedicated to her. She is widely venerated in Europe and is associated with organs, harpsichords, cellos, lutes, and other images relating to music; she often wears a crown of roses or lilies, and her neck may show the marks of her beheading. Among the most beautiful works of art in her honor are the splendid sculpture (1600) by Stefano Maderno in the church of S. Cecilia (☞ *63*), which depicts her as she was found when her tomb was opened in 1595, and a fresco cycle (1616–1617) by Domenichino in S. Luigi dei Francesi (☞ *84*).

Stereotypes were also applied to hermits. Probably based on the model of the temptations of Christ in the desert, hermits were usually said to have been subjected to temptations by the devil. They were also believed to have the power to tame ferocious beasts, as did some martyrs: St. Thecla is modeled after Daniel in the lion's den; St. Jerome is often depicted translating the Bible with a tamed lion at his feet. Early bishops seized on these images as part of their commitment to combating paganism and heresy.

CROSSES, SWORDS, AND STAFFS: HOW TO IDENTIFY THE SAINTS

Saints' faces were not very important in early Christian art. Martyrs, particularly, were thought of as exemplary models rather than as real people. Their physiognomic characteristics were pronounced relatively unimportant in a polemic against pagan art, which had reached great formal heights in Hellenistic portraiture and continued to influence Roman art until the end of the empire. This art must have appeared too individualistic in the eyes of the church. Instead of identifying saints by portraying physical features, a name sufficed to identify a saint, and names often appear next to images in the mosaics in early Christian churches. From the 4th century on, elements of the late ancient tradition began to reappear, including facial features and halos, which had once been an attribute of emperors. Images of the two principal saints repeat the iconography of ancient philosophers; Peter has white hair and a white beard, and Paul appears bald and lean-faced, with a short, black beard.

All the other saints could be identified at first glance only by their clothing, which indicated the category to which they belonged. Apostles were depicted wearing royal mantles and pallia, hermits and anchorites were shown in habits, soldiers in cuirasses, bishops with a shepherd's crook and miter, kings with a crown, and so on. Intellectuals, including evangelists, prophets, church fathers, and doctors, hold a book or scroll; knights a weapon; pilgrims and hermits a staff. It is only in Western Christianity, particularly with the flowering of the Gothic style, that personal attributes became common. These referred to a salient event, often martyrdom, in the saint's life: a gridiron for St. Laurence, a

FACES OF SAINTS

Many saints and prophets appear in the altarpiece of the Adoration of the Trinity (1592), by Francesco Bassano, in the Chiesa del Gesù, and they are almost always depicted with their attributes. Here are some of them.

Moses with the tablets of the Law.

St. Martin with his cloak.

King David with his harp.

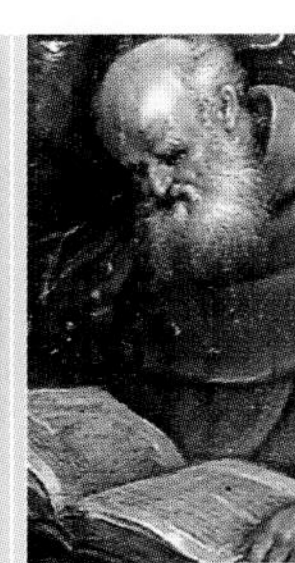

St. Anthony Abbot with a book.

wheel for St. Catherine, an organ for St. Caecilia, eyes for St. Lucy, the Christ child for St. Christopher, keys or a cross for St. Peter, a sword for St. Paul (who was beheaded), and the like.

PAINTINGS AND SCULPTURES: THE ICONOGRAPHY OF SAINTS

Dignity, heroism, devotion, and controversy describe the representational universe of the saints. Throughout the Middle Ages and until the late 15th century, saints were portrayed in dignified fashion. Images were almost never violent, not even the rare depictions of scenes of martyrdom. Violence appeared only in representations of the Last Judgment that were meant to admonish and frighten the viewer. Saints were presented as examples of how good Christians should live their mortal lives. During the Renaissance, with its humanistic attitudes, saints were shown as heroic, following newly rediscovered classical models.
The Counter-Reformation, which sought to return Christianity to the purity of its early days, inherited the image of the saint as hero but pushed for a more devotional, less titanic characterization.

Counter-Reformation doctrine dictated that images must be immediately recognizable, even by laypersons. In the struggle against the contempt of the Protestant world toward saints and images of saints, sacred art became charged with polemical significance. The more iconoclastic the Protestant countries became, the more the Roman Church urged the worship of images. Jean de Bolland brought attention to saints who were previously unknown, such as Praxedes, Pudentiana, and Agnes. Ironically, just as the representations of saints were taking on a universal, atemporal quality, historical studies uncovered new facts about saints, and the information found its way into works of art, to the point of esotericism (with the consequence that in certain altarpieces, there are saints whose names we still don't know). Martyr saints were depicted in increasingly bloody fashion as role models in the Catholic struggle against the Protestant Reformation, which did not recognize their cult. These representations served a

ST. CATHERINE OF ALEXANDRIA

Removed from the liturgical calendar after the Vatican II (1969), St. Catherine of Alexandria was one of the most venerated martyr saints. Martyred around 306, she was immensely popular from the 13th century until the end of the Middle Ages, and again during Baroque times, during which time she was honored and worshiped almost as much as the Virgin. Many legends exist about her life, and her protection is believed to extend to children, virgins, wives, and everyone working in any occupation that requires the use of wheels and knives. Before being beheaded, she was placed between two hooked wheels, which were meant to turn and lacerate her flesh. Lightening destroyed the infernal machine, and the iconography typically represents her with a fragment of hooked wheel or a sword. Two Roman churches—S. Caterina dei Funari (☞ *84*) and S. Caterina della Rota—and two chapels—in S. Maria Maggiore (☞ *126*) and in S. Clemente (☞ *105*)—are dedicated to her.

Masolino's St. Catherine Freed by the Angels, detail of the fresco (1428–1431) in S. Clemente.

St. Catherine with the wheel.

St. John the Baptist with his cross-shaped staff.

St. Laurence with a gridiron.

St. Francis with the stigmata.

St. Paul with a sword.

SAINTS WORTHY OF DEVOTION

Almost all saints, particularly the oldest ones, are attributed to one or more patronages, whose origins, whether rooted in history or legend, have often been lost. The following are some of the patron saints widely venerated in Rome (and their feast days):

St. Sebastian (January 20): Martyred in 288 in Rome, he is the patron saint of the dying, merchants of hardware, potters, plumbers, gardeners, soldiers, and fountains. He also protects livestock from disease and plague.

St. Blaise (February 3): Martyred in 316 in Sebaste, Armenia (now Turkey), St. Blaise is the patron saint of doctors, cobblers, tailors, plasterers and bricklayers, bakers, milliners, musicians, and domestic animals. He is also patron saint for good weather and protector against sore throats, coughs, hemorrhages, toothache, and plague. On his feast day, candles, wine, and bread are consecrated and are still distributed in the church of S. Biagio della Pagnotta (☞76).

St. Vitus (June 15): A popular child saint who, according to tradition, was martyred in Rome in 304, at the age of 7, Vitus is patron saint of innkeepers, actors, blacksmiths and miners, domestic animals, springs, and people who are deaf or mute. He is also protector against epilepsy, hysteria, cramps, lightening, and bad weather.

dual purpose as devotional icons and as didactic mementos for novices destined for Protestant or non-Christian lands. Future missionaries filed past the *Martyrology* in S. Stefano Rotondo (☞ *108*), to better know the fate that awaited them.

The Counter-Reformation was neither brief nor painless for religious art. Clement VII attempted to obliterate Michelangelo's *Last Judgment*, and hundreds of other works that did not follow the prescriptions laid down by the Council of Trent were renounced or destroyed. The church sometimes intervened directly, issuing directives about the postures and attributes that artists could depict and even the colors that they could use. Perhaps this was the beginning of the transformation of religious art, to which the West owes so much, into an art frozen in time, an art that with rare exceptions has seemed unable to absorb and reflect contemporary culture since the 19th century.

THE WORLD PROTECTED BY SAINTS

In addition to being models of behavior, saints almost immediately became intercessors with God and patrons (a term derived from the Latin for "protector" or "supporter"). The concept of protection by a saint is deeply rooted. Almost all Indo-European divinities presided over some activity and protected something or someone, and in this sense the saints performed a function of the old gods. In the frescoes of the Catacombs of Domitilla are the earliest examples of "personal" protection, where the patron saint places a hand on the shoulders of the person being protected. The idea of the saint as protector began to spread in the 11th century, when Europe experienced urban and economic rebirth, and continued to grow during the 14th century, when the Western world underwent one of its longest crises as a result of famine, the Black Death (1347–1348), and a sharp decline in population, which would not be restored to its original levels until the second half of the following century.

During both these periods, everyone and everything—person, house, profession, confraternity, corporation, religious order, city, domain, or nation—had a patron saint; nothing in the world was without one. Particularly during the 14th century,

THE TRIUMPH OF GOLD

On the city's altars, light filtering through windows, or flickering from a multitude of candles, is reflected in warm colors by Rome's gilded treasures.

① **S. Pietro** (☞ *52*)
In front of Bernini's tribune, an immense gilded sunburst (detail at right) hangs over the monumental black and gold bronze throne, which encloses the so-called Chair of St. Peter.

② **S. Eustachio** (☞ *84*)
This church was founded by Constantine on the site where St. Eustace suffered his martyrdom. In the church a high altar in bronze and polychrome marble, by Nicola Salvi, is surmounted by a beautiful baldacchin by Ferdinando Fuga.

③
Chiesa del Gesù
(☞ *80*)
The altar of St. Ignatius is emblematic of the splendor and decorative richness of Jesuit art. Four monumental lapis lazuli columns surround a statue of the saint, whose tomb lies beneath the altar (*left*).

④
S. Maria in Campitelli
(☞ *115*)
This "glory" of gilded angels (*above*) is a splendid Baroque composition by Carlo Rainaldi, with a miraculous image of St. Maria in Portico Campitelli (11th century) at the center.

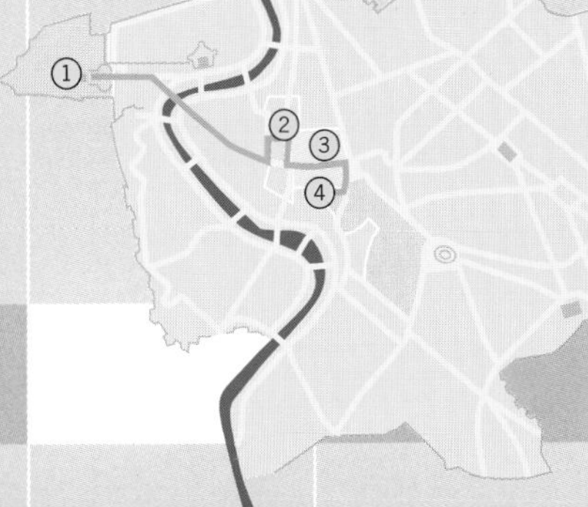

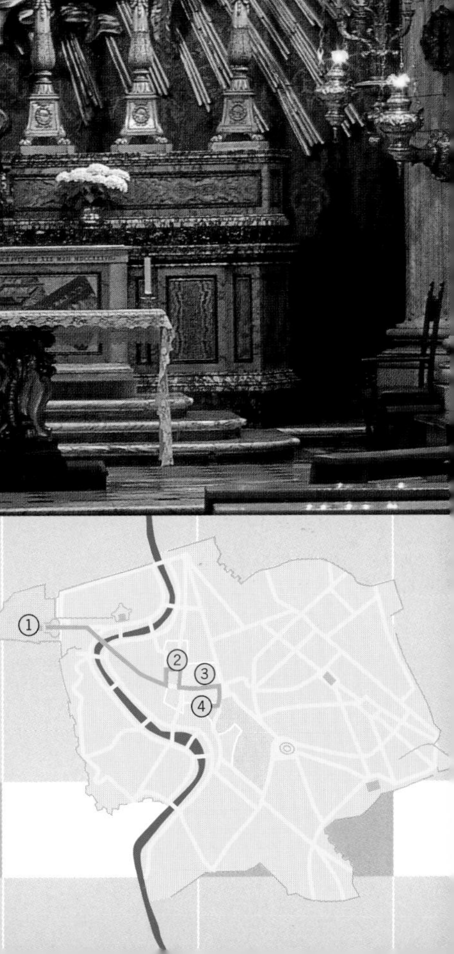

SAINTS WORTHY OF DEVOTION

St. Ignatius of Loyola (July 31): Patron saint of soldiers, children, spiritual exercises, and pregnant women, He is protector against guilty consciences, livestock diseases, and plague.
In Rome, the waters of St. Ignatius (holy water in which a relic of the saint or a small medal with his image has been immersed) are thought to have miracle-working properties.

St. Laurence (August 10): Patron saint of librarians, archivists, cooks, brewers, innkeepers, laundresses, ironers, firemen, vinedressers. He is also protector against eye and skin maladies, sciatica, fevers, and fires.

St. Bibiana (December 2): Martyred in Rome in 367, she protects against cramps, headaches, alcoholism, epilepsy, and accidents. Until the 18th century, the dust from the column to which she was bound during martyrdom (☞124), and the mint that grew around her tomb were used as a remedy for epilepsy.

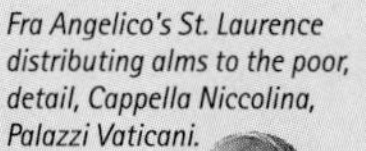

Fra Angelico's St. Laurence distributing alms to the poor, detail, Cappella Niccolina, Palazzi Vaticani.

patron saints functioned as talismans against evil; they were protection against specific illnesses, storms, attacks from pirates, and so on. By invoking the right saint, it was believed that evil could be kept at bay.

PATRON SAINT OF ROME

Agnes, whose name means pure and innocent, is patron saint of Rome, along with Peter, Paul, Laurence, and Frances of Rome. Very little is known about Agnes; her martyrdom occurred during the persecution of Diocletian. The epigraph on her tomb, written by the poet-pope Damasus I (366–384), mentions her age: 12. She became a symbol of virginity because it was said that a mass of hair grew to cover her body, preventing her violation. As a result of this legend, hair became an attribute of virgins. The episode is depicted in a bas-relief in the vaults of the church dedicated to her in Piazza Navona (☞*70*). Tresses completely cover the body of the young girl, who is accompanied by two soldiers. The vault area is part of what remains of the stadium of Domitian, presumably the site where the girl's martyrdom took place. Agnes' head is kept in the same church, and her tomb is in the catacombs on Via Nomentana, where the basilica of S. Agnese Fuori le Mura stands (☞*130*).

THE WORSHIP OF RELICS

Before and after the era of Diocletian (284–305), when the last great persecutions took place, two dates are significant in the Christian world. The first is 260, when emperor Gallienus granted Christians the right to practice their religion freely and ordered the restoration of church property that had been confiscated. The second is 311, just two years before Costantine's edict that established freedom of worship to all religions, when co-emperor Galerius issued an edict that authorized the end of the great persecution. Although there were still innumerable obstacles in the late ancient world, these decrees allowed Christians to practice their religion openly. Homage began to be paid to the martyrs. The deification was accompanied by a phenomenon of relic-

IN THE NAME OF MARY

"...You are blessed among women and blessed is the fruit of your womb...." The populace has always exhibited great passion for the Mother of God and has always asked a great deal from her—healing, recovery from wounds, intercession...

① **S. Maria in Trastevere** (☞*65*)
This was the first church dedicated to the Madonna and probably the first in the city officially open to her worship. Domenichino painted the *Assumption of the Virgin* in the central section of the coffered ceiling (*below*).

② **S. Maria in Aracoeli** (☞*115*)
According to legend, Augustus, after seeing a vision of the Virgin, ordered that an "altar to the Son of God" be built. On the fourth column to the left, in the central nave, a fresco depicts the Madonna "Refugium peccatorum."

③ **S. Agostino** (☞*82*)
One of the earliest Renaissance churches in Rome, S. Agostino contains Jacopo Sansovino's *Madonna del Parto*, widely venerated as a protectress of women in childbirth. The church also houses the *Madonna of the Pilgrims* by Caravaggio (*right*).

creation, and places and objects that came into contact with the diva or "divine one" (from the Latin *divus*, "divine") became relics. Temples were built on the sites of the martyrs' tombs or places of martyrdom, and parts of their bodies—known as relics (from the Latin *reliquus*, "that which remains")—were safeguarded and became objects of veneration. Relics were protected by specially commissioned containers, known as reliquaries, that were often masterpieces of goldsmithery. Everything connected to the saints became invested with a certain sanctity. During the Middle Ages, when saints' relics were venerated with particular fervor, European cities and monasteries vied and paid high prices for real and presumed bones of martyrs and fragments of clothing; one even acquired feathers from the archangel Gabriel. As the center of Christianity, a holy city, and the destination of a constant stream of pilgrims, Rome has always been rich in relics related to the best-known saints and to the life of Christ.

AN EXCEPTIONAL CASE: RELICS OF CHRIST

The remains of Christ's time on Earth are located in three of the four patriarchal basilicas, seat of the patriarchs, the highest ranking bishops in the Church of Rome. These relics are tied almost exclusively to two events: his Passion and his death. The so-called Column of the Flagellation was brought from Jerusalem to the church of S. Prassede (☞*108*) in 1223. S. Croce in Gerusalemme (☞*124*) houses the relics of the true cross—three pieces of wood, a nail, and part of the inscription (INRI), that hung at the top of the cross. S. Giovanni in Laterano (☞*105*) contains the table from the Last Supper, four columns that during the Middle Ages were thought to correspond to the height of the Savior, the stone slab on which the soldiers played dice for his tunic, and the so-called Well of the Samaritan. Near the Basilica of S. Giovanni is the Scala Santa (☞*109*), the largest relic in the Christian world. These so-called Holy Steps are said to be the staircase from the Praetorian Palace, where drops of Jesus' blood fell after he was flagellated in front of Pontius Pilate. The spots where the blood fell

ALEXIUS, THE BEGGAR SAINT

Several saints renounced all material possessions for a life of mendicancy on the fringes of society. One of the most famous of these so-called beggar saints, who lived almost semisecret lives in Rome, was St. Alexius, patron saint of beggars and vagabonds. He lived in the 4th or 5th century and was the son of a wealthy Roman family. According to some sources, he renounced his wealth on his wedding day and went to live in Edessa (Turkey); returning to Rome, he hid beneath the staircase of his paternal home, unknown to his family, and lived on charity. Baroque Rome celebrated his person—the Jesuits pointed to him as a model of chastity—and he became the subject of musical and theatrical portrayals. Bernini staged one of these, commissioned by the Barberini family, and traces of the sets, in the form of a monumental reliquary in stuccoed wood by Andrea Bergondi, can be seen in the church of S. Alessio (☞*119*).

④
S. Maria della Concezione in Campo Marzio (☞*90*)
The present-day church, probably buit on a pre-existing 7th-century structure and rebuilt in the 17th century, houses on the high altar a 12th-century Byzantine icon of the *Madonna Advocata*, originally from Constantinople (*above*).

⑤
S. Maria Maggiore (☞*126*)
In the world's largest church dedicated to the Virgin Mary, a beautiful mosaic by Jacopo Torriti depicts one of the nine choirs of angels that take part in the coronation of the Virgin by the Redeemer, in the *Triumph of the Virgin*.

are now well protected, framed in metal and glass. In reality this is the stairway of honor from the Lateran Palace, installed here to provide access to the popes' private chapel. The steps were identified with the Praetorian Palace during the 15th century, and pilgrims today still climb them on their knees in profound devotion. The church makes pronouncements of authenticity only after very thorough examination, but as with the Scala Santa, veneration of a relic often persists, even when it may not be warranted.

The Basilica di S. Pietro (☞*52*) in the Vatican contains the veil of Veronica, who stopped to wipe Jesus' face when she met him on the road to Calvary. His image remained on the cloth, which was brought back from Jerusalem by the crusaders. The church also contains part of the wood from the cross and part of the lance with which Longinus pierced the Savior's side. All three relics are exhibited to the faithful during Holy Week.

"WE DESCEND LIVE INTO THE INFERNO"

> *"As a boy, when I was studying in Rome, my friends and I used to visit the tombs of the apostles and martyrs on Sundays. We would enter the tunnels carved out of tufa stone and entirely covered with tombs, so that the prophetic saying, 'We descend live into the inferno,' seemed to be fulfilled. Occasional rays of life from the surface lessened the shadows a bit.... We proceeded slowly, one step at a time, completely enveloped in darkness"* (Commentary to Ezekial, 40:5).

When you visit the catacombs today, you may well have the kind of experience recounted above by St. Jerome (347–420), the church father who translated the Bible into Latin. For centuries an aura of legend—related to the worship of saints' relics, places of martyrdom, and tombs—has surrounded the catacombs. These intricate networks of underground tufa passages were never hiding places or places of worship. They were immense cities of the dead, the bodies buried in niches carved into the walls. The names of Rome's catacombs are those of the saints, martyrs, and popes who were entombed there, including

A GOOD DEATH

Given the high mortality rates until the modern era, the church calendar is full of patron saints of the so-called "Good Death" saints dedicated to the physical and spiritual assistance of people who are ill and dying.
St. Camillus de Lellis (1550–1614), friend of St. Philip Neri and founder of the Camillini (1586), is one of the most beloved of these saints in Rome and was venerated for quite some time as the patron saint of the city. The Camillini, also known as the Ministers of the Sick, contributed significantly to health reform in Rome: they taught people to isolate those with contagious diseases, they considered diet as a function of illness, and they reorganized the hospital ward system.
St. Camillus is buried in the church of S. Maria Maddalena (☞*99*), whose walls are frescoed with scenes from his life.

St. Camillus de Lellis healing the sick during the 1598 flooding of the Tiber (1746) by Pierre Subleyras, Museo di Roma.

UNDERGROUND ROME

This hidden city is rich in itineraries to its ancient core: tombs of early Christians, forgotten and buried churches, sites of esoteric sects and cults.

① **Catacombe di S. Callisto** (☞*129*)
The official burial ground of the Roman church lay along the Via Appia Antica. Fifty martyrs and some 16 popes from the early centuries of Christianity are buried here.

The Good Shepherd, 2nd- to 3rd-century, Catacombs of St. Calixtus.

② **S. Sebastiano** (☞*132*)
Built at the behest of Cardinal Borghese, this church occupies the site of a Constantinian basilica and stands above the catacombs. The *triclinium*, a porticoed space with graffiti-painted walls, is where early Christians used to worshipped Sts. Peter and Paul.

③ **Catacombe di Priscilla** (☞*129*)
This catacomb complex stands along the ancient Via Salaria, where Romans buried their dead. In one of the burial chambers is a Madonna and child fresco (*rigth*), the oldest representation of the Madonna (mid-2nd century).

Sebastian, Callistus, Agnes, and others; or of the people who gave the land where they were established, such as Priscilla and Flavia Domitilla. Many catacombs contain significant pictorial decorations that document the transition of art from Roman to early Christian styles. Even after the catacombs' funerary function ended in the 5th century, pilgrims continued to come—to worship and to look at and touch the tombs and even the bodies of the saints. Here and there *fenestellae*, or small slits, were opened, through which pilgrims would reach in and touch the remains with small pieces of fabric. Others were content to leave with a bit of oil that burned in the lamps near the tombs. It is not difficult to understand how, in the pilgrim's tales of their visits, those bits of fabric that had touched the body of a saint became parts of the saint's clothing. These, too, became relics, precious memories of the long and dangerous voyage to Rome.

ROME OF THE DEAD

At the foundation of Roman culture was the peoccupation, even obsession, with boundaries. In ancient times a boundary—the walls—separated the city of the living from the city of the dead, who reposed in necropolises along the consular roads. In the 5th century, the dead began to be buried inside the city walls, in orchards, churches, crypts, vaults, and monasteries. Those who could afford it were buried near the tomb of a martyr or next to a high altar. One way or another, people tried to be close to one who had been closer to God. Thus the dead entered the city.

As barbarian incursions and earthquakes made life appear increasingly precarious, and the distance between the world of the living and that of the dead began to shrink, Christians stood fast in their belief that life and death were stages on the path toward eternal life. Faith in the Resurrection and the new concept of a hereafter, where the just were rewarded and the wicked punished, made death seem less traumatic.

Throughout the Middle Ages and for much of the modern and contemporary era in the West, death was a familiar presence. Famines, wars, epidemics, and poor hygiene took lives indiscriminately. In his *Cantico di Frate Sole*

FRANCIS IN ROME

St. Francis of Assisi, patron saint of Italy since 1939, lived in Rome between 1181 and 1226. During the period he worked to have his new order approved, first by Pope Innocent III in 1210, then by Pope Honorius III in 1223 (who granted definitive approval). In 1224, the saint received the stigmata—bodily marks resembling the wounds of the crucified Christ that miraculously appeared on him— and some of the bandages that covered his wounds are housed in S. Francesco alle Stigmate, next to the Pantheon. In the church of S. Francesco a Ripa (☞ *64*), a monk accompanies visitors to a small room where the saint resided, the only remaining portion of the ancient Hospice of S. Biagio; there, a stone that St. Francis used as a pillow is preserved (protected by a grate), along with a spectacular reliquary dating from 1696.

Detail of Federico Barocci's St. Francis receiving the stigmata, Vatican Pinacoteca.

④
S. Prisca
(☞ *121*)
Beneath this church, built prior to the 5th century on the remains of a Roman structure, is a 2nd- to 3rd-century Mithraeum. Preceded by a vestibule where victims were sacrificed, the room has frescoed walls.

⑤
Basilica di Porta Maggiore
(☞ *124*)
Hidden beneath the roadbed of the Rome–Naples railway, this church is believed to have been the site of a neo-Pythagorean worship. Perfectly preserved, it is divided into three naves, its walls and vaults covered with beautiful stuccowork.

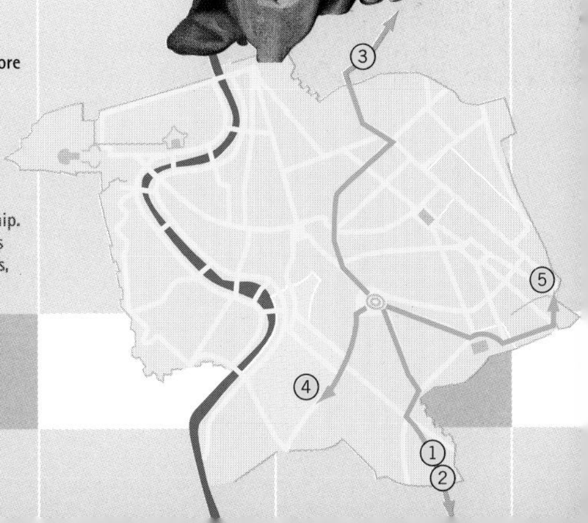

THE COMPANY OF IGNATIUS

St. Francis Xavier (1506–1552), co-founder of the Jesuits, proselytized throughout Japan, China, and India, and the church proclaimed him the patron saint of the Indies, of missionaries, and of missions in the East. His body remains in Goa, but his arm is housed in the chapel dedicated to him in the right transept of the Chiesa del Gesù (☞ *80*) opposite the chapel dedicated to his confrère, Ignatius of Loyola, with whom he was canonized in 1622. In 1679, Carlo Maratta painted the altarpiece illustrating his death (below).

(1224), St. Francis of Assisi praised God for "Bodily death our sister." The everyday relationship with death gave meaning to burial; it was one of the acts of mercy. Joseph the carpenter, one of the world's most venerated saints and the protector of grave diggers and the dying, was one of the saints to whom people prayed for a good death. Confraternities and religious orders, the first of which were the Franciscans, were founded to bury the dead and assist the dying or those condemned to the gallows.

Baroque Rome dramatized death through spectacular and in some cases macabre representations of the passage from life. With advances in anatomical knowledge, decorations imitating tibias, femurs, and skulls were used on tombstones or monuments inside churches. The Franciscans decorated crypts and chapels with real bones; in the church of S. Maria della Concezione dei Cappucccini(☞ *126*) the remains of 4,000 cadavers create a complex of chapels decorated with friars' bones and mummies. An hourglass and scythe motif emphasizes the precariousness of life, and an inscription reminds the visitor: "I am what you will become. I was what you are."

ROME OF THE LIVING

The image of Rome as a city of God has been shaped by more than the worship of the dead and their relics. A great many saints, some of whom are inextricably bound to the Eternal City, lived, studied, and worked here. St. Frances of Rome (1384–1440), forced by her parents to marry, was an exemplary wife and mother. Upon her husband's death in 1436, she became the Mother Superior of the Benedictine Oblates of Tor de' Specchi, a community dedicated to charitable work. One of the 15th century's great mystics, she was in constant contact with her own guardian angel, in whose company she is often depicted, and many prayed to her for help and counsel. Her body rests in the church dedicated to her (☞ *113*).

Rome owes a great deal to the Spaniard Ignatius of Loyola (1491–1556), founder of the Society of Jesus and author of the *Spiritual Exercises* (1548), which was in the vanguard of the Counter-Reformation. This militant order, which would become one of the most powerful in the church, was dedicated to mis-

THE TOUR OF THE SEVEN CHURCHES

The first great Roman basilica dedicated to St. Peter and the six other basilicas have always been pilgrimage destinations. In 1577 St. Philip Neri introduced the Tour of the Seven Churches, a route necessary to obtain plenary indulgence.

①
S. Pietro
(☞ *52*)
This is the largest church in the world. In 326 Pope Sylvester consecrated the first basilica, which had been established by Constantine on the site of the apostle's martyrdom and burial. A symbol of Christianity, it houses priceless treasures

Above S. Pietro's central nave and baldachin.

sionary work and, from the beginning, active in every sector of public life. To combat heresy and convert non-Christians, Ignatius expected his followers to undergo rigorous cultural and educational preparation. Jesuit colleges became famous throughout the world and provided instruction for the ruling classes of Europe. The Chiesa del Gesù (☞ *80*), one of Rome's most beautiful churches, was erected on the occasion of Ignatius's canonization (1622). Beneath the ornate altar in the left transept, the saint's remains rest in an urn; next to the church are the rooms where Ignatius lived.

"BE GOOD, IF YOU CAN"

St. Philip Neri (1515–1595) was extremely popular among Romans, who nicknamed him Pippo Bono (Good Phil). An itinerant preacher in the city, he was known as the Apostle of Rome, and the entire city wept at his funeral. He took in poor children for instruction, removing them from squalor. Immensely patient, he told the children to "be good, if you can," a phrase that became almost a refrain in Rome. The saint was a friend and counselor to popes and cardinals, including St. Charles Borromeo, archbishop of Milan. He is also the patron saint of humorists, and there are many anecdotes about his cheerfulness and ready wit. When an aristocrat slapped him, tired of Neri's continual requests for money for orphans, Neri responded, "This is for me; and for my children?" The rooms where he worked and an altar dedicated to him are in S. Maria in Vallicella (also know as the Chiesa Nuova ☞ *68*). In this church he taught the faithful to sing religious hymns and invented the musical form of the oratory; the order he founded in 1575 goes by the name Oratorians.

A MILANESE IN ROME: CHARLES BORROMEO

One of the most beautiful domes in Rome belongs to Ss. Ambrogio e Carlo al Corso, a church dedicated to two Milanese bishops that lived 12 centuries apart. St. Ambrose, who died in 397, is one of the distinguished Doctors of the Church; St. Charles Borromeo (1538–1584), patron saint of pastoral workers and seminarians, left an indelible mark on church his-

ST. BENEDICT, FATHER OF WESTERN MONASTICISM

Benedict of Norcia (c. 480–547) spent little time in Rome: he studied here and immediately fled, horrified by the dissoluteness of his schoolmates. But his influence on church history was profound, and in 590, Gregory I, a member of the order St. Benedict founded and that bears his name, was elected pope. The remains of Benedict's room are in the church of S. Benedetto in Piscinula (☞ *63*), which was built around them; the saint is depicted in a 15th-century panel with a gold background on the high altar and a fresco at the church entrance. One of the most beautiful images of St. Benedict, Pierre Subleyras's *The Miracle of St. Benedict* (1744), depicts Benedict raising a gardener's son from the dead; it is in the sacristy of the church of S. Francesca Romana (☞ *113*).

② **S. Maria Maggiore** (☞ *126*)
Legend has it that the basilica stands on the site of a miraculous snowfall, which is why it is also known as S. Maria della Neve (of the Snow). Built by Sixtus III, it is held up by 40 monolithic columns and has a beautiful mosaic pavement.

S. Maria Maggiore at night (left)

③ **S. Giovanni in Laterano** (☞ *105*)
Pope Miltiades established this basilica in the 4th century, on property owned by the Laterani family. Damaged and pillaged numerous times, it was renovated by Borromini for the 1650 Jubilee.

The facade emerges from behind the Roman walls of Porta S. Giovanni (left).

④ **S. Croce in Gerusalemme** (☞ *124*)
This church was founded by Constantine in 320 to house the relics of Christ's Passion, brought back from the Holy Land by his mother, St. Helena. In addition to these important relics, soil from Calvary is said to lie beneath the floor of the church.

ST. ANDREW

Among the many churches in Rome dedicated to Andrew, at least three are well known: S. Andrea delle Fratte (☞ *97*), S. Andrea al Quirinale (☞ *104*), and S. Andrea della Valle (☞ *70*). This apostle's popularity dates from 1462, when his remains were brought to Rome at the request of Pope Pius II. Churches, paintings, and sculptures were dedicated to the saint from that time on, especially during the first half of the 17th century. Outside Italy in the late 15th century, iconography of St. Andrew began to include an *X*-shape cross, as seen in in the paintings by Domenichino in S. Gregorio Magno (☞ *113*) and those by Mattia Preti in S. Andrea della Valle (*below*), and it is with this cross that the saint has almost always been depicted since then.

tory. Charles Borromeo spent a few years in Rome, as special secretary to his uncle, Pope Pius IV. He became archbishop of Milan in 1564, but his work had a broader resonance in the Italian church, as did his reputation as a model pastor. He was an important figure during the Council of Trent and a promoter of the immediate application of its provisions. He is one of the exemplary saints of the Counter-Reformation, along with Ignatius of Loyola and Philip Neri. His activity during the plague of 1576 in Milan made him so popular in Rome that he displaced as a protector from plague medieval saints such as St. Roch. Fine portrayals of St. Charles in prayer, in procession, and among those afflicted by plague may be seen in the church of Ss. Ambrogio e Carlo al Corso (☞ *92*) and in the churches of S. Carlo ai Catinari (☞ *82*) and S. Carlo alle Quattro Fontane (☞ *104*).

ROME WITHOUT SAINTS

The last 300 years of the millennium seem like one long conspiracy against the saints. The Eternal City was secularized first by the Enlightenment; then by the Risorgimento (the "Resurgence," a nationalist struggle angainst the Austrian-Hungarian Empire), which culminated in the unification of Italy and taking of Rome (1870); and finally by the modern era. During these times saints appeared to wane from the capital of Christianity. But 2,000 years of faith—and an almost equal period of secular power for the papacy—are not easily erased. In this holy city, saints have left a tangible legacy, as present as the churches and the monuments of Rome. The many religious orders established by them are strongly rooted in the city and throughout Italy: Jesuits, Oratorians, Piarists, Trinitarians, Camilliani. The dozens of religious orders, whether strictly cloistered or fully involved in charitable works, were and continue to be the tool through which the church remains in continuous touch with the world of men

Facing page: Detail of the opulent decoration of the church of S. Andrea al Quirinale.

5
S. Lorenzo Fuori le Mura (☞ *131*)
The present-day basilica was formed by merging two ancient churches: S. Lorenzo (4th century) and the Chiesa della Vergine Maria (8th century). The current 13th-century appearance is the result of restoration work following World War II bombings in 1943.

6
S. Sebastiano (☞ *132*)
This basilica was built in the 4th century on the site of a Christian necropolis. Initially dedicated to Sts. Peter and Paul, it was later named for St. Sebastian, the Roman soldier martyred during the persecutions of Diocletian.

7
S. Paolo Fuori le Mura (☞ *131*)
After S. Pietro, this is the largest basilica in Rome. It was built by Constantine on the site of a small existing chapel and was dedicated to St. Paul.

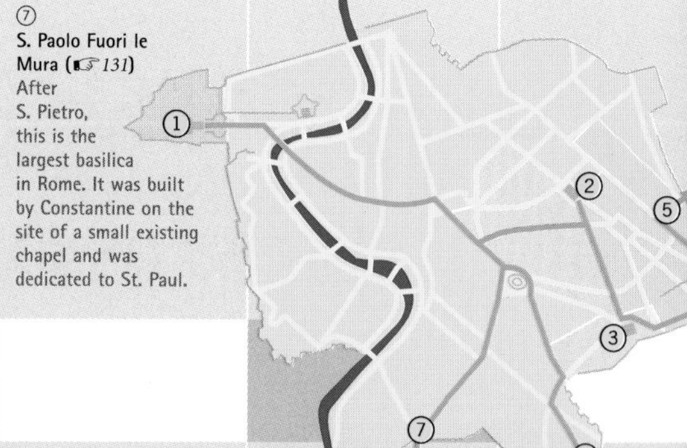

ROME'S JUBILEES

Origins and Chronology

In the Beginning

THE WORDS OF THE BIBLE

"You shall count off seven weeks of years, seven times seven years, so that the period of seven weeks of years gives 49 years. Then you shall have the trumpet sounded loud: on the 10th day of the 7th month—on the day of atonement—you shall have the trumpet sounded throughout all your land. And you shall hallow the 50th year and you shall proclaim liberty throughout the land to all its inhabitants. It shall be a jubilee for you: you shall return, every one of you, to your property and every one of you to your family. That 50th year shall be a jubilee for you: you shall not sow, or reap the aftergrowth, or harvest the unpruned vines. For it is a jubilee; it shall be holy to you: you shall eat only what the field itself produces."
Leviticus, 25:8–13
(*The New Oxford Annotated Bible*)

In the Old Testament (Leviticus, 25), one of the dictates God communicated to Moses on Mount Sinai was that of the Jubilee, a sabbatical celebration of a year of remission, to be held every 50 years. During this year, normal work activities were to cease, slaves were to be freed, and debts and punishments forgiven. It is difficult to say if this tradition came from Egypt or if it was imported there. A hieroglyphic describes Ramses II, the ruling pharaoh at the time of Moses, as "rich in jubilee celebrations." The festive trumpeting of the ram's horn that announced the year of remission was called a *yôbêl*, the derivation of the Latin term *iubilaeum* and the English word jubilee.
When Christianity adopted the concept of a great periodic indulgence, the idea of the forgiveness of accumulated material debts was replaced by the remission of spiritual and moral debts—that is, sins. Medieval man was much more concerned with these debts than with material ones, because of his vivid conception of hell and purgatory, places where eternal and interim punishments were carried out.
During the Middle Ages, a pilgrimage was the best means of obtaining forgiveness for sins and redemption from guilt. Although the tradition of making pilgrimages to holy sites dates from the early centuries of Christianity, starting in the 8th century pilgrimages could earn sinners expiation from even the gravest sins, including murder and adultery. Special manuals indicated the number of pilgrimages and penances required to atone for each sin, a tariff calculated to correspond with the severity of the crime. In a liturgical ceremony, the worldly clothing of the guilty was removed and replaced with the garments of pilgrims: a staff with a metal point, a long dress of rough texture, sandals, a short cape, and a leather bag to carry food and money. In their quest for rehabilitation, pilgrims could travel as far as their pilgrimage destination under church protection, but they remained excluded from society until they had redeemed their sins.
With the advent of Benedictine monasticism in the 9th and 10th centuries, this practice was more strictly regulated, in part because of the social disorder that the presence of criminals in

RELICS AND RELIQUARIES

Mortal remains of saints, martyrs, and heroes of the church are relics, treasures of faith, and objects of intense devotion.

① **S. Pietro** (☞ 52)
The basilica, which rises above the tomb of the apostle Peter, houses the veil of Veronica, a portion of the wood of the cross, and part of the lance that pierced Christ's side. The Treasury of S. Pietro contains an extensive collection of reliquaries.

Reliquary of the image of Christ of Edessa. Papal Sacrist (left).

② **S. Clemente** (☞ 105)
The apse mosaic of the Triumph of the Cross (*detail, above left*) contains fragments from the holy cross of Golgotha. The crypt beneath the ciborium contains the saint's body.

③ **Scala Santa** (☞ 109)
Sixtus V had this building constructed to preserve the ancient private chapel of the popes (the chapel of S. Lorenzo, known as the Sancta Sanctorum). The stairway has been falsely identified as the one traversed by Jesus during his trial (*right*).

View of Rome at the time of Pope Sixtus IV (oil on canvas, c. 1550). Mantua, Palazzo Ducale.

free circulation inevitably might provoke.

Principal pilgrimage destinations at that time were Jerusalem, considered the center, not only of Christianity, but also of the universe; Rome; and Santiago de Compostela, in Galicia, a region of northwest Spain, where the tomb the apostle James, evangelizer of Spain, is located. During this period, although Rome housed the tombs of Sts. Peter and Paul, the city was just a stop along the route to the Holy Land. Italy served as a natural and cultural bridge between West and East.

The Crusades for the liberation of Jerusalem from the "infidels," —as Muslims were called by medieval Christians—marked the apex of the armed pilgrimage movement. By participating in the Crusades, even financially, Christians were able to obtain plenary indulgence, or the remission of all temporal penance inflicted on the sinner in expiation for his or her sins.

FROM JERUSALEM TO ROME

With the passage of time, Arab incursions throughout the Mediterranean made pilgrimages to the Holy Land increasingly difficult. For centuries Arab forays constituted a threat to the Christian West, particularly to Spain. From the late 11th century to the mid-13th century, Crusades ensured European access to Biblical sites. But by the late 13th century, Christian Europe had lost control of the Holy Land. In 1270, the Seventh (and final) Crusade, against Tunisia, ended in defeat for the Christians, whose forces were decimated by plague; France's Louis IX, later St. Louis, was among the dead. Then, in 1291, the Crusades lost

ROME'S APPEARANCE

Throughout the Middle Ages and almost until the dawn of the Renaissance, pilgrims coming from the most distant locales, from as far away as northern Europe, arrived in Rome after a long and tiring trek. Looking down on the city for the first time from the surrounding heights, they saw hundreds of fortified and crenellated towers rising up amid the classical ruins. Each of these towers corresponded to one of the families that were vying for control of the city. Writer Piero Bargellini described the city, which stood amid vast areas of countryside:

"[Rome] still looked Medieval, with its enclosing walls, crenellated towers and campaniles pierced with windows: a city without domes, other than the flattened one of the Pantheon. The four major basilicas, with sloping roofs, formed arch-vaulted islands, spread out in four locations, distant from one another: S. Pietro, near the Tiber, S. Paolo Fuori le Mura, S. Giovanni in Laterano and S. Maria Maggiore."

④
S. Croce in Gerusalemme (☞ 124)
Also called the Basilica Sessoriana (*Sessorium* was the term for the imperial residence in the late empire), the church was erected by Constantine to house and honor relics of Christ's Passion, brought back from the Holy Land.

⑤
S. Susanna (☞ 100)
During the Middle Ages, this church was a pilgrimage destination because of its numerous relics of martyrs and saints (including St. Susanna), and well as relics of the cross, the tomb of Christ, and the Virgin's garments and hair.

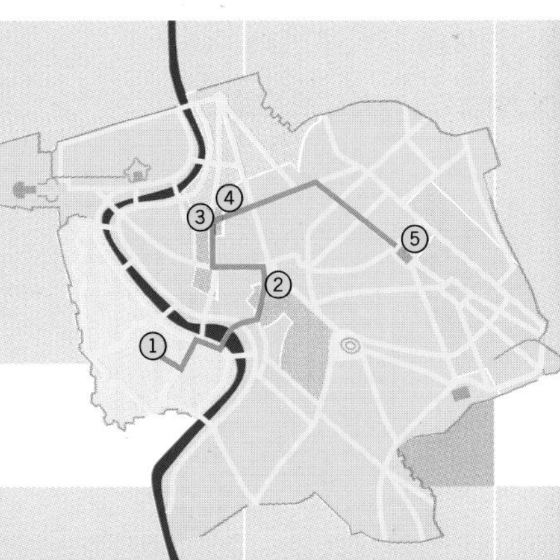

Pilgrims arriving in Rome, from Giovanni Sercambi's Chronicles, early 15th century. Lucca, State Archives.

the last Christian bulwark in the Near East, St. John of Acri (now Akko, in Israel).

The likelihood of a reconquest of the Holy Sepulcher became increasingly remote, and the center of the Christian world almost naturally shifted to Rome, site of the papacy and a holy place because of the presence of the tombs of Sts. Peter and Paul.

Many evangelical sites were difficult to reach, so sanctuaries where relics were kept and venerated, even relics of dubious authenticity, became pilgrimage destinations in the West. These relics arrived in Europe by two routes: some came from the Holy Land, having been donated by crusaders or bought by monasteries, and others were plundered from the imperial treasury in Costantinople, the capital of the Eastern Empire and, in a major turn of events, the site to which the Venitians had diverted the Fourth Crusade (1202–1204) from its original intended destination, Egypt. In this way the West, lacking in sacred objects, was able to satiate its hunger for relics. News spread through the Christian world of miracles wrought by the relics, and the relics' new homes—churches, monasteries, sanctuaries—became centers of Christianity and destinations of popular devotion.

"DISCOUNTS" FOR VISITING THE BASILICAS

At the end of the 14th century, the city's four patriarchal churches were S. Giovanni in Laterano, S. Pietro, San Paolo Fuori le Mura, and S. Maria Maggiore. Pilgrims who visited each basilica were granted an indulgence "bonus": a deduction of one year plus 40 days from the length of the punishment to be suffered in the afterlife. Those who visited other less "important" churches in Rome received a partial indulgence of only 40 days.

HOLY ROUTES

As the major monastic and mendicant orders were established, numerous abbeys and routes were constructed to connect them, which made it less difficult and dangerous to reach holy sites. The routes to Santiago de Compostela and Rome were dotted with sanctuaries that housed miraculous relics, which in turn transformed the sanctuaries into cultural centers and ultimately commercial hubs. New settlements developed because of the presence of pilgrims, and they vied with one another for the presence of worshippers, who came searching for parts of saints' bodies and

A REFUGE FOR PILGRIMS

Foreign communities had *scholae*, recognized institutions equipped with churches, hospitals, cemeteries, and hospices for the benefit of pilgrims from specific countries.

① **S. Maria dell'Anima** (☞ *71*)
Approved by Boniface IX, this was a hospice for Germans, who were guaranteed food and lodging for 10 days.

② **Nostra Signora del Sacro Cuore** (☞ *68*)
Next to the church of S. Giacomo degli Spagnoli (the original name) was a Spanish hospice, which offered food and lodging for three days.

③ **S. Luigi dei Francesi** (☞ *84*)
Since the late 15th century, this institution welcomed French pilgrims, who could stay up to three days and received a cash subsidy upon leaving (*right:* the church's ceiling).

objects connected to their memories.

As stories of miracles multiplied, and as the number of new cults surrounding martyrs and saints mushroomed, restoration projects were undertaken to create glorious settings worthy of the sacred mementos. The acquisition of precious objects of worship took on economic as well as spiritual importance, and a speculative market in relics soon developed.

INDULGENCES

Visiting sacred sights yielded indulgences of various types, either partial or plenary. Bishops were soon granting indulgences in exchange for money and subcontracting their distribution, and the privilege was abused to the point where the practice was compromised irremediably.

The 13th century brought a canonic examination of the practice of indulgences, and the bishops' assembly convoked for the Lateran Council IV (1215) reestablished full papal authority, the *plenitudo potestatis*, over this matter. St. Thomas Aquinas (1225–1274), the great philosopher and theologian of the time, addressed the issue in definitive terms: "The power to grant indulgences resides exclusively with the pope."

Doctrine legitimized the principle of indulgence when it affirmed that the church is not only the fiduciary custodian of the Communion of Saints—that is, the saints' community—but also the guardian of the treasury of merits acquired by them. The church may distribute part of this limitless "moral capital" to the faithful. When Boniface VIII proclaimed plenary indulgence for the Jubilee of 1300, he simultaneously seized for himself, as representative of Peter on Earth, the right to distribute this immense reserve of salvation.

In 1295, just five years before that first Jubilee, plenary indulgence was granted to pilgrims who had gone to the church of S. Maria in Collemaggio in Aquila and to Assisi, while those who had visited the patriarchal basilicas in Rome received only a partial indulgence. At the same time, the prized remissions of sins were also granted, for a variety of different reasons, to believers who had not made pilgrimages. Among the beneficiaries were

KEEP TO THE RIGHT

The first Jubilee brought about innovations in transportation and traffic. In 1300, one-way traffic was introduced on the two sides of the Ponte S. Angelo. Dante Alighieri may have participated in this Jubilee, of which he wrote:

"thus the Romans, because of the great throng, in the year of the Jubilee, have taken measures for the people to pass over the bridge, so that on one side all face toward the castle and go to S. Pietro, and on the other they go toward the Mount."

—Dante's *Inferno*, translation by Charles S. Singleton, 1970, Princeton University Press (Bollingen Series)

Papal procession over the Ponte S. Angelo. 17th century.

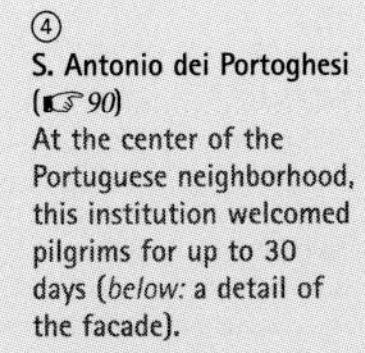

④ **S. Antonio dei Portoghesi** (☞ *90*)
At the center of the Portuguese neighborhood, this institution welcomed pilgrims for up to 30 days (*below:* a detail of the facade).

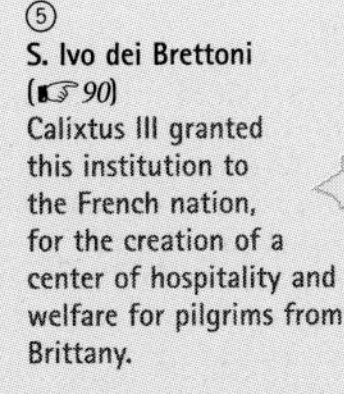

⑤ **S. Ivo dei Brettoni** (☞ *90*)
Calixtus III granted this institution to the French nation, for the creation of a center of hospitality and welfare for pilgrims from Brittany.

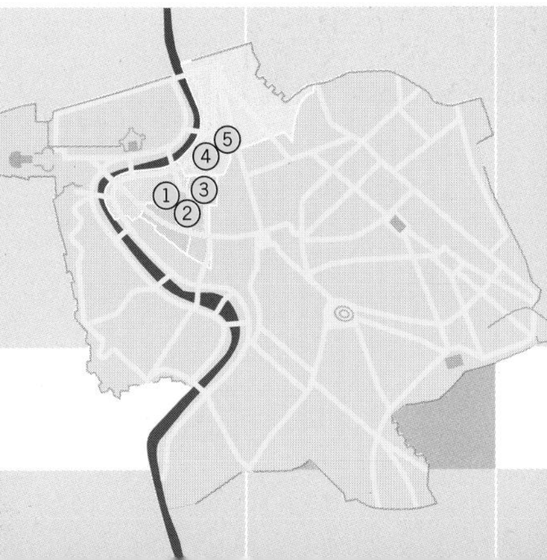

WHAT IS A PAPAL BULL?

In Medieval Latin, a *bulla* was a seal of authentication on official documents; it was affixed to the parchment with a silk or hemp thread. The word later came to mean the documents promulgated by papal or imperial authority. Thus a papal bull is a letter from the pope that can address various issues (subjects of faith, but also affairs of state), and which is proclaimed or delivered to recipients. Papal bulls are still written in Latin, the official language of the church, and in the historiography they are identified by the first words of the text. The first Jubilee (1300), for example, was declared with the papal bull *Antiquorum habet fida relatio* ("The elderly are circulating a trust-worthy account").

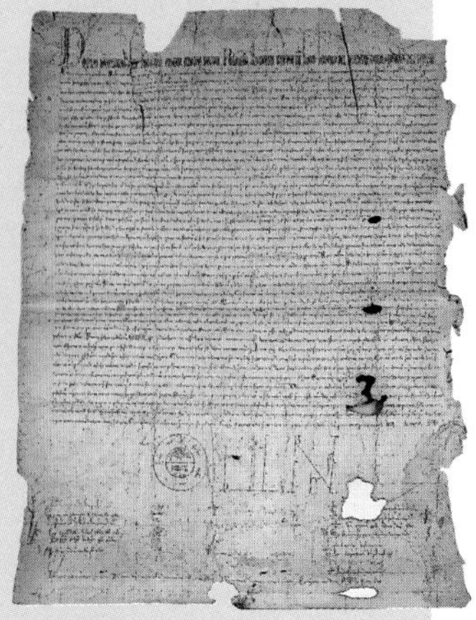

Papal bull by Honorius III, dated March 15, 1218.

Franciscans, missionaries to the Tartars; the pope's allies in the war against the Sicilians; and all those who fought against the Colonna, Rome's powerful patrician family and mortal enemies of Pope Boniface VIII, who was a member of the rival Caetani family.

ROME, THE NEW JERUSALEM

For centuries, Jerusalem was the center of the world of the faithful, but now this role fell to Rome. Calling itself the Cradle of Christianity and site of the throne of Peter, the city designated itself the direct heir to Jerusalem. Where it was once necessary to join the Crusades to obtain an indulgence, the establishment of the Jubilee put indulgences within the reach of anyone who completed a penitential journey, *ad limina apostolorum*, to the tombs of the apostles. Important relics—such as the veil of Veronica (the sudarium of Christ, with the impression of his face) and fragments of the true cross and the holy lance, all preserved in Rome—attracted multitudes of pilgrims.

Legend has it that the pilgrims who went to Rome for Christmas 1299, when Christmas coincided with New Year's, spread the word that the pope was about to proclaim a grand indulgence on the occasion of the century's close. An account of the events, written by Cardinal Jacopo Stefaneschi, relates that Boniface VIII, looking for a precedent, consulted the archives to see if there was any mention of such a custom, but he found no doctrinal justification that might endorse such an initiative. It was at that point that an elderly pilgrim came forward with a story in support of a precedent. He told the pope that he had participated, along with his own father, in the plenary indulgence granted at the close of the preceding century. His father had then requested that the son, if still alive a century later, return to Rome to complete a similar pilgrimage.

> *"The elderly are circulating a trust-worthy account that those who go to the honored Basilica of the Prince of Apostles in Rome are granted great remissions and indulgences of sins."*

FAITH ENROUTE

Beautiful shrines, with painted Madonnas, signs of widespread and popular devotion, decorate corners of Rome's pilgrimage roads. Like beacons at the sea's edge they capture the traveler's eye.

① **Via della Lungara** (☞ 67)
Designed by Bramante, this street, along with the parallel Via Giulia, is considered a sacred route because of the flow of pilgrims that traveled it, en route to S. Pietro. The street is a continuum of 16th-century villas and palaces.

② **Via del Pellegrino** (☞ 79)
Opened in 1497, this was part of the ancient Via Peregrinorum that lead toward the Vatican; at the corner of the Arco di S. Margherita is a beautiful stucco shrine with a Madonna and child.

③ **Via dei Coronari** (☞ 73)
Many pilgrims traveled this street to cross Ponte S. Angelo and arrive at the basilica of S. Pietro. *Coronari*, or rosary-makers, gave the street its name; they were merchants who sold rosaries to the faithful along this route.

The oldest shrine in Rome, on Via dei Coronari.

Pilgrims stopping at a sanctuary, from Giovanni Sercambi's Chronicles (15th century).

Thus begins the papal bull *Antiquorum habet fida relatio*, in which Pope Boniface VIII proclaimed the first Jubilee year in 1300. The first Jubilee marked the beginning of a custom that has endured many ups and downs ever since. In the papal bull *Antiquorum habet*, the pope decreed that the Jubilee would take place in every centennial year. But one of Boniface VIII's successors, the French pope Clement VI (1342–1352), proclaimed a second Jubilee as early as 1350 and decreed that the Jubilee should be celebrated every 50 years. This schedule would be changed numerous times, and extraordinary Jubilees were added to ordinary ones. As a result, Jubilees have long been held every 25 years. Over the centuries, Jubilee celebrations have reflected the political, social, and cultural situations of their times, but the principal players remained the pilgrims, who faced the long, difficult journey to Rome, full of hope and faith that their path would lead to salvation.

A DANGER-FILLED JOURNEY

During the Middle Ages, only soldiers, merchants, and pilgrims habitually traveled the perilous roads that linked different cities and countries. Merchants and pilgrims, particularly, ran numerous risks along the way. Merchants traveled to acquire material riches; pilgrims hoped to acquire gifts and wealth of another nature: indulgences and grace. Both abandoned familiar, safe places to face the unknown and danger, with no certain guarantee of ever returning home.

THE SPECTACLE OF FAITH

Michel de Montaigne, a 16th-century philosopher and traveler, wrote in his *Italian Travel Journal* (1580–1581):

"The splendor of Rome and its principal grandiosity consist in the conspicuousness of devotion; it is quite wonderful, these days, to observe the religious zeal of so vast a multitude. . . . The most notable and amazing thing I have ever seen, here or elsewhere, was the incredible quantity of people scattered throughout the city that day for devotions, and above all the quantity of confraternity members. For in addition to the great number of those who were seen by day, gathering in S. Pietro, as soon as the city grew dark, a fire appeared for each of those monks, who set out in a line, toward S. Pietro, each holding a torch, in most cases a white candle. I believe that at least 12,000 torches passed before me, since this procession filled the street from eight in the evening until midnight, during which time I saw neither space nor interruption."

④
Piazza di Tor Sanguigna (Piazza Navona) (☞ *70*)
A theatrical shrine, depicting the Assumption of the Virgin, dominates the piazza in front of the facade of Palazzo Grossi. A painting inserted within an exuberant frame is surrounded by putti (*above right*).

⑤
Via del Plebiscito (Galleria Doria Pamphilj) (☞ *80*)
On Palazzo Pamphilj's facade, an opulent shrine with a sunburst design, with an image of the Madonna at the center.

VOICES FROM THE PAST

In his description of the millennial Jubilee celebrations of 1300, German historian Ferdinand Gregorovius quoted Giovanni Villani, a Florentine merchant and banker, eyewitness of the event, and author of the *Nuova Cronica*:

"Rome offered the spectacle of throngs of pilgrims coming and going ... such a mob of people ... Men from their own countries were ready to welcome them at the gates ... and urban officials ... who pointed out to them places where they could find lodgings

... For an entire year, Rome was a seething field of pilgrims, a true Babel in its confusion of languages. They say that every day, 30,000 pilgrims came and went and every day there were 200,000 foreigners in the city..."

It is difficult for the modern traveler to imagine the significance of the sacrifices that a pilgrimage implied in the Middle Ages. The pilgrim left his land and loved ones, and they, in turn, were deprived of his labor for as long as he traveled. The journey also entailed additional expenses for the family, which had to supply their pilgrim with a sum sufficient to live on for a period of time that was difficult to estimate.

Once a pilgrim made the decision to go, the bishop blessed him in a solemn ceremony and presented him with the pilgrim's staff of penitence, a curved staff that symbolized his new condition. The pilgrim was then accompanied in a procession beyond the city gates. A few privileged pilgrims departed on horseback or astride mules, but most went on foot. Before leaving, many made their wills.

All roads led to Rome, it was said, because it was from there that, in ancient times, pilgrims had departed. In antiquity, the efficiency of communication routes contributed to the expansion of the empire, but since its collapse in AD 476, the Roman system of well-constructed roads, which had led from the capital of the ancient world through Europe to the East and to Africa, had slowly and inexorably deteriorated. Time had damaged the paving, bridges had collapsed, and major routes often changed-because of interruptions and detours. Along the principal routes, pilgrims found a dense network of inns and places of shelter, as well as numerous minor sanctuaries and abbeys where they could rest and take refreshment. At dusk, a bell, called the *smarrita* (for "those gone astray") rang out from places of shelter, to indicate the way to those who were still on the road. The *smarrita* was renamed the Ave Maria (Hail Mary) when St. Bonaventure ordered his monks to recite a prayer three times for those who might be lost during the night.

During medieval times, those who could took advantage of water routes, which were quicker and more direct, although made dangerous by Saracen pirates, who all too frequently intercepted pilgrims' ships and sold the travelers as slaves in distant lands. The difficulties, dangers, and sufferings of a pilgrimage—including the tolls, duties, and taxes along the road; the perpetual danger of bandits; and the threats of illness and inclement weather—served

CHRISTMAS IN ROME

Christmas crèches of all sizes and styles are scattered throughout the city, in the piazzas and in almost every church in Rome. They can be visited in a citywide itinerary from mid-December mid-January.

① **S. Pietro** (☞ 52)
During the festivities, city residents and tourists gather in the embrace of Bernini's colonnade to admire the tall fir tree decorated for the holiday, and the traditional crèche at the foot of the obelisk. The recent custom of a Christmas tree in Piazza S. Pietro was introduced by Pope John Paul II. (*left*).

② **Piazza Navona** (☞ 70)
Both before and after its Baroque transformation, the piazza was a theater for famous festivals and processions. Today, during the Christmas season and until Epiphany, the piazza is filled with stalls selling small figures for crèches and toys.

③ **Ss. Ambrogio e Carlo al Corso** (☞ 92)
The church contains an elaborate 18th-century crèche that reflects, in its details, the period of its creation (*below*).

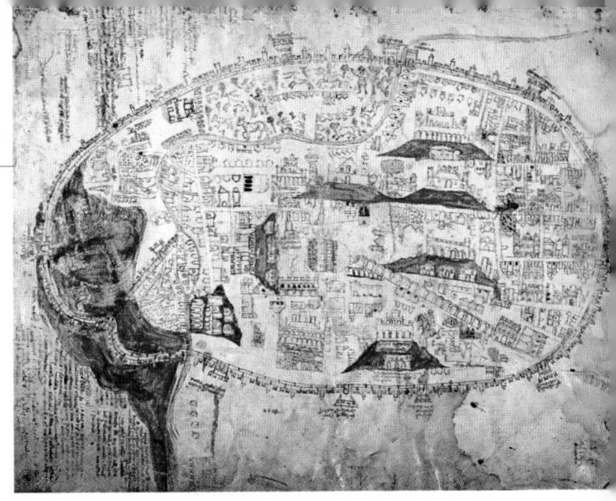

to increase the value of the venture as an atonement for misdeeds and a source of indulgences.

HELP ALONG THE WAY

Since antiquity, guidebooks have described the itinerary to Rome from the most remote parts of Europe. Some, such as the *Itinerary of Einsiedeln* and the *Notitia ecclesiarum urbis Romae*, both dating from the Carolingian era, limited themselves to written descriptions of the route and stopping places. Others were embellished with images or maps and included information about distances, in days on foot, and suggestions about which direction to take. Two of the most well-known were the *Chronica Maiora* by Matthew Paris, written in the 13th century, and the *Tabula Peutingeriana*, a 23-foot scroll taken from an original source dating from late antiquity.

These precious aids were accessible to very few pilgrims, both because of their value and because most people were illiterate or did not know Latin. The majority of wayfarers trusted oral descriptions and information, and they reached the principle communication routes and joined forces with other pilgrims who had the same destination. From throughout Europe, they gathered en route to Rome along Via Francigena (the road from France) also called Via Romea (the road to Rome), which, depending on the era, coincided with stretches of Via Aurelia, Via Cassia, and Via Flaminia. The route arrived at Rome over the Ponte Milvio (Milvian bridge) and passed through the Porta del Popolo, or from the present Via Trionfale, descending from the Monte Mario hill.

Once in Rome, the *Mirabilia Urbis Romae*, an illustrated, handwritten guidebook, described for voyagers the legends, between history and myth, about the ruined monuments of antiquity. The vestiges of ancient Rome were scattered among the urban outgrowths that crowded around the major churches, separated from one another by vast areas of countryside and vineyards.

In subsequent centuries, the institution of Jubilees in Rome contributed significantly to the renewal of the city and to its return to a splendor that, even today, attracts millions of visitors—pilgrims and non-pilgrims alike.

Plan of Rome in 1345.

Opposite: Pilgrims at S. Giovanni in Laterano; detail from a fresco in the Biblioteca Apostolica Vaticana.

VOICES FROM THE PAST

"A chronicler who was among the pilgrims in 1300 described it thus: 'Bread, wine, meat, fish and oats were traded in abundance and at reasonable prices; but hay was rather expensive and inns extremely so.

... The Romans claim to number 2 million men and women in all. And in that crowd, I often saw someone fall and be crushed beneath the feet of the multitudes and it was only with great effort that I myself, more than once, escaped such misfortune.'

... We can imagine the quantity of ancient artifacts, coins, gems, rings, sculptures, marble fragments and manuscripts—which pilgrims took back to their countries."

—Storia della Città di Roma nel Medioevo
(1859–1873)

④
Piazza di Spagna
(☞ *89*)
As in many Italian cities, life-size crèches are installed in the piazzas of Rome. On January 6, on the Spanish Steps, the Three Kings arrive, bearing gifts for the infant Jesus (*left*).

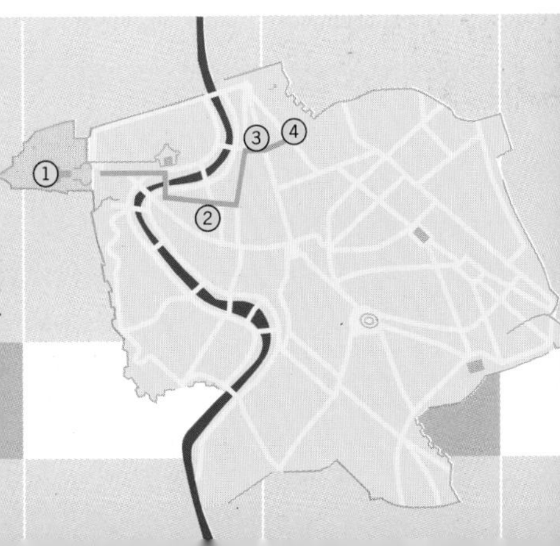

The Tumultuous Middle Ages in Rome

1300 **THE FIRST JUBILEE**
Pope Boniface VIII (1294–1303) issues the papal bull *Antiquorum habet fida relatio,* proclaiming the first Jubilee. It is written to address popular expectations at the century's end and is promulgated two months after the New Year. Approximately 200,000 pilgrims are in Rome. Giotto is commissioned to execute a fresco in S. Giovanni in Laterano, depicting Boniface VIII proclaiming the Jubilee, and a mosaic of the Navity in S. Pietro.

1302 With the papal bull *Unum Sanctam,* Boniface VIII proclaims the supremacy of the papacy over secular authority. This is the first sign of a rupture between the church and the French monarchy, the most powerful of the time.

1303 Boniface VIII establishes the Rome's university, now the Università della Sapienza (from the name of the Palazzo della Sapienza, where it was located from the 15th century until 1935). Philip IV, king of France, reacts to the publication of *Unam Sanctam* by having Boniface VIII captured while at his residence in Anagni (south of Rome). Freed by popular insurrection, the pope returns to Rome, where he dies in October of that year.

1309 Pope Clement V (1305–1315) transfers the papal see to Avignon, France, marking the beginning of the so-called Avignon captivity, which lasts until 1377, during which time the papacy is subject to the French crown.

1341 The River Tiber floods the city.

1343 Motivated by the success of the Holy Year, particularly for the city's economy, a Roman delegation appears before Pope Clement VI (1342–1352) in Avignon, to convince him to proclaim a new Jubilee before the end of the century

1347 For a few months, Cola di Rienzo, a common man, assumes power in a popular revolt as tribune of the people, with the initial support of the papacy. His political model, based on republican and imperial Rome, contributes to reawakening interest in the monuments of antiquity. He is killed on the Campidoglio in 1354, during an uprising.

1348 The stairway of S. Maria in Aracoeli (☞*115*) is opened. In September, the most terrible earthquake since the founding of Rome destroys both recent structures and ancient monuments. The facade of S. Giovanni in Laterano collapses and the basilica of S. Pietro is damaged. The Black Death strikes the city.

1350 **THE JUBILEE WITHOUT A POPE**
Clement VI remains in Avignon and sends two cardinals to celebrate the Holy Year. A visit to S. Giovanni in Laterano (☞*105*) is added to the visits to the basilicas of S. Paolo Fuori le Mura (☞*131*) and S. Pietro (☞*52*) recommended by Boniface VIII for the first Jubilee. To gain indulgence, Romans must visit the three basilicas once a day for 30 days; pilgrims coming from outside the city must make the daily visit for 15 days.

1377 The end of the Avignon captivity is confirmed by Gregory XI's reentry into Rome. The pope's residence is moved from the Lateran to its new headquarters at S. Pietro. This move reflects the shift of Rome's city center, which now lies in the area within the bend of the Tiber, between the Campidoglio and the Vatican. Because of the plague and the continuing economic crisis, the population, which stood at approximately 35,000 inhabitants in 1300, declined to approximately 25,000.

1383-1388 The plague further decimates the population of Rome.

1389 With the papal bull *Salvator Noster Unigenitus,* Pope Urban VI (1378–1389) proclaims a new Jubilee year for 1390 and changes the interval between one Jubilee and another from 50 to 33 years (the number of years in the life of Jesus). The change is meant to accommodate the average human life span, which at the time was less than 50 years, but the unexpected proclamation also has several political motives, such as addressing the

ELSEWHERE IN ITALY

Approaching the13th century, the struggle between Guelphs, aligned with the Papal States of central Italy, and the Ghibellines, aligned with the German Holy Roman Emperor, becomes a feature of medieval life in Italy,

1200
Italy's population numbers about 8.5 million

1204
Crusaders, led by Venetian doge Dandolo, capture Constantinople.

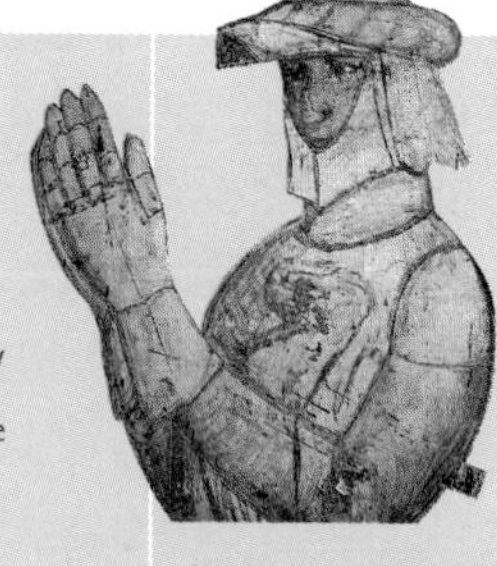

A crusader; 14th-century fresco. Naples, Cathedral.

1250
Holy Roman Emperor Frederic II dies in Apulia. In Florence the Guelfs get the upper hand and establish a new democratic order.

1262
Florentine bankers issue Europe's first bills of exchange.

1264
Charles I of Anjou invades Italy, intervening in the continuing Guelph–Ghibelline conflict.

antischismatic struggle against the antipope in Avignon and papal control over the city of Rome, which is torn by clan rivalries.

1390 **THE UNEXPECTED JUBILEE**
Pope Boniface IX (1389–1404) has only a few months to organize and manage an unforeseen Jubilee in a devastated city. Within the city's walls, vast uninhabited areas alternate with small settlements; the layout of the road network has almost disappeared; churches are crumbling; and the baronial families have taken possession of the ancient ruins, transforming them into fortresses from which they control urban points of access and transit. The church is without funds, and to face its grave economic problems, it is forced to seek loans and take out mortgages from Tuscan bankers. S. Maria Maggiore (☞ *126*) is added to the list of three basilicas to be visited. To prevent an outbreak of plague, a decree is issued on May 31, specifying that pilgrims need only visit the basilicas for a single week, but the plague returns nonetheless. The pope retreats to nearby Rieti. The church reaps considerable income from the Jubilee, in part because of a new practice of granting of indulgences outside Rome. For the first time, penitents' economic situations are taken into account in determining the amount that they must pay to obtain indulgences without making a pilgrimage to the city.

1399 In the spring, the Flagellanti Bianchi (White Flagellants), members of a popular religious movement, traverse Italy to the cry of *pace e misericordia* (peace and mercy). They flagellate themselves as a sign of penitence, dress in white (hence their name), and wear hoods. They enter Rome, where the pope receives them on September 7.

1400 **THE UNOFFICIAL JUBILEE**
This Jubilee is not officially proclaimed by the usual papal bull, but rather is commanded by throngs of the faithful flocking to the city

Taddeo di Bartolo's plan of Rome (early 15th century). Siena, Palazzo Pubblico.

(120,000 according to some sources) in September 1399. With the arrival of hot weather, the plague returns, claiming up to 800 victims a day. On the outskirts of the city, roads are littered with corpses. The Hospice of S. Maria dell'Anima (☞ *71*) is established to accommodate German pilgrims. The pope institutes a building commission for the restoration of S. Paolo Fuori le Mura.

1415 A flood strikes Rome.
1422 An outbreak of the plague and a flood devastate the city.

1423
1425 **AN UNKNOWN JUBILEE**
Scant documentation provides differing accounts of the precise date of this Jubilee. As soon as he is elected by the Council of Constance to remedy the Western Schism, Pope Martin V (1417–1431) initiates the difficult task of restoring the social, economic, and cultural life of the city. He begins reconstruction projects to improve the image of the papacy and the church, and basilicas, churches, and palaces are renovated. During this period, various painters work under the patronage of the pope and cardinals: Gentile da Fabriano (the frescoes in S. Giovanni in Laterano that depict scenes from the life of John the Baptist), Pisanello, Masaccio, and Masolino (*Triptych of the Snow* in S. Maria Maggiore). For the first time, papal documents mention the opening of the Porta Santa (Holy Door) in S. Giovanni in Laterano.

1271
Marco Polo (1254–1324) begins his voyage to the East.

1290–1375
Dante Alighieri (*left*, in a fresco by Domenico di Michelino in the Florence Cathedral), Francesco Petrarch, and Giovanni Boccaccio lay the groundwork for modern Italian literature.

1377
The Avignon captivity ends. Pope Gregory XI reestablishes the seat of papal power in Rome (*right:* the event in a fresco by Giorgio Vasari, in the Sala Regia of the Vatican). The election of this French anti-pope leads to the Western Schism (1378–1417).

The Splendors of Rome's Renaissance

1450 THE NEW FACE OF ROME
Nicholas V (1447–1455), the humanist pope, continues restoration work in the city. He establishes the basis for the Vatican Library's first collection of books, acquiring codices and manuscripts; he is also establishes the Vatican Botanical Garden. A period characterized by patronage and advances in the arts begins. The contract for the Holy Year treasury is granted to Cosimo de' Medici, who strikes a medal called a Giubileo, which pilgrims take home as souvenirs, along with copies of Veronica's veil. The areas traversed by pilgrims traveling from one basilica to another are sparsely inhabited and unsafe. On the occasion of the Jubilee, to encourage development of these areas, the pope resorts to incentives, exonerating inhabitants from payment of taxes and lining streets with new elm trees. A new outbreak of plague forces pilgrims to spend only five days in the city. The pope blesses the pilgrims every Sunday at S. Pietro, and the Veronica's veil is exhibited to the public every Saturday. Parts of the old Constantinian basilica of S. Pietro are demolished, others expanded. Architect Leon Battista Alberti begins construction of the Vatican Palaces (☞*54–58*).

1452 Two important projects took place during this year: the improvement of three roads (Via dei Pellegrini, which leads into the present-day Ghetto; Via Papale, which leads to the Campidoglio; and Via Recta, the present Via dei Coronari) and the rebuilding of the Leonine City that lies between Castel S. Angelo and S. Pietro. The latter calls for the demolition of the old medieval Borgo district and the creation a new small city layed out on three rectilinear streets.

1455 The construction of Palazzo di Venezia (☞*81*) begins.

1458 Enea Silvio Piccolomini, humanist, patron, one of the leading figures in the cultural renewal of Rome, is elected pope. He takes the name Pius II (1458–1464).

1462 With the papal bull *Cum Almam Nostram Urbem*, Pius II promotes the protection of ancient monuments.

1473-1475 In preparation for the Jubilee of 1475, Sixtus IV (1471–1484) begins an urban renewal plan that addresses problems with roads, sanitation, the restoration of monuments, and the construction of new buildings, with attention paid to the aesthetic and commemorative aspect of the new architecture. Some of the many projects include the construction of the Ponte Sisto (☞*76*), the only bridge built over the Tiber between antiquity and the 19th century; the straightening of many medieval streets; the demolition of exterior stairways, overhangs, and balconies from residential buildings; and the enclosing of porticoes and passageways. These measures were also meant to reduce crime in a city where pilgrims were frequently assaulted in the dark recesses of porticoed streets. Renaissance Rome begins to take shape.

1475 THE SISTINE JUBILEE
Plague affects this Holy Year, which is extended until Easter 1476. The pope sanctions the 25-year Jubilee period and the cancellation of all indulgences outside Rome during the Jubilee year. The city becomes the definitive center of the Catholic world. Pilgrims included many crowned heads: King Ferrante of Naples; Queen Dorothy of

Above: Sixtus IV nominates Platina prefect of the Vatican Library (1477), in a painting by Melozzo da Forlì. Pinacoteca Vaticana.

1402
The Visconti of Milan repelled Robert of Bavaria's attempted invasion.

1407
The Banco of S. Giorgio, Europe's first public bank, is established in Genoa.

1427
Masaccio paints the fresco of the Trinity in S. Maria Novella in Florence. He dies a year later in Rome at age 27.

1443
Brunelleschi's (1377–1446) cupola is completed on Florence's Duomo.

1451
Christopher Columbus (*below*) is born in Genoa

1455
Beato Angelico dies in Rome

1469–1492
Florence is ruled by Lorenzo de' Medici (1449–1492), known as "the Magnificent," one of history's greatest patrons of the arts.

1498
Dominican friar Girolamo Savonarola (1452–1498), right in a painting by Fra' Bartolomeo della Porta, was hanged and burned in Florence as a heretic. After the expulsion of the Medici family (1494), he had established a democratic republic based on a moralistic philosophy.

Denmark; Mattia Corvino, king of Hungary; Federico da Montefeltro, duke of Urbino; and Charlotte of Lusignano, former queen of Cyprus. With the papal bull *Ad decorem militantis Ecclesiae*, Sixtus IV establishes the Biblioteca Apostolica Vaticana (☞*55*). Reconstruction projects continue under Sixtus IV, including S. Maria del Popolo (☞*92*) from 1475 to 1477; S. Agostino (☞*82*) from 1479 to 1483; S. Maria della Pace (☞*71*) in 1482; the Sistine Chapel (☞*55*) from 1475 to 1481; the Ospedale di S. Spirito in Sassia (☞*61*) from 1473 to 1478; and the Palazzo della Cancelleria (☞*69*) in 1485.

1500 **THE JUBILEE OF THE GREAT MASTERS**

Pope Alexander VI (1492–1503) establishes the ritual of the opening and closing of the Porta Santa in each of the four major basilicas. The passage through the door becomes a condition for obtaining indulgence. Resuming a project of Pope Nicholas V, the Via Alessandrina is constructed, corresponding to the new Porta Santa of S. Pietro (inaugurated December 24, 1499, with the beginning of the Holy Year). Bramante designs the cloister of S. Maria della Pace and the tempietto of S. Pietro in Montorio (☞*71*), his first two projects in Rome. Michelangelo creates the *Pietà*, his first work in Rome.

1503 Julius II (Giuliano Della Rovere), one of Rome's greatest patron of the arts, is elected pope. He is pope until 1513.

1508–1512 Michelangelo paints the frescoes for the Sistine Chapel.

1509 Raphael (1483–1520) begins work on his Stanze in the Vatican (☞*52*).

1510 Martin Luther visits Rome and is scandalized by the dissolute habits of the popes and by the sale of indulgences.

1517 Lateran Council V concludes in Rome, during which Pope Leo X declares that the church's work of self-reformation is completed.

1523 Another devastating plague strikes the city.

Domenico del Massaio's plan of Rome, 1472. Biblioteca Apostolica Vaticana.

1525 **THE TRIUMPH OF MONEY**

The sale of indulgences flourishes; believers are no longer required to complete a pilgrimage and can simply pay to receive absolution. The plague and the possibility of obtaining indulgence without going to Rome result in a very small number of pilgrims during the Jubilee. Pope Clement VII (1523–1534) opens the Via del Babuino (formerly the Via Clementia, then the Via Paolina, completed in 1543, under Paul III). Thus the so-called trident of the Campo Marzio district takes shape, with its vertex at Piazza del Popolo (☞*88*), the principal northern point of entry for pilgrims. In subsequent centuries, numerous inns and hotels open here to houses artists and travelers. Antonio da Sangallo and Baldassarre Peruzzi continue working on S. Pietro in the Vatican. Raphael designs the Hall of Constantine.

1526 The first historically reliable census in the modern era counts 55,000 inhabitants.

1527 Charles V's imperial troops pillage the city in what will be known as the Sack of Rome.

1542 Paul III establishes the congregation of the Santo Uffizio as a custodian of Catholic orthodoxy.

1546 Antonio da Sangallo, who is overseeing the construction of the new basilica of S. Pietro and the Palazzo Farnese, dies. Michelangelo Buonarroti takes over these projects.

Above: a gold ducat coined by Clement VII for the Jubilee of 1525. Museo Nazionale Romano.
Below: S. Pietro and the Vatican. Vatican, Barracks of the Noble Guards.

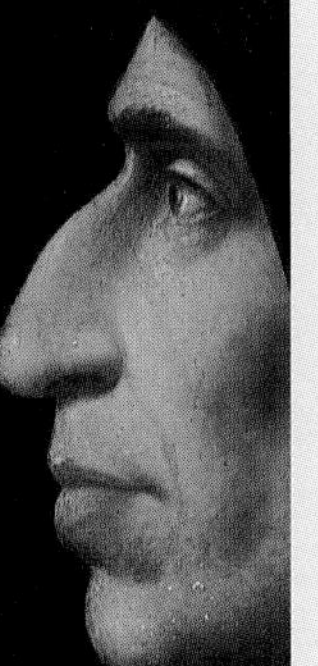

1499
Leonardo da Vinci (1452–1519) completed the *Last Supper* for the refectory of S. Maria delle Grazie in Milan.

1513
The Prince by Machiavelli (1469–1527) was the strongest expression of Renaissance political thought.

1521
Pope Leo X (Giovanni de' Medici, 1513–1521) excommunicates Martin Luther (1483–1546), precipitating the Protestant Reformation.

1545–1563
The Council of Trent formulates the Catholic response to the Reformation.

Counter-Reformation and the Baroque Era

1550 **THE JUBILEE OF THE "NEW" ROME**
The death of Paul III in 1549 delays the opening of the Holy Year, which is inaugurated by Julius III (1550–1555) during Carnival of 1550. To avoid speculation and unjustified price increases, rents are frozen for pilgrims' lodgings. Ignatius Loyola and Philip Neri actively participate in the Jubilee. Julius III allows Michelangelo, now elderly, to visit the seven churches on horseback. The appreciation and restoration of ancient monuments continues, intended to spur an ideological revival of classical Rome's pomp and splendor, and to sanction the continuity between the Roman empire and the papacy.

1551–1555 Julius III builds a suburban villa, the Villa Giulia (☞*134*), a compendium of Mannerist culture.

1555 Pope Paul IV (1555–1559) issues a papal bull that establishes the Ghetto (☞*81*) in the area of the ancient Circus Flaminius; it will be the compulsory residence of the Jewish community until 1870.

1561 Pius V (Antonio Ghislieri), persecutor of the heretics, is elected pope. He will later become saint.

1568 Construction of the Chiesa del Gesù (☞*80*), designed by Vignola, begins.

1575 **THE JUBILEE OF THE COUNTER-REFORMATION**
At the height of the Counter-Reformation, the Holy Year becomes an ideological celebration of the church in defense of the Catholic religion and a call for unity among believers. The law *Quae Publice Utilia,* written at the behest of Gregory XIII (1572–1585), introduces the concept of building for the public good. The pope grants a permanent headquarters to the Archconfraternity of the Santissima Trinità, which will play an important role in welcoming pilgrims during this and future Jubilees. Carlo Borromeo, archibishop of Milan, participates in a pilgrimage and travels barefoot over the prescribed itineraries. With the establishment of the Itinerary of the Seven Churches, an initiative by Philip Neri, work on the roads connecting the major basilicas becomes necessary; the Via Merulana and Via Gregoriana are opened (1576).

Portrait of Pope Julius III, in the Galleria Spada.

1584 The Vertuosa Compagnia de' Musici (Company of Virtuous Musicians), also known as the Academy of S. Cecilia, is established; it will remain the most important musical institution in Rome.

1585–1590 These years mark Sixtus V's papacy, during which the advent of the use of carriages mandates the broadening or redesign of numerous streets, including Via Felice, Via Panisperna, Via dei Serpenti, and Via Maggiore.

1586 Under the direction of Domenico Fontana, the Vatican obelisk is placed in the center of Piazza S. Pietro (☞*54*); the "memorable undertaking," as contemporary accounts call it, takes six months to complete.

1592 A malaria epidemic strikes the city.

1598–1599 Once more, the Tiber overflows its banks and floods the city.

1599–1602 Caravaggio paints three canvases dedicated to St. Matthew for the church of S. Luigi dei Francesi (☞*84*).

1600 Philosopher Giordano Bruno is burned as a heretic in Campo de' Fiori (☞*74*).

1600 **THE JUBILEE OF THE GREAT PROCESSIONS**
In preparation for the Jubilee, Clement VIII (1592–1605) creates two commissions to oversee the organization of the spiritual and material aspects of the event. New piazzas are created in front of various churches, including S. Prisca

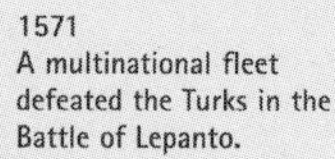
1571
A multinational fleet defeated the Turks in the Battle of Lepanto.

1633
Galileo Galilei (1564–1642) faces the Inquisition.

1678
Composer Antonio Vivaldi (*above*) was born in Venice. He died in 1741 in Vienna, totally forgotten.

(☞*121*), S. Gregorio Magno (☞*113*), S. Nicola in Carcere (☞*85*), and S. Giovanni in Laterano; the titular basilicas are restored; and new churches are consecrated, among them Chiesa Nuova (☞*68*).
Approximately 500,000 pilgrims converge on the city. Confraternities, many of which are founded during this period, organize retinues and processions. Members and participants wear cloaks and mantles of different colors. The spectacle of processions, with standards, banners, and the sound of liturgical songs against the backdrop of ancient and modern monuments, gives this Jubilee an air that is more theatrical than pious.

1614 Rome's first public library, the Biblioteca Angelica, is founded.
1622 Carlo Maderno creates the dome of S. Andrea della Valle (☞*70*), the second tallest in Rome after that of S. Pietro; the church is consecrated in 1650.
1623–1624 Gian Lorenzo Bernini begins work on the bronze baldachin for S. Pietro, using bronzes from the Pantheon portico; this project is completed in 1633.

1625 THE WARTIME JUBILEE

The city suffers a new plague and another flood. Fearing contagion, visits to the basilicas outside the city walls are replaced with visits to S. Maria in Trastevere (☞*65*), S. Lorenzo in Lucina (☞*99*), and S. Maria del Popolo. With the papal bull *Pontificia Sollicitudo,* Pope Urban VIII (1623–1644) grants indulgence to hermits, monks, prisoners, the ill, and all those who are unable to make to journey to Rome, as well as to those who pray for peace in a Europe suffering the torment of the Thirty Years' War.

1626 The new basilica of S. Pietro is consecrated.
1638 Francesco Borromini begins construction of the church of S. Carlo alle Quattro Fontane (☞*104*).

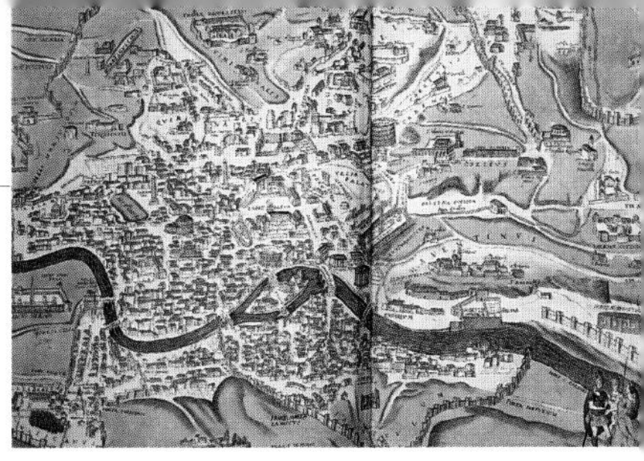

Plan of Rome, 1588.

1650 THE HEIGHT OF BAROQUE ROME

For the Jubilee of Innocent X (1644–1655) there is a great flow of pilgrims (approximately 700,000), and once again the confraternities, particularly the Filippini and the Gonfalone, distinguish themselves in welcoming the multitudes. The tone of this Jubilee is worldly, with retinues, receptions, and gaudy processions organized by rival confraternities. On Easter, the Spanish confraternity sponsors spectacular fireworks in Piazza Navona. Bernini conceives the Fontana dei Quattro Fiumi (Fountain of the Four Rivers) for the piazza; the project is completed the following year. Borromini designs the church of S. Ivo alla Sapienza (☞*84*).

1667 The colonnade of Piazza S. Pietro, designed by Bernini, is completed; the project was begun in 1656.

1675 THE QUEEN'S JUBILEE

The elderly and tired Clement X (1670–1676) inaugurates the 15th Jubilee in the presence of Queen Christina of Sweden, who converted to Catholicism. For the papacy, her conversion is a symbol of the victory of the church over the Lutheran religion. Bernini creates a statue of the *Blessed Ludovica Albertoni*, housed in the church of S. Francesco a Ripa (☞*64*).

1694 Carlo Fontana completes the Palazzo di Montecitorio (☞*97*), begun in 1653 by Bernini.

Ponte Sisto in a series of views of Rome by Gaspare Vanvitelli, housed in the Musei Capitolini.

707
ustrian domination
ver Italy replaces the
rench.

714
Vith the Peace of
astadt, France
ecognizes the new
alian possessions:
ombardy, Sardinia,
nd the kingdom of
aples.

1720–1790
The Great Age of the Grand Tour: northern Europeans visit Italy and start the vogue for classical studies. Among the famous visitors are Edward Gibbon (1758), Jacques-Louis David (1775), and Johann Wolfgang von Goethe (1786).

From the Enlightenment to the Present Day

1700 **THE JUBILEE OF THE TWO POPES**
The Jubilee proclaimed by Innocent XII (1691–1700) is brought to conclusion by Clement XI (1700–1721). The tone of this Holy Year is sober, with less of the pomp and frivolity that had distinguished previous Jubilees. The city administration issues edicts for street cleaning and for the maintenance of churches. Indulgences are granted to pilgrims who visit S. Giovanni in Laterano on St. Thomas's feast day and to those who follow the pope on his visit to the four basilicas.

1704 Reconstruction of the Porto di Ripetta, Tiber's ancient port "della Posterula," used for small river traffic from Tuscany and Umbria, begins. This is Rome's largest urban renewal project in 18th century.

1725 **THE JUBILEE OF THE NEEDY**
Pope Benedict XIII (1724–1730), a Dominican, emphasizes providing pilgrims with hospitality and assistance during their journey. He visits the ill and the imprisoned, devotes himself to assisting the needy, and shows little interest in the political vicissitudes of the time.

1726 Piazza di Spagna is linked to the Pincio by the steps of Trinità dei Monti (☞*88,90*).

1729 The Hospital of Ss. Maria e Gallicano (☞*62*), designed by Filippo Raguzzini, is completed; it is a model for 18th-century hospital architecture.

1743 The names of the various rioni are placed on plaques and nailed to the walls of houses at street intersections.

1750 **THE JUBILEE OF ENLIGHTENMENT**
Religious fervor and participation in the celebration of the Holy Year (as well as the flow of pilgrims) decreases. Benedict XIV (1740–1758) entrusts Frà Leonardo da Porto Maurizio with the spiritual preparations for the Jubilee; he preaches in Piazza Navona, S. Maria in Trastevere, and S. Maria sopra Minerva. The Stations of the Via Crucis are moved into to Coliseum, reinterpreting this ancient monument in Christian terms as a place of martyrdom. Luigi Vanvitelli reorganizes the interior of the Basilica of S. Maria degli Angeli (☞*125*) and is involved in the building of S. Pietro.

1762 Pope Clement XIII (1758–1769) inaugurates the Trevi Fountain (☞*94*).

1763 German archaeologist Johann Joachim Winckelmann (1710–1768), spiritual father of neoclassicism, is put in charge of Rome's antiquities.

1771 Clement XIV (1769–1774) establishes the Museo Pio-Clementino (☞*57*); the transformation of the Vatican Palaces into museums begins.

1773 Clement XIV disbands the Jesuits. The order will be reinstated in 1814.

1775 **THE LAST JUBILEE OF THE ANCIEN RÉGIME**
The Jubilee is celebrated by Pius VI (1775–1799), who welcomes Maximilian of Austria and Tanucci, minister of the Kingdom of Naples, to Rome; both these men harbor Enlightenment and anticlerical ideas, a sign of the church's opening to modernity.

1789 Antonio Canova creates the funerary monument of Clement XIV, housed in the basilica of SS. Apostoli (☞*101*). It is his first work in Rome.

1798 Napoléon's French troops occupy Rome; the Republic of Rome is proclaimed, and Pope Pius VI is exiled and dies in France.

1799 A conclave is held in Venice, and Pius VII (1800–1823) is elected pope. He arrives in Rome on July 3, after traversing an Italy occupied by the French. The Jubilee of 1800 is not celebrated.

1816–24 Architect and urbanist Giuseppe Valadier redesigns Piazza del Popolo.

1823 Fire destroys the basilica of S. Paolo Fuori le Mura.

1778
Teatro alla Scala is completed in Milan.

1796
Napoléon begins his Italian campaigns, annexing Rome and imprisoning Pope Pius VI four years later.

1804
Napoléon crowns himself emperor (*right:* a detail of a painting by J.-L. David) in the presence of Pope Pius VII.

1815
Austria controls much of northern Italy after Napoléon's downfall.

1820–1831
Insurrections and revolutionary movements strike many Italian States and cities.

1848–1849
New popular revolts for national independence from Austria.

1825 **THE JUBILEE OF THE RESTORATION**
After the riots of 1820–1821, Leo XII (1823–1829) proclaims the Jubilee amid a tense climate, full of suspicion and fears that the crowd of pilgrims will be infiltrated by revolutionary elements. The confraternities of SS. Stimmate di S. Francesco, Orazione e Morte, and SS. Trinità dei Pellegrini oversee hospitality; special new laws prohibit improper behavior and regulate women's clothing.

1848 Riots, inspired by Giuseppe Mazzini's republican ideals, result in the creation of the short-lived Roman Republic, defended militarily by Giuseppe Garibaldi's volonteers. Pope Pius IX (1846–1878) retreats to Gaeta, near Naples, and doesn't return to Rome until April 1850, after the French troops of Napoléon III retake the city.

1850 The Jubilee of 1850 is not declared.

1863 Poet Giuseppe Gioachino Belli (1791–1863) dies; his work in Roman dialect, published posthumously, reveals him to be one of the greatest writers of italy's dialect literature.

1868 Cholera claims 8,500 victims in Rome.

1870 Vatican Council I pronounces the dogma of papal infallibility in matters of faith. The Tiber floods the city. After a short siege, Italian troops occupy Rome, the last city to fold in this 10-year-old kingdom. This event completes the Italian territorial unity and constitutes the end of the church's secular power.

1871 Rome becomes the new capital of Italy.

Above: View of Rome after the breaching of Porta Pia (1870). Museo del Risorgimento.
Below: Carlo De Paris's Presentation of the keys of the city to Pius IX, who returned to Rome on April 12, 1850. Museo Storico Vaticano.

1875 **THE JUBILEE OF POLEMICS**
After the proclamation of the unification of Italy, and in open polemics with the Italian State, the Holy Year, proclaimed with the papal bull *Gravibus Ecclesiae et huius Saeculi Calamitatibus*, is celebrated stealthily, without public ceremonies and without the opening of the Porta Santa.

1876 After the disastrous 1870 flood of the Tiber, construction begins on river embankments, a project that is completed in 1900.

1881 With more than 270,000 inhabitants, Rome is now the third largest city in Italy, after Naples and Milan.

1891 Pope Leo XIII (1878–1903) publishes the encyclical *Rerum Novarum*, which signals an attempt to seek a political balance between the Italian State and the church, and a new social role for the church within the new state.

1900 **THE JUBILEE OF THE NEW CENTURY**
Contributions to the Jubile by welfare and charitable organizations, which played such a large role in assisting pilgrims, is sharply reduced by political transformations. The pope appoints a permanent pontifical commission to assist pilgrims.

1922 The fascist march on Rome concludes with Benito Mussolini assuming the task of forming a new government.

1924 Socialist House Representative Giacomo Matteotti is assassinated by the fascists.

1925 The governorship of Rome is established; the city administration depends directly on the Ministry of the Interior, and the capital assumes unique administrative status.

1860
Garibaldi (*right*) defeats the Bourbon rulers in Sicily and Naples.
The Kingdom of Italy is established a year later.

1870
Rome is captured by Italian troops and is declared capital of Italy.

1900
King Umberto I is assassinated by an anarchist;
he is succeeded by King Victor Emmanuel III.

1915
Italy enters World War I on the side of the Allies.

1925 **THE JUBILEE UNDER FASCISM**
During the Jubilee, pilgrims can obtain indulgences by praying for the unity of Christians, peace among people, and a solution to the Palestinian problem. Different commissions organize the reception of pilgrims, and a large Missionary Exposition spreads the word about the activities of Catholic missions in the world and celebrates the church's evangelical work. Pope Pius XI reopens the exterior loggia of S. Pietro and gives the blessing *Urbi et Orbi* ("to the city and the world").

1929 The Lateran Treaty is signed. The treaty defines the relationship between church and state and declares the independence of the Vatican City; the Italian State grants payment to the church for expropriation of its property.

1933 The Via dell'Impero, the present-day Via dei Fori Imperiali, opens.

1943 On July 19, U.S. planes bomb the S. Lorenzo quarter; on September 10, Italian and German soldiers clash at Porta S. Paolo; on October 16, the Jewish community of Rome is rounded up and deported.

1948 Pope Pius XII (1939–1958) establishes the Holy Year Central Committee, which will oversee Jubilee preparations.

1950 **THE JUBILEE OF RECONSTRUCTION**
Pilgrims flow into the city, and the Casa del Pellegrino is established, on the new Via della Conciliazione, to accommodate them; the Hospice of SS. Trinità dei Pellegrini is restored. The pope proclaims this Holy Year a "year of great return, a year of great forgiveness."

1957 The Treaty of Rome is signed, and Italy becomes a founding member of the European Economic Community.

1975 **THE JUBILEE ON TELEVISION**
This Jubilee, proclaimed by Paul VI (1963–1978), is the first to be broadcast on worldwide television. The world has changed a great deal, and the pope expresses his opinion about the church with regard to social and moral changes through numerous encyclicals, which address issues of birth control, celibacy of priests, and the relationship between the church and the world. Paul VI undertakes numerous pastoral trips worldwide.

1991 Rome's population numbers more than 2,700,000 inhabitants.

1996 The Italian State votes into law its commitment to the Jubilee. The law sets aside money for development of accommodations, transportation, and infrastructures for the health and safety of pilgrims in the new millennium. A large number of sites undergo restoration and improvement, following what has become a centuries-long tradition of preparing the city for the event.

2000 **THE JUBILEE OF THE THIRD MILLENNIUM**
With the papal bull *Tertio millennio adveniente*, Pope John Paul II (1978) proclaims the Jubilee for the year 2000. It acquires special significance because of its dual role of celebrating the Holy Year and marking mankind's path toward a new millennium.

1925
Mussolini, prime minister since 1922, establish a fascist dictatorship.

1940–1944
During World War II, fascist Italy fights with Axis powers until it is forced to capitulate (1943), and Mussolini flees Rome. Italian partisans and Allied troops compel the eventual withdrawal of German troops from Italy.

1968–1979
Years of violence, when terrorists from both the extreme left and the extreme right resorted to bombs, destruction, and attacks, culminate in the kidnapping and murder of former prime minister Aldo Moro (1916–1978).

1991
Waves of refugees from neighboring Albania flood southern ports on the Adriatic.

1993
Italians vote for sweeping reforms after scandal exposes widespread political corruption.

1999
NATO alliance planes bomb Yugoslavia in an effort to resolve a situation of ethnic strife in Kosovo.

Above:
Pope John Paul II.

Facing page:
One of two 17th-century fountains at the focal point of the ellipse of Piazza S. Pietro.

PONT MAX

Opposite page:
The altar with the sarcophagus of S. Catherine of Siena, in the church of S. Maria sopra Minerva.

Holy Rome

Area by area, churches, ancient temples, palaces of the powerful and pilgrims' routes, catacombs and relics. These sites have been part of the history of the Church and have transformed the Eternal City into the Holy City.

1

Vatican, Borgo, and Prati

VATICAN CITY

(A) The majestic dome of the basilica of S. Pietro, seen from the Ponte Vittorio Emanuele II.

(B) The baldacchino and the throne of St. Peter, created by Bernini for the basilica of S. Pietro.

Much of the history and development of this tiny state was determined by the presence of St. Peter's tomb, located a short distance from the Circus of Caligula, where the apostle was martyred between AD 64 and AD 67. In 800, Charlemagne was crowned emperor in the basilica founded by Constantine, and the district acquired worldwide political significance. In the Middle Ages, after the construction of the city walls by Pope Leo IV, the area became a fortified citadel and, after the Avignon exile, the definitive seat of the pontiffs. The Renaissance and Counter-Reformation patron-popes were responsible for majestic projects that remodeled the city as the capital of a modern state, while later interventions organized the immense art collections into museums. After the Lateran Treaty of 1929, the Vatican City became independent from Italy, with the pontiff granted full legal, political, and administrative sovereignty. In addition to the area contained within the walls, the Vatican also has sovereignty over the Lateran, Cancelleria, and Propaganda Fide palaces; the Hospital of the Bambino Gesù; Castel Gandolfo; and the Cybo and Barberini villas. The Vatican has its own armed forces, police, and mint; maintains its own communications network; and publishes L'Osservatore Romano, *the official newspaper of the Holy See.*

Basilica di S. Pietro ① (St. Peter's Basilica)

⊞2 D3. In approximately AD 320, in honor of the first apostle and commemorating his divine investiture ("You are Peter..."), the emperor Constantine had an impressive basilica constructed on the site of the hallowed tomb of St. Peter. Ancient documents marvel at the magnificence of this church, resplendent with mosaics, art treasures, and gold, a sight that rewarded the arduous travels of pilgrims who arrived from every corner of the world. When the popes returned from exile in Avignon (1377), the more than 1,000-year-old basilica was in disrepair. After some ineffective restorations, Julius II decided to demolish it to make space for a new, even grander edifice to symbolize the supremacy of the Church of Rome. Famous architects succeeded one another in directing the works, but the turning point came with Michelangelo, who designed the monumental dome. In 1626 (before the construction of Bernini's colonnade), the basilica was opened, following innumerable polemics. The enormous facade by Carlo Maderno, too wide in proportion to the height, seems more suitable to a palace than to a religious edifice. Five doors lead to the sanctuary, which is symbolically guarded by the equestrian statues of Constantine and Charlemagne. The last door to the right is the **Porta Santa,** or Holy Door, that is opened and closed by the pope only during Jubilee years. At the center of the facade is the grand loggia, set aside for the traditional blessing, *Urbi et Orbi* (to the city and to the world). The basilica was conceived as a symbol of the church's eternity, and most of its fragile decorations have been removed over the years. Pieces that do remain include the beloved statue of St. Peter and Michelangelo's *Pietà*. Tradition has it that the former, attributed to Arnolfo di Cambio (13th century), was created by melting down a statue of Jupiter; the right foot has been worn away from being rubbed by the hands and lips of the faithful. The *Pietà* is the only statue signed by Michelangelo, supposedly because he became furious at hearing it attributed to another sculptor. The basilica's interior bears the dominant and sumptuous imprint of Baroque art, particularly that of Bernini, who is responsible for the dramatic *cattedra* (throne) of St. Peter and the majestic *baldacchino* (canopy) above the apostle's tomb. The loggias inserted between the piers of the dome safeguard the basilica's most precious relics, including Veronica's veil, which has an imprint of a male face that, since the early Middle Ages, has been believed to belong to Jesus. The pontiffs' many funerary monuments, created over the centuries by illustrious artists, make this vast Christian sanctuary a "triumphal" space.

Beneath the central nave of St. Peter's Basilica is the **Sacre Grotte Vaticane** (Crypt of St. Peter's), which occupies the space between the current basilica and the old basilica of Constantine. In addition to the tombs of numerous popes, the grottoes also hold early Christian sarcophagi, architectural fragments, and monuments from the old basilica. Excavations have determined the location of the Circus of Caligula (beneath the left nave) and, just next to it, a pre-Constantinian necropolis. This cemetery area, with pagan and Christian tombs, was in use from the 1st to the 4th centuries AD and includes well-preserved mausoleums belonging to the families of wealthy freedmen, with interiors decorated with stuccowork, frescoes, mosaics, and sarcophagi. The presence of Christians can be ascertained from the inscriptions and

NI CAELORVM TV ES PETRVS
B
FIDES
MVNDO

(A) Piazza S. Pietro's 17th-century fountain.
(B) The last rays of sun penetrate the colonnade of the piazza.

images, including (in the mausoleum of the Giulii) one of Christ depicted on the chariot of the sun, in the typical iconography of the god Apollo. On the site of the current Altar of Confession (beneath Bernini's baldacchino) is a modest monument with two superimposed niches, next to a wall on which is written, in Greek letters, Peter Is Here. This has always been an object of great veneration and interest, and the 4th-century basilica was constructed so the tomb would be at the center of the presbytery, visible to the faithful. ⊠*Piazza S. Pietro.*

Casina di Pio IV
(Garden House of Pius IV)
▦**2 C3.** In 1561 Pirro Ligorio created this elegant structure, a typical example of late Renaissance garden architecture, in the Vatican Gardens. It has two separate buildings and two side pavilions; the smaller building, laid out behind a fountain, is lightened in its upper portion by a loggia and decorated with mosaics at its base. The larger building has a facade ornamented with floral and figurative stuccowork. Today the building contains the Pontifical Academy of Sciences, established in 1936 by Pope Pius XI and counting among its members scientists from all over the world, including those not of the Catholic faith. ⊠*Giardini Vaticani.*

Collegio e Camposanto Teutonico
(German College and Cemetery)
▦**2 D3.** The college and cemetery were established in 799 on a plot of land donated by Pope Leo II to Charlemagne and, according to legend, with earth brought from Calvary. This was the location of the Schola Francorum, a hospice for pilgrims and the oldest German institution in Rome. The current church was built in the 15th century according to German prototypes of the time, and the Confraternity of Santa Maria della Pietà in Campo Santo was established for the German and Flemish community, which continues to look after the nearby cemetery. The German College, which grew out of the former hospice, houses an institute of historical-archaeological studies, an archaeological and ecclesiastical history library, and a small museum with sculptures, inscriptions, and various vestiges of early Christianity. ⊠*Piazza dei Protomartiri Cristiani.*

Giardini Vaticani
(Vatican Gardens)
▦**2 C2–C3–D1–D2.** Spread over the slopes of the Monte Vaticano, the gardens were laid out in a typical 16th-century Italian style, which combines the precise geometry of French gardens with the more fanciful plantings of English design. Wooded areas alternate harmoniously with geometric divisions defined by hedges and flowering parterres, and the landscape is further "furnished" with kiosks, artificial grottoes, small structures, and fountains.

Museo Storico Artistico—Tesoro di S. Pietro (Historical Art Museum—Treasury of St. Peter's)
▦**2 D3.** The objects of liturgical use and the many works of considerable artistic value displayed here survived the sack of Rome, first by the Saracens (846) and later by the imperial troops of Charles V (1527) and Napoléon. One of the treasury's many masterpieces is the *Colonna Santa* (Holy Column), on which, according to tradition, Christ rested in the Temple of Solomon in Jerusalem, but which actually dates from the 4th century AD. The collection also includes a dalmatic (a ceremonial tunic), said to have belonged to Charlemagne, but which dates from the Byzantine era; a cross donated by Byzantine emperor Justin II to the city of Rome (6th century); the *Monument of Sixtus IV* (1493), a masterpiece by Pollaiuolo; a canopy by Donatello (1432); and the *Sarcophagus of Giunio Basso,* prefect of Rome in 359, decorated with scenes from the Old and New Testaments. ⊠*Piazza S. Pietro.*

Piazza S. Pietro ②
(St. Peter's Square)
▦**2 D3–D4.** The space in front of the basilica was designed by one of the most talented artists of the Italian Baroque, Gian Lorenzo Bernini. The elliptical design (built between 1656 and 1667 for Alexander VII, with heated disagreements between artist and client) has four rows of columns that appear to be a single row when viewed from two focal points. At the center is the **Obelisco Vaticano** (Vatican Obelisk), which stood in the Circus of Caligula, where Peter was martyred. In the Middle Ages the obelisk was the source of various popular myths, including that the bronze globe at the tip contained the ashes of Julius Caesar. Perhaps to combat such pagan beliefs, Sixtus V had a cross containing a fragment of the true cross placed atop the obelisk. Two wings link the semicircular colonnades to the basilica; the one on the right ends at the Scala Regia, another spectacular invention by Bernini.

③

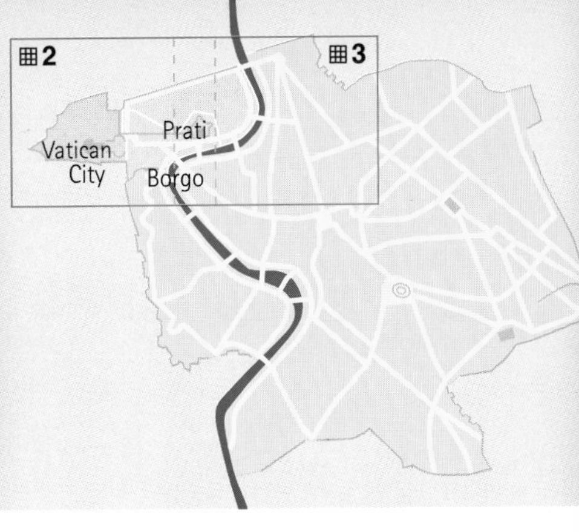

Conceived as the last of the imperial forums, this piazza as "Christian forum" has multiple meanings. It is a refuge within the fold of the mother church, symbolized in the embrace of the colonnade. It also has a typically Baroque element of theater, with metaphorical representations of the city (the elliptical form is derived from the Coliseum; the obelisk is typical of Roman circuses), the world (with reference to the elliptical orbits of the planets, according to Copernicus's new theories), and the universe (at the piazza's center is the obelisk, a solar symbol that measures time and space and celebrates the pope as "solar" sovereign, similar to Louis XIV, king of France).

MUSEI E PALAZZI VATICANI
(Vatican Museums and Palaces)
▦**2 B3–C3.** The Vatican has been the official papal residence since 1377, when the exile in Avignon ended. Before that, the popes lived in the Lateran and maintained only a small, fortified building in the Vatican. Beginning in the 15th century, the pontiffs transformed and expanded that building into a magnificent dwelling, intended as a manifestation of the glory of God and the victory of faith. The palaces contain the Vatican Museums, a complex of art collections that is unqiue not only because of the value and variety of the objects on display, but also because of the beauty and sumptuousness of the spaces that contain them. The immense papal collections, originally organized in accordance with criteria of Renaissance collecting, began to be arranged as museums in the late 18th century, when the existing buildings were converted to that use and other spaces were designed specifically for exhibition purposes. All the museums are accessed via the same entryway. ✉ *Viale Vaticano,* ☏ *06/698–84947.*

Appartamento Borgia
(Borgia Apartment)
▦**2 B3–C3.** Borgia Pope Alexander VI, notorious for his avarice and his libertine way of life, entrusted the decoration of his Vatican apartment to Betto di Biago, also know as Pinturicchio (1492–1494), whose work here is a testament to his talent. The most sumptuous of the building's spaces is the **Sala dei Santi** (Hall of Saints), which, despite its name, fully reflects the anything but saintly temperament of this pope. The room is a Renaissance homage to ancient Egyptian civilization, evoked in the myth of Isis and Osiris, where the goddess appears as the personification of wisdom and the mythical progenitor of the pontiff. The heraldic bull of the Borgia family is identified with Hapi the bull, or Osiris resurrected, who triumphs at the center of the vault. Part of the collection of modern religious art established by Paul VI in 1973—or approximately 800 works of painting, sculpture, and graphics donated by artists and collectors from around the world—is housed here.

Appartamento di S. Pio V
(Apartment of St. Pius V)
▦**2 B3–C3.** The apartment of Pius V (1566–1572), the stern Counter-Reformation pope who ceaselessly lashed out at the immorality of the Curia and the city, is made up of the eponymous gallery, two drawing rooms, and a chapel. Today the gallery contains a series of tapestries, including valuable 15th-century examples from the Tournai workshop. The two drawing rooms display a collection of medieval and Renaissance ceramics and a collection of precious miniature mosaics.

Biblioteca Apostolica Vaticana
(Vatican Apostolic Library) ③
▦**2 C3.** Established in 1475 at the behest of Pope Sixtus IV, the library enjoyed extraordinary growth during the Counter-Reformation and continued to expand until it became one of the most important libraries in the world. It contains 800,000 printed books, in addition to thousands of codices, manuscripts, and incunabula (books produced from movable type, in the earliest period of printing). Over the course of time it has absorbed entire historical libraries, as well as the library holdings of numerous popes. The original **Salone Sistina,** by Domenico Fontana (1587–1589), has magnificent frescoes from the late 16th century.

Cappella Sistina (Sistine Chapel)
▦**2 D3.** Pope Sixtus IV had the chapel built (1475–1481) and entrusted the decoration of the side walls and the wall opposite the altar (with scenes from the life of Moses and Christ and portraits of the pontiffs) to some of the most celebrated painters of the time, including Botticelli, Signorelli, Perugino, Ghirlandajo, and Pinturicchio. The magnificent ceiling fresco, executed by Michelangelo for Pope Julius II (1508–1512), illustrates the history of mankind before the coming of Christ: nine stories from Genesis in the central zone; monumental figures of *Sybils* and *Prophets,* the forerunners of Christ; and the miraculous salvation of Israel serve as the historical introduction to the path of Redemption. The *Creation of Adam* is one of the symbols of the Renaissance; the contact between the index finger of God the Father and that of Adam releases the spark of a higher intelligence that is showered down upon humanity. Although the undertaking left Michelangelo exhausted and ill, 24 years later he accepted Paul III's commission to paint the disturbing *Last Judgment* on the back wall of the chapel. The fresco has been restored to its original splendor. The drama of religious crisis during those years and the

④ Ancient statues in the Neoclassical Braccio Nuovo of the Museo Chiaramonti.

Hermes and the famous Laocoön group in the Museo Pio Clementino ⑤.

personal tribulations of the artist take shape in a terrible image that brings to mind the gloomy verses of the *Dies Irae* rather than the words of the Bible, with an almost unbearable emphasis on the tragedy of man, shattered by divine turmoil. Michelangelo spent five years working alone, and the immense fresco, which is organized in superimposed bands, revolutionized the traditional iconography of the subject. All partitions are filled with the swirling motion of the resurrected and the damned. Even the Madonna seems to draw back in fright at the explosive power of Christ. Among the saints, the solemn figures of Peter and Paul can be identified, and Michelangelo left an anguished self-portrait in the flayed skin of St. Bartholomew. Below, angels sound the trumpets of judgment, and all around a battle rages between angels and devils vying for souls. The work is one of the milestones of European culture. When it is time to elect a new pope, the College of Cardinals meets in conclave here, surrounded by these images.

Cortile della Pigna
(Courtyard of the Pinecone)

▦**2 C3.** The vast Belvedere Courtyard, designed by Bramante and famous during the Renaissance for its tournaments, was subsequently divided into three sections, one of which is this courtyard. In the Middle Ages a colossal bronze pinecone was discovered on an ancient public building in the Campo Marzio, which is the derivation of the Pigna district's name. For centuries the pinecone adorned the atrium of the ancient basilica of St. Peter before being moved to its current location.

Galleria delle Carte Geografiche
(Map Gallery)

▦**2 B3–C3.** The gallery's name comes from the 40 geographical maps of Italian regions and church possessions that Pope Gregory XIII had painted between 1580 and 1583, based on cartoons by Egnazio Danti, an eminent mathematician and cosmographer of the time. To distribute the maps clearly on the walls, Danti adopted the Appenines as a dividing element. On the walls facing the Belvedere Courtyard he represented the regions bounded by the Ligurian and Tyrrhenian seas, and on the wall facing the gardens, the regions bounded by the Alps and the Adriatic. Many of the maps show panoramic views and city plans, and some indicate sites of famous battles. As a group, they constitute an important document of 16th-century geography and cartography.

Museo Chiaramonti ④
(Chiaramonti Museum)

▦**2 C3.** The Museo Chiaramonti, which takes its name from its founder, Pope Pius VII (1800–1823), was laid out and organized by Antonio Canova. It displays almost 1,000 ancient sculptures and a rich collection of epigraphs. The Museo Chiaramonti proper occupies part of a gallery designed by Bramante and contains Roman copies of Greek statues, portraits, reliefs, urns, and sarcophagi from the Roman era. The **Galleria Lapidaria** (Gallery of Stone Tablets), located in the remaining part of the gallery, displays pagan and Christian epigraphs that were first collected by Pope Clement XIV. The **Braccio Nuovo** (New Wing) is a Neoclassical gallery created after the return of sculptures removed by Napoléon. It contains some famous and important works: a statue of Augustus, found in Livia's villa in Prima Porta, is the most famous portrait of the first Roman emperor. Other Roman copies of Greek sculpture include the *Wounded Amazon*, restored by Thorvaldsen; the *Satyr in Repose*; the *Spear-bearer*; and the *Athena Giustiniani*. A colossal statue of the Nile, flanked by sphinxes, crocodiles, and 16 putti, which symbolize the fertility guaranteed by the river's flood, is based on a Hellenistic original.

Museo Gregoriano Egizio
(Egyptian Museum)

▦**2 B3.** Established by Pope Gregory XVI in 1839, the museum was first organized by Luigi Ungarelli, one of the first Italian scholars of Egyptology. It was reorganized in 1989 by Jean-Luc Grenier, who regrouped the exhibits according to dynasty. The museum houses a significant collection of epigraphs ranging from the 3rd century BC to the 6th century AD, numerous statues, sarcophagi, mummies, steles, and other remains from funerary rites. The works from the Roman era, inspired by Egyptian art, are of particular interest and bear witness to Roman society's enthusiasm for Egyptian culture. Many of the pieces came from Hadrian's villa in Tivoli, others from the important sanctuary of Isis in Campo Marzio in Rome.

Museo Gregoriano Etrusco
(Etruscan Museum)

▦**2 B3.** Created by Pope Gregory XVI in 1837, this museum contains materials that, for the most part, were obtained from excavations carried out by the church in southern Etruria during the 19th century. The princely Regolini-Galassi tomb (named for the men who discovered it) from Cerveteri yielded splendid jewels and furnishings from the 7th century BC. The famous *Mars of Todi*, one of the masterpieces of Italian bronze work, from the 5th century BC, depicts a young warrior pouring an offering before leaving for battle. According to the epigraph engraved on the breastplate, the donor was

⑤

Celtic. The museum has a collection of gold from Vulci; a substantial collection of Greek, Etruscan, and Italiot (from southern Hellenized Italy) ceramics; and a small collection of antiquities from Rome and Lazio.

Museo Gregoriano Profano
⊞**2 B2–B3.** This collection of antiquities was established by Pope Gregory XVI in 1844 in the Lateran Palace and moved to its current location by Pope John XXIII in 1970. It includes materials from excavations within the papal state. A significant section is devoted to original Greek works, including some sculpture fragments from the Parthenon, an Attic funerary relief (5th century BC), and a head of Athena. Roman copies of Greek sculptures include a statue of Marsyas, copies of a famous bronze group by Myron (460 BC) that once stood at the entrance to the Acropolis in Athens, and the *Niobid Chiaramonti*, probably after a work by Skopas or Praxiteles. There are numerous significant examples of Roman sculpture, including the monumental funerary edifice of Vicovaro, the imperial statues from Cerveteri, fragments from the tomb of the Haterii, and an impressive series of sarcophagi.

Museo Missionario Etnologico (Ethnological Missionary Museum)
⊞**2 B3–C3.** Established by Pope Pius XI in the Lateran Palace, the museum was transferred here by Pope John XXIII. It displays materials from the 1925 Jubilee missionary exhibition and various gifts from individuals and missionary congregations, presenting extensive documentation of cultures and traditions outside Europe. On exhibit are objects, reconstructions, and texts related to local religions, death rituals, the introduction of Christianity, social organization, artistic production, and daily life (with a vast array of garments, furniture, household goods, arms, and furnishings).

Museo Pio Clementino ⑤
⊞**2 B3.** This first major component of the Vatican Museums was a result of the efforts of popes Clement XIV and Pius VI. Its founding went beyond the mere organization of a papal collection, and occurred within the framework of a broader plan to safeguard works of art that were well known in the late 16th century. Clement XIV wanted to design a location for the substantial collection that had been accumulating in the Belvedere Palace since the times of Julius II. Pius VI completed the new installation, which was begun in 1771 and financed with proceeds from a lottery. For centuries, many of the sculptures exhibited here influenced art throughout the world: the *Apoxiomenos* (a Roman copy of a work by Lysippus, 4th century BC); the *Apollo di Belvedere, Laocoön*, and *Hermes* statues in the Octagonal Courtyard (all Roman copies of Greek masterpieces), and the *Perseus Triumphant* by Canova. The collection also includes the *Apollo Killing a Lizard* (from a bronze by Praxiteles, 4th century BC), the much-admired *Sleeping Ariadne* (from a 2nd-century BC Hellenistic original), and the *Torso del Belvedere* (1st century BC), which inspired Michelangelo for his Sistine Chapel nudes.

Museo Pio Cristiano
⊞**2 B2–B3.** Founded by Pope Pius IX in 1854, the museum contains artifacts from the catacombs and from the early Christian basilica. Housed here is an impressive series of early Christian sarcophagi, mosaics, architectural fragments, and sculpture. Also displayed is a comprehensive collection of Christian epigraphs of a funerary, public, commemorative, and religious nature dating from the 1st to 7th centuries AD. These objects provide a a glimpse into the religious ideas, social composition, everyday life, and spoken language of the early Christian communities. The most precious monument is the funeral pillar of Abercius, bishop of Hierapolis of Phrygia, who lived during the time of emperor Marcus Aurelius (AD 161–AD 180). An inscription in Greek bears the epitaph dictated by him: "Wherever my faith pushes me, and prepares for my meal, fish from streams . . . untainted, which the pure Virgin takes and each day places before her friends so that they might eat, with excellent wine that she offers, mixed with bread." If the Christian interpretation of the text is correct, this is the most ancient Christian epigraph about the Eucharist.

Museo Profano
⊞**2 C3.** This single exhibition room preserves the rich original furnishings designed by Luigi Valadier. Founded by Clement XII, the museum displays artifacts from the Etruscan, Roman, and medieval eras. Artifacts were culled from 18th-century collections such as those of Carpegna and Albani and from early 19th-century excavations.

Museo Sacro
⊞**2 C3.** Created by Pope Benedict XIV, this museum displays early Christian and Byzantine antiquities from various sources, including some from Roman catacombs. The

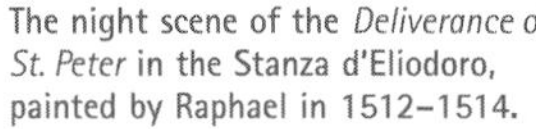

The night scene of the *Deliverance of St. Peter* in the Stanza d'Eliodoro, painted by Raphael in 1512–1514.

holdings of the museum include a Byzantine mosaic depicting St. Theodore (14th century); a case for the head of St. Sebastian (9th century), formerly in the church of the Ss. Quattro Coronati; early Christian and Coptic textiles; a rich collection of lamps and ceramics with Christian, pagan, and Jewish symbols; and an Eastern-style water vessel used for washing the hands after meals (8th–9th century), which, according to legend, was used by St. Laurence.

Museo Storico Vaticano
(Vatican Historical Museum)
▦**2 C3.** Located in the Lateran Palace, this is a department of the institution of the same name. Created by Pope Paul VI in 1973, it contains a collection of means of transport used by various popes and cardinals: black landaus, the daily means of transportation for popes until the early years of the papacy of Pius XI; coaches, designed to endure long trips over rambling roads; formal carriages, including one built for Leo XII by the celebrated Roman carriage builder Gaetano Peroni; and numerous sedans, such as the extremely elegant, red damask one used by Leo XIII.

Pinacoteca Vaticana ⑦
▦**2 C3.** This extraordinary collection of paintings was established by Pope Pius VII (1816), who welcomed the Congress of Vienna's decision that works plundered by Napoléon's troops should be returned from France and kept in public collections. Other works of art were added from various sources, creating a vast and multifaceted group of paintings, with emphasis on Italian works, ranging from pre-Renaissance to 17th-century works. The museum also contains 10 tapestries made in Brussels from cartoons by Raphael, depicting scenes from the Acts of the Apostles; Pope Leo X commissioned these to decorate the walls of the Sistine Chapel. Giotto's *Stefaneschi polyptych,* originally painted for the high altar of the old St. Peter's, is the best preserved work by this 14th-century artist in Rome. The museum's Renaissance sections include other masterpieces, such as *Sixtus IV Nominating Platina Prefect of the Vatican Library* (1477) by Melozzo da Forlì; Raphael's *Coronation of the Virgin* (1503), *Madonna of Foligno* (1512), and *Transfiguration* (1517); and Leonardo da Vinci's *St. Jerome.* There is an extensive collection of works from the 17th century, the apogee of religious painting in Rome, including Caravaggio's dramatic *Deposition* (1604), Pietro da Cortona's *Pietà,* Domenichino's *Communion of St. Jerome* (1614), and Guido Reni's *Crucifixion of St. Peter.*

Stanze di Raffaello
(Raphael Rooms) ⑥
▦**2 D3.** These rooms constituted the official portion of the apartment of Julius II; the decorative scheme was entrusted to Raphael, who worked here between 1508 and 1525. The first room, the **Stanza della Segnatura,** illustrates the highest attributes of the human spirit: Divine Truth, investigated by Theology (*Disputation of the Sacrament,* depicting the debate about the mystery of the Eucharist), and Rational Truth, investigated by Philosophy (*School of Athens*); Beauty, represented by *Parnassus;* Goodness, expressed by the *Theological and Cardinal Virtues;* and Law, both civil (*Justinian, the Emperor, Handling the Pandects*) and ecclesiastic (*Gregory IX Handling the Decretals*). Many of the figures in the two major scenes resemble men of Raphael's time: Julius II is portrayed dressed as Gregory IX, Leonardo as Plato, Bramante as Euclid. Frescoes in the second room, the **Stanza d'Eliodoro,** illustrate a series of divine interventions to protect the church: faith threatened (*Mass at Bolsena,* representing an episode when blood issued from the communion wafer held by a doubting priest); the person of the pontiff (*The Deliverance of St. Peter from Prison*); in its see (*Meeting of Attila with Leo the Great*); and the church's legacy (*Expulsion of Heliodorus,* portraying the thief trampled by the horse of the divine envoy). The **Stanza dell'Incendio** extolls the new pope, Leo X, in four episodes from the lives of popes with the same name (Leo III and IV). In the scene from which the room takes its name, the blessing given by Leo IV miraculously stops the fire that is destroying the Borgo district; in the *Battle of Ostia,* the same pope thanks God for a storm that dispersed the Arab fleet. Leo III is the protagonist of the *Coronation of Charlemagne* and the *Oath,* where he refutes the false charges of the nephews of Hadrian I. The **Stanza di Costantino** was decorated by pupils of Raphael from his drawings. The theme is the victory over paganism and the establishment of the church in Rome (*Baptism of Constantine, Battle of Ponte Milvio, Apparition of the Cross,* and the *Donation of Rome*).

The Deposition ⑦, a work of rare dramatic power, painted by Caravaggio in 1604.

View of Castel S. Angelo ⑧, built in the 2nd century as a tomb for the emperor Hadrian.

⑧

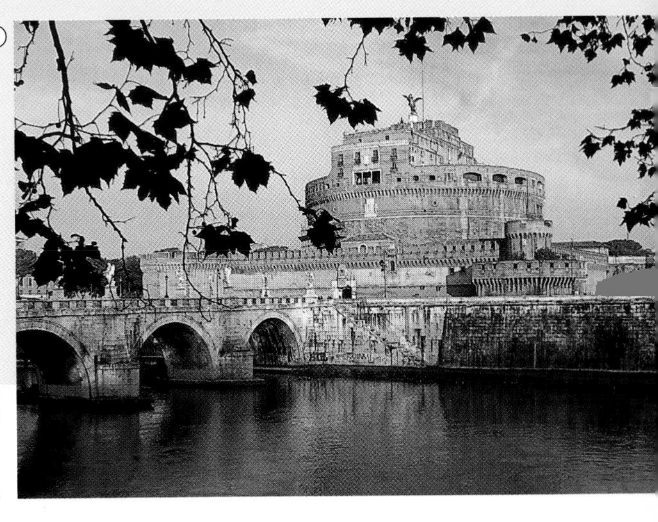

BORGO AND PRATI

Beginning in late antiquity, Christian Rome emerged in the vast area defined by the right bank of the Tiber River, Castel S. Angelo, and the Vatican, almost in opposition to the pagan city on the opposite bank. As the numbers of pilgrims to the tomb of St. Peter increased, the communities of Christianized northern Europe urged that a permanent facility be established. The result was the Borgo district (the word "borgo" derives from the Gothic word "burg," or town). The sack of Rome by the Saracens (AD 846) pushed Pope Leo IV to build a wall, defining an area known as Città Leonina, which included St. Peter's, Borgo, and Castel S. Angelo. The development of the district, which did not become an official rione *(region) until 1586, took place during the urban development of the Vatican. Its building fabric remained intact until the defacements of the 20th century, the most serious of which was the opening of the Via della Conciliazione. The Prati district, the last of the modern rioni, is also on the right bank. Prior to the postunification building explosion, the area was filled with meadows (*prati*), vineyards, orchards, and marshes that were scattered with huts and inns for hunters.*

Castel S. Angelo ⑧

⊞2 C6–D6. Over the course of its long existence, Castel S. Angelo has played various roles, from mausoleum to fortress, from notorious prison to sumptuous papal residence, and it has been the setting for some of the most dramatic events in Rome's history. It was built as the monumental tomb of the emperor Hadrian (2nd century AD), who wanted to create a work that would convey the power and wealth of the Roman Empire, heir to the splendor of the Eastern monarchies. Its inclusion within the Aurelian Wall (AD 275) inaugurated its new purpose as a citadel, capable of resisting the assaults of the Visigoths (410) and the Ostrogoths (537). In addition to being a mighty fortress, it was located at a meeting point between ancient and medieval Rome and the new Vatican, which had grown up around the tomb of St. Peter. Its Christianization, including its name, dates from the year 590 and is linked to an apparition by the Archangel Michael, who announced to Pope Gregory the Great the end of the plague. The event is evoked in the large bronze statue atop the structure. Between the 10th and 15th centuries, the fortress passed into the hands of various patrician families and became the property of various popes. Each strengthened the building's military function and opulently decorated its interior spaces, turning it into an emblem of power and renewed authority after the exile to Avignon and the Great Schism. Today it is the site of the **Museo Nazionale di Castel S. Angelo,** which includes, in addition to a collection of ancient arms, the luxurious papal apartments, decorated stucco, friezes, frescoes, tapestries, and ceramics. Its terrace, made famous by Puccini's *Tosca,* provides one of the most beautiful views of the city's historic center. ✉ *Lungotevere Castello 50,* ☏ *06/687–5036.*

Chiesa and Facoltà Valdese di Teologia
(Waldensian Church and Theological Institute)

⊞3 C2. The unique style of the facade, which brings together Romanesque, German, and Byzantine forms, was chosen to differentiate the building from Catholic churches and, through the cylindrical side towers, to resolve the problem of linking it to the structures that lie behind. The interior, which has a basilican plane and a women's gallery, has no sacred images, in accordance with Waldensian dictates; the stained-glass windows are embellished with Christian symbols and floral motifs. The church was erected between 1911 and 1914, a few years after the establishment of the adjacent theological institute, which has a vast library. ✉ *Via Dionigi 57.*

Museo delle Anime del Purgatorio
(Museum of the Souls of Purgatory)

⊞3 C3. In 1897 the priest Victor Janet began to collect textiles, skullcaps, breviaries, Bibles, wood panels, nightshirts, and other objects that, in his opinion, showed the traces of fire left by the souls of the departed. The small museum displays this disconcerting evidence of celestial life, submitted from various regions of Europe, although the Catholic Church has made no pronouncements as to the significance of the materials. The museum is contained within space belonging to

A

Ten statues of angels, bearing symbols of Christ's Passion, rise along the parapet of the Roman Ponte S. Angelo. They were created from drawings by Gian Lorenzo Bernini (the two sculpted by Bernini himself are now in S. Lorenzo alle Fratte).

the church of the Sacro Cuore del Suffragio (1894–1917), a rare example of neogothic architecture in Rome, apparently inspired by Milan's cathedral. ✉*Lungotevere Prati 12,* ☎*06/688–06517.*

Ospedale di S. Spirito in Sassia (Hospital of St. Spirito in Sassia)

▦2 D5–E5. Created by Pope Innocent III in 1201 on the site of the Schola Saxonum (the hospice for Saxon pilgrims, from which the appellation "in Sassia" is derived), the Hospital of S. Spirito in Sassia was established to assist the sick, the poor, and orphans. It achieved considerable economic power, which was further consolidated in 1605 with the establishment of the Banco di S. Spirito. A religious order of the same name spread throughout Europe, with institutions similar to the Roman model. Sixtus IV completely rebuilt the edifice (1473–1478), and his successors added various wings. The hospital's long history as an important teaching and research institution is amply documented in the **Museo Storico Nazionale di Arte Sanitaria** (National Historical Museum of Health Services), which exhibits anatomical charts, gynecological and surgical instruments, and a collection of pharmacy vessels. The impressive and unfinished door of S. Spirito, designed by Antonio Giamberti da Sangallo the Younger at the time of Paul III, is clearly inspired by ancient triumphal arches. ✉*Lungotevere in Sassia.*

Palazzo dei Penitenzieri

▦2 D5. For many years this building was the center of operations for the Jesuits, who functioned as confessors (with particular powers for granting absolution) in St. Peter's Basilica. Erected between 1480 and 1490 for Cardinal Domenico della Rovere, it has an stately facade inspired by the Palazzo Venezia, an unusual two-story courtyard, and refined frescoes attributed to Pinturicchio, who, at the time, was working on the Borgia Apartment. Today the building is used as a hotel and as offices for the Equestrian Order of S. Sepolcro di Gerusalemme. ✉*Via della Conciliazione 33.*

Ponte S. Angelo ⑨

▦2 D6. Built by the emperor Hadrian to link his mausoleum with the Campo Marzio, this bridge became the principal crossing point for pilgrims going to St. Peter's. Pope Clement VII (1534) had two statues, depicting St. Peter and St. Paul, placed on the end opposite the mausoleum. Pope Clement IX (1668) later transformed the bridge into one of the most theatrical monuments of the Roman Baroque, embellishing it with 10 statues of angels holding the symbols of the Passion. These were executed by various sculptors from drawings by Gian Lorenzo Bernini. These raging youthful figures, their faces misshapen by grief, their garments in disarray, summarize 17th-century devotion with a wedding of physicality and spirituality. The two angels created by Bernini himself (one with a scroll, another with a crown of thorns) were considered too fine to remain exposed to the elements and were moved to S. Andrea delle Fratte.

S. Maria in Traspontina

▦2 D5. The name of the church comes from its location, beyond the S. Angelo Bridge ("Trans pontem," or "across the bridge"). Its monumental construction was part of a plan to renew the Borgo, which had been largely abandoned by its most prosperous residents after the 1527 sack of Rome. Begun in 1566 and completed in 1668, the church has a Latin cross plan surmounted by a dome without a drum, so the artillery stationed at Castel S. Angelo could have an unencumbered range of fire. On the high altar, designed by Carlo Fontana with a crown-shaped baldachin surmounted by angels, is an icon of the Virgin brought to Rome from the Holy Land, perhaps in 1216 by the Carmelites. ✉*Borgo S. Angelo 15.*

S. Spirito in Sassia

▦2 D5. Currently part of the vast hospital complex of the same name, the church replaced the ancient S. Maria in Sassia, which was annexed to the hospice for Saxon pilgrims during the 8th century. It was rebuilt at the behest of Pope Paul III by Antonio Giamberti da Sangallo the Younger, who employed sober Renaissance forms, and completed by Sixtus V (1585–1590). The medieval church of S. Maria was the site of a solemn procession, instituted by Pope Innocent III in 1208, which brought Veronica's veil from the Vatican basilica. Pilgrims who were present were asked, in exchange for a year of indulgences, to make donations to the hospital, which had just been established. ✉*Via dei Penitenzieri 12.*

2

Trastevere

Trastevere's centuries-long separation from the rest of the city and its history have resulted in distinctive customs, traditions, and even a dialect, all of which contributed to the legendary pride of its population and the frequent disputes with the inhabitants of the opposite bank. The district's working-class character has origins in antiquity: in Roman times it was inhabited by foreign merchants who traded at the port of Rome and by the city's Jewish community (which later moved across the river). During subsequent eras Trastevere continued to be occupied by people devoted to trade and by settlements of foreigners, including Venetians, Corsicans, and Genoese. Until modern times very few buildings in the district had been restored, although there are a number of architectural treasures, particularly from the Renaissance and Baroque periods. During the second half of the 19th century, various initiatives transformed the structure of the neighborhood. The most drastic changes involved the construction of an embankment and the opening of the Viale Trastevere, which destroyed numerous historic buildings and much of the ancient street fabric. Today, large areas of the district retain the old mysterious, noisy, genuine flavor that constitutes Trastevere's unique charm.

Fontana dell'Acqua Paola

▦**5 D2.** Buit in 1612 for Pope Paul V (from whom it takes its name), the fountain celebrates the restoration of the aqueduct of Trajan. Marble from the Forum of Nerva and columns from the first basilica of St. Peter were used. In 1690, Pope Alexander VIII commissioned Carlo Fontana to design the broad piazza, which offers an excellent view of the fountain, and the semicircular basin. The compact volumes of the structure, inspired by Roman triumphal arches, are extended by three arcades and surmounted by a multilinear coping, and the theatrical effect fits perfectly within the landscape of the Janiculum. ✉ *Via Garibaldi.*

Gianicolo (Janiculum)

▦**5 A1–D2.** The Janiculum was indispensable to the city's defense from ancient times until the arduous battles between Garibaldi and the French troops in 1849. But the hill, well known for its silhouette of pine and cypress trees highlighted at sunset and its splendid views, is one of Rome's most gentle and suggestive locations. Solitary and contemplative types such as Tasso, Leopardi, and Chateaubriand favored the site, as have legions of artists, who, since Renaissance times, have come here to capture some of the most beautiful images of the city. According to one legend, this is the site where St. Peter, crucified upside down, gathered the entire city in an unencumbered visual embrace. After 1870 the celebrated *passeggiata* (promenade) dominated the crest of the hill, which was thus preserved in its natural beauty and consecrated to patriotic memories.

Ospedale dei Ss. Maria e Gallicano

▦**5 D4.** The hospital, built between 1724 and 1729, was founded by Benedict XIII to aid those suffering from skin afflictions (a tradition that has been maintained in today's dermatological hospital). These people were often rejected by other hospitals, with the exception of the Hospital of S. Lazzaro, on the Via Trionfale. Architect Filippo Raguzzini created a model for hospital architecture of the time, and the anatomy theater, a source of pride for this institution in the 19th century, still has a stuccowork frieze depicting the legend of Aesculapius and the Tiber Island and portraits of famous physicians. ✉ *Via S. Gallicano 25/A.*

Ospizio Apostolico di S. Michele a Ripa Grande

▦**5 E5–F5.** Established in the late 17th century as a boys' reformatory, the hospice later became the city's principal institution for education and welfare, named after the Archangel Michael, long the subject of special devotion in Rome. In the mid-18th century it opened its doors to orphans of both sexes, single women, the elderly, the disabled, and the destitute, and also served as a women's prison. The building, designed by Carlo Fontana and Ferdinando Fuga, incorporates the churches of S. Michele and the Madonna del Buon Viaggio. In addition to its function as an institution of public assistance, the hospice played an important role in Rome's artisanal history. It was the site of a wool mill, a famous tapestry factory, and a foundry (one of its last creations was the equestrian group for the Victor Emmanuel Monument). Today it houses the Ministry of Cultural Affairs. ✉ *Via S. Michele 22.*

Palazzo Corsini

▦**5 B3.** Built in the 16th century, the palace became famous during the 17th century, when it was inhabited by Queen Christina of Sweden, who made it the center of Rome's cultural life. In the 18th

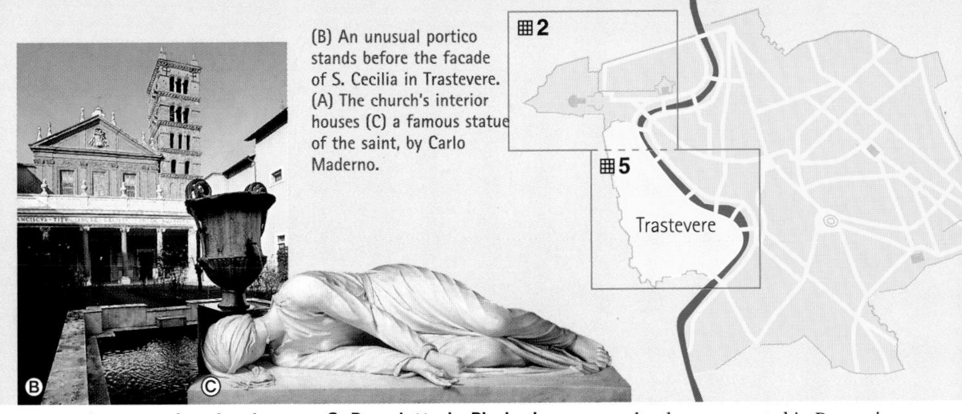

(B) An unusual portico stands before the facade of S. Cecilia in Trastevere. (A) The church's interior houses (C) a famous statue of the saint, by Carlo Maderno.

century it was purchased and expanded by the Corsini family to accommodate their gallery of paintings and their family library, which included a rich collection of early books and manuscripts. Since 1883 it has been the property of the state and the location of the Accademia Nazionale dei Lincei, the most authoritative cultural and academic institution in Italy, founded in 1605. The **Galleria Corsini** (which, together with the gallery in the Palazzo Barberini, constitutes the Galleria Nazionale di Arte Antica) was founded by Cardinal Neri Corsini, nephew of Pope Clement XII, and is the only 18th-century Roman collection to survive intact. It displays Italian and foreign painting from the 17th and 18th centuries. In 1883, the palace garden became the Botanical Garden of the University of Rome and now contains environments that simulate various climatic conditions. The 19th-century greenhouses shelter various species of citrus fruits, orchids, and succulents. ✉ *Via della Lungara 10,* ☎ *06/688–02323.*

S. Agata

▦5 D5. The simple Baroque church of S. Agata is linked to the religious traditions of Trastevere because of its wooden sculpture of the Madonna del Carmine. Every year in July, the Festa de' Noantri is celebrated with a series of outdoor spectacles, illuminations, fireworks, and a tremendous consumption of watermelons and wine. It is an example of the secular festival, dating from the 1920s, superimposed on a traditional religious festival. The celebrations begin with a procession that transfers the statue (dressed each year in new embroidered garments) from the church of S. Agata to the nearby church of S. Crisogono. ✉ *Largo S. Giovanni de Matha 9.*

S. Benedetto in Piscinula

▦5 D5. Erected between the 11th and 12th centuries, this church preserves the cell of St. Benedict, part of the saint's house according to tradition. It has a small Romanesque bell tower with two rows of mullioned windows and a Neoclassical facade. The Cappella della Madonna holds a 14th-century fresco of a *Madonna and Child.* The principal nave, flanked by columns with ancient and medieval capitals—plundered from other locations—has traces of a mosaic floor and, on the high altar, a gold-topped table with a 15th-century image of St. Benedict. ✉ *Piazza in Piscinula 40.*

S. Callisto

▦5 D4. After being a slave to a Christian and leading a less than impeccable life, Callistus became papal secretary and then, in AD 217, pope. He was one of the most active and important of the early popes, and he was a protagonist in the first schisms in the church's history. About a century after his death he began to be venerated as a martyr. According to legend, he was thrown into a well, his neck tied to a stone (the well has been identified as the one in the garden of the former monastery annexed to the church). During the 8th century this small building was erected on the site of his presumed martyrdom, and it was rebuilt in the 17th century. Callistus was buried in the Calepodio Cemetery, on the Via Aurelia, not in the cemetery that bears his name. ✉ *Piazza S. Calisto.*

S. Cecilia in Trastevere ①

▦5 D5. In addition to being one of the most interesting churches in the city, this is one of the very few oases of solitude in the turbulent Trastevere district. The Passion of the young martyr, who lived during the first half of the 3rd century and has been venerated in Rome since early Christian times, is in large part legendary. According to tradition, the first place of worship was the house of Caecilia's family or of her husband, Valerian, who was also a saint and martyr. The church encompasses the remains of a calidarium, the room with hot baths, where she was confined for three days, exposed to the steam in an attempt to suffocate her, before she was finally beheaded. Pope Paschal I rebuilt the edifice as a basilica in 821 to safeguard the saint's body, which was recovered intact in the catacombs of S. Callisto. In 1595, the sarcophagus was opened and the body was found exactly as it had been buried, turned on one side, the face turned down, and three of her fingers extended, which was taken to allude to the mystery of the Trinity. Stefano Maderno immortalized the miraculous event in his famous statue, which is located beneath the high altar (1600). The sarcophagus of this saint and other martyrs is kept in the crypt, where many tombs have been recovered (Christians aspired to be buried as close as possible to the martyrs), along with frescoes, including a 5th-century image of St. Caecilia at prayer. A magnificent 9th-century mosaic in the apse depicts Christ offering a benediction, flanked by saints and by Pope Paschal I, who commissioned the work. The pope is portrayed with a square halo, because he was still alive at the time the work was executed. The basilica contains two pivotal works by two late 13th-century masters of the figurative revival, both of whom attempted to restore the plastic values of the ancient world. At the center of the presbytery is a ciborium, or altar canopy (1293), by Arnolfo di Cambio, a masterpiece of Gothic sculpture, executed at the same time that Pietro Cavallini was completing his magnificent *Last*

② Bernini's statue of the *Blessed Ludovica Albertoni* (1674), in S. Francesco a Ripa.

(A) The high altar and baldacchino by Carlo Rainaldi in S. Maria della Scala, adjacent to a monastery well known for its (B) pharmacy, which dates from the 18th century ③.

Judgment on the opposite wall. Today St. Caecilia is considered the patron saint of music and the makers of musical instruments, although without any precise historical reference. The Accademia Nazionale di S. Cecilia is one of the most famous conservatories in the world. ✉ *Piazza S. Cecilia 22.*

S. Crisogono

▦**5 D5.** The current church is the result of a radical 17th-century restoration of a Romanesque (12th century) structure, which in its turn had been built above the remains of a 5th-century basilica (one of the most ancient in Rome) dedicated to St. Chrysogonus, who was martyred at the time of the Diocletian persecutions. There are some interesting fresco remains (8th–11th centuries) from the early Christian building, with figures of saints and hagiographic episodes: *Pope Sylvester Capturing the Dragon, St. Pantaleone Healing the Blind Man, St. Benedict Healing the Leper,* and the *Rescue of St. Placid.* The later building, with three naves and a beautiful mosaic floor, has seven altars, each with its own relics (as in great basilicas), and on St. Chrysogonus's feast day (November 24) pilgrims and worshipers receive plenary indulgence. The painted coffered ceiling from the Baroque era is one of the most beautiful in Rome. ✉ *Piazza Sonnino 44.*

S. Dorotea

▦**5 C3.** The church appearance is a result of the 18th-century reconstruction of the original Romanesque building, first called S. Silvestro and later named after Dorothy, a 3rd-century Eastern martyr. At the beginning of the 16th century the church was the assembly place for a religious confraternity, the Oratorio di Divino Amore, established by St. Cajetan (1480–1547), co-founder (with Peter Caraffa, later Pope Paul IV) of the Theatines religious order, which, along with the Jesuits, became one of the forces of the Counter-Reformation. In the adjacent house, St. Joseph Calasanctius opened the first free public school in Europe, in 1592. ✉ *Via S. Dorotea 23.*

S. Francesco a Ripa ②

▦**5 E4–E5.** The church was built on the site of the former S. Biagio (10th century), where, according to a deeply rooted tradition, St. Francis of Assisi stayed during his sojourns in Rome. The current appearance dates from the partial renovation in the late 7th century. The side chapels, rich in works of art, bear witness to the particular devotion of certain Roman noble families to the saint of Assisi. In the Paluzzi-Albertoni Chapel is Gian Lorenzo Bernini's statue of the *Blessed Ludovica Albertoni* (1674), a masterful blend of mysticism and theatricality, along the lines of his *Ecstasy of St. Teresa* in the church of St. Maria della Vittoria. The architectural cornice and the skillful use of light focus attention on the vibrant figure of this Roman mystic (1474–1533), who had a gift for making miracles and prophecies. The only surviving space from the ancient Hospice of S. Biagio is the Chapel of S. Francesco, whose theatrical wooden reliquary (1696), inspired by Bernini, has a copy of a panel attributed to Margaritone d'Arezzo, considered an actual portrait of St. Francis. (The original is in the Pinacoteca Vaticana.) ✉ *Piazza S. Francesco d'Assisi 88.*

S. Giovanni Battista dei Genovesi

▦**5 D5.** The Genoese community in Rome had its residences and mercantile warehouses near the port of Ripa Grande. In 1481, Meliaduce Cicala, a Genoese nobleman, left a bequest for the construction of a church dedicated to the patron saint of Genoa and a hospital for sailors. The hospice building, completely renovated outside, has an evocative late 15th-century cloister with a portico with arches and octagonal columns and an architraved loggia. The church, which has been renovated many times (most recently in 1864), contains a beautiful funerary monument to its donor. The spaces above the cloister contain the Archive of the Confraternity of St. Giovanni, which includes hospital documents. ✉ *Via Anicia 12.*

S. Maria dei Sette Dolori

▦**5 C3.** Beginning in 1643, Borromini built this church and convent for the Order of Augustinian Oblates. The master designed a facade (unfinished) almost completely without openings, animated solely by a double order of pilasters and niches, as if to express visually the strict cloistered life of the monastic order by turning the wall into an element of isolation and defense. As in the Oratory of St. Philip Neri, the church is developed along an axis parallel to the facade. Inside, a high cornice twists uninterruptedly around the arches of the side chapels and the presbytery; above the entrance, the cornice breaks into two curved volutes, the building's most significant element, unifying and strengthening the space. The atrium alternates curved and rectilinear segments, most likely inspired by a space in Hadrian's Villa in Tivoli. ✉ *Via Garibaldi 27.*

S. Maria dell'Orto

▦**5 E5.** The current 16th-century church has its origins in a chapel erected during the 15th century to celebrate an image of the Virgin with child, which had been removed from a garden wall. The facade has two rows of columns

③

punctuated by pilasters, arched portals, and a crowning element of small obelisks. Inside, the exuberant 18th-century stucco and gilded decoration radically transform the spatial equilibrium of the Renaissance layout. The building was the site of numerous "universities" (corporations) of arts and crafts, the names of which are recorded in the dedication of the chapels. The Luigi Huetter Study Center on Roman Confraternities and Universities of Arts and Crafts, which has a library and a small museum, is annexed to the church. ✉ *Via Anicia.*

S. Maria della Luce

▦5 D5. The name of the original church (3rd or 4th century) was S. Salvatore in Corte, perhaps refering to an ancient public edifice. It was rebuilt in the 12th century on a basilica plan, with an elegant bell tower with triforium and a transept with an apse (visible from the Vicolo del Buco). After the miraculous image of a Madonna, who restored the sight of a blind man, was transferred here, the name and structure of the church were changed. In 1730, the interior space was rebuilt in its current form, with luminous, late Baroque elements embellished by stuccowork. ✉ *Via della Luce.*

S. Maria della Scala ③

▦5 C3. Like many churches in Trastevere, this was built (1593–1610) to house an image of the Madonna, painted above a stairway and considered miraculous. Inside the church are works by 17th-century artists, such as Carlo Rainaldi, Cavaliere d'Arpino (Giuseppe Cesari), and Pomarancio. Important works of art include the *Beheading of the Baptist* by Gerrit van Honthorst, a Dutch painter who was profoundly influenced by Caravaggio. Carlo Saraceni's *Death of the Virgin* replaced a painting of the same subject by Caravaggio, now in the Louvre, because the latter work was rejected by the monks as lacking in "decorum" and because they suspected that the model was a prostitute who had drowned in the Tiber. The adjoining monastery administers a famous pharmacy that dates from the 17th century, that supplied the papal court, and that still has the original furnishings and equipment. ✉ *Piazza della Scala 23.*

S. Maria in Cappella

▦5 E6. The name is derived from the makers of *cupelle,* or barrels, who were given the church as the site for their confraternity in the 15th century. A hospital was later added to the 11th-century church, and the entire complex was completely renovated in the 19th century by the Doria Pamphili family to become Rome's first home for the aged. ✉ *Vicolo S. Maria in Cappella 6.*

S. Maria in Trastevere ④

▦5 D4. The basilica of St. Maria in Trastevere is one of the most important churches in Rome, overshadowed only by the four patriarchal basilicas. Founded by Pope Julius I in the mid-4th century, it was the first place of worship dedicated to the Madonna. During Jubilee years afflicted by calamities or pestilence, this church was often preferred by pilgrims to the distant S. Paolo. Tradition links the dedication to Mary to the miraculous source of a fountain of mineral oil that was later interpreted by Christians as a sign auguring the birth of Christ. An inscription near the apse marks the spot where the miracle is said to have occurred. In the 9th century, Pope Gregory IV constructed a crypt to hold the remains of certain martyrs that had been moved from catacombs threatened by the Saracens' sack of Rome. The current church (12th century) was built by Innocent II and decorated with celebrated mosaics in the apse depicting Christ and Mary enthroned with saints. In 1291, another mosaic by Pietro Cavallini, illustrating *Scenes from the Life of the Virgin,* was added at the height of the windows. This mosaic's refined and delicate colors and the plastic strength of the figures were an innovative departure from Byzantine canons and can be compared to developments in the work of Cimabue and Arnolfo di Cambio. Bertoldo Stefaneschi, a member of one of the most important families in Trastevere, commissioned the frescoes. He is portrayed in prayer, in a lower

4
PIVS IX PONT MAX
INSTAVRAVIT
PONT ANNO XXII
PETRVS
IVLIVS

The apse mosaics (left), created in two phases (those in the spherical vault date from the 12th century, those in the lower band from the 13th), are among the treasures within S. Maria in Trastevere ④.

The tempietto of S. Pietro in Montorio ⑤, designed in the early 16th century by Bramante, is a milestone of Renaissance architecture .

panel, with the Madonna and St. Peter and St. Paul. The most venerated image in the church is the monumental icon of the *Madonna of Mercy,* in the Altemps Chapel; this 6th- to 7th-century encaustic panel depicts the Virgin and child enthroned between two angels. Considered a miraculous sacred image, created by a direct emanation of divinity, it was the object of great care and devotion by certain Roman pontiffs. Gregory III (731–741) covered it in silver leaf, and Leo III (795–816) donated a large purple veil to hang in front of the sacred image. ⊠*Piazza S. Maria in Trastevere.*

S. Onofrio al Gianicolo

▦2 F5. Dedicated to the venerated 4th-century hermit, this monastery complex was built during the 15th and 16th centuries on the site of an ancient hermitage. It is linked to the poet Torquato Tasso, who stayed here, dying in 1595. He was posthumously granted a crown of laurel on the Campidoglio. Beneath the Renaissance portico of the church courtyard, three lunettes (1605) by Domenichino depict scenes from the life of St. Jerome (in memory of the hermits who resided here in the 15th century). The interior has an opulent decorative scheme by, among others, Domenichino, B.B. Ricci, students of Annibale Carracci, and, perhaps, Baldassare Peruzzi (*Scenes from the Life of Mary*). A cloister with frescoed scenes from the life of St. Onuphrius is attached to the church. The monastery houses the **Museo Tassiano,** which has manuscripts and editions of his works. ⊠*Piazza S. Onofrio 2.*

S. Pietro in Montorio ⑤

▦5 D3. Ferdinand and Isabella of Spain built this church (1481–1500) and dedicated it to St. Peter, who, according to an unfounded tradition, was crucified here. The name "in Montorio" is derived from the ancient Latin name for the Janiculum, *Mons Aureus* (Mount of Gold), so-called because of the yellow sand that is visible at twilight. Numerous works of art decorate the church, including the *Flagellation of Jesus* (1518) by Sebastiano del Piombo, perhaps based on a drawing by Michelangelo. The site's main attraction is Bramante's **Tempietto,** commissioned in 1502 as a commemorative chapel to the martyrdom of Peter. This minuscule edifice holds a place of primary importance in 16th-century architecture, with its perfect elaboration of the central plan and its obvious reference (including its name) to Greco-Roman architecture. Bramante's rigorous treatment of the geometric elements of the circle and cylinder define an architectural model of universal value and symbolize the synthesis between Christian and Renaissance Rome and the ancient city. ⊠*Piazza S. Pietro in Montorio 2.*

Via della Lungara

▦2 E5–E6; 5 A2–B3. One of the roadways most frequently traveled by pilgrims on their way to S. Pietro, the Via della Lungara ("street along a river") was also called the Via Santa, or Holy Way. It was built between 1508 and 1512 by Pope Julius II, at the same time the Via Giulia was laid out, along the other bank of the Tiber. The task was entrusted to Bramante, who, in addition to being a talented architect, had a profound interest in designing urban spaces. The stately character of the street, which is flanked by villas, palaces, and churches built between the 16th and 18th centuries, is now diminished by the Tiber embankment that partially demolished and lowered what had been one of most spectacular streets in Rome.

Villa Farnesina

▦5 B3. Agostino Chigi built this sumptuous residence (1507–1509) in the midst of suburban gardens along the Tiber. It was the principal backdrop for Roman society and cultural life at the culmination of the Renaissance, until the dramatic sack of Rome in 1527. Chigi welcomed as guests numerous cardinals, ambassadors, and princes, and the host of artists and intellectuals who gravitated around the court of Pope Leo X. Baldassare Peruzzi designed this "villa of delights," which was later acquired by the Farnese family, hence the building's name. Peruzzi combined a typical 15th-century city palace structure with a loggia and projecting side wings, emphasizing the relationship between building and nature. The best painters in Rome contributed to the opulent interior decorations, which are dominated by mythological and astrological subjects. In addition to Sebastiano del Piombo, Il Sodoma, and Domenico Beccafumi, Chigi engaged the painter Raphael, whose *Triumph of Galatea* (1513–1514) is a showpiece of classicism, both in its subject and in the figures and colors. The artist also conceived the decorative scheme for the loggia overlooking the garden, transforming the vault into a luxuriant pergola that frames scenes from the adventures of Psyche. ⊠*Via della Lungara 230.*

3

Ponte and Parione

During the early Middle Ages, much of Rome's population was concentrated in the area within the bend of the Tiber that is closest to the Vatican. People were drawn here by the proximity to the Holy See and by the presence of the Ponte S. Angelo, one of the few ancient Roman bridges still standing and considered important enough to have lent its name to the entire district. The surrounding area was scattered with ruins of ancient monuments, and the name Parione may derive from the Latin paries *("wall"). Along today's Via dei Banchi Nuovi, Via Governo Vecchio, Via di S. Pantaleo, Via dei Banchi Vecchi, Via del Pellegrino, Campo de' Fiori, and Via dei Giubbonari, which closely follow the outlines of the ancient city, a dense urban fabric developed, full of small churches, inns, warehouses, and exchange banks. The urban renewal promoted by Renaissance and Baroque popes transformed the two districts, which were enriched with churches, palaces, and elegant houses. There was tremendous commercial activity, and the transfer of the market from the Campidoglio to Piazza Navona further contributed to the quarter's liveliness. The opening of the Corso Vittorio Emanuele II and other postunification projects altered the earlier urban plan and accelerated the deterioration of many structures.*

①

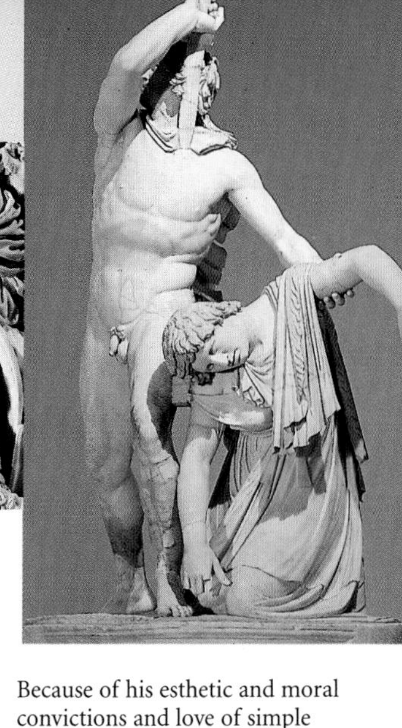

Detail of the Ludovisi sarcophagus (showing a battle between the Romans and the Barbarians) and a statue of a Galatian committing suicide, in the Museo Nazionale Romano in the Palazzo Altemps.

Chiesa Nuova ②

▦3 E2–F2. In 1575, the pope gave the little church of S. Maria in Vallicella to the Congregation of the Oratory, which was founded by St. Philip Neri, and they immediately began its reconstruction. The building's design recalls that of the Chiesa del Gesù, and the 10 side chapels, personally requested by St. Philip Neri, celebrate episodes from the life of the Madonna. The interior decoration expresses not only the ascetic orientation of the Oratorians, but also the ideals of the "triumphant" church of the Counter-Reformation and the diversity of tastes of the chapels' private patrons. These range from Federico Barocci's delicate *Visitation,* commissioned by St. Philip Neri, to typical Counter-Reformation devotional painting. There are also works by Caravaggio (*The Deposition,* 1604, now in the Vatican Pinacoteca); by Rubens, who was commissioned to paint the three presbytery paintings in 1608; by Guido Reni, who painted a famous altarpiece with the portrait of the saint; by Il Guercino; by Alessandro Algardi; and a by host of stuccoworkers, who, according to a writer at the time, bathed the church in a "shower of gold." Pietro da Cortona's frescoes cover the dome, apse, and nave and depict the apparition of the Virgin to St. Philip during the demolition of the ancient little church. The frescoes are the artist's most ambitious rendering of a sacred subject. Next to the magnificent church the Oratorians built a vast monastery complex, the **Palazzo dei Filippini,** characterized by an austere design. Because of his esthetic and moral convictions and love of simple materials, architect and sculptor Borromini was perfectly suited to the order's spirit of charity and good works, and he carried out the assignment brilliantly, creating the oratory, the **Torre dell'Orologio,** and the extraordinary concave facade, a metaphor for the embrace of the faithful that was echoed by Bernini in St. Peter's. The palace houses many cultural institutions, including the Roman Newspaper Archive, which contains nearly all Roman newspapers from the 18th century to the present; the Capitoline Historical Archive; and the Vallicelliana Library, established by St. Philip Neri in 1581, also designed by Borromini, and one of the oldest libraries in Rome open to the public. ✉*Piazza della Chiesa Nuova.*

Nostra Signora del Sacro Cuore

▦3 F3. This is the real name of the church of S. Giacomo degli Spagnoli, built on the occasion of the 1450 Jubilee. The church was long the site of the Spanish court's celebrations and rituals of mourning. The solemn Easter celebrations in Piazza Navona organized by the Confraternity of the Resurrection, headquartered in the church, were particularly famous. After the focus of Spanish court life shifted to **S. Maria in Monserrato,** these activities declined, but the church continued to be used as a loggia for viewing spectacles in the piazza. The works of art and funerary monuments were transferred to the new Spanish church. Some Renaissance works remain, such as a chancel in polychrome marble, the marble backdrop behind the high altar,

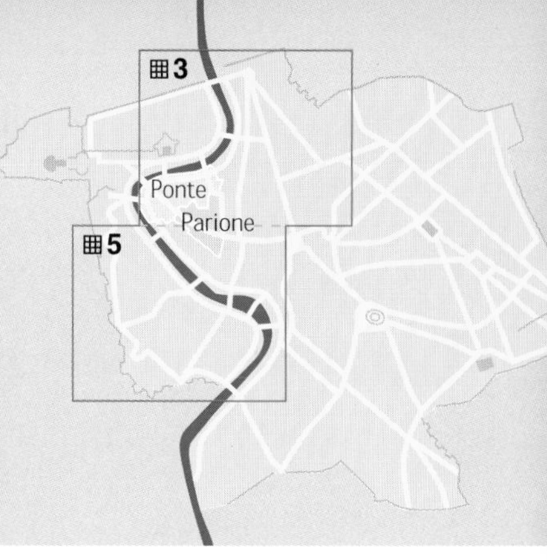

② S. Maria in Vallicella, better known as Chiesa Nuova, was rebuilt at the request of St. Philip Neri, beginning in 1575.

and the S. Giacomo Chapel. ✉ *Piazza Navona.*

Palazzo Altemps, Museo Nazionale Romano ①

⊞3 E3. Built at the end of the 15th century, the Palazzo Altemps is crowned by a beautiful covered roof terrace with arcades and four obelisks, the work of Martino Longhi the Elder, who also finished the extraordinary courtyard in travertine and stucco. The palazzo was restored so it is possible to appreciate fully the impressive pictorial scheme and the wooden ceilings inlaid with mother-of-pearl. But the contents are even more precious than the container: the palazzo is one of the locations of the **Museo Nazionale Romano** and contains more than 200 antiquities from collections of some of the city's aristocratic families. The most noteworthy group of works is from the Ludovisi collection, which was created by Cardinal Ludovico (1595–1632), nephew of Gregory XV, to embellish his immense villa. The cardinal's villa was demolished as a result of postunification building speculation and to make space for the neighborhood that now exists off the Via Veneto. The cardinal's collection, which was originally much richer, is a testament to the Roman aristocracy's passion for antiquities and classical art. ✉ *Piazza S. Apollinare 44,* ☎ *06/683–3566.*

Palazzo Braschi

⊞3 F3. This Neoclassical edifice (1791–1811) is the last palazzo built in Rome for the family of a pope (Pius VI). The building's grand staircase was designed by Giuseppe Valadier and embellished with statues and stucco decorations. In 1871, the palazzo became the property of the state, and it now houses offices for various cultural institutions. One of these is the **Museo di Roma,** which contains paintings, sculptures, drawings, and other art objects that illustrate various aspects of the city's life and culture, from the Middle Ages to the present. Some of the most interesting works are paintings inspired by Roman costumes and festivals and the collection of men and women's costumes from the 18th and 19th centuries. The palazzo also houses the **Gabinetto Comunale delle Stampe,** the municipal photo archive and print room, which contains precious documentation of transformations in the city and its territory between the 16th and 20th centuries. ✉ *Piazza S. Pantaleo 10,* ☎ *06/687–5880.*

Palazzo della Cancelleria

⊞5 A4. Construction of the palazzo began in 1485, at the request of Cardinal Raffaele Riario, nephew of Sixtus IV, with contributions by the pope's other nephew, Julius II (both pontiffs' coats of arms appear on the facade). In 1517, Leo X confiscated the building from the cardinal, who was guilty of organizing a plot against the pontiff, and shortly thereafter it became (and still is) the location of the Apostolic Chancellery, the office that publishes papal decrees. Today it houses various cultural institutions and the Tribunale della Sacra Rota, the Vatican's highest court. The building's authorship is uncertain, although Bramante was certainly involved, most obviously in the courtyard. Other noteworthy elements are the extremely long facade, the elegant balcony overlooking the Campo de' Fiori and Via del Pellegrino, the Salone dei Cento Giorni (which Vasari claimed to have frescoed in 100 days), and the Study, with a vault painted by Perin del Vaga. During the second half of the 17th century the palazzo became a lively center for musical and theatrical life, featuring the most important artists of the time, and one room was used as a theater. The palazzo incorporates the basilica of **S. Lorenzo in Damaso,** which in the late 15th century replaced the church established in 380 by Pope Damasus to house various relics. ✉ *Piazza della Cancelleria 1.*

Palazzi dei Massimo

⊞3 F3. For centuries, the ancient Massimo family owned an entire block, and the most important building on that block was the **Palazzo Massimo "alle Colonne,"** rebuilt by Baldassarre Peruzzi (1532–1536) after the sack of Rome. It was one of the first and most significant attempts to restore the devastated city. The curved line of the facade follows the shape of Domitian's *Odeon,* over which the building was erected. The most celebrated of the sumptuous interiors is the chapel, in which Paolo Massimo is said to have been recalled from the dead by St. Philip Neri on March 16, 1584; on that day every year the chapel is open to the public. The **Palazzo Massimo di Pirro** gets its name from a statue of Mars, now in the Capitoline Museums. In the Piazza dei Massimi, which lies behind, is the oldest of the palaces, known as **Istoriato** and decorated with historical scenes; in 1467, this became the site of the first printing office in Rome. The facade is one of the few surviving examples of the painted decorations that were common in Rome during the Renaissance. ✉ *Corso Vittorio Emanuele 141; Corso Vittorio Emanuele 145; Piazza dei Massimi 1–3.*

Piazza Navona contains three fountains; the Fountain of the Four Rivers, by Bernini, is embellished with statues that personify the world's great rivers.

Pasquino

▦3 **F3.** Leaning against a corner of the Palazzo Braschi is a marble statue in great disrepair. It was discovered a short distance away and placed here in 1501 by Cardinal Oliviero Carafa. The statue is a Roman copy of a Greek sculpture (Menelaus supporting the corpse of Patroclus), but the people of Rome gave it the name of a local tailor, Pasquino, famous for his invective against those in power. From the time of its discovery, anonymous authors attached to it sarcastic comments and political denunciations, generally against the papal government (thus our word "pasquinade"). For centuries, the statue was the most famous and loquacious of Rome's "talking statues" (the others were the Madama Lucrezia in Piazza Venezia and the Marforio, formerly in Via del Campidoglio, now in the Capitoline Museums). The papal administration generally ignored these expressions of popular discontent, but there were cases when those considered guilty of having spoken through Pasquino had to pay harshly for their temerity. The area came to be populated by printers, booksellers, and publishers, and the piazza became known as the Piazza dei Librai. ✉ *Piazza di Pasquino.*

Piazza Navona ③

▦3 **E3–F3.** Along with S. Pietro and the Campidoglio, this is one of Rome's most well known attractions, and for centuries it has been one of the most animated spaces in the city. It stands above the ancient Stadium of Domitian (AD 81–96) and echoes that site's unusual plan and dimensions. The piazza's dramatic setting is the work of Innocent X Pamphilj (1644–1655), who wanted to transform it into a place for the glorification of his own family and entrusted its execution to the great masters of the Baroque. The result was the palazzo, the church of S. Agnese, and the fountains, the most spectacular of which is the **Fontana dei Fiumi,** in which Gian Lorenzo Bernini expressed all his theatrical talents: a carved rock, with personifications of the major rivers of the four continents, holds up an obelisk surmounted by the dove of the Pamphilj coat of arms. The piazza's ancient function was echoed in its use as a place for tournaments, processions, jousts, and the extraordinary spectacle of a mock naval battle that concluded with the appearance of a gilded ship in the piazza, which had been transformed into a lake and was framed by fireworks. The adjacent **Piazza di Tor Sanguigna** contains both the ruins of Domitian's stadium and one of the most magnificent shrines from the 18th century, attached to the facade of the Palazzo Grossi Dondi. It depicts an Assumption of the Virgin, painted on canvas and surrounded by putti, with two angels below pointing up to the image.

Piazza di Ponte S. Angelo

▦3 **E1.** Located at the end of the Ponte S. Angelo and for centuries the principal access route to the Vatican, the piazza was an important junction and busy commercial and banking center. Because of its location, it was chosen as the site for capital executions, the most famous of which was that of Beatrice Cenci and her accomplices in 1599 (☞Palazzo Cenci Bolognetti, *74*).

S. Agnese in Agone

▦3 **E3.** In the early Middle Ages an oratory was built on the ruins of an ancient Roman stadium, in memory of the martyrdom of St. Agnes. Here, according to tradition, the young Christian, dragged naked to her death, was covered by her hair, which grew miraculously (the event is immortalized in a marble relief by Alessandro Algardi in one of the spaces belowground). Innocent X wanted to rebuilt the church in more majestic form. The structure bears Borromini's unmistakable touch, and the concave facade, tall side towers, and tilt of the dome create a powerful image from every point in the piazza. The church's interior presents a vast panorama of Roman sculpture from the second half of the 17th century, with works of the most significant artists in Bernini's circle. ✉ *Piazza Navona.*

S. Andrea della Valle ④

▦5 **A5.** S. Andrea, modeled on the Chiesa del Gesù, is one of the most solemn and characteristic churches of the Counter-Reformation. The stateliness of the church's dimensions and wealth of its ornamentation express the triumphant reality of Catholicism. It was built between 1591 and 1665 for the Theatine congregation, which played a primary role in this period of ecclesiastic history. Carlo Maderno created one of his greatest works in the majestic, soaring dome, second in size only to that of St. Peter's. The young Borromini collaborated with Maderno and invented the unusual capitals for the lantern of the dome, with cherubim that echo the Iconic volutes. The facade is by Carlo Rainaldi, who accentuated

S. Andrea della Valle's magnificent dome is second in size only to the dome of S. Pietro.

vertical and plastic effects in accordance with accepted principles of the Baroque. Artists of note contributed to the church's sumptuous pictorial decoration, including Domenichino, who frescoed the bowl-shaped vault of the apse with *Scenes from the Life of St. Andrew,* and Giovanni Lanfranco, who painted the *Heavenly Glory with the Assumption of the Virgin,* which marked the beginning of a taste for illusionistic effects, culminating in the clamorous success of 17th-century painting. ✉ *Piazza S. Andrea della Valle.*

S. Apollinare

▦3 E3. The present-day church is the result of a renovation (1741–1748) by Ferdinando Fuga of an early medieval church that was also dedicated to the bishop-saint of Ravenna. The entrance vestibule has a venerated fresco of the Madonna (15th century). From 1574 to 1773 the adjacent **Palazzo di S. Apollinare** was the headquarters of the Collegio Germanico, established by St. Ignatius of Loyola and restored by Fuga in the sober, monumental style that is characteristic of Jesuit architecture. ✉ *Piazza S. Apollinare 49.*

S. Giovanni dei Fiorentini ⑤

▦2 E5–E6. Beginning in the 15th century, a sizable Florentine colony developed along the initial portion of the Via Giulia. The area had warehouses, residences, and a consulate that governed the district's activities. Leo X built a church there for his fellow townsmen and dedicated it to the patron saint of Florence, St. John the Baptist. The construction of the church had the strong support of the Compagnia della Pietà, a confraternity of Florentines established to aid and bury plague victims. Jacopo Sansovino began the building in 1519, and work was continued by Carlo Maderno, who created the unusual elongated dome. The facade was built in 1734 by Florentine Alessandro Galilei, who was asked to design the facade for S. Giovanni in Laterano two years later and who received both commissions from Clement XII Corsini, also from Florence. ✉ *Via Acciaioli 2.*

S. Maria dell'Anima

▦3 E3. This is the national church for German-speaking Catholics. It was founded, along with a hospice, after the Jubilee of 1350 by two wealthy German pilgrims, and it was completely rebuilt in its current form on the occasion of the 1500 Jubilee. The tall Renaissance facade is surmounted by the coats of arms of the empire and Hadrian VI, who was teacher and counselor to Charles V. Hadrian was also the last non-Italian pope until the election of John Paul II in 1978. German models inspired the church interior, conceived as a large hall with three naves of equal height, separated by tall, slender cruciform pillars. Impressive funerary monuments attest to the secular presence of Germans in Rome. ✉ *Via S. Maria dell'Anima.*

S. Maria della Pace

▦3 E2. The church, built at the behest of Sixtus IV during a period of political and social unrest, has its origins in a miraculous event, when an image of the Madonna (kept in an earlier church and now on the high altar) was struck by a stone and issued forth blood. The pope proclaimed it the Madonna della Pace (Madonna of Peace) and ordered a church built as an offering for peace in Italy. It was completed in 1656 by Pietro da Cortona, who designed a convex facade preceded by a semicircular portico, and it is one of the most typical and harmonious examples of the Roman Baroque. The interior contains the Chigi Chapel, with four figures of sibyls painted by Raphael, who was clearly influenced by Michelangelo's Sistine Chapel sibyls. Baldassare Peruzzi frescoed the Ponzetti Chapel, and the choir and high altar are by Carlo Maderno. The adjacent cloister, Donato Bramante's first work in Rome (1500–1504), is noteworthy for the harmony of its proportions and the compact

⑥

⑦

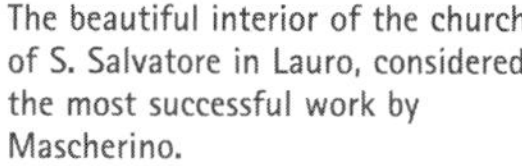
The beautiful interior of the church of S. Salvatore in Lauro, considered the most successful work by Mascherino.

structure of its space. It is close in spirit to the classical models that are its principal sources of inspiration, and like S. Pietro in Montorio (the "Tempietto"), it seems solemn and monumental, despite its modest size. ✉ *Via della Pace 5.*

S. Nicolò in Agone
(Nicola dei Lorenesi)

▦3 E3. This is the national church of the Lorrainers, who, breaking away from S. Luigi dei Francesi, obtained the church of S. Caterina in 1622. They rebuilt that church (1636) and changed its name to S. Nicolò di Mira (3rd century), after the figure who, in addition to being the patron saint of Lorraine, is also the protector of marriages. Roman couples often pray at this church on the eve of their nuptials. ✉ *Via S. Maria dell'Anima.*

S. Pantaleo

▦3 F3. A small church dating from the Middle Ages, S. Pantaleo acquired a certain importance when Paul V granted it to St. Joseph Calasanctius (1557–1648). This Spanish priest and theologian was transferred to Rome, where he found many homeless and derelict children, who had been in many cases orphaned by epidemics. He founded the first free public school in Europe (located in S. Dorotea, in Trastevere) and the congregation of the Scolopi, or Piarists, whose schools are to this day attended by thousands of children throughout the world.
Construction of the present church began in 1681 and was completed with a simple Neoclassical facade by Giuseppe Valadier (1806); St. Joseph Calasanctius's remains are beneath the ornate high altar. The church's namesake is Pantaleon, a 4th-century martyr who was a physician of exceptional talent. He is the patron saint of doctors, midwives, and wet nurses. ✉ *Piazza S. Pantaleo.*

S. Salvatore in Lauro ⑥

▦3 E2. The name "in Lauro" may refer to bay trees that were planted along the Tiber embankment at the time the church was built. The original building, known as far back as the 12th century, was destroyed by fire in 1591 and rebuilt according to the plan of Ottaviano Mascherino; the Neoclassical facade was added in 1857. At one time entrusted to the Celestines, in 1669 the church passed into the hands of the Confraternity of the Piceni, who dedicated it to the Madonna of Loreto. The luminous interior, inspired by Palladian models, has a Latin cross plan with 34 grand travertine columns along the walls. The church contains a *Nativity* by Pietro da Cortona. The monastery complex adjacent to the church includes an elegant Renaissance cloister, and the refectory has a large painting by Cecchino Salviati depicting *The Wedding at Cana* (1550). ✉ *Piazza S. Salvatore in Lauro 15.*

Via dei Banchi Nuovi

▦3 E1–E2. This was once part of the ancient Papal Way, the itinerary newly crowned popes followed from the Vatican to the Lateran residence. The street was opened by Sixtus IV and got its name from the 16th-century "new" bank of Agostino Chigi, the wealthy owner of the Farnesina Villa (a counterpoint to the offices of the 15th-century banking offices, know as the *banchi vecchi,* or old banks). As soon as the street was opened, it became a desirable address for members of the curia, which explains the homogenous character of the residential buildings.

Via dei Banchi Vecchi ⑦

▦3 F1. Along with Via del Pellegrino, Campo de' Fiori, and Via dei Giubbonari, this was part of the ancient Via Peregrinorum and takes its name from the numerous bankers' offices once located here. The street is lined by various notable Renaissance structures. At number 123 is the 16th-century **Palazzo degli Accetti,** with a rusticated ground floor and a top floor with a loggia; at number 22 the so-called **Palazzo dei Pupazzi** (Palace of the Dolls, 1538–1540), built by the Milanese jeweler Giovan Pietro Crivelli, has refined stucco cupids and female nudes, explaining the building's unusual name. The **Palazzo Sforza Cesarini,** built in 1458–1462 by Cardinal Rodrigo Borgia (later Pope Alexander VI), overlooked this street before the construction of the 19th-century facade on the Corso Vittorio Emanuele (number 282). It housed the papal chancellery until that office was transferred to the Palazzo Riario; in 1536 the building passed into the hands of the Roman branch of the Sforza family from Milan. During the Middle Ages the church of **S. Lucia del Gonfalone,** at 12 Via dei Banchi Vecchi, was the national church of the Bohemians, who had their ancient hospice nearby. It took on great importance after the

installation in the late 15th century of the Archconfraternity of the Gonfalone. Founded by St. Bonaventure in the 13th century, this group worked zealously to aid hospitals and pilgrims. Made up of members of the aristocracy and the highest social classes, it wielded considerable economic and political power. The nearby oratory (☞ *74*) also belonged to the confraternity.

Via dei Coronari ⑨

▦3 E2. The *coronari,* sellers of rosaries (*corone*), were once quite numerous along this street, which for centuries was thronged with pilgrims. After the opening of the Corso Vittorio Emanuele, it lost much of its traditional character. The street bears vestiges of the Roman Via Recta, which was reorganized by Sixtus IV as part of his extensive building program. It preserves its Renaissance and Baroque appearance almost intact, despite the deteriorated state of many of the buildings. The **Palazzo Lancellotti,** from the late 16th century, has a lovely main entrance with columns and a balcony designed by Domenichino. The sides of the facade have two stucco shrines, one with an image of Christ the Redeemer surrounded by a sunburst and supported by an angel and cherubs' heads, the other with an image of the Madonna. At the corner of the Vicolo Domizio is a famous **Immagine di Ponte,** a shrine by Antonio Giamberti da Sangallo the Younger (1523–1527) with a *Coronation of the Virgin* by Perine del Vaga, in great disrepair. It is the oldest of the once numerous sacred shrines that ornament the streets of Rome. The number, variety, and decorative wealth of

A shrine in Via dei Coronari; the street once housed shops where rosaries were sold, resulting in the name.

the shrines impressed travelers throughout the ages. For the most part dedicated to the cult of the Virgin, they also influenced local custom. They were outfitted with oil lamps that lit the streets at night, and people made a habit of placing small altars nearby, decorated with flower and candles, a practice that led to popular open-air celebrations and novenas, often with musical accompaniment.

Via del Banco di S. Spirito

▦3 E1. This street takes its name from the **Palazzo del Banco di S. Spirito** (number 31), designed in 1521–1524 by Antonio Giamberti da Sangallo the Younger. It served as both an elegant backdrop for those coming from Castel S. Angelo and a dividing point between the Via dei Banchi Vecchi and the Via dei Banchi Nuovi. The building housed the mint until 1541 and, after 1666, the Banco di S. Spirito, founded by Paul V in 1605 to support the numerous welfare, religious, and social activities of the hospital of the same name. The slightly concave facade has a triumphal arch on a rusticated base, with windows on the sides and, on the pediment, Baroque statues of *Charity* and *Thrift.* The church of **Ss. Celso e Giuliano** (entrance at 12 Vicolo del Curato), which dates from the 5th century but was rebuilt in the 18th century, contains a beautiful altar by Pompeo Girolamo Batoni (*Christ in Glory,* 1738). The **Palazzo Gaddi** (1430), at number 42, has a harmonious courtyard embellished with niches with statues and a stucco decorative scheme.

Via del Governo Vecchio ⑧

▦3 E2–F2. The street gets its name from the presence, at number 39, of the **Palazzo del Governo Vecchio,** which has an elegant marble entrance with diamond point rustication. It was built by Cardinal Stefano Nardini (1473–1477), governor of Rome, and it was initially called Via del Governo. When government offices were moved to Palazzo Madama, the street acquired its current name. Like the Via dei Banchi Nuovi, it was part of the medieval Papal Way between St. Peter's and the Lateran; today it is known for its antiques shops. Both noble and simple buildings, most of which date from the 16th or 17th century, flank the street. Some of the facades preserve traces of frescoes and stucco decorations. The street also houses the church of **S. Tommaso in Parione** (entrance at 33 Via Parione), built in 1582 and known to Romans as the site of St. Philip Neri's ordination.

4
Regola

Lively Campo de' Fiori is the site of a daily food market; by evening it is a popular gathering place for the young people of Rome. In times past it was the designated site for capital executions.

Bordered for a long stretch by the Tiber, from the Mazzini Bridge to the Lungotevere Cenci, this district takes its name from deposits of river sand, or arenula *(corrupted to* reula, *then* regola*). Like Ponte and Parione, it experienced considerable urban development and building between the 16th and 17th centuries, when new streets were opened, piazzas designed, and luxurious palaces erected, such as those for the Farnese and Spada families. But traces of the medieval fabric remain, linked to the path of the Papal Way and the pilgrims' route, such as S. Paolo's picturesque complex of 13th-century houses, near S. Paolo alla Regola.*

Campo de' Fiori ①

▦5 A4. Until the 15th century this area was covered with flower-filled fields, most likely the origin of the name. In addition to being the site of a market (still held daily), many inns and bookstores, and residences of famous courtesans, it was also a place for public executions. In 1600, Giordano Bruno was accused of heresy by the Inquisition and burned at the stake; he was later honored with a statue, which, in its severe expression, recalls the sternness of his denunciations against corruption and vice. The installation of the monument in 1889, nearly three centuries after Bruno's death, provoked violent polemics between Republicans and partisans of the pope.

Oratorio del Gonfalone

▦3 F1. The powerful Confraternity of S. Lucia del Gonfalone, which also held the nearby church of S. Lucia (☞ 73), established the oratory (1544–1547). All institutions of this type had both a public church and a private oratory set aside for prayer, worship, and meetings. The building has a modest facade and a sumptuous interior, embellished with a painting cycle (1572–1575) depicting *Scenes from the Passion of Christ,* one of the most interesting examples of Roman Mannerism. The room is surrounded by choir stalls and has a wooden ceiling. ✉ *Vicolo della Scimmia 1/B.*

Ospizio dei Cento Preti
(Hospice of the Hundred Priests)

▦5 B4. After the construction of the Tiber embankment, very little remained of this structure, which was built by Domenico Fontana in 1587 for Sixtus V. It was erected to accommodate an ambitious welfare project, which placed all the city's beggars in a single institution. The hospice was dedicated to St. Francis of Assisi and was administered by a congregation of 100 priests. At the beginning of the 18th century, Clement XI decided to transfer the facility to the apostolic hospice of S. Michele, after which this structure housed an institution for girls and an ecclesiastic hospital. ✉ *Via dei Pettinari.*

Palazzo Cenci Bolognetti
(Piazza delle Cinque Scole)

▦5 B5. The mound on which the palazzo of the famous Roman Cenci family rises probably rests atop the ruins of the Statilio Tauro Amphitheater, the first one in Rome built of brick (29 BC). The palazzo is made up of various elements, unified in the 16th century by flat stucco rustication. Across from the palazzo is the aristocratic chapel of **S. Tommaso ai Cenci,** known as far back as the 12th century but rebuilt during the second half of the 16th century and chosen by Francesco Cenci as the family's burial site. Francesco and his family were protagonists in the darkest event of the time: Having molested his daughter, Beatrice, Francesco was killed by her, with the help of her brother and lover. The following year (1599) the murderers were publicly beheaded in Piazza di Ponte. ✉ *Piazza delle Cinque Scole 23.*

Palazzo Farnese ②

▦5 A4–B4. In 1514, Cardinal Alessandro Farnese began work on his new palazzo. After he became Pope Paul III, his plans for the building became much more solemn and grand and involved Antonio Giamberti da Sangallo the Younger (principal and side facades), Michelangelo (the impressive cornice and much of the courtyard), and Giacomo della Porta (the rear facade and large loggia facing the Via Giulia). The result is perhaps the most beautiful palazzo in Rome, characterized by the perfect equilibrium of its majestic mass. An array of artists contributed to the drawing rooms' magnificent decoration, which includes the barrel vault of the gallery, frescoed by Annibale and Agostino Carracci (1597–1600) with *The Triumph of Love over the Universe,* which advances beyond Renaissance equilibrium and initiates the spatial illusionism of

2

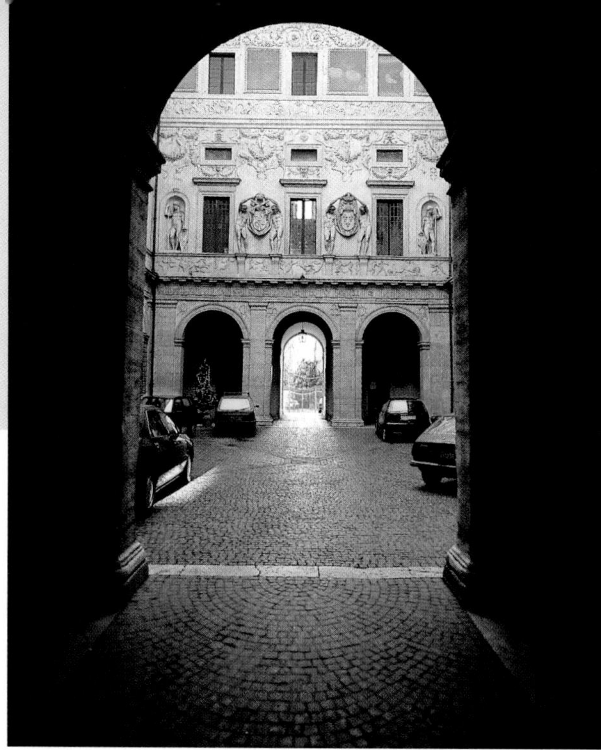

③ The courtyard of Palazzo Spada, a 16th-century building ennobled by Borromini's ingenious work is the site of the State Council, as well as the Galleria Spada, an important collection of Baroque paintings.

Baroque art. Today the building houses the French Embassy and the French School, a prestigious institute of historical and archeaological studies. In the past the piazza hosted numerous spectacles: a weekly horse market; bullfights; and a festival celebrating the presentation by the king of Naples to the pope of the *chinea*, a white mule, symbol of vassalage. During the 19th century it was also a gathering place for people from the countryside and a place for hiring laborers. At number 96 Piazza Farnese is the church of **S. Brigida,** erected by Boniface IX on the site of a house where the mystic Swedish saint had stayed; it was rebuilt in the 18th century. Until the Protestant reformation it was the location of a Swedish hospice. ✉*Piazza Farnese 67.*

Palazzo del Monte di Pietà

▦5 B5. Monte di Pietà was established in 1539 by a friar, Giovanni Mattei de Calvi, as a public lending institution to combat the usury practiced by Jewish lenders of the time. Working-class borrowers secured loans at extremely modest rates of interest against personal possessions left as collateral. Patrons repossessed their property upon repayment of the loan. Private citizens or confraternities often cancelled debts as an act of charity. The Palazzo del Monte di Pietà thus carried out a function of primary importance during times of economic crisis and in the absence of sufficient welfare institutions. The 16th-century palazzo, acquired by the Monte and later expanded, has an extremely simple facade that is embellished only by a shrine depicting Christ in the tomb and four coats of arms. ✉*Piazza del Monte di Pietà.*

Palazzo Spada ③

▦5 B4. This is one of the most refined and celebrated Roman residences, because of both its elaborate stucco decorative scheme on the facade and courtyard (by Giulio Mazzoni, 1556–1560), and the extraordinary contribution of Francesco Borromini. Built for Cardinal Girolamo Capodiferro in the mid-16th century, it was later acquired and renovated by the Spada family. The courtyard contains the gallery designed by Borromini in 1653, an exceptional example of perspectival illusionism. Although it is only 30 feet long, it simulates a length four times greater, and the statue that stands at the back, which appears very tall, is in reality quite small. The **Galleria Spada,** created in the 17th century by Cardinal Bernardino Spada (1594–1661), is a rare intact example of small patrician gallery. The room, which has its original furnishings, frescoes, and brick floors, contains predominantly Italian and Flemish paintings from the 17th century. ✉*Piazza Capo di Ferro 13,* ☎*06/686–1158.*

Ponte Sisto ④

▦5 B4–C4. In the wake of the collapse of Ponte S. Angelo during the Jubilee of 1450, when it was crowded with pilgrims, Sixtus IV decided to restore an ancient bridge to the Janiculum in time for the 1475 Jubilee. The bridge was built during Roman times and probably collapsed during the flood of 589. This project was one of the cornerstones of the urban renewal program of Sixtus IV and his successor, Julius II. Until the late 19th century the bridge was the only one in the city remaining from the time of the Roman Empire. The structure, which links Trastevere to the Regola and Parione districts, incorporates part of the ancient bridge and is made up of four arcades and a large circle for runoff in the central pier, which for centuries was used as a water gauge.

S. Biagio della Pagnotta

▦3 F1. The church was erected in the 12th century, rebuilt in the 18th century, and restored during the following century. The name is derived from the custom of distributing a roll that has been blessed to the faithful on St. Blaise's feast day, February 3. The church is in the care of Armenian Catholic priests. ✉*Via Giulia 64.*

S. Caterina da Siena

▦5 A4. Erected between 1766 and 1776 by the Sienese Archconfraternity, this church is located on the site of a 16th-century oratory. The entire block was set aside for the welfare and hospitality of Sienese citizens. Two orders of columns modeled on Borrominian motifs decorate the building's concave facade. ✉*Via Giulia.*

S. Eligio degli Orefici ⑤

▦5 A3. St. Eligius (588–600), a talented goldsmith and counselor to the French kings, was bishop of Noyon and devoted himself to

④

spreading the faith among the people of Flanders. As patron saint of goldsmiths and blacksmiths, his veneration quickly spread from France and Flanders throughout the west (there is a second Roman church dedicated to him: S. Eligio dei Ferrari, near Piazza Bocca della Verità). The design of this church (1509–1575) is attributed to Raphael; the facade was completed in the 17th century. The interior, on a Greek cross plan, is somber and harmonious, punctuated by gray pilaster strips against a white backdrop, and clearly reveals Bramante's influence. The noteworthy hemispherical dome probably was designed by Baldassarre Peruzzi. ✉ *Via S. Eligio 8/A.*

S. Girolamo della Carità

▦5 A4. The building (1654–1660) is closely linked to the memory of St. Philip Neri, who lived in the adjacent monastery and established his institutions here. To the left of the high alter is a chapel designed by Filippo Juvarra (1705) and dedicated to the saint. Inside the church are a refined marble decorative scheme, an intricate coffered ceiling, and an unusual chapel by Borromini that was commissioned by the Spada family in 1660. It is a shallow space, separated from the nave not by the usual balustrade, but by a pair of angels that support a faux drapery of jasper (one of the wings revolves on a hinge, allowing access to the chapel). The small alcove feels like a domestic space, with two chests topped with statues of the reclining figures of Spada family members, flowered tapestries, family portraits, and images of saints. Marble inlays on the walls mimic damask, and the floor is designed with a floral motif that alludes symbolically to the inexorible passage of time. ✉ *Via Monserrato 62/A.*

S. Maria in Monserrato

▦5 A4. The church was begun in 1518, following the design of Antonio Giamberti da Sangallo the Younger, for the Confraternity of S. Maria di Monserrato (Montserrat is a famous sanctuary near Barcelona), which was established by Alexander VI in 1495. It was the national church, first for the people of Aragon and Catalonia, then for all Spaniards, replacing the church of S. Giacomo (now Our Lady of the Sacred Heart). Many of the church's most beautiful works come from S. Giacomo, including the statue of *St. Jerome* by Jacopo Sansovino, funerary monuments, and the marble flooring. The building also contains Annibale Carracci's *St. Diego di Alcantara* and the funerary monuments of two popes, Callistus II and Alexander VI, both Spaniards, transferred here from the Vatican grottoes. Above the 18th-century entrance is a group of the *Madonna and Child Sawing the Rock,* which refers to the serrated shape of the mountain on which the Catalonian sanctuary is located. ✉ *Via Monserrato at Via di Montoro.*

S. Maria dell'Orazione e Morte

▦5 B4. The strange name—St. Mary of the Oration and Death—has its origins in the charitable activity of the Company of Good Death, established in 1535 to gather unburied corpses. This group built a church in 1576, and rebuilt between 1733 and 1737 according to a design by Ferdinando Fuga. The elaborately decorated interior has an elliptical plan surmounted by a high dome. Two winged skulls over the central doorway allude to the builders' profession, and beneath the church is a subterranean cemetery in which approximately 8,000 bodies were buried over the course of three centuries (from 1552 to 1896). ✉ *Via Giulia at Via del Mascherone.*

⑤

S. Maria del Pianto

▦5 B5. The church was established in 1616 to house an image of the Madonna from the nearby Portico di Ottavia that was said to have cried following a deadly brawl on the site. The fresco is located on the high altar. The building was designed along a Greek cross plan, with large pilasters and a dome on pendentives decorated in stuccowork; its facade has remained unfinished. During the Counter-Reformation the church hosted a popular catechism competition among boys from various parishes, which concluded with the proclamation of an "emperor of Christian doctrine." The victor was carried in triumph before the pope, from whom he could request a favor. ✉ *Via S. Maria dei Calderari 29.*

S. Maria della Quercia ⑥

▦5 B4. The church has the same name as the important Renaissance sanctuary located near Viterbo. Dating from the early 16th century, the building was erected for the populous colony of Viterbo natives in the district; the project had the backing of Julius II, whose heraldic symbol was the oak tree or *quercia.* The building's appearance is the result of a 1727 reconstruction that introduced a Greek cross plan surmounted by a hemispherical dome and a convex facade crowned by a high attic. ✉ *Piazza della Quercia 27.*

S. Paolo alla Regola

▦5 B5. This church was built in the late 17th century on the site of a house where, according to tradition, St. Paul had lived. The street of the same name bears traces of an important medieval street called Strada della Regola (from

6

7

the name of the district), which, prior to modern demolitions, preserved much of the original residential fabric. Still standing are some 13th-century buildings (in great disrepair), known as the **Case di S. Paolo,** with porticos, loggias, and towers. A short distance away is the church of **S. Maria in Monticelli** (at number 28 of the street of that name), perhaps named for the ruins that lie below. An extremely ancient structure, it was restored by Paschal II (1101) and again transformed during the 18th and 19th centuries. The interior has a fragment of mosaic in the apse, with the head of Christ the Redeemer (12th century) and a 14th-century crucifix. ✉ *Via S. Paolo alla Regola 6.*

S. Salvatore in Onda

▦**5 B4.** The name of this church, which refers to the flooding of the Tiber, is mentioned as far back as the 12th century, but numerous later restorations have completely altered its original appearance. Attached is a monastery that has housed the Hermits of St. Paul, the Augustinians, and the Conventual Friars. During the early 19th century, the church was the base for the pastoral activity of St. Vincent Pallotti, who Romans consider the second Philip Neri because of his tireless works of charity and welfare, particularly with prisoners, the sick, and the young. In 1835 he founded a society for Catholic missionary work, the members of which were called Pallottines. Initially the order was made up of only 12 priests, but later the order expanded to include laypersons and spread worldwide. Pius XI called the saint a precursor of Catholic Action, the lay apostolic movement. The present-day church is within the Pallottine motherhouse. ✉ *Via dei Pettinari 51.*

S. Spirito dei Napoletani

▦**5 A3.** Founded in 1619 by the Confraternity of Neapolitans, this church was rebuilt between 1701 and 1709 by Carlo Fontana. The two-story facade with a sculpted entry and rose windows was reconstructed in 1853. Inside the building is a painting by Luca Giordano (1705): *The Martyrdom of St. Gennaro,* patron saint of Naples. In 1630, the adjacent hospice became the site of the Collegio Ghislieri, founded by Roman physician Giuseppe Ghislieri for the instruction of the poor, and, like the many other city institutions, made possible through private philanthropy. ✉ *Via Giulia 34.*

S. Tommaso di Canterbury

▦**5 A4.** This church is located in a renovated (1864) earlier church, SS. Trinità degli Scozzesi, an 8th-century edifice that itself was rebuilt in 1575 to repair damage inflicted during the sack of Rome. The building is contained within the Collegio Inglese, founded by Gregory XIII in 1579 to strengthen unstable ties between the Catholic Church and England. This initiative, like the creation of the Greek and German colleges, was part of the ecumenical approach that guided the policies of this pope, who wanted cosmopolitan Rome to be a tangible symbol of the opening of the Catholic Church to the world. But Gregory's projects failed, and many of the priests who were educated in the college were killed in England during 17th- and 18th-century persecutions. ✉ *Via Monserrato 45.*

Ss. Giovanni Evangelista e Petronio dei Bolognesi

▦**5 B4.** In 1575 the Bolognese community in Rome acquired the complex of S. Giovanni Calibita on the Tiber Island. With the support of Pope Gregory XIII, who was from Bologna, they abandoned the first church and established a new church on this site (1582), dedicated to St. John and to St. Petronius, the patron saint of their own city. The Bolognese community was quite large, particularly during the 16th and 17th centuries, and ties between Rome and Bologna were very close. Many Bolognese artists contributed to the city of the popes, including Guido Reni, Domenichino, the Carracci, and the sculptor Alessandro Algardi, who is buried in this church. ✉ *Via del Mascherone.*

SS. Trinità dei Pellegrini

▦**5 B4.** In 1548, St. Philip Neri founded a community of priests to tend the growing crowds of pilgrims, particularly during Holy Years, and the sick. This group took the name of the Archconfraternity of Pilgrims and Convalescents. It was one of the most significant manifestations of the desire for strong religious renewal in Rome during the second half of the 16th century. The group's activities had incredible results, and during the 1575 Jubilee alone, approximately 170,000 pilgrims were offered assistance and hospitality, with additional help from numerous laypersons. Paul IV gave this church to the confraternity in 1558; it was rebuilt in between 1603 and 1616, and the facade was completed in 1723. The high altar has a *SS. Trinità* by Guido Reni. ✉ *Via dei Pettinari 36/A.*

Via dei Giubbonari

▦**5 B5.** The numerous clothing shops that line this street follow a

An evocative section of the Via Giulia ⑦, the 16th-century street laid out for Pope Julius II by Donato Bramante.

The final section of the Via dei Pettinari ⑧ and, at the end, the Ponte Sisto, built in 1473.

secular tradition that is perpetuated in its name (*giubbonari* are jacket-makers). It has always been a thriving area, thanks in part to the fact that the street was part of the Via dei Pellegrini. Midway the street opens into the Largo dei Librari with the little church of **S. Barbara dei Librari,** founded in the 11th century on the ruins of the Theater of Pompey and under the aegis of the Università dei Librari, a corporation of printers, bookbinders, and scribes that rebuilt the church in 1680.

Via Giulia ⑦

▦5 A3–B4. Continuing the urban renewal projects of his uncle Sixtus IV, Julius II decided to replace the narrow, winding medieval streets that led to the Vatican with broad, rectilinear stretches that were more elegant and also more easily traveled by pilgrims. The pope commissioned Bramante (1508) to design two parallel streets on the opposite banks of the Tiber, the Via della Lungara and the Via Giulia, which were linked by the Ponte Sisto and by another bridge, never built, opposite the Hospital of S. Spirito. According to Julius II's plans for the street that bears his name, the principal public buildings of the papal state were to face each other, but this never came to fruition. Despite the demolitions of the modern era, the Via Giulia has preserved a certain stylistic homogeneity and is now one of the most harmonious streets in Rome and one of the most popular, thanks to its galleries and antiques shops. Many notable palazzi line the street, such as the **Palazzo Falconieri** (number 1), designed by Borromini, with large Baroque sculptures at the sides of the facade and a magnificent loggia facing the Tiber. The memorable **Palazzo Sacchetti** (number 62) was erected in 1552 and has a reception hall decorated with scenes from the life of David by Cecchino Salviati (1554) and a gallery with Pietro da Cortona's *Holy Family* and *Adam and Eve.* Near the **Carceri Nuove** (number 52), the prisons built by Innocent X (1655), are part of what was meant to be the grand **Palazzo dei Tribunali,** planned by Julius II and designed by Bramante, but never completed. Vestiges of the rusticated foundation, with projecting benches that have long been known as the Via Giulia sofas, remain.

Via di Monserrato

▦5 A3–A4. The street assumed this name immediately after the construction of the church of S. Maria di Monserrato, which in its turn was named after a famous Catalan sanctuary. In earlier times the street contained the houses and prisons of the powerful Savelli family and was know as the Via di Corte Savella. It is distinguished by elegant buildings and churches, including the **Casa di Pietro Paolo della Zecca** (Paul II's superintendent of coinage), which dates from the late 15th century and has traces of frescoes on its facade. The 16th-century **Palazzo Incoronati de Planca** (number 152) has the Planca family coat of arms over the entrance. The two facades of the **Palazzo Ricci** are covered with frescoes (from ca. 1525), representative of a fashion that was popular during the Renaissance, but which has very few surviving examples in Rome.

Via del Pellegrino

▦5 A4. The name refers to the ancient Via Peregrinorum, which took pilgrims from the Tiber Island area and the market of S. Angelo in Pescheria toward Ponte S. Angelo. Alexander VI expanded the street in 1497, following an urban reorganization plan begun by Nicholas V and Sixtus IV. Near the **Arco di S. Margherita** is one of the most original and decorative shrines in the city. It depicts a *Madonna and Child* against an architectural background; the image is surmounted by a sunburst "glory" interwoven with a crown supported by putti; the figure of St. Philip Neri appears below. The sculpture also depicts in stucco the so-called procession "machines" that were widely used during the 17th and 18th centuries. These wooden, cardboard, or plaster structures reproduced altars, temples, or statuary compositions of sacred subjects, and they were transported through the streets of the city during the religious processions of the Baroque era, along with hundreds of crucifixes, candlesticks, and banners painted with religious scenes.

Via dei Pettinari ⑧

▦5 B4. Sixtus IV renovated this street at the time of the rebuilding of the Ponte Sisto to link Trastevere to the commercial zones of the Ponte, Parione, and Regola districts. Like many others the area—such as Via dei Cappellari (hat-makers), Via dei Giubbonari (jacket-makers), Via dei Chiavari (key-makers), Via dei Baullari (chest-makers), Via dei Chiodaroli nail-makers), Via dei Falegnami (carpenters), Via dei Funari (rope-makers) , and so forth—this street's name refers to one of the commercial activities that was carried out here (in this case the making and selling of combs).

5

S. Eustachio, Pigna, and S. Angelo

During the Roman period this area had many significant public buildings and sites, including the Pantheon, the Theater of Marcellus, and the sacred zone of Largo Argentina. Many other sites were destroyed or incorporated into later buildings. Throughout the Middle Ages the quarter remained inhabited, preserving much of the ancient road network. Beginning in the 13th century it experienced new vitality as the center of various artisan and commercial activities. Traces of that era are still present in place names, in the winding lanes, and in some buildings that escaped Renaissance and Baroque expansion. This is particularly evident in the district of S. Angelo, where, in 1555, the Jewish Ghetto was established. When the popes returned from Avignon, the three districts, like others contained within this bend of the Tiber, received crowds of pilgrims making their way toward the Ponte S. Angelo. Many palaces and churches (some of the city's most famous) testify to the monumental urban development that took place between the 15th and 18th centuries. The continuity of the area's urban fabric was damaged by interventions carried out between the 19th and 20th centuries, including the opening of the Corso Vittorio Emanuele and the Corso Rinascimento and the expansion of the Palazzo Madama.

① 

② 

Velázquez's portrait of Innocent X hangs in the Galleria Doria Pamphilij, established by that same pontiff.

Chiesa del Gesù ①

⊞5 A6. The original appearance of the church, which was built for the Jesuits between 1568 and 1584, was quite different. The designs of Giacomo da Barozzi (know as Vignola) and Giacomo della Porta were completely in keeping with the principles of sobriety and austerity expressed by the Council of Trent and were also in accordance with the evangelical poverty preached by St. Ignatius of Loyola, founder of the order. The magnificent Baroque decoration dates from the second half of the 17th century, when the order decided that the church should offer a more explicit demonstration of the triumphs of the Catholic Church and the Jesuit order, then at the height of its power. Giovanni Battista Gaulli, called Baciccia, frescoed the vault of the nave with *The Triumph of the Name of Jesus,* one of the most majestic and original attempts at dominion over infinite space, typical of Baroque art. The altar of St. Ignatius (who is buried here) is the largest and most ornate in Rome; conceived by Andrea Pozzo, it was created by more than 100 artists and craftsmen and is made up of a profusion of white and colored marble, gilded bronze, silver, lapis lazuli, and semiprecious stones. Opposite is the altar of St. Francis Xavier, a Jesuit missionary who performed significant work in India and Japan. Designed by Pietro da Cortona, it contains a reliquary with the saint's arm. ⊠*Piazza del Gesù.*

Collegio Romano

⊞3 F4–F5. The austere edifice was built in 1582 to house the oldest and most prestigious Jesuit scholastic institution, which the order's founder, St. Ignatius of Loyola, called the "universal seminary." Internationally famous instructors teach here, and during its history important cultural institutions have been located on the premises, including the Astronomical Observatory, the Museo Kircheriano, the Spezieria, and an extensive library. After 1870 the first state high school (Ennio Quirino Visconti) of the new Italian capital was established here. In 1930 the Jesuit university moved to the Palazzo della Pontificia Università Gregoriana, in Piazza della Pilotta. ⊠*Piazza del Collegio Romano.*

Galleria Doria Pamphilj ②

⊞3 F5. The Palazzo Doria Pamphilj, one of the grandest in Rome, is one of the few that is still inhabited by the family from which it takes its name. It houses an extraordinary art gallery, established by Innocent X in 1651, that displays works from the 16th and 17th centuries and two splendid portraits of Innocent by Diego Velázquez (1650) and Gian Lorenzo Bernini. When Camillo, the pope's nephew, married Olimpia Aldobrandini, the original collection was enriched with important works by Raphael, Titian, Beccafumi, and Parmigianino, as well as outstanding paintings from the Ferrara school. Camillo patronized the most famous artists of his time (Bernini, Borromini, Algardi, Pietro da Cortona, and Caravaggio) and acquired numerous paintings by Bolognese artists and landscapes by Claude Lorrain. The union with the Doria family (1760) brought to the gallery masterpieces by Sebastiano del Piombo and Bronzino, as well as some tapestries. The magnificent drawing room of the private apartment is also open to visitors. On the

③

facade along the Via del Plebiscito is a magnificent 18th-century shrine that contains a group of angels and cherubs above a dense sunburst shape and supporting an oval frame with an image of the Madonna. ✉*Piazza del Collegio Romano 2,* ☏*06/679–7323.*

Ghetto ③

⊞5 C6. The Jewish community in Rome, originally established in Trastevere, began to move into the S. Angelo district, near the Tiber Island, during the 13th century. A papal bull by Paul IV in 1555 established the Ghetto, imitating the one created in Venice shortly before. The area was surrounded by walls and became the obligatory and exclusive place of residence for the Roman Jews, who lived here in overcrowded and demeaning conditions. In 1848 the walls were taken down, and beginning in 1888 the Ghetto was demolished and replaced with four blocks completely disconnected from the surrounding urban fabric. The **Synagogue** (1899–1904), which replaced an earlier edifice destroyed by fire in 1903, stands out amid the city's architecture, with its pavilion-roof dome on a square drum and its Assyrian-Babylonian decorative motifs that recall the original land of the Jewish people. The facade on the Via del Tempio has Jewish symbols (a seven-arm candelabrum, the tablets of the Ten Commandments, a star of David, a palm branch). The building houses the **Museo d'Arte Ebraica,** which contains archaeological remains, sacred objects, vestments, liturgical furnishings, manuscripts, and documents. ✉*Synagogue and Museum: Lungotevere dei Cenci,* ☏*06/684–0061.*

Palazzo Madama

⊞3 E3–F3. Built in 1503 as the Roman residence of the Medici family, the palazzo takes its name from "Madama" Margaret of Austria, widow of Alessandro de' Medici, who had lived here. The building changed hands many times and experienced many architectural transformations over the centuries. In 1871 it became the seat of the Italian Senate. ✉*Piazza Madama.*

Palazzi dei Mattei

⊞5 B6. In the 15th century the large block defined by Via Caetani, Via Paganica, Via delle Botteghe Oscure, and Via dei Funari was occupied by the Mattei family. The family gradually built a series of palaces that bore the names of the estates of the various family branches. The oldest is the **Palazzo di Giacomo Mattei** (17–19 Piazza Mattei), erected in the mid-15th century and expanded in the 16th century. The **Palazzo Mattei Paganica,** at 4 Piazza dell'Enciclopedia Italiana, was begun in 1541 and houses the National Encyclopedia Institute. Beneath the building are the remains of the Theater of Balbo (13 BC). Behind these ruins was a large portico, the vestiges of which housed, in medieval times, various commercial and manufacturing activities, giving the street the name *botteghe oscure,* or "dark shops." The impressive **Palazzo Mattei di Giove** (31 Via dei Funari), designed by Carlo Maderno (1598–1618), has a courtyard richly decorated with ancient sculptures and stuccowork. The building houses various cultural institutions. On the facade is a simple shrine with an image of the Virgin enclosed in an oval frame decorated with stars and stuccowork flowers. ✉*Piazza Mattei.*

Palazzo di Venezia

⊞6 A1. This building is the first important expression in Rome of the Renaissance canons for civil architecture theorized by Leon Battista Alberti. It was constructed in 1455 for the Venetian cardinal Pietro Barbo, who later became Paul II. It was designed as a block on a rectangular plan, with corner towers and a central courtyard with portico and loggia. The basilica of S. Marco became the Palatine Chapel, and the piazza, which was designed to complement the palace and as the monumental end for the road, became the famous end

④ Piazza Mattei: the Fontana delle Tartarughe, a masterpiece by Giacomo della Porta (1581–1584), was embellished in 1658, perhaps by Bernini.

The dome of the Pantheon ⑤ (AD 118–AD 125), a majestic realization of imperial architecture, summarizes Romans' knowledge of building; it was used as a model by Brunelleschi for the Duomo in Florence.

point for the Corsa dei Bàrberi, a riderless horse race held at Carnival. The designer of the complex still has not been identified, but Alberti's influence is clear, both in the overall design, in the vault of the entrance hall off the piazza, and in the extremely beautiful courtyard. The name is derived from the fact that the building was given to the Venetian Republic in 1564 to house its embassy. Today it contains the **Museo di Palazzo di Venezia,** which includes paintings from the 13th to the 18th centuries, sculptures in marble and wood, bronzes, porcelain, glasswork, ivories, and tapestries. ✉ *Via del Plebiscito 118,* ☎ *06/699–94319.*

Pantheon ⑤

▦3 F4. This is the best preserved monument from ancient Rome, thanks to its transformation into a church (S. Maria ad Martyres) in 609. It is said that the day the building was consecrated, 28 wagons of martyrs' bones were transported here, taken from various city cemeteries. This event is the origin of All Saints' Day (November 1), instituted by Gregory IV in the 9th century. The ancient temple was built by the emperor Hadrian (AD 118–AD 125) on the site of a temple from the Augustan age (AD 27–AD 25) that was dedicated to the worship of all the gods (thus the name). It is a wonderful example of the technical skill of the Roman architects. The dome is the largest ever built in brick (142 feet in diameter; St. Peter's is 139 feet), and because the height of the dome from the floor is equal to the diameter, it defines a spherical space inserted into a cylinder, producing a sensation of perfect and simple harmony. During the Middle Ages the building was used as a fortress; in 1625, Pope Urban VIII gave Gian Lorenzo Bernini the bronze from the portico to make the baldacchino for S. Pietro and cannons for Castel S. Angelo (provoking the famous pasquinade: "What the barbarians didn't do, the Barberini did"). After Raphael was buried here, during the Renaissance, the Pantheon became a burial site for artists, and in 1878 it was chosen as the site for the tombs of the kings of Italy. The **Piazza della Rotonda,** which opens up in front of the Pantheon, is one of the most popular and liveliest in Rome. In addition to the splendid, ancient monument, it is noted for its fountain, designed by Giacomo della Porta. ✉ *Piazza della Rotonda.*

Piazza Mattei ④

▦5 B6. This small piazza is like a jewel box, surrounding one of the most beautiful fountains in Rome, the **Fontana delle Tartarughe,** designed by Giacomo della Porta (1581–1584), with the tortoises added later, perhaps by Gian Lorenzo Bernini. The piazza is flanked by the **Palazzo Costaguti** (number 10), which dates to the mid-16th century. Its rooms, which cannot be visited, are famous for the number and quality of paintings and the richness of the furnishings. Some of the greatest 17th-century artists worked here, including Guercino, Domenichino, and the Zuccari.

Piazza della Pigna

▦3 F4. The name is derived from the large bronze pinecone that adorned one of the many Roman monuments in the area (it is now in the Cortile della Pigna in the Vatican). The small church of **S. Giovanni della Pigna** (51 Vicolo della Minerva) was known in the 10th century and given by Gregory XIII to the Company of Piety Toward Prisoners (1577), which had it rebuilt in 1624. Inside are tombs of two members of the aristocratic Porcari family. In 1453, Stefano Porcari was put to death here by Pope Nicholas V for organizing a plot to install a republican government. The remains of the Porcari houses are incorporated into a 19th-century building at the back of the piazza, on the Via della Pigna.

S. Agostino

▦3 E3. Built in 1420, this is one of the first Renaissance churches in Rome, although it was later expanded and altered. It contains many artworks, and the high altar, designed by Gian Lorenzo Bernini, includes a Byzantine icon of the Virgin, which was brought from Constantinople after the Turkish conquest (1453). Romans venerate Jacopo Sansovino's *Madonna del Parto* (1521), and numerous ex-votos surround the sculpture. The church also has a painting of *The Prophet Isaiah* by Raphael (1512), a sculpture group of *St. Anne and the Madonna with Child* by Andrea Sansovino (1512), and a 15th-century panel depicting *God the Father.* But the church's most famous work is the *Madonna dei Pellegrini* by Caravaggio (1605), which caused an uproar from the start because of the lowly and domestic setting it portrays and the realism of its dirty and tattered pilgrims. To the side of the church is the **Biblioteca Angelica** (8 Piazza S. Agostino), the first public library in Rome, established in 1614 by the Augustinian Angelo Rocca and specializing in ecclesiastical and historical-literary studies. It contains more than 1,000 books, manuscripts, incunabula, and prints, as well as two globes, celestial and terrestrial, from 1599–1603, the only ones of this type in Italy. ✉ *Piazza S. Agostino.*

S. Carlo ai Catinari ⑦

▦5 B5. The name of this church refers to both St. Charles Borromeo and to the bowl-makers who worked in the district. It was

5

⑥

⑦

built for the Barnabites in 1610–1620, in honor of the most important figure of the Catholic Reformation and the inspiration for the political and apostolic action of Pius IV. The architect was Rosato Rosati, and the soaring dome is one of the most beautiful in the city. The church has many paintings inspired by the life and works of the titular saint, including works by Domenichino, Pietro da Cortona, and Guido Reni. ✉ *Piazza Cairoli*

S. Caterina dei Funari

⊞ **5 B6.** The church's name refers to the rope-makers who worked in the ruins of the portico of the Theater of Balbo, vestiges of which were discovered in the area behind the church. An earlier medieval church, given by Paul III to St. Ignatius of Loyola (1537), became the seat of the Confraternity of the Miserable Virgins and was rebuilt in 1564. The beautiful travertine facade has two rows of Corinthian pilasters, festoons, and other relief ornamentation. ✉ *Via dei Funari*

S. Eustachio

⊞ **3 F3.** According to one of the many legends related to his life, Eustace was a valiant general in the troops of the Emperor Trajan (2nd century AD). He converted to Christianity after encountering a stag with a cross on its head during a hunting party. A stag's head with a cross can be seen on the tympanum of the church, which Constantine founded, supposedly on the site of the saint's martyrdom. The church was restored in the 12th century (the bell tower belongs to this phase) and partially rebuilt during the 18th century. The interior has a notable high altar in bronze and polychrome marble by Nicola Salvi (1739), surmounted by a baldacchino by Ferdinando Fuga (1746). ✉ *Via S. Eustachio 19.*

S. Gregorio della Divina Pietà

⊞ **5 C6.** Legend has it that the church stands on the site of the birthplace of St. Gregory the Great (ca. 540–604). The church's current appearance dates from 1729, when Benedict XIII renovated it and gave it to the Congregazione degli Operai della Divina Pietà, which assisted aristocratic families that had fallen upon hard times. A plaque on the facade has a biblical passage in Hebrew and Latin that reproaches the Jews for persevering in their faith. The church stands near one of the entrances to the Ghetto and was used for the compulsory sermons to the Jewish community. ✉ *Piazza Monte Savello 9.*

S. Ivo alla Sapienza ⑥

⊞ **3 F3.** This church is incorporated within the **Palazzo della Sapienza,** which was the site of the University of Rome until 1935 and now houses the State Archives. Urban VIII wanted to transform the ancient university chapel and entrusted the work to Borromini, who best expressed his talent in the church of S. Ivo (1642–1660). As in S. Carlino, the architect adopted a central plan, but one based on a hexagon, unusual in Italian architecture. The same motif is repeated in the light-filled dome and, on the exterior, in the multifoiled drum. Most amazing, however, is the twisting spire surmounted by an aerial structure in iron. The structure must have looked disconcerting and almost scandalous in a the city filled with serene, rotund domes. It is no accident that there is nothing else like it in Rome. With its powerful vertical thrust and the blinding whiteness of the interior, S. Ivo is one of the most accomplished expressions of the period's quest for spiritual renewal. ✉ *Corso Rinascimento 40.*

S. Luigi dei Francesi ⑧

⊞ **3 E3.** In the late 15th century the French colony acquired a small church and made it the center of their public assistance services. They planned a renovation, which was carried out in 1589. All the figures on the facade are French: below, Charlemagne and St. Louis (Louis IX, king of France, who died during the Eighth Crusade in 1270); above, St. Clotilde (5th-century queen of the Franks and patron saint of women) and St. Joan of Valois (daughter of Louis XI, founder of the Order of the Nuns of the Annunziata in 1500). St. Louis is honored in the fresco at the center of the vault (1756). The high altar has an *Annunciation* by Francesco Bassano, and one of the chapels has Domenichino's *Scenes from the Life of St. Caecilia* (1616–1617). The church's principal attraction is the chapel painted by Caravaggio for the French cardinal Mathieu Cointrel (1599–1602, ☞ *151*), also known as the Cantarelli chapel. The three canvases (*Martyrdom of St. Matthew, The Calling of St. Matthew,* and *St. Matthew with the Angel*) reveal miracles occurring in the midst of everyday reality, an event shared by all and perennially relevant. Light plays a new and decisive role in these paintings, which later artists could not ignore. Numerous tombs testify to the continuous French

S. Carlo ai Catinari's ⑦ wonderful dome, from 1620, has pendentives with paintings by Domenichino depicting the *Cardinal Virtues*.

The broad and solemn 16th-century facade of S. Luigi dei Francesi ⑧, created in travertine; one of the numerous masterpieces contained within is Caravaggio's canvas of *St. Matthew with the Angel*.

⑧

presence in Rome, and the painter Claude Lorrain (1600–1682), who spent decades lovingly studying the Roman countryside, is buried here. Next to the national French church is the **Palazzo di S. Luigi,** the facade of which, on the Via di S. Giovanna d'Arco, has a theatrical entrance surmounted by a loggia. For centuries it was the principal institution offering assistance to French pilgrims and residents of the city. ✉*Piazza S. Luigi dei Francesi 5.*

S. Marco

▦**6 A1.** Completely renovated by Paul II during the second half of the 15th century, this basilica became the private chapel for the pope's newly built Palazzo di Venezia. But its origins are much earlier; it was founded in the 4th century by Pope St. Mark in honor of the evangelist of the same name. It was rebuilt by Gregory IV in the 9th century, and the mosaics in the apse are from this period. They depict a standing Christ, flanked by various saints including the evangelist Mark and Pope Mark, as well as the donor, Pope Gregory, holding a model of the church. The solemn facade, with a three-arch portico surmounted by a loggia, was constructed with materials from the Coliseum and the Theater of Marcellus. The gilded and blue coffered ceiling is one of two 15th-century ceilings that survive in Rome (the other is in S. Maria Maggiore). The church's outstanding artistic patrimony includes works by Palma the Younger, Melozzo da Forlì, and Antonio Canova. The granite tomb in the presbytery contains the remains of Pope Mark and the Christian martyr saints Abdon and Sennen. ✉*Piazza S. Marco 48.*

S. Maria sopra Minerva ⑨

▦**3 F4.** The church gets its name from the ruins of the Roman temple of Minerva Calcidica, believed to lie below. Entrusted to the Dominicans, it was rebuilt beginning in 1280 and was altered and expanded many times over the centuries, up to an unfortunate Gothic-style renovation in the 19th century. The Dominicans, always firm supporters of the church, particularly in matters of doctrine, became especially powerful during the Counter-Reformation, when they dominated the Inquisition Tribunal. This explains the importance assumed by this church, its sumptuous aristocratic chapels, and the extraordinary wealth of its artistic patrimony. The statue of the *Resurrected Christ* by Michelangelo (1519–1520), the frescoes by Filippino Lippi (1488–1493) in the Carafa Chapel, the funerary monuments of Clement VII and Leo X by Antonio Giamberti da Sangallo the Younger (1536–1541), and the funerary monument of Francesco Tornabuoni by Mino da Fiesole (1480) are some of the many works of art in this church. Two famous Tuscans are also buried here: St. Catherine of Siena (☞ *51*), patron saint of Italy, who died in Rome in 1380, and Fra Angelico, Dominican painter of the monastery of S. Marco in Florence, who died in 1455. The monastery contains the **Biblioteca Casanatense,** which specializes in theology and church history. ✉*Piazza della Minerva.*

S. Maria in Monterone

▦**3 F3.** The name derives from the Sienese Monterone family, who founded a hospice next to the church for their compatriots. The building, mentioned as far back as 1186 and entirely rebuilt in 1682, has eight Ionic columns in the interior. In 1728, the Mercedari, then in possession of the church, had the adjacent monastery built with an elegant rococo facade. ✉*Via Monterone 75.*

S. Maria in Via Lata

▦**3 F5.** According to ancient tradition, the church stands on the spot where Sts. Peter and Paul and the evangelists John and Luke stayed. Storerooms from the Roman Empire were discovered beneath the edifice and were transformed into an oratory during the 5th century. When an upper level was added to the church in the 9th century, these structures were enclosed. The building was renovated in the 17th century, when Pietro da Cortona created the elegant facade and portico. The interior is decorated with frescoes and Baroque-era marble and stuccowork. The high altar, attributed to Gian Lorenzo Bernini, has a 13th-century panel with an image of the *Vergine Advocata,* which is kept in a case adorned with precious gems. The painting is venerated by pilgrims and Romans alike because of the numerous miracles attributed to it. The name of the church derives from the name of the ancient Roman street, which corresponds to the present-day Via del Corso, the urban portion of the Via Flaminia. ✉*Via del Corso 306.*

S. Nicola in Carcere

▦**5 C6.** This church has ancient origins (perhaps 7th century) and stands on the ruins of three Roman temples. It was rebuilt in 1128 and renovated numerous times during subsequent centuries. It was probably attended by the Greek colony that resided in the district, which may explain its dedication to a Greek saint; "in carcere" refers to a prison that existed on the site during the 8th century. The simple facade, which incorporates two ancient columns, is by Giacomo della Porta (1599).

9

The Carafa Chapel, entirely covered with frescoes by Filippino Lippi (1488–1493), is one of the treasures of S. Maria sopra Minerva ⑨, which is extraordinarily rich in outstanding masterpieces.

Part of the elegant front of the Portico d'Ottavia ⑩, a monument from ancient Rome and, in the back, a view of the dome of S. Angelo in Pescheria.

⑩

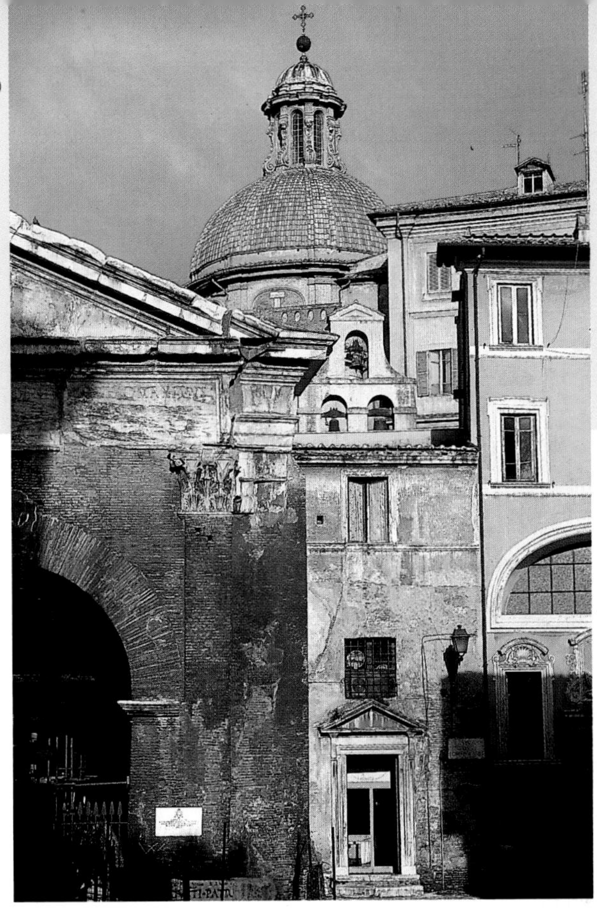

In Roman times this area was bounded by the slopes of the Campidoglio, the Theater of Marcellus, and the Tiber port, where the vegetable market (Foro Olitorio) was located. Vestiges of the three ancient temples are visible both outside and inside the church; these have been identified in ancient writings as the temples dedicated to Hope, Janus, and Juno the Deliverer. ⊠ *Via del Foro Olitorio*

S. Stefano del Cacco

⊞5 A6. The church was built on the ruins of the Temple of Isis, the most important sanctuary of the Egyptian cult in ancient Rome. A statue of an Egyptian divinity with the head of a monkey (a *macaco*, or croo monkey) was discovered nearby, hence the name of the church. Already known in the early Middle Ages, the church was restored many times (the bell tower and apse are from the 12th century). In 1607, it was renovated by the Sylvestrine monks to whom the church had been granted in 1563 and who still serve here. ⊠ *Via S. Stefano del Cacco 26.*

Via delle Coppelle

⊞3 E3–E4. The street takes its name from the barrel-makers who worked in the area during the Middle Ages. The **Palazzo Baldassini** at number 35 was designed by Antonio Giamberti da Sangallo the Younger (1514–1525) and is organized around a courtyard with a portico and loggia; some traces of Renaissance frescoes, grotesques, and stuccowork remain. Today it houses the Luigi Sturzo Institute, which promotes studies in the political, historical, and social sciences. The institute has a specialized library and extensive archive with documents relating to the working-class Catholics who played a decisive role in founding the Christian Democratic Party and in postwar Italian politics. Since 1663 **S. Salvatore alle Coppelle** (72b Piazza delle Coppelle), rebuilt over an older church in the 18th century, has been the headquarters for the Confraternity of Perseverance, which was established to assist foreigners who are taken ill.

Via del Portico d'Ottavia ⑩

⊞5 B6–C6. The Portico d'Ottavia was an enormous square portico, built in the 2nd century BC and rebuilt by the emperor Augustus (23 BC), who dedicated it to his sister Octavia. During the Middle Ages it was the site of a busy commercial center; a fish market, which dated to that time, functioned until 1880. The only trace of the Roman building that remains is the majestic propylaea, which function as the entrance to the church of **S. Angelo in Pescheria** (6 Via di Tribuna Campitelli), built in the 8th century but restored on numerous occasions. Next to the church is the **S. Andrea dei Pescivendoli** oratory (1689), which has a beautiful facade decorated in stuccowork. The street has some medieval and Renaissance buildings, such as the 13th-century **Torre dei Grassi** (at number 25), the 15th-century **Case dei Fabi** (at numbers 8 and 13), and the **Casa di Lorenzo Manilio** (1468), which is decorated with ancient sculptures and epigraphs.

6 Campo Marzio

In ancient times this district was dominated by large public monuments, and it remained sparsely inhabited for a long time thereafter. During the 15th century it began to be more densely populated when the commercial mooring on the Tiber, near the tomb of Augustus, attracted groups of foreign merchants (Dalmatians, Illyrians, Bretons, and others), and numerous sites were established to assist the growing influx of pilgrims and foreigners who arrived in the city at Porta del Popolo. The creation of the trident, formed by Via del Corso, Via del Babuino, and Via di Ripetta, during the 16th century initiated a period of gradual urbanization, which increased over the next two centuries. In addition to churches and aristocratic palazzi, the district was embellished with various infrastructures to accommodate foreigners making the grand tour (including many artists and writers), who increasingly made Rome one of their stops. Numerous inns were opened, then hotels, cafés, artists' studios, and artisan workshops, which soon turned the Campo Marzio into a center of international tourism for the city.

Ara Pacis Augustae

▦3 C3. The peace established by Augustus after a century of bloody civil wars was celebrated with this monument, erected between 13 BC and 9 BC in the Campo Marzio. The remains of the altar were discovered in various stages, beginning in the 16th century. The monument consists of a marble enclosure, entirely decorated in reliefs that, high above a flight of steps, surround the actual altar. The reliefs on the long sides depict a procession of figures from the imperial family and allude to the dynastic continuity necessary for the stability of the empire. Four panels on the short sides show the majestic figures of *Pax*, portrayed as a woman in a luxuriant landscape, and the goddess *Roma*. Two other mythological scenes (*Aeneas Making a Sacrifice* and *Lupercalia*) evoke the origins of the capital city. The Altar of Peace has been protected inside a glass pavilion since the 1930s. ✉ *Piazza Augusto Imperatore.*

Chiesa di Gesù e Maria

▦3 B4. Both the church and the adjacent convent were built in between 1672 and 1675 by the Discalced Hermit Monks of St. Augustine as a monastery for contemplatives and mendicants. The sober facade reflects the austerity of the order's life, while the magnificent interior, rich in polychrome marble, stuccowork, and paintings, expresses the Baroque taste for theatricality and sumptuous decoration. The single barrel-vaulted nave houses four funerary monuments of the Bolognetti family (1678–1690), conceived as theater stages for the figures. The confessionals below are masterpieces of cabinetmaking. ✉ *Via del Corso 45.*

Chiesa del Divino Amore

▦3 D4. During the 12th century a church was erected here, dedicated to St. Caecilia, on the site where, according to tradition, the house of the saint's father stood. In 1729, the structure, which was also dedicated to St. Blaise, was rebuilt by the mattress-makers' guild, following a design by Filippo Raguzzini that preserved the ancient bell tower with two stories of three-mullioned windows. In 1801 the church was given to the Confraternity of the Madonna del Divino Amore, hence its current name. The confraternity, founded in 1744, was previously located in a sanctuary of the same name on the Via Ardeatina. ✉ *Vicolo del Divino Amore.*

Chiesa della Trinità dei Monti

▦3 C5. The church was financed by the sovereigns of France, who were overwhelmed by the sanctity and miracles worked by Francis of Paola, the famous Calabrian hermit who was sent by Sixtus IV to the bedside of Louis XI, king of France, and was for many years an advisor to Louis's son, Charles VIII. The latter provided the saint with the means to establish a monastery for his order, the Minim Friars, with a church dedicated to the Trinity. Its position atop the Pincio, overlooking the city, and its soaring facade flanked by two bell towers have made it one of the most well-known sites in Rome. The church houses a wealth of artwork, including one of the most famous frescoes in Rome, Daniele da Volterra's *Deposition*, which shows the strong influence of Michelangelo. The monastery refectory was decorated by Andrea Pozzo (1694), the cloister by other Mannerists, who painted scenes from the life of St. Francis of Paola. The piazza of the same name, with the obelisk of Sallust at its center, marked the beginning of the Strada Felice, the long, straight street conceived by

② 

Sixtus V, linking Trinità di Monte with S. Croce in Gerusalemme. ✉*Piazza Trinità dei Monti 3.*

Colonna dell'Immacolata Concezione

▦3 C5. In 1845 Pius IX proclaimed the dogma of the Immaculate Conception of Mary, after centuries of study and debate on the subject. To celebrate this event, a monument was erected that incorporated a column of marble that was discovered in the Campo Marzio a century before. A broad octagonal base embellished with statues of the prophets Moses, Isaiah, Ezekial, and David supports the column, which in turn is surmounted by a bronze statue of the Virgin. Since 1929 there has been a tradition to leave flowers at the column on the Feast of the Immaculate Conception (December 8), which is marked with popular celebrations and the participation of the pope. ✉*Piazza di Spagna.*

Palazzo Borghese

▦3 C4–D4. In 1596 Cardinal Camillo Borghese purchased this palazzo, which had been built a few years earlier. After he became Paul V, he had the building enlarged by Flaminio Ponzio, who transformed it into a palace for the Borghese family. The Largo della Fontanella Borghese leads to the majestic courtyard with two-story arcades decorated with ancient statues. At the back of the courtyard is a magnificent pool, called the Bath of Venus, embellished with Baroque statues and fountains. The palace used to house a famous art gallery, which was moved to the Villa Borghese in 1891. The large building opposite the main facade of the palazzo was set aside for employees and stables. For approximately 50 years, Piazza Borghese has been the site of a famous stamp and rare book market. ✉*Piazza Borghese.*

Palazzo Ruspoli

▦3 C4–D4. Built by Bartolomeo Ammannati (1556–1586) for the Ruccellai family, the building passed into the hands of the Caetani, and then, in 1776, the Ruspoli family. Martino Longhi the Younger designed the famous grand staircase (1640), considered one of the jewels of civil Roman architecture, and the Mannerist Jacopo Zucchi frescoed the gallery of the piano nobile. The ground-floor rooms used to house the Caffè Nuovo, a favorite meeting place in 19th-century Rome. ✉*Piazza S. Lorenzo in Lucina.*

Piazza del Popolo ①

▦3 A3–A4. In medieval times, well before the piazza took on its current theatrical appearance, this was the principal entrance point to the city for pilgrims and travelers from the north, who arrived along the Via Flaminia near the church of S. Maria del Popolo. The piazza's appearance began to take shape when Sixtus V erected the Egyptian obelisk of Ramses II in 1589 to punctuate the junction of the trident made up of the Via di Ripetta, Via del Corso, and Via del Babuino. The growing influx of visitors necessitated further reorganization of the space, which was designed by Giuseppe Valadier in the early 19th century and completed with the creation of two large semicircles and ramps that climb to the Pincio belvedere. For centuries the piazza was the point of departure for solemn processions of sovereigns and ambassadors; it was also the site of Carnival festivals, games, and fairs. The **Porta del Popolo**, the ancient Porta Flaminia in the Aurelian Wall, has a majestic interior facade by Gian Lorenzo Bernini, created on the occasion of the arrival of Queen Cristina of Sweden (1655). When she converted to Catholicism, Pope Alexander VII gave her a triumphal welcome to the city, in part because the event represented a Catholic victory after the humiliation the church suffered in the Peace of Westphalia.

Piazza di Spagna ②

▦3 C5. The name dates from the 17th century (it was previously called Piazza della Trinità), when the Spanish Embassy was installed in the Palazzo Monaldeschi. This period also marked the beginning of a violent rivalry for possession of the piazza between Spain and France, which owned the church overlooking the space. In 1629, an unusual fountain in the form of a semisubmerged boat (the

S. Maria dei Miracoli, in foreground, and S. Maria di Montesanto ③, the twin churches of Piazza del Popolo, were commissioned by Alexander VII and designed by Carlo Rainaldi to mark the beginning of Via del Corso.

The soaring interior of S. Maria della Concezione in Campo Marzio ④ contains numerous works of art from Eastern Rite churches.

Barcaccia) was erected at the center of the piazza at the behest of Urban VII, who wanted to commemorate the disastrous flood of 1598. The fountain design was entrusted to Pietro Bernini, but the clever solution of the street-level basin (to get around the difficulty of poor water pressure) reveals the imagination of Pietro's son, Gian Lorenzo. The finishing touch to the piazza's theatrical design is the **scalinata,** the stairway leading up to the church (on axis with the Barcaccia and the Via Condotti). It was built in between 1723 and 1726, after decades of proposals, and was designed by Francesco De Sanctis, who replaced two existing tree-lined streets. Triumphal and yet simple, the stairway of Piazza di Spagna is one of the most magnificent and characteristic creations of the early 18th century. On the right is the **Casina Rossa,** where the poet John Keats died in 1821 and which now houses the Keats-Shelley Memorial House, one of the most complete libraries of the English Romantic period. ✉*Casina Rossa: 26 Piazza di Spagna,* ☎*06/678–4235.*

S. Antonio dei Portoghesi

▦3 D3. The church was built around the mid-17th century in a district with a Portuguese community, on the site of a hospice for Portuguese pilgrims. The fanciful Baroque ornamentation of the church's facade includes two virile figures that support the side volutes and two angels with trumpets on the tympanum. ✉*Via dei Portoghesi 2.*

S. Giacomo in Augusta

▦3 B4. This was the church of the ancient hospital of S. Giacomo degli Incurabili; its name comes from its location near the tomb of Augustus. The church was rebuilt in 1592–1600 by Francesco da Volterra and Carlo Maderno, on an elliptical plan with an imposing facade and, for the first time in Rome, two bell towers to the sides of the apse, instead of flanking the facade. In the 16th century the **Ospedale di S. Giacomo,** founded in 1338, specialized in incurable diseases, particularly syphilis, which was known as the French disease because it was introduced to Roman citizens by the troops of Charles VIII. The great need for shelters at the time necessitated a partial renovation of the hospital, which became one of the most important charity and welfare institutions in the city. The hospital pharmacy became famous for the preparation of an infusion known as Holy Wood, which was thought to be particularly effective for alleviating the effects of syphilis. ✉*Via del Corso 499.*

S. Girolamo degli Illirici

▦3 C3. A community of immigrants from Illyria and Croatia, threatened by the Turks, moved to Rome in the 14th century. In 1453, they obtained from the pope the little church of S. Marina, near the port of Ripetta, and they rededicated the building to their national saint. Sixtus V had the church rebuilt by Martino Longhi (1588) the Elder, with a Renaissance facade in travertine, with two orders of pilaster strips and a small bell tower. ✉*Piazza Porto di Ripetta.*

S. Ivo dei Brettoni

▦3 D3. The present-day church is the result of a 19th-century renovation of an older house of worship, given by Callistus III to the French community from Brittany, to which it still belongs. It became a center of hospitality and assistance for pilgrims from that region. St. Ivo Hélory (1253–1303), patron saint of Brittany, was particularly dedicated to the legal protection of the poor, and the future confraternities of St. Ivo were inspired by his example. ✉*Vicolo della Campana*

S. Maria della Concezione in Campo Marzio ④

▦3 E4. This is an Eastern, Antiochene rite Catholic church, founded around 750 by Pope Zacharias for a group of nuns from the Convent of St. Anastasia in Constantinople. The nuns had been forced to flee the persecutions of Emperor Leo III (717–741), who forbade the making and worship of holy images. The church housed a great number of Byzantine icons, one of which—the 12- to 13-century *Madonna Advocata*—still adorns the high altar; it depicts the Virgin in a gesture of intercession, her right arm raised and her left on her chest. During later years, the church and convent complex were taken over by Benedictine nuns and gained the support of various Roman aristocratic families. The building was completely redesigned in its current Baroque form between 1668 and 1685. The former Convent of S. Maria encompasses the medieval church of **S. Gregorio Nazianzeno** (3 Vicolo Valdina), which has frescoes dating from the 11th and 12th centuries and a beautiful Romanesque bell tower (12th–13th century) with four rows of mullioned windows. ✉*Piazza Campo Marzio 45.*

S. Maria di Montesanto and S. Maria dei Miracoli ③

▦3 A4. These "twin" churches act as monumental entrances to the Via del Corso and are essential elements in the theatrical design of Piazza del Popolo and the trident (Via del Corso, Via di Ripetta, Via del Babuino) that radiates out from the piazza. Alexander VII understood the urban necessity for these two structures, which were begun by Carlo Rainaldi and

4

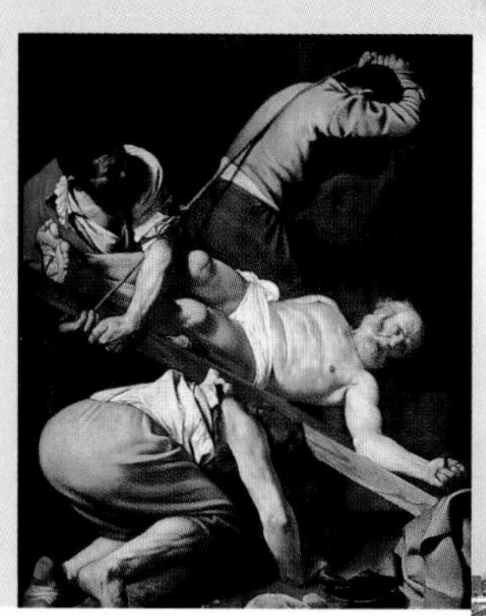

⑤

completed by Gian Lorenzo Bernini and Carlo Fontana in the late 17th century. Both churches have a central plan and are preceded by an open vestibule with four columns with statues, but their appearances differ. S. Maria di Montesanto has an elliptical plan and a dodecagonal dome; S. Maria dei Miracoli has a circular plan and an octagonal dome. The former church has statues of saints (1674) on its facade, perhaps conceived by Bernini, and houses a late 14th-century panel depicting the Virgin of Montesanto, as well as bronze portraits of various popes. S. Maria dei Miracoli takes its name from a painting of the Madonna over the high altar. The facade has statues of saints that show the influence of Bernini and an extremely elegant 18th-century bell tower. ✉*Piazza del Popolo.*

S. Maria del Popolo ⑤

▦3 A4. The current building was preceded by a chapel erected by Paschal II in 1099, at the end of the First Crusade. The name most likely reflects the fact the Roman people financed the construction. Reconstruction, which began in the late 15th century, involved numerous illustrious architects. Bramante redesigned the choir, Raphael designed the Chigi Chapel, Carlo Fontana the Cybo Chapel, and Gian Lorenzo Bernini made various contributions to the structure and furnishings. The interior is a treasure trove of works of art. The choir contains monuments of Cardinals Ascanio Sforza and Girolamo Basso della Rovere (1505–1507), masterpieces by Andrea Sansovino; above these are precious painted windows by Guillaume de Marcillat (*Childhood of Christ* and *Scenes from the Life of the Virgin*, 1509). Pinturicchio painted the beautiful frescoes on the vault (*Coronation of Mary, with Evangelists, Sibyls, and Doctors of the Church*, 1508–1510), and Raphael provided the drawings for the mosaics in the dome (*God, Creator of the Firmament, with Symbols of the Sun and the Seven Planets*, 1516). The church's most famous artworks are Caravaggio's two masterpieces, in the first chapel in the left transept: *The Crucifixion of St. Peter* and *The Conversion of St. Paul* (1601–1602). Luther stayed at the Augustinian monastery attached to the church. ✉*Piazza del Popolo 12.*

S. Maria Portae Paradisi

▦3 B4. The origin of this church's name (St. Maria of Heaven's Gate) is uncertain. It was rebuilt in 1523 by Antonio Giamberti da Sangallo the Younger. Above the entrance is a marble relief of a *Madonna and Child* by Andrea Sansovino. The octagonal interior beneath the dome has rich decorative frescoes and stuccowork and includes, among other things, notable funerary monuments of Matteo Caccia (1645) by Cosimo Fancelli and of Antonio di Burgos by Baldassarre Peruzzi (1526). ✉*Via Canova 29.*

S. Rocco

▦3 C3–C4. Built in 1499 by the Confraternity of the Porto di Ripetta, the church was rebuilt in the 17th century and underwent a later Neoclassical restoration. The hospital of the confraternity, adjacent to the church, was transformed in 1517 into a lying-in hospital that welcomed "honest but unmarried women." Women were assisted in absolute confidentiality, so their pregnancies were never known to the world outside. Inside the church, to the left of the presbytery, an elegant chapel has a venerated image of the *Madonna delle Grazie* (17th century). ✉*Largo S. Rocco 1.*

Ss. Ambrogio e Carlo al Corso ⑥

▦3 C4. St. Ambrose and St. Charles Borromeo were, respectively, the bishop of Milan in the 4th century and the archbishop of the same city in the 16th century. The two saints, who played a defining role in the history of the church, are the most venerated in Lombardy, and the community from that region was responsible for the building of this house of worship, beginning in 1612. The project was entrusted to Onorio Longhi and to Martino Longhi the Younger, then to Pietro da Cortona, who designed the dome (one of the most beautiful in the city) and the interior decoration. The floor plan is unique in Rome, with a continuation of the side naves in an ambulatory, within the presbyteryan—obvious reference to Gothic models, such as Milan's cathedral. The magnificent interior has an extremely rich Baroque decorative scheme, much of which celebrates St. Charles. The most noteworthy artwork is the high altar by Carlo Maratta (1685–1690), which has a *Glory of Sts. Ambrose and Charles.* In the ambulatory, in a niche behind the high altar, is a fine 17th-century reliquary containing the heart of St. Charles. ✉*Via del Corso 437.*

Via del Babuino

▦3 A4–B4–B5. The straight line that joins Piazza del Popolo to Piazza di Spagna was laid out by Clement VII and Paul III during the first half of the 16th century and takes its name from an ancient statue of a silenus, now next to the church

The *Crucifixion of Peter*, a masterpiece by Caravaggio, is one of two splendid canvases by the artist in S. Maria del Popolo (5). The church is adjacent to the beautiful park on the Pincio that is filled with pine trees.

Ss. Ambrogio e Carlo al Corso (6), dedicated to two major Lombard saints, is surmounted by a late Baroque dome of great interest. It was built in between 1668 and 1669 by Pietro da Cortona.

(6)

(7)

of S. Atanasio. Along with the nearby Via Margutta, the new street was soon inhabited by out-of-towners (predominantly Neapolitans) and by artists. It then became well known for its art and antiques trade, which still makes it one of most popular streets in the historic center. At number 149 is the Greek Catholic church of **S. Atanasio** (1580–1583), with an unusual and charming interior; at number 153b is the interesting English evangelical church of **Ognissanti** (All Saints), one of the few neo-Gothic structures in Rome (1882–1887).

Via dei Condotti

▦3 C4–C5. This is one section of the long Via Trinitatis, laid out by Paul III (1534–1549), which linked the church of Trinità dei Monti to the Tiber. The street takes its name from the important waterlines (*condotti*) that ran beneath, supplying the entire Campo Marzio. Today the street is famous for its luxury clothing and jewelry shops, but during the 18th and 19th centuries it was the heart of the city, with the most exclusive and renowned hotels and cafés frequented by artists, intellectuals, and travelers. Of these, the oldest (1760) and most famous is the **Caffè Greco** (number 86), which over the years was patronized by Gogol, Stendhal, Modigliani, and Toscanini, and which still has some of the original furnishings. The street has other elegant buildings, including the **Palazzo dell'Ordine di Malta** (Palace of the Knights of Malta, number 68), built in the 17th century and expanded in the 19th century, with some original wooden ceilings still visible. Nearby is the church of the **SS. Trinità dei Spagnoli** (at number 441 of the street of the same name) and the adjacent monastery, built in 1741–1746. The church has various paintings depicting Giovanni di Matha and Felice di Valois, the two French priests who, in the late 12th century, founded the Trinitarians. The order worked devotedly, first in Europe, then throughout the world, for the liberation of prisoners and slaves.

Via del Corso (7)

▦3 A4–F5. This is a section of the ancient Via Flaminia and was for centuries the principal access route to the city for visitors and pilgrims from the north. During the early centuries of Christianity, the street was lined some of the most ancient churches in the city, including S. Marcello, S. Lorenzo in Lucina, S. Maria in Via Lata, S. Maria in Aquiro and S. Silvestro in Capite. The **Ospedale di S. Giacomo** (1339) was instrumental to the street's subsequent development. The Renaissance and Counter-Reformation popes made the street more uniform, with the transformation of the modest existing houses into aristocratic palazzi; they also built numerous new churches (S. Giacomo in Augusta, Ss. Ambrogio e Carlo al Corso, Gesù e Maria). During this time the street became a setting for festivals, parades, and spectacles, particularly the famous Carnival races, from which the street gets its name and which, until the late 19th century, were the most widely attended events in the city. Artists, writers, and musicians from throughout Europe popularized an extremely lively image of Roman Carnival, contributing to the widespread image of the extroverted, boisterous Roman.

Via dei Prefetti

▦3 D4. During medieval times, prefects (citizen governors) had their offices on this street. The most important building today is the 16th-century **Palazzo di Firenze** (number 27), so-called because of the Medici family from Florence. The building now houses the Dante Alighieri Society, dedicated to the dissemination of Italian language and culture throughout the world. Midway down the street is the small **Chapel of the Madonna della Pietà** also known as the Chapel of Divino Amore, because of its proximity to the church of the same name. It is dominated by an impressive 17th-century Madonna and child.

Via di Ripetta

▦3 A4–D3. Laid out at the behest of Leo X in 1518, the street was called Via Leonina until the 18th century, when it was renamed for its proximity to the Ripetta embankment. The design of the Tiber embankment, which entailed the destruction of the Porto di Ripetta (one of the most important examples of 18th-century Roman architecture) and the isolation of the tomb of Augustus, eliminated a precious portion of the ancient building fabric along the street. There are, however, still significant buildings to be seen. In addition to two imposing monuments erected by the first Roman emperor (the Ara Pacis and the tomb of Augustus), there are also the churches of S. Girolamo degli Illirici, S. Maria Portae Paradisi, and S. Rocco.

7

Trevi and Colonna

With the excepftion of the areas adjacent to the Trevi and SS. Apostoli piazzas, the Trevi district was sparsely inhabited until the Renaissance. Urbanization began during the papacy of Sixtus V, with the opening in 1585 of the Strada Felice. During the two subsequent centuries the area was enriched with new churches and palazzi, both in the lower zone, near Piazza SS. Apostoli, and around the papal residence on the Quirinal Hill. Rome's new function as a capital city brought transformations, such as the construction of government buildings on the Quirinal and the opening of the Via del Tritone, Via Barberini, Via Bissolati, and the King Umberto I Tunnel. The Colonna district, which in medieval times had many residences and churches along the Via del Corso, continued to develop, thanks to the interventions of Gregory XIII and Sixtus V. Between the 18th and 19th century, the area adjacent to Via del Corso became the social heart of the city, the site of popular celebrations, cafés, and the first political demonstrations. The area at the foot of the Pincio has preserved its original character, but the zone around Montecitorio underwent profound transformations after 1870. This became the political city (Palazzo di Montecitorio, Palazzo Chigi) that replaced entire city blocks and continues to expand.

Chiesa del SS. Nome di Maria

▦6 A2. Built in 1737 for the Confraternity of the Most Holy Name of Mary, the church was founded as a sign of gratitude to the Virgin for the victory over the Turks in Vienna (1683). The architecture, clearly inspired by the nearby church of S. Maria di Loreto, is complex and laden with decorative elements. The high altar has a venerated panel with an image of the Virgin and child (13th century), which comes from an earlier, small church, S. Bernardo della Compagnia. ✉*Foro Traiano 89.*

Fontana di Trevi ①

▦3 E5. The Trevi Fountain, the most spectacular and majestic of Rome's fountains, was created at the behest of Clement XII over a 30-year period (1732–1751). The fountain's water comes from the Aqua Virgo, the aqueduct built in 19 BC, which is fed from a source that, according to legend, was pointed out to some thirsty soldiers by a young girl (*virgo*). At the center of the fountain is the ocean god, whose shell-shaped chariot is drawn by seahorses guided by Tritons. The statues in the side niches represent Abundance and Salubrity, and the entire sculptural group rests on jagged rocks rising out of the sea (represented by the basin with raised edges). This fountain is linked to a great many legends and popular traditions, including the belief that those who throw a coin in its waters are sure to return to Rome. It is possible that this derives from the extremely ancient custom of pilgrims leaving coins on St. Peter's tomb. ✉*Piazza di Trevi.*

Galleria dell'Accademia di S. Luca

▦3 E5. The National Academy of S. Luca continued the activity of the University of Painters, which was founded in the 15th century and whose members met in a church dedicated to St. Luke, on the Esquiline Hill (the evangelist saint is the patron of painters and artists in general, as well as notaries, butchers, and doctors). Since 1932 the academy and the art gallery of the same name have been located in Palazzo Carpegna (redesigned by Borromini in 1643–1647). The gallery houses sculpture and a collection of important paintings by Italian and foreign artists from the 16th to the 19th centuries. The works are gifts or bequests from patrons and artists, following a tradition, begun in the the 17th century, for academy members to donate at least one of their works to the institution. The academy houses a notable collection of members' portraits, prize-winning canvases, and the controversial *Madonna with St. Luke,* begun by Raphael and perhaps completed by another artist. ✉*Piazza dell'Accademia di S. Luca 77,* ☏*06/679–8850.*

Galleria Nazionale d'Arte Antica ②

▦4 D2. Pope Urban VIII wanted his new family palazzo to be near his Quirinal residence. This building was begun in 1625 by Carlo Maderno, who designed a structure with a central element and open wings that combined aspects of an urban palazzo and a garden villa. Gian Lorenzo Bernini designed the garden facade and the staircase, and Francesco Borromini is responsible for the spiral stair-

(2)

Raphael's *Fornarina*, which, according to tradition, is a portrait of the artist's beloved. The portrait hangs in the Galleria Nazionale di Arte Antica in the Palazzo Barberini.

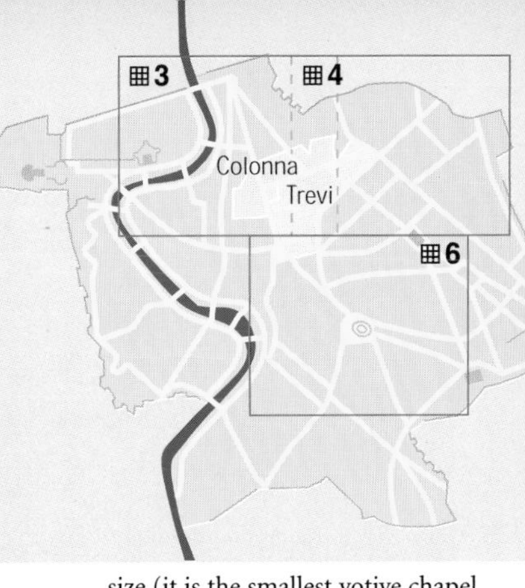

case in the right wing. The luxurious residence was built to accommodate official functions and entertainments of the Barberini family. The palazzo included a theater and ball court, and the broad space in front of the building was used for cavalcades and tournaments. Most rooms have frescoed ceilings, the most famous of which is the main drawing room, painted by Pietro da Cortona with *The Triumph of Divine Providence*, a dramatic and theatrical celebration of the pope and his family. At the center, Divine Providence triumphs over Time and gives the Barberini coat of arms to Immortality. The side scenes illustrate the virtues of Urban VIII and the projects accomplished during his papacy. Acquired by the state in 1949, the Palazzo Barberini now houses the Galleria Nazionale d'Arte Antica, established in the late 19th century as a repository for works from various private collections (Corsini, Torlonia, Sciarra, Chigi, Barberini, and others), legacies, and acquisitions. The collection, one of the most important in Rome, includes paintings by the most famous Italian and foreign masters from the 13th to the 18th centuries. The most admired paintings are Raphael's *Fornarina*, Hans Holbein's *Portrait of Henry VIII*, and Caravaggio's *Judith and Holofernes* and *Narcissus*. The collection also includes Filippo Lippi's *Madonna and Child;* Tintoretto's *Adulteress;* Titian's *Venus and Adonis;* Il Bronzino's *Portrait of Stefano Colonna;* and El Greco's extraordinary sketches, *The Adoration of the Shepherds* and *The Baptism of Christ.* The apartment has an extensive collection of majolica, porcelain, glass, furniture, and clothing from the 17th and 18th centuries. ✉ *Via Quattro Fontane 13,* ☎ *06/481–4591.*

Galleria Colonna

⊞3 E5. The foremost private collection in the city, along with the Doria Pamphilj, is housed in one of the largest residential complexes in Rome. Pope Martin V built the Palazzo Colonna in the early 15th century, on the ruins of a medieval castle. It was expanded and rebuilt in 1730 by Filippo Colonna, incorporating a palazzo built in 1484 for Cardinal Giuliano della Rovere (the future Julius II), first a rival but later related to the Colonna family. The sobriety of the exterior contrasts with the sumptuous scale and decorations of the interiors, which include the splendid gallery that has often been compared to Versailles. The ceilings are sumptuously decorated with frescoes that celebrate the glories of the Colonna family, particularly Marcantonio, victor over the Turks in the Battle of Lepanto. Large mirrors, chandeliers, gilded stuccowork, inlaid floors, and antique statues create a magnificent frame for the painting collection, which was begun in the 17th century and offers works from the 14th to the 18th century. The high points of the gallery and adjoining spaces are the ornate great hall, the hall of landscapes (which contains two jewel caskets and 17th-century French and Flemish landscapes), a room with a ceiling fresco of *The Apotheosis of Martin V,* and the throne room, designed to receive visits from the pope. ✉ *Via della Pilotta 17,* ☎ *06/679–4362.*

Oratorio del Crocifisso

⊞3 E5. Built in 1568 by Giacomo della Porta for the Order of the Confraternity of the Crucifix, this building was established to venerate the famous crucifix in the nearby church of S. Marcello al Corso. The chapel of the **Madonna dell' Archetto** (1851) is located on the adjacent Via di S. Marcello, at number 41B. Despite its very small size (it is the smallest votive chapel in Rome), the chapel is a space of extraordinary architectural and decorative harmony. It was built by Marchese Alessandro Papazzurri (owner of the palazzo next door, now known as the Palazzo Balestra) to accommodate a revered holy image of the Madonna (*Madonnae Causa Nostrae Letitiae*) painted on majolica-covered stone in 1690. ✉ *Piazza dell'Oratorio.*

Palazzo Capranica

⊞3 E4. One of Rome's first Renaissance-style palazzi, this was built before Bramante's arrival in the city. It was begun in 1451 by Cardinal Domenico Capranica to house an ecclesiastical college (the first of its type in Rome) that he established. Most of the building is taken up by the Capranica Cinema, one of the oldest theaters in the city, that began as a private theater built by the Capranica family in 1694. According to tradition, the palazzo stands on the site where St. Agnes once lived, and a chapel within the Collegio is dedicated to her. ✉ *Piazza Capranica.*

Palazzo Chigi

⊞3 E4. It took more than a century to complete this grand palazzo, which has housed government cabinet offices since 1961. Begun in 1580 by the Aldobrandini family, the work continued during the papacy of Clement VIII (a member of that family), and the building was considerably expanded in the following century during the papacy of Alexander VII, a member of the wealthy Tuscan Chigi family known for their patronage of the arts. The solemn entrance on Piazza Colonna, the courtyard fountain, and the rich decoration of the interior spaces date to the 18th century. An elegant and original decorative scheme in stucco squares adorns the courtyard, and

③

④

a grand staircase adorned with antique sculptures rises to the second floor, which houses the Cabinet Room. On the third floor is the sumptuous Gold Room, decorated in Neoclassical style. Between the 17th and 18th centuries, when the palazzo was one of the liveliest centers of Roman social life, the general populace was involved in the festivities held here and received generous donations of food, wine, and money. ✉*Largo Chigi/Piazza Colonna.*

Palazzo di Propaganda Fide ④
▦3 C5. The Congregation of Propaganda Fide, established by Gregory XV in 1622, is the church's central agency for missionary work. Established during a period of great excitement about geographic discoveries and grave spiritual crisis caused by the Reformation, the Propaganda Fide represented a milestone in the history of Catholicism and a turning point in the evangelical process. The 16th-century palazzo was transformed gradually, with successive interventions by various architects, including Bernini (1644). But the most innovative contribution was made by Borromini (1646–1667), whose design was one of his last and most significant creations. The facade on Via di Propaganda Fide looms over the narrow street, and the walls seem animated by an uncontainable internal pressure that pushes and compresses the window frames, which are barely held back by the tall pilaster strips. The same intense vibration, although attenuated by diffused light, is found in the **church of the Re Magi,** inside the palazzo. ✉*Piazza di Spagna 48.*

Palazzo del Quirinale ③
▦3 E6. A cornerstone of Baroque Rome, this palazzo has always been a seat of political power. First it was the summer residence of the popes, then the papal palace, the royal palace, and finally the official residence of the president of Italy. The construction of the building, begun under Gregory XIII, was completed during the papacy of Clement XII (1730–1740). The most celebrated architects of the Counter-Reformation and Baroque periods participated in its construction. The solemn facade is animated by Carlo Maderno's entrance (1615), with statues of St. Peter and St. Paul, and by the Loggia of Benedictions above, designed by Bernini (1638), who was also responsible for the circular tower on the left. The inner courtyard, which has a severe Counter-Reformation appearance, is used for receiving heads of state. The rooms contain works by Botticelli, Pietro da Cortona, Claude Lorrain, Lorenzo Lotto, Melozzo da Forli, and Guido Reni, who executed the wonderful frescoes for the private chapel of Paul V, the so-called Chapel of the Annunciation. The spacious gardens in the back of the palazzo have an unusual Organ Fountain, built for Clement VIII, and an elegant Coffeehouse, erected at the most scenic point for Benedict XIV (1741). The Palazzo Quirinale overlooks a piazza of the same name that dominates one of the most beautiful views of the city. Numerous popes were involved in the planning of this piazza, from Gregory XIII to Pius IX. The focus of activity in the piazza is the **Fontana di Monte Cavallo,** with the **Dioscuri**, two colossal statues of Castor and Pollux holding back their horses, which came from the Baths of Constantine, and, at the center, an **obelisk** that was once graced the facade of the tomb of Augustus. ✉*Piazza del Quirinale.*

Piazza Barberini
▦4 D2. The piazza assumed its modern urban character toward the end of the 19th century, with the building of the Via del Tritone and Via Vittorio Veneto, which intersect here. Before that time, the area was dominated by fields, with scattered houses, workshops, and inns populated by artists. Since 1625 the piazza has borne the name of the Barberini family, whose palazzo and gardens extended as far as Via XX Settembre. The family of Urban VIII commissioned Gian Lorenzo Bernini to create two well-known fountains. At the center of the piazza is the spectacular **Fontana del Tritone,** created for the pope in 1642–1643, with four dolphins with the Barberini heraldic bees raising up a shell on which the Triton stands. At the corner of the Via Veneto is the **Fontana delle Api** (Fountain of the Bees, 1644), which also sports the Barberini coat of arms.

Piazza Colonna ⑤
▦3 E4–E5. Until the late 19th century the piazza was the center of the papal city. Its monumental development resulted from its position at an important intersection of two streets traveled by pilgrims, one linking Porta Salaria to Ponte S. Angelo, the other going from Porta del Popolo to the Campidoglio. In the late 16th century Sixtus V began the demolition of the modest houses that faced the piazza, and these were replaced with patrician palaces. Later this was the site of the papal post office, as well as the location of numerous popular cafés. The central **column** that gives the piazza its name was erected in AD 180–AD 193, to celebrate the victories of Emperor Marcus Aurelius against the barbarians at the eastern boundaries of the empire. The

The Palazzo di Propaganda Fide (4), on which both Bernini and Borromini worked, is the site of the historical congregation of the same name that is in charge of the coordination of various missionary activities of the church.

The column of Marcus Aurelius stands at the center of Piazza Colonna (5); it was erected in 180–193 to celebrate the eastern victories of the emperor against the Marcomanni, the Quadi, and the Sarmatians and depicts his military undertakings.

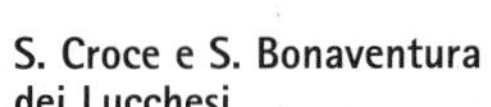

imperial statue that originally topped the monument was lost in medieval times, and Sixtus V replaced it with a bronze statue of St. Paul (1588–1589). The late Baroque church of **Ss. Bartolomeo e Alessandro** was built by an 18th-century confraternity of the people of Bergamo, who dedicated it to the patron saints of their city.

Piazza di Montecitorio

⊞**3 E4.** The piazza was laid out by order of Clement XII Corsini (1730–1740) to create a suitable urban space in front of the palace of the same name. Innocent X (1653) commissioned Gian Lorenzo Bernini to design the **Palazzo di Montecitorio,** which was later converted into law courts and was known as the Curia Innocenziana; today the building houses the Chamber of Deputies. The structure's legal function made it significant in people's lives, particularly because during the 19th century, its largest bell rang out to indicate the beginning of the school day and the opening of offices. In front of the palazzo is an Egyptian **obelisk** from the 4th century BC, which the emperor Augustus used as the gnomon of a sundial. It was moved here in 1796 by Pius VI, who restored its function. The pierced bronze globe, embellished with heraldic symbols of the pope, is traversed by the sun's rays, which indicated the hours on special fillets inserted into the pavement of the piazza.

Pontificia Università Gregoriana

⊞**3 E6–F6.** The impressive palazzo of the Pontificia Università Gregoriana was erected in 1927–1930 to accommodate the prestigious institution founded by St. Ignatius of Loyola in 1551 and previously located in the palazzo of the Collegio Roman and in the Palazzo Borromeo. Today it is an active center for research and study in religion and philosophy. The facade, which has a wealth of classical motifs, recalls the architectural lines of the Collegio Romano. The corner house between Via dei Lucchesi and Via dell'Umiltà has a **17th-century shrine** with a painted image of a crucifix, perhaps related to the nearby Capuchin monastery. ✉ *Piazza della Pilotta.*

S. Andrea delle Fratte

⊞**3 D5.** The name of the church recalls the original rural location, on the periphery of the city (*fratte* means "thickets"). The present-day church was begun in 1612 for the Marchese Paolo Del Bufalo, on the site of an older church that had belonged first to the Scottish community, then to the Minim Friars of St. Francis of Paola. The church's most interesting features are the creations of Francesco Borromini, who worked here from 1653 until 1665. The unusual bell tower conveys a measure of his inspired invention of new forms. Several architectural orders, each different, are superimposed, culminating in the complex crowning element with volutes that support the insignia of the saint (the diagonal cross) and the donor family (the buffalo), surmounted by a metal crown. Inside the church are two marble statues of angels made by Gian Lorenzo Bernini for the Ponte S. Angelo. These are the only statues for the bridge that the artist personally executed, and they were never located there because Clement IX wanted to protect them from the elements. Like all the other angels in the series, they carry symbols of Christ's Passion: the scroll and the crown of thorns. ✉ *Via S. Andrea delle Fratte 1.*

S. Croce e S. Bonaventura dei Lucchesi

⊞**3 E6.** The national church for the people of Lucca (1682–1695) is sober on the exterior but has a surprising interior similar to a drawing room, with exuberant furnishings in marble and gold, and stucco friezes. It was erected over the ruins, still visible below, of the church of S. Nicola de Portiis (9th century), which belonged to the Minorite Capuchin Friars and was given to the people of Lucca by Urban VIII in 1631. In the courtyard is the **Palazzo di S. Felice,** which takes its name from St. Felix of Cantalice, a humble Capuchin friar and friend of St. Charles Borromeo and St. Philip Neri. For more than 40 years St. Felix wandered the streets of Rome, begging for contributions for his order, singing praises to the Madonna, and telling edifying stories. ✉ *Via dei Lucchesi 3.*

S. Ignazio (6)

⊞**3 E4–F4.** The piazza (1727–1728) on which the church stands is a refined urban Rococo creation. The facades of three buildings feign the presence of symmetrical streets converging in the wide space, defining a sort of theatrical backdrop. The church (1626–1685), commissioned by Gregory XV to honor the founder of the Jesuits, imitates, in its facade and interior, the Chiesa del Gesù. The pictorial decoration was for the most part created by the Jesuit Andrea Pozzo, a mathematician, set designer, and student of perspective who was extremely well versed in the use of optical devices to create fictitious spaces. Because there were no funds to construct a dome, he resorted to an ingenious trompe l'oeil, a gigantic canvas depicting a sumptuous dome with a broad drum on columns, in place of the dome that had been planned. The *Entry of St. Ignatius*

6

The ornate altar in the left transept, a precious creation from the Baroque period, includes the *Annunziata*, a marble altarpiece by Filippo della Valle, one of the most notable of the many works in S. Ignazio ⑥.

An evocative view of S. Maria di Loreto, SS. Nome di Maria, and Trajan's Colum ⑦, three well-known monuments that form a fascinating corner of Rome, between Piazza Venezia and the Forum of Trajan.

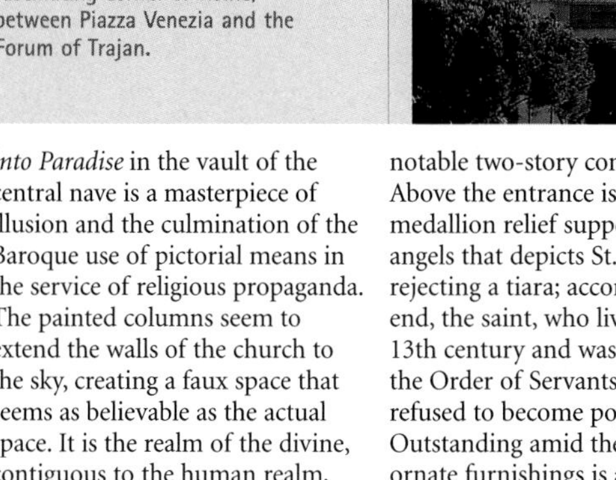

into Paradise in the vault of the central nave is a masterpiece of illusion and the culmination of the Baroque use of pictorial means in the service of religious propaganda. The painted columns seem to extend the walls of the church to the sky, creating a faux space that seems as believable as the actual space. It is the realm of the divine, contiguous to the human realm, miraculously perceivable beyond the terrestrial experience. ⊠*Piazza S. Ignazio.*

S. Lorenzo in Lucina

▦**3 D4.** The name may derive from the house that stood here in Roman times and that belonged to a rich matron named Lucina. The building was later transformed into a church. It was rebuilt by Paschal II in the 12th century (the portico and bell tower remain) and radically redesigned in the 17th century for the Order of Minorites. There is a particularly interesting chapel designed by Gian Lorenzo Bernini for Innocent X's physician, Gabriele Fonseca, whose vivid portrait is by the same master. The high altar has a famous *Crucifixion* by Guido Reni and, behind it, a marble throne with an inscription that recalls the placement by Paschal II (1112) of relics of St. Laurence in the altar, including a fragment of the martyr's gridiron. ⊠*Via in Lucina 16/A.*

S. Marcello al Corso

▦**3 F5.** The church was erected over a 4th-century building dedicated to Pope Marcellus I (308–309), who, according to legend, was forced by the emperor Maxentius to work in the stables of the central post office until he died of exhaustion. Between the 16th and 17th centuries the church was rebuilt, with contributions by Jacopo Sansovino, Antonio da Sangallo the Younger, and Carlo Fontana, who is responsible for the notable two-story concave facade. Above the entrance is a beautiful medallion relief supported by angels that depicts St. Philip Benizi rejecting a tiara; according to legend, the saint, who lived in the 13th century and was a member of the Order of Servants of Mary, refused to become pope. Outstanding amid the church's ornate furnishings is a funerary monument for Cardinal Giovanni Michiel by Jacopo Sansovino. The cardinal was a nephew of Paul II and was poisoned by the Borgia family in 1503. ⊠*Piazza S. Marcello 5.*

S. Maria in Aquiro

▦**3 E4.** No convincing explanation has come to light for the title "in Aquiro," and there is no information about the origins of this church, although it is quite ancient and is mentioned in relation to a restoration carried out by Gregory III (731–741). In 1389 Urban VI called it S. Maria della Visitazione, recalling the biblical episode of Elizabeth's visit to Mary. In the 16th century it was granted to the Confraternity of Orphans and was rebuilt. In addition to 17th- and 19th-century paintings, the church contains a highly regarded detached fresco (*Madonna and Child with St. Stephen*), dating from the 14th century. ⊠*Piazza Capranica 72.*

S. Maria di Loreto ⑦

▦**6 A2.** Begun in 1507 by order of the Confraternity of Bakers, this church combines Bramante's classic style with the new Mannerist tendencies inaugurated by Michelangelo. The two styles are clearly evident in the facade, where a square base punctuated by Corinthian pilaster strips and niches is surmounted by a large dome on an octagonal drum, culminating in a fanciful empty lantern. The sculptural group on the entrance tympanum, depicting *The Virgin and the Blessed House of Loreto,* may be by Andrea Sansovino (1550). The most admired works in the church are the two angels by Stefano Maderno and the *St. Susanna* by François Duquesnoy (1629–1633), the Flemish sculptor who collaborated with Bernini on the baldacchino and various statues for S. Pietro. In this work he expressed his artistic ideals, which were based on the rigorous study of nature and antiquity; the substantial and harmonious forms and the grace of the figure of St. Susanna became a model for much 17th- and 18th-century sacred statuary. ⊠*Piazza Madonna di Loreto 26.*

S. Maria Maddalena

▦**3 E4.** The church was built in the 17th century at the behest of the Ministers of the Sick, an order founded by St. Camillus de Lellis in 1582 to minister physically and spiritually to the sick. The facade (added in 1735), which has a concave silhouette and a wealth of statues, niches, and ornamentation, and the sacristy, with its extremely refined decorative scheme, are among the most representative examples of the Rococo style in Rome. Many of the paintings in the church depict scenes from the life of St. Camillus, whose order acted heroically during various epidemics of plague and cholera in Italy. The order also deserves great credit for improving health care, along the lines achieved earlier in Spain by St. John of God. St. Camillus and his followers isolated those with contagious diseases, studied their diets, improved hospital structures, and worked to aid the dying. The church contains the tomb of St. Camillus and his death mask. ⊠*Piazza della Maddalena 53.*

S. Maria dell'Umiltà

▦**3 E5.** The church was built in the early 17th century for Francesca

⑧

The high altar and crypt of S. Silvestro in Capite ⑧ houses an important relic, the head of S. John the Baptist. The church is sumptuously decorated according to Baroque taste.

Created by Carlo Maderno in 1603, the facade of S. Susanna ⑨ represents an important transition in Baroque style.

Baglioni of Perugia, who, after being widowed, founded a religious community that lived by Dominican precepts. The facade by Carlo Fontana (1680) was modified in 1853, when the entire convent complex was adapted to accommodate the North American College, which is still located here. The ornate interior decorations of marble and stuccowork were also created by Fontana for a wealthy nun who financed the project. ✉ *Via dell'Umiltà.*

S. Maria in Via

⊞3 D5. Mentioned in the 10th century, the church was rebuilt in 1256 to hold an image of the Madonna miraculously discovered in the waters of a well (still visible to the right of the altar). The current Baroque appearance is the result of a renovation for the Servite Order, completed in 1670. Within the simple interior, the first chapel on the right contains the venerated *Madonna of the Well*, a fragment of a 13th-century painting. The church is popular in Rome for its yearly Christmas installation of dramatic crèches set in Roman landscapes. ✉ *Largo Chigi.*

S. Nicola da Tolentino

⊞4 C3. Erected in 1599 by the Discalced Augustinians, the church honors the famous preacher saint of the Augustinian Hermits, who was venerated in both Europe and America. After the mid-17th century it was rebuilt with a solemn yet complex facade. The interior has a rich decorative scheme of polychrome marble, paintings, and stuccowork. At the center of the high altar is a sculpture that depicts a vision of St. Nicholas; the doves, which appear in the sculpture and throughout the building, refer to the coat of arms of the Pamphilj, for whom the church was built. Since 1883 the building has belonged to the Armenian Pontifical College, founded that year by Leo XIII, to whom there is a monument. ✉ *Salita S. Nicola da Tolentino 17.*

S. Silvestro in Capite ⑧

⊞3 D5. The name "in Capite" refers to the relic of St. John the Baptist's head, which is kept in the church. The building was erected in the 8th century by Stephen II on the ruins of the ancient Temple of the Sun, and the Baroque elements are the result of various interventions carried out between the late 16th century and the early 18th century. The lovely 12th-century Romanesque bell tower was preserved intact. The sumptuously decorated interior contains, among other things, an ornate choir and organ (1680), an elegant 16th-century marble altar (in the main chapel), and various paintings that illustrate events from the life of St. Sylvester, who was pope from 314 to 335, during a decisive period for the history of the church, when the emperor Constantine granted Christians the freedom to practice their religion. ✉ *Piazza S. Silvestro.*

S. Silvestro al Quirinale

⊞3 F6. A widening of the street in 1877 caused the original late 16th-century facade to be replaced by the current modest one. The large, single nave has an opulent coffered ceiling, gilded and painted with scenes in relief, and abundant pictorial decoration. The most artistically interesting work is the sumptuous Bandini Chapel (at the back of the left transept), by Ottaviano Mascherino (1585); it has an octagonal plan and a dome ornamented with biblical scenes frescoed by Domenichino (1628) and stucco statues by Alessandro Algardi (*Magdalen* and *St. John*, 1628) and Francesco Mochi (*St. Joseph* and *St. Martha*). When conclaves met in the Quirinal Palace, the procession of cardinals often left from this church. ✉ *Via XXIV Maggio 10.*

S. Susanna ⑨

⊞4 C3–D3. The church stands above a building that, according to tradition, was the residence of St. Gabinus, father of St. Susanna, and next to the house of Pope Caius (283–296), Gabinus's brother. Remains of Roman houses are visible below the church. The original construction (2nd–4th century) was restored in 796 by Leo III and completely rebuilt beginning in the late 16th century. Throughout the Middle Ages, it was a destination for pilgrimages because of the numerous relics of martyrs and saints and the presence of the bodies of St. Susanna and her father, to which were added relics of the true cross, the holy sepulchre, and the clothing and hair of the Madonna, which were mentioned in old guidebooks to lend prestige to the church. The solemn facade by Carlo Maderno (1603) is one of the first examples of the Roman Baroque; some of the paintings in the church are dedicated to the

(9)

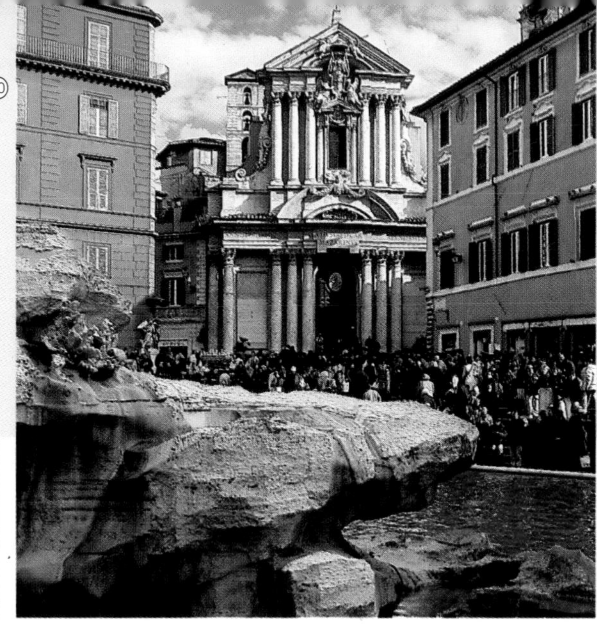

(10)

titular saint, about whose life very little is known with certainty. A 6th-century tradition relates that she suffered martyrdom in 304 because she refused to marry the son of the emperor Diocletian. It is now the national church of American Catholics. ✉*Piazza S. Bernardo.*

SS. Apostoli

▦**3 F5.** Founded in the 4th century, the basilica (consecrated to Sts. Philip and James) was given a grand and complete renovation by Carlo and Francesco Fontana in the early 18th century. The Neoclassical facade (1827) is preceded by a 15th-century portico, which was embellished in 1675 with statues of Christ and the apostles. The interior, resplendent with 18th-century gold work, frescoes, and stucco, creates a sensation of vastness, in part because of the soaring vault, frescoed by Baciccia with a depiction of *The Triumph of the Franciscan Order,* which echoes the triumphal and illusionistic forms expressed earlier in the Chiesa del Gesù. The most famous of the church's many funerary monuments is one of Clement XIV, the first work in Rome by Antonio Canova (1783–1787), who achieved tremendous success reinterpreting Bernini's style in classical terms. ✉*Piazza SS. Apostoli.*

Ss. Vicenzo e Anastasio (10)

▦**3 E5.** The reconstruction of this church was ordered in 1650 by Cardinal Giulio Mazzarino, whose elaborate coat of arms appears on the facade between four angels. The Neoclassical decoration of the interior is the result of a complete renovation during the 19th century. The church has a macabre reputation because it contains the heart linings of popes Sixtus V to Leo XIII, whose organs were removed during embalming. Most of these popes died in the papal palace on the Quirinal, for which this was the parish church. On the corner of Via dei Ss. Vincenzo e Anastasio and Via della Dataria is a **17th-century shrine** depicting kneeling angels in flight and supporting a baldacchino; the painted image, now illegible, depicted the holy family. ✉*Piazza di Trevi*

Via delle Quattro Fontane

▦**4 D2–E3.** This street corresponds to a section of the Strada Felice, the long straight road created by Sixtus V in 1585, and takes its name from the monumental fountain complex at the summit, at the intersection with the axis of Via XX Settembre and Via del Quirinale. The layout of the crossroads was one of the most significant episodes of urban planning by Sixtus V in this district. At the corners of the intersection are fountains and niches embellished with statues of the Arno, the Tiber, Diana, and Juno. In addition to a number of aristocratic palaces, the street is flanked by the Scottish Presbyterian church of S. Andrea, built at the time of Clement VIII (1592–1605) and which functioned as a refuge for Scottish fugitives during the religious struggles of that time.

Via del Seminario

▦**3 E4.** The street takes its name from the Roman seminary established in the Palazzo Borromeo by Pius IV (1560), who erected the building to fulfill the Council of Trent's provisions for training the clergy. At the beginning of the street (number 120) is the little church of **S. Macuto,** known in the 12th century and rebuilt in 1579 by the Confraternity for the People of Bergamo, before passing into the possession of the Jesuits.

Via Sistina

▦**3 C6–D6.** The name of the street celebrates Pope Sixtus V, who planned the long artery to link Trinità dei Monti to the basilica of S. Croce in Gerusalemme (the Strada Felice). The street corresponds to the section of that road between Trinità dei Monti and Piazza Barberini. The considerable privileges granted by the pope to those who constructed buildings along the street ensured its immediate success and helped to make Piazza di Spagna a center of activity for foreigners in Rome. Beginning in the 17th century, many patrician palaces were built here. The facades of some of these buildings bear plaques listing the important artists who stayed there, such as Piranesi, Gogol, Thorvaldsen, and Canina. Via Sistina's international character, reflected in its numerous and popular fashion boutiques, persists today.

8 Monti

Trajan's Column, with its splendid reliefs that unfold for 656 feet; in the background, S. Maria di Loreto.

Until the unification of Italy, when enormous urban development necessitated the creation of new rioni, Monti was the largest district in Rome, occupying more than a third of the city's area. Today it is still one of the largest districts, and it incorporates part of the Quirinal, Viminal, and Esquiline hills. In addition to the Imperial Forums, it includes one of the principal basilicas, S. Giovanni in Laterano. During the Middle Ages, the presence of this Christian monument assured the quarter's important strategic position amid the infighting of Rome's aristocratic families, and in various ways encouraged the popes to intervene in the urban plan. The architectural face of the district was modified radically in the 19th and 20th centuries, but in some areas, between Via Panisperna and Via Cavour for example, traces of the medieval city survive.

Battistero Lateranense
(Lateran Baptistery)
⊞**7 E1.** S. Giovanni in Fonte, better known as the Lateran Baptistery, was built (313–318) by Constantine at the same time as the adjacent basilica. In the early Christian era, proximity to a church was necessary, because baptism required immediate participation in the Eucharist. The interior's octagonal plan was a reminder of the *ogdòade,* the eighth day, dedicated to God, and a reference to the Resurrection of Christ as well as man, who, through the sacrament of holy water, is reborn to new life and destined for salvation. This is described in the inscription that Pope Sixtus III (432–440) had engraved on the architrave of the building's interior. The green basalt font was initially used for adult baptisms by immersion. The chapels contain precious works of art, including 5th- and 7th-century mosaics and 12th-century bronze doors. ✉ *Piazza S. Giovanni in Laterano 4.*

Colonna Traiana ①
(Trajan's Column)
⊞**6 A2.** To commemorate the conquest of Dacia, Trajan (AD 98–AD 117) not only created the most magnificent of the Imperial Forums, but also erected a tall column, decorated with a spiral frieze that circled 23 times from the bottom up, for a total length of 656 feet. It was a history book written in marble. But it is the quality of the formal language, not the dimensions of the work, that make this perhaps the most important surviving monument of Roman art. The Christian Middle Ages contributed to the column's preservation by constructing the church of S. Nicola "de Columna" around the column (vestiges of the building are still visible on the base). One reason for the column's immense fame is its endurance as a symbol of sovereignty, reflected in the great number of reproductions throughout Europe. At the time of Pope Sixtus V, a statue of Trajan that had surmounted the column, but which disappeared during the Middle Ages, was replaced with one of St. Peter, and the monument was blessed with a solemn consecration and "purged of all traces of paganism." ✉ *Piazza S. Maria di Loreto.*

Domus Aurea (Golden House) **and Colle Oppio** (Oppian Hill)
⊞**6 C4.** The Colle Oppio Park contains the ruins of extraordinarily important Roman monuments, particularly the Domus Aurea (the name was chosen by Nero, according to Suetonius), an immense residence the emperor built after the fire of AD 64 (for which he blamed the Christians). The structure takes up approximately 198 acres and includes hundreds of rooms, *nymphaea* (rooms with fountains), reception rooms, and porticos, with thousands of square feet of frescoes, marbles, and stuccowork, as well as gardens, woods, and a lake. The complex, the object of harsh moral condemnation in its time, disappeared within a few years, dismantled mainly by Trajan, who used it as the foundation for his monumental baths. In the 15th and 16th centuries, painters such as Pinturicchio, Filippino Lippi, Perugino, and Raphael descended into its underground passages. They were amazed by the grottoes' fanciful grottesque decorations, which they went on to reproduce in their own work, including Raphael's loggias in the Villa Farnesina and the Villa Giulia. It was here that the *Laocoön,* now in the Vatican Museums, was discovered. Recent times brought another discovery: an enigmatic fresco with the image of a Roman city seen from above, perhaps dating from the late 1st century AD, the oldest and largest urban landscape from antiquity. ✉ *Via del Monte Oppio.*

Foro di Augusto
(Forum of Augustus)
⊞**6 B2.** The Forum of Augustus, with its Temple of Mars Ultor (Mars the Avenger), was built as a result of a vow made by Octavius Augustus before the Battle of Philippi (42 BC), in which Brutus and Cassius, the murderers of

③

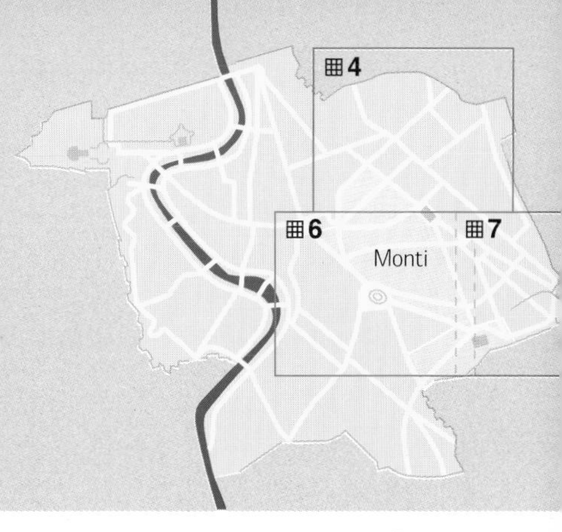

Julius Caesar, died. The piazza provided new spaces for the crowds that thronged the old forums (the Roman Forum and the Forum of Caesar), but served principally to celebrate the undertakings and triumphs of the emperor, who decorated the forum with statues of historical and mythical figures. To isolate the complex and protect it from the frequent fires that broke out in the popular quarter that lay behind, a large wall was built at the far end. There were two openings through the wall; the passageway on the right was given the name Arco dei Pantani (Arch of the Marshes) during the Middle Ages, because of the surrounding swamps. For the same reason the medieval church of S. Basilio, which was built above the temple and incorporated its columns, was known as Noah's Ark. In the late 12th century, the order of the Knights of St. John of Jerusalem (later the Knights of Malta) established its Roman priory above the church and monastery. In the 15th century the head of the order, Cardinal Marco Barbo, nephew of Pope Paul II, built the existing structure, with its elegant loggia overlooking the Imperial Forums. In 1932 Mussolini opened the Via dei Fori Imperiali to link Piazza Venezia to the Coliseum, and, in the process, destroyed the medieval and Renaissance fabric of the district, along with the clear separation between the Roman and Imperial Forums. ✉ *Piazza del Grillo 1.*

Madonna dei Monti

⊞6 B3. This church, perhaps Giacomo della Porta's masterpiece, was built in 1580, following a public collection of funds (with the approval of Gregory XIII), to celebrate the discovery of a miraculous image of Mary amid the ruins of an ancient convent of the order of Poor Clares. It is one of the most interesting churches of the transitional period between the Renaissance and the Baroque. The elegant facade, with two rows of pilasters connected by volutes, was inspired by the Chiesa del Gesù, as was the interior, which is filled with paintings and stuccowork. The altar holds the remains of Giuseppe Labre, a Franciscan saint who lived as a beggar at this church and died here. On the same square is the extremely old church of **Ss. Sergio e Bacco,** the Ukrainian Catholics' parish church, which is also known as the Madonna del Pascolo (Madonna of the Pasture), because of the image venerated within. ✉ *Via della Madonna dei Monti 44.*

Ospedale di S. Giovanni

⊞7 E1. One of the oldest and most glorious Roman institutions, the hospital was founded in 1348 by the Confraternity of St. Salvatore del Sancta Santorum, during the Black Death that ravaged Europe. This society was established to safeguard and honor the image of the Savior (still in the Sancta Sanctorum), which, in medieval times, was venerated because it was considered to be the work of angels. In 1288 substantial donations from Cardinal Pietro Colonna allowed the confraternity to undertake numerous works of charity and to assist the sick. The hospital was also the recipient of donations by the Romans; in 1381 the Senate donated to the hospital one-third of the Coliseum, to be used as a quarry. The institution has been sustained during all eras by bequests and donations. The expansion toward Piazza S. Giovanni in Laterano was made possible by a private donation in 1462. Later additions transformed it into a large, modern hospital-city, continuing a tradition deeply rooted in Roman civic life. ✉ *Piazza S. Giovanni in Laterno.*

Palazzo della Consulta ③

⊞4 E2–F2. This magnificent building, on the east side of the Piazza del Quirinale, was built at the behest of Clement XII, who wanted to create a suitable context for the newly completed grand papal residence. Designed by Ferdinando Fuga (1732–1734), it held the Council of State (which dealt with issues regarding the temporal affairs of the church) and the barracks for the Corazze and the Cavalleggeri (the cavalry troops assigned to defend the pontiff). In 1924, the building was turned over to the Ministry of the Colonies, and since 1955 it has been the location of the Constitutional Court. ✉ *Piazza del Quirinale.*

Palazzo Lateranense ② (Lateran Palace)

⊞7 E1. Sixtus V (1585–1590) commissioned Domenico Fontana to design this palace to replace the old papal residence (the Patriarchio, or Patriarchate), then in ruins as a result of fire and abandonment by the popes, who had taken up residence in the Vatican after the exile in Avignon. Built in a very short time, as were all Sixtus's projects, it is one of the most solemn and balanced examples of Roman Baroque architecture. Turned into a museum in the 19th century, it now houses the vicariate of Rome and the **Museo Storico Vaticano,** dedicated to the history of the papacy, with extensive documentation related to papal ceremony. The magnificent papal apartment occupies 10 sumptuously decorated rooms. Here, on February 11, 1929, the representatives of the Holy See and the Italian State signed the Lateran Treaty, whereby Italy granted the church sovereignty over the territory that became known as the Vatican City, and which would become an independent state. The Holy See, in turn, recognized the

Kingdom of Italy with Rome as the capital. ✉ *Piazza S. Giovanni in Laterano,* ☎ *06/698–86386.*

Palazzo Pallavicini Rospigliosi
▦4 F2. Cardinal Scipione Borghese, nephew of Paul V, the first pontiff to reside at the Quirinal Palace, decided to build a residence in the immediate vicinity of the new papal see. The building, completed by Carlo Maderno in 1616, changed hands numerous times before passing to the Rospigliosi family in the late 17th century. The new owners enlarged the building and embellished it. The wedding of Gian Battista Rospigliosi (1646–1722) with Maria Carmela Pallavicini brought the palace into the possession of the Pallavicini family, its current owners. In 1614, Guido Reni painted the ceiling fresco of the Casino Pallavicini with a splendid *Aurora,* the result of his passionate study of Raphael and classical statuary; it is a fundamental work in the history of the classical ideal. The **Galleria Pallavicini,** one of the few galleries of the great families that still survives, contains paintings by Botticelli, Signorelli, Pietro da Cortona, Lorenzo Lotto, Paul Bril, Luca Giordano, Rubens, Tintoretto, the Carracci, and Velásquez. ✉ *Via XXIV Maggio 43,* ☎ *06/474–4019.*

S. Agata dei Goti
▦6 A3. Founded in the 5th century, this church was the center of an Arian cult in the Goth community in Rome, the only evidence of such practice in the capital. In 593, Gregory I reconsecrated the church to the Catholic religion and gave it its present name. A porticoed atrium leads to the facade, which was rebuilt during the 18th century. The interior preserves part of the original structure and has Baroque and 19th-century additions. The church has three naves, divided by 16 granite Ionic columns. In 1933, a 12th- to 13th-century mosaic canopy was reinstalled in the presbytery. Agatha was born in Catania and martyred there around 251; her breasts were cut off and she was placed on burning coals. She is venerated as a protector against breast cancer and fires. ✉ *Via Mazzarino 16.*

S. Andrea al Quirinale ④
▦4 E2. Gian Lorenzo Bernini designed this jewel of Baroque architecture (1658–1661), which was commissioned by Cardinal Camillo Pamphilj for the Jesuit novitiate. The artist adopted an elliptical plan, one of his favorite schemes, with the main axis parallel to the entrance. Inside, the compelling rhythm of the large piers draws your eye toward the central altar niche, which contains an image of St. Andrew borne aloft to heaven. The intense colors of the marble and the light of the stuccowork and gilding enhance the spectacular nature of the miraculous event. The facade's two curved wings, which invite and welcome passersby, is equally brilliant. It is said that Bernini's sole payment for his work was a donation of daily bread, sent to him from the novitiate's oven. In the adjacent monastery are the rooms of St. Stanislaw Kostka, who came to Rome as a Jesuit novice and died here at the age of 17, in 1568. The beautiful statue in polychrome marble by Pierre Legros (1703) shows him lying on his deathbed. Stanislaw is the patron saint of novices and of university students throughout the world. The Jesuits still place flowers in the rooms where he lived and died. ✉ *Via del Quirinale 29.*

S. Carlo alle Quattro Fontane
▦4 E2. Commissioned by the Spanish Trinitarian fathers, this was Rome's first church dedicated to St. Charles Borromeo after his canonization in 1610. Francesco Borromini was the talented architect, and this, his first autonomous project, gave proof of the revolutionary power of his art. The small size of the space forced him to devise ingenious building plans. Vigorous columns that emphasize the undulating line of the walls punctuate the elliptical interior space. An oval dome, a fanciful geometric lacework of cross-shaped, hexagonal, and octagonal coffers, soars above. The coffer shapes diminish as the ceiling rises, creating the illusion of exaggerated height, and the abundant light from the lantern highlights the compact unity of the space and the complexity of its internal tensions. The facade's concise juxtaposition of concave and convex walls, largely unfettered by decorative elements, creates an effect of heightened tension. This facade was completed some years later and was the last work by the great mas-

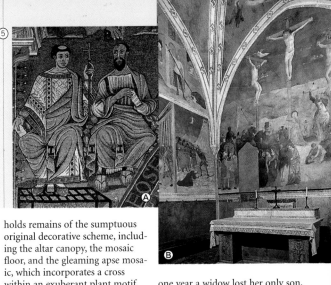

(A) Under the spectacular dome of S. Andrea al Quirinale ④, the faithful gather at the center of the liturgical celebration in a triumph of light; (B) the facade's sinuous forms, which invite visitors to enter, are by Bernini.

S. Clemente ⑤ (upper church): (A) detail of the mosaic decoration of the bowl-shaped apse vault and (B) the Chapel of St. Catherine (1428–1431), frescoed by Masolino da Panicale, probably in collaboration with Masaccio.

⑤

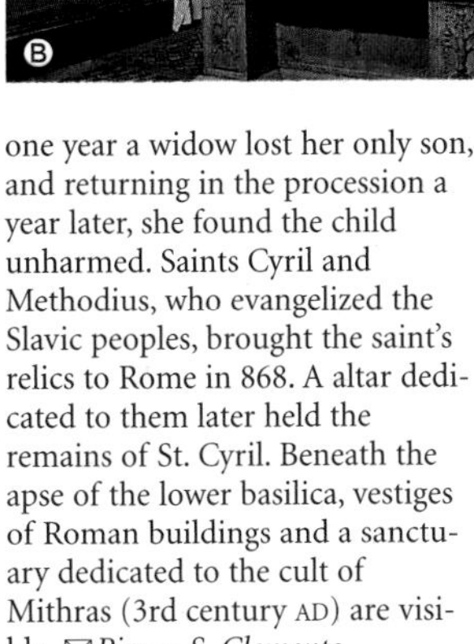

ter, who in his youth had been deeply affected by the austere piety of St. Charles, and who wanted to conclude his career by returning to this, his first creation. In 1667, exhausted and isolated, Borromini committed suicide by throwing himself upon his sword. ✉ *Via del Quirinale 23.*

S. Caterina a Magnanapoli

▦6 **A2.** This church was founded around 1575, along with the convent of Dominican nuns, who brought with them some relics of St. Catherine of Siena. Rebuilt between 1628 and 1641, the facade has two architectural orders of the same width. A 20th-century double staircase leads to a portico with three arches surmounted by the second row, with a large window and niches. The interior, with a single nave and three side chapels, has ornate 17th- and 18th-century decorations. Carlo Marchionni's monumental high altar (1787) has a tabernacle in agate, lapis lazuli, and gilded bronze, and a sculptural group by Melchiorre Caffà, made from colored marble and stucco, depicting the *Ecstasy of St. Catherine.* Caffà, one of the most successful interpreters of Bernini's vocabulary, was in this case clearly inspired by the *Ecstasy of St. Teresa* in S. Maria della Vittoria. The convent, which in 1619 also included the nearby **Torre delle Milizie,** was demolished in 1924. ✉ *Largo Magnanapoli.*

S. Clemente ⑤

▦6 **D5.** Named after Peter's third successor (88–97), this basilica offers a a centuries-long collection of monuments that traverses most of the city's history, from the 1st century AD to the threshold of the modern era. According to tradition, the upper church, commissioned by Pope Paschal II (1099–1118), was built over the house where the saint was born. It holds remains of the sumptuous original decorative scheme, including the altar canopy, the mosaic floor, and the gleaming apse mosaic, which incorporates a cross within an exuberant plant motif. The political significance of the image is clarified by the inscription, which says that law alone withers vines, which, instead thrive beneath the sign of the cross. The image is also a container for relics, and it holds fragments of the cross from Golgotha. Masolino da Panicale (perhaps with Masaccio) painted the frescoes (1428–1431) in the Chapel of St. Catherine, one of the most venerated Christian martyrs in the capital. Some 18th-century frescoes in the central nave depict significant episodes from the life of St. Clement. In AD 97 Clement was condemned to exile and forced labor in the famous marble quarries of Chersoneso, in the Crimea, where he continued his missionary work. There was no water in the quarries, and prisoners risked dying of thirst. Clement, having seen a lamb scraping the earth with its hooves, began to dig at that spot, from which a spring burst forth. Trajan had Clement thrown into the Black Sea with an anchor around his neck. Clement is also the subject of most of the frescoes in the lower church (4th century), executed between the 9th and 11th centuries. This group of work includes, among others, the *Legend of Sisinius,* prefect of Rome, who ordered his soldiers to arrest the pope. Blinded by God, they instead imprisoned a column (the scene is well known thanks to the inscriptions in crudely realistic vernacular, to which Clement replies in formal Latin). Another miracle immortalized here has always attracted popular devotion. It recounts how the sea waters opened up once each year, to allow the faithful to pray at the martyr's watery grave. According to legend, one year a widow lost her only son, and returning in the procession a year later, she found the child unharmed. Saints Cyril and Methodius, who evangelized the Slavic peoples, brought the saint's relics to Rome in 868. A altar dedicated to them later held the remains of St. Cyril. Beneath the apse of the lower basilica, vestiges of Roman buildings and a sanctuary dedicated to the cult of Mithras (3rd century AD) are visible. ✉ *Piazza S. Clemente.*

S. Francesco di Paola

▦6 **B3.** Francis of Paola (ca. 1436–1507), a hermit saint, came from Calabria. In 1632, a wealthy believer from the same region donated the funds for the construction of this church, which was set aside for the order of Minim Friars, who dedicated themselves to a rigorously ascetic life. The church became the national church of the Calabrians. The ornate lower portion of the travertine facade, articulated by pilasters, contrasts with the simplicity of the upper order, which was refinished in plaster in the 18th century. Inside is Giovanni Antonio de Rossi's dramatic high altar (ca. 1655), a magnificent stucco drapery made to look like bronze and supported by angels, is noteworthy. The nearby **Torre dei Margani** (12th century), in Piazza S. Pietro in Vincoli, was transformed into the church bell tower. It is a massive, square structure that terminates in a balustrade and still has a medieval coat of arms. ✉ *Piazza di S. Francesco di Paola 10.*

S. Giovanni in Laterano ⑥

▦7 **E1–F1.** As cathedral of the bishop of Rome, S. Giovanni in

⑥

Ⓐ Ⓑ

(A) The monumental facade of S. Giovanni in Laterano, the cathedral of Rome, is an elegant, solemn creation by Florentine architect Alessandro Galilei (1732–1735); (B) a view of the cloister, created in the early decades of the 13th century; (C) the tabernacle, built in 1367, is decorated with frescoes. The silver reliquaries contain the heads of the Apostles Peter and Paul.

Laterano is called the mother of all churches. It was built in the 4th century over the barracks of the Equites Singulares (the emperors' mounted guards), in the area that Constantine donated to Pope Miltiades. According to medieval legends, the Lateran was the place where Pope Sylvester baptized the emperor, ill with leprosy, who, when he was healed, converted to Christianity. Pope Gregory I, who consecrated the basilica to St. John the Baptist and St. John the Evangelist, performed the dedication of the church. The basilica is also known as the Redeemer, because of both the icon preserved in the nearby chapel of the Sancta Sanctorum and the legend of the apparition of the face of Christ on the day of the consecration. Thanks in part to Constantine's donations, the church has always had precious ornaments, and it is popularly believed to contain exceptional relics. The most important are those related to St. John the Evangelist: the chalice from which he drank poison, the chain with which he was bound, and the miraculous tunic he used to raise three people from the dead. Some of the many other relics are the sackcloth of John the Baptist, the cloth Jesus used to dry the feet of his disciples, and the red garment Jesus was given by the soldiers of Pontius Pilate. In 1370, the remains of the heads of Peter and Paul were brought from the Sancta Sanctorum. The church then acquired a prestige even greater than that of the basilicas of Sts. Peter and Paul and was considered the true heart of Christendom. The original structure underwent numerous and radical transformations over the course of the centuries, up to the Baroque renovations by Borromini. The central entrance on the facade has bronze doors from the Curia (the site of the Roman Senate) in the Forum, while the last door on the right is the Porta Santa, or Holy Door, and is opened only during Jubilee years. The long history of the building is manifested in the extremely rich interior decoration, and the cloister is a masterpiece of mosaic art. ✉ *Piazza S. Giovanni in Laterano 4.*

S. Lorenzo in Fonte

▦6 A4. This small church, also known as Ss. Lorenzo e Ippolito, is linked to the imprisonment of the martyr St. Laurence. Because of the presence of underground structures from Roman times and a well, this was believed to be the place where the saint was incarcerated and where he baptized his jailer, Hippolytus (the painting on the high altar depicts this legend). The current structure, which dates from a 1656 renovation, is very simple, with a Neoclassical facade. ✉ *Via Urbana 50.*

S. Lorenzo in Panisperna

▦6 A4. According to tradition, the church was built in the time of Constantine, on the site of the saint's martyrdom, but the current building is the result of a 1576 renovation. The adjacent Convent of the Poor Clares at one time distributed bread and ham on the saint's feast day (August 10), in remembrance of deacon Laurence's distribution of the church's treasures to the poor of Rome before his death. It is probably that custom that gave the street its name, "panisperna," from the words for bread (*pane*) and ham (*perna*). The outer gate leads to a courtyard, in which stands a rare example of a medieval house with an exterior staircase. In the presbytery, a dramatic painting depicts the martyrdom of St. Laurence. ✉ *Via Panisperna 90.*

S. Lucia in Selci

▦6 B5. Enclosed within a 17th-century Augustinian convent, the church of S. Lucia in Selci was built, certainly no later than the 8th century, over an ancient Roman building (the portico of Livia, none of which is still visible). Reconstructed by Carlo Maderno in 1604, it has a rectangular interior space with a barrel vault, two altars, and paintings depicting the *Martyrdom of St. Lucy* and the *Vision of St. Augustine.* The altar canopy in polychrome marble and gilt and alabaster statues are attributed to Maderno, the choir to Francesco Borromini. ✉ *Via in Selci 82.*

S. Martino ai Monti

▦6 B5. The church, located in an area rich in archeological finds from Roman times (partially visible in the vicinity and belowground), was founded in the early 6th century by Pope Symmachus, who dedicated it to St. Sylvester and St. Martin of Tours (ca. 316–397). The latter was known for his ascetic and missionary life, particularly for the episode where he gave his cloak to a beggar. It is not certain if this was the location of the ancient *titulus Equitii,* where the early Christians of the quarter used to meet. The building has been restored many times, and its current appearance is the result of a 17th-century renovation. The interior has three naves divided by ancient columns. The side naves have precious 17th-century wooden ceilings and noteworthy paintings. A central staircase descends to the dramatic crypt, animated by a great number of columns that contain the remains of various martyrs. The crypt leads to spaces that still have structural elements and architectural fragments from Roman and medieval times and frescoes from the 9th century. ✉ *Via Monte Oppio 28.*

PIVS·IX·PONT·MAX
ANNO·D·MDCCCLI
XIII·CELLAM·MAXIMAM·VE
VETVS·MVSIVVM·MVLTI
ET·IN·NOVAM·ABSIDEM·OP
LAQVEARI·ET·CONTIGNATI
CENDAM·LAXANDAMQVE·CVRAVIT
QVVM·EXEMPLAR·RESTITVI
SFERRI·AVLAM·TRANSVERSAM
CCCCLXXXIV·SACRI·PRINC·VII

S. Pietro in Vincoli ⑦

▦6 B4. In the 5th century Pope Sixtus III ordered a church to be built to hold a precious relic: the chains (*vincula* in Latin, from which the name "in Vincoli" is derived) that bound St. Peter in the prisons of Jerusalem. According to legend, the chains were found adjacent to those of the apostle's Roman imprisonment, and they miraculously welded together, forming a single chain, which is kept here, beneath the high altar. Cardinal Giuliano della Rovere, the future Pope Julius II, made radical changes to the church (1471–1503), and other alterations were made in the 18th century. The basilica's many works of art include an early Christian sarcophagus (in the crypt), paintings by Guercino and Domenichino, and a Byzantine mosaic from the 7th century that depicts St. Sebastian with a beard. These works are eclipsed, however, by Michelangelo's renowned *Moses,* the only work the artist completed for the tomb of Julius II. The original project called for a much more opulent presentation (a structure on many levels, crowded with biblical figures) and a more prestigious and momentous location that was selected by Julius II himself: beneath the dome of St. Peter's and above the tomb of the apostle. ✉ *Piazza S. Pietro in Vincoli 4/A.*

S. Prassede ⑨

▦6 A5. According to tradition, Praxedes was the sister of St. Pudentiana and the daughter of Senator Pudens, in whose house the apostle Peter stayed. Legend has it that St. Praxedes collected the remains and the blood of martyrs, and the legend is recounted in an inscription on a round porphyry well cover in front of the entrance. The 5th-century church was completely rebuilt in 822 by Pope Paschal I, on the occasion of the transfer of the relics of 2,300 martyrs from the catacombs. In the apse a mosaic depicts *Christ Offering a Benediction, Surrounded by Saints,* above a frieze showing 12 lambs (the apostles) and the two celestial cities, Jerusalem and Bethlehem. Paschal I built the Chapel of S. Zeno (called the "Garden of Paradise") as a mausoleum for his mother, Theodora. It is entirely covered with mosaics, which portray the Virgin and child, Sts. Praxedes and Pudentiana, and Christ with the apostles. The dome contains an image of Christ supported by four angels, and medallions with busts of male and female saints frame the door. Another chapel contains the so-called Column of the Flagellation, brought from Jerusalem in 1223. A reliquary contains three thorns, said to be from Christ's crown. ✉ *Via S. Prassede 9/A.*

S. Pudenziana ⑧

▦4 F4. Tradition states that the church dedicated to Pudentiana, the sister of St. Praxedes, was built over the house of their father, Pudens, and that he himself transformed it into a place of worship. The current building, which dates from the late 4th century but has been altered many times, has an apse decorated with the oldest Christian mosaics that survive from a place of worship. They almost certainly can be dated from the papacy of Innocent I (401–417), according to an inscription, now lost. In the solemn central image, Christ is seated on a jewel-studded throne, surrounded by the 12 seated apostles, and two women place crowns of martyrdom on the heads of Peter and Paul. It is likely that the women symbolize the two essential components of the early Christian community, one stemming from Judaism and the other from paganism. The scene is surmounted by an impressive jeweled cross, next to which are the symbols of the four evangelists, the so-called "tetramorph," inspired by the Apocalypse of St. John, which appears here for the first time. Here, as in the church of St. Praxedes, popular myth spread the belief of the existence of a well, in which St. Pudentiana was thought to have gathered the blood of 3,000 martyrs. In 1610, a eucharistic miracle, similar to the one in Bolsena, where blood spilled from a consecrated vessel to rekindle the faith of a doubting priest, is said to have occurred in the Caetani Chapel. ✉ *Via Urbana 160.*

S. Stefano Rotondo

▦6 F5. The church was built in the 5th century to hold the remains of St. Stephen, the first Christian martyr, who was the object of widespread veneration after the discovery of his tomb near Jerusalem in 415. The word "Rotondo" refers to the church's circular plan, modeled on the church of the Holy Sepulchre in Jerusalem and utilized here for the first time in a church in Rome. Two centuries later, Pope Theodore I transported the remains of the martyrs Primus and Felician to the church and had a mosaic created with their images on either side of a jeweled cross. According to tradition, they were two Roman brothers who renounced their pagan faith and were baptized at the time of the terrible persecutions under Diocletian. They tirelessly preached their new faith and aided imprisoned Christians, until they were put to death publicly in 305, after enduring atrocious tortures. The outer wall of the church is frescoed with 34 moving scenes of *Martyrology* (1572–1585), commissioned by Pope Gregory XIII. ✉ *Via di S. Stefano Rotondo 7.*

The mosaic apse in the church of S. Pudenziana (8) dates from the founding of the present-day building in the late 4th century.. The mosaic depicts Christ enthroned with the apostles and Sts. Pudentiana and Praxedes.

(A) Detail of the early Christian mosaics of the Chapel of S. Zeno, the principal Byzantine monument in Rome, located in the right nave of the basilica of S Prassede (9); (B) a view of the central nave of the same church.

(9)

S. Vitale

▦4 E2. The church was founded by Pope Innocent I in 402, thanks to the generosity of Vestina, widow of a Roman notable. It was built to hold the remains of Sts. Gervase and Protase and their father, Vitalis, which were removed from Bologna and Milan after the discovery of their tombs by St. Ambrose. In the 6th century, Pope Gregory the Great established a procession of widows, in memory of the church's benefactress. The building originally had three naves, but was reduced to a single nave by Sixtus IV on the occasion of the Jubilee of 1475. In 1598, Clement VIII ceded the church to the Jesuits, who linked it to the church of S. Andrea al Quirinale and carried out a complete restoration. The interior is decorated with scenes from the lives of martyrs and prophets and from the martyrdom of St. Vitalis. ✉ *Via Nazionale 194/B.*

Scala Santa

▦7 E2. While he was overseeing the construction of the new Lateran Palace, Pope Sixtus V decided to save the private chapel of the popes (dedicated to St. Laurence), which was part of the ancient Patriarchate, the papal residence during the Middle Ages. The building was also called the Sancta Sanctorum, because of the relics it contained, connected to Christ, the apostles, and to significant figures of the Christian faith. The old palace's staircase was also salvaged and moved to the chapel. According to a 15th-century tradition, the stairs are identified with those ascended by Christ during his Passion, in Pontius Pilate's palace, and since that time worshippers have climbed them on their knees. The restored mosaics and frescoes in the chapel date from the 13th century. The most important of the many treasures is a miraculous sacred image of Christ, thought to be "not painted by human hands." The 5th- to 6th-century panel is now in the Museo Sacro in the Vatican. ✉ *Piazza S. Giovanni in Laterano 14.*

Ss. Domenico e Sisto

▦6 A3. The Baroque-era church was preceded by a small house of worship from the first millennium, known as S. Maria a Magnanapoli, which housed the Dominican nuns of the Convent of S. Sisto at the baths of Caracalla. At the behest of Pope Pius V, a Dominican, an opulent monastic complex was built on the site of and encompassed the small ancient church. This new structure was given the name of Ss. Domenico e Sisto, in remembrance of the old convent. Some of the most famous architects of the time were involved in the century-long building project (1569–1663), which concluded with the creation of the elegant facade, dramatic in its height and staircase. The interior has a single nave covered with a barrel vault and three altars on each side. Gian Lorenzo Bernini designed the first altar on the right and the high altar. ✉ *Largo Angelicum 1.*

Ss. Marcellino e Pietro

▦6 D6. This structure, built in 1751, replaced a 4th-century church that stood near the Via Labicana Catacombs. In 1256, the remains of the two martyrs to whom the building is consecrated were brought to the church. Even earlier it was an important destination for pilgrims, because of the presence of a hospice, entrusted in 1276 to the Confraternity of those Commended to the Savior. The cube-shaped exterior, divided by pilaster strips, presages neoclassicism, and the stepped dome and the interior are clearly inspired by Borromini. ✉ *Via Merulana 162.*

Torre de' Conti

▦6 B3. This is one of the most imposing remnants of medieval Rome, a city crowded with the towers and fortresses of the nobility, often erected, as in this case, on the solid remains of ancient edifices. The tower was built by Innocent III in 1203, over part of the Forum of Vespasian. It then passed into the hands of Innocent's family, the Conti di Segni, one of the most prominent families in the history of the church, to which it contributed 12 popes and 25 cardinals. Conceived not only as a private building, but also as a symbol of papal power, the tower was part of an extensive fortification system that was partially destroyed by the earthquake of 1349 and partially collapsed in 1644. ✉ *Largo Ricci.*

Torre delle Milizie

▦6 A2. According to legend it was from this tower that the emperor Nero watched Rome burn, while he composed verses and songs. In reality its construction is much more recent, and it represents an important example of civic architecture from medieval Rome. Built in the early 13th century by the powerful Conti di Segni family, it passed into the hands of the Annibaldi and then Boniface VIII. Boniface turned it into a stronghold in the struggle between the Caetani and Colonna families. In the 17th century it was incorporated into the Dominican Convent of S. Caterina a Magnanapoli. Damaged by lightening numerous times, the tower lost its third floor during the earthquake of 1348, which also caused the ground to sink and the tower to tilt markedly, a characteristic that is still visible. ✉ *Largo Magnanapoli.*

9 Campitelli and Celio (Campitelli and the Coelian Hill)

The Campitelli includes the most important archaeological zones in the city: the Campidoglio, the Palatine, and the Roman Forum. In postclassical times the district was predominantly occupied by ancient ruins. The slopes of the Campidoglio, which was the principal commercial center of the city during the early Middle Ages, had the area's only residential concentration. During the 20th century, this disctrict was terribly scarred by fascist demolition, which led to the isolation of the Campidoglio from the rest of the neighborhood and the opening of the Via del Mare (now the Via del Teatro di Marcello). The Coelian Hill and district were also long ignored and sparsely populated. Even during ancient times there were few patrician residences or public buildings here, and the district was animated only when the Coliseum hosted spectacles. During the Middle Ages and Renaissance the hill became depopulated; some villas and small farms remained, but the only significant buildings were Christian places of worship, some of the most ancient in the city (Ss. Giovanni e Paolo, Ss. Quattro Coronati, S. Maria in Domnica). In the 20th century, the area's relative proximity to the center made it a site for considerable urban development.

Arco di Costantino ②
(Arch of Constantine)

▦6 D3. Located on the ancient Via Trionfale, which was traveled by victorious generals and emperors, the Arch of Constantine is Rome's grandest and best-preserved ancient arch. It was dedicated to the emperor by the Roman senate and people to celebrate the victory over Maxentius (312), achieved, as the epigraph reads, "by divine inspiration": legend tells of the appearance of the cross to Constantine before his decisive battle. The arch is a miscellany of sculptures and reliefs from earlier monuments, juxtaposed with those made during the time of Constantine. During this historical period in Rome, which had lost its position as capital to Constantinople, it must have been very difficult to find sufficient skilled labor to create the decoration for a large public monument. Thus started the practice of reusing ancient materials, a custom that lasted throughout the Middle Ages and made the Arch of Constantine a precious gallery of official Roman sculpture. The composite nature of the monument did not escape Raphael, whose harsh judgment of the reliefs from the Constantinian era ("very silly, without any good art or design") remained the prevailing opinion about late-ancient art until a few decades ago. ✉*Piazza del Colosseo, corner of Via di S. Gregorio.*

Carcere Mamertino
(Mamertine Prison)

▦6 B2. This is part of the ancient state prison, where many illustrious enemies of Rome met their deaths. The medieval legend, according to which the apostle Peter was imprisoned here and baptized his jailers with water from a source that sprang from underground, seems to be without basis. In 1726, the building was transformed into a house of worship, S. Pietro in Carcere. Above the prison is the church of **S. Giuseppe dei Falegnami,** created for the association of carpenters in 1598. The Chapel of the Crucifix, which has a venerated 16th-century wooden crucifix, is located in a space excavated between the floor of the church and the ceiling of the prison. ✉*Clivio Argentario 1.*

Colosseo

▦6 C4–D4. The largest amphitheater in the Roman world (it could hold more than 70,000 spectators) was built by the emperors of the Flavian dynasty between AD 72 and AD 80, on a site earlier occupied by the artificial lake of Nero's immense Domus Aurea. Indeed its ancient name was the Amphitheater of Flavius, and the present name, which dates from the 8th century, derives from the colossal bronze statue of Nero, no longer in existence, that was more than 114 feet high. Here ancient Romans attended gladiator combats and hunts of wild animals. Romantic tales about the sacrifice of Christians to wild beasts have no historical basis. But the Coliseum has always provoked a number of legends and popular fantasies, making it a symbol of the city and its rule. The Venerable Bede's prediction (8th century) is well known: "As long as there is the Coliseum, there will be Rome; as long as there is Rome, there will be the world." The last Coliseum spectacle we know of took place in 523, a date that marks the beginning of the monument's abandonment and deterioration. During subsequent centuries it was used as a quarry

2

The Arch of Constantine, with three barrel vaults, and, on the right, the Amphitheaterof Flavius, universally known as the Coliseum.

for building materials. During the baronial struggles of the Middle Ages, it was transformed into a fortress and later occupied by various institutions (hospitals, confraternities, and artisan associations) that profoundly altered its structure. The popes were the greatest exploiters of its stones, and between the 15th and 17th centuries the travertine of the ancient amphitheater provided material for major building projects, from S. Giovanni in Laterano to S. Pietro, from the Palazzo Venezia to the Palazzo della Cancelleria, from the Palazzo Barberini to the Porto di Ripetta. In light of this merciless plunder, Bernini took a remarkable stance in opposition to the practice, and planned the overall renovation of the complex for the 1675 Jubilee. These plans called for the construction of a church at the center of the arena, to be consecrated to the martyred saints who supposedly died on this site (there was already a chapel here). The project was never built, but the 1675 Jubilee decreed the sanctity of the site, an act confirmed by Benedict XIV in the mid-18th century, with the building of the 14 stations of the Via Crucis and with an edict prohibiting the monument's desecration. During the 19th century there was an increase in restoration, consolidation, and excavation work, and the Coliseum gradually was cleared of the vegetation that had covered it and structures that had been added over the course of time. ⊠*Piazza del Colosseo.*

Foro Romano ①

▦6 C2. Throughout the entire republican period the Roman Forum was the center of the city's political, commercial, and religious activity; the repository of its mythological and historical traditions; and, with home to its statuary, edifices, and commemorative monuments, a site of celebration of Rome's power. The long history of the Forum begins with the origins of the city (8th century BC) and ends in the 7th century AD, when the area was abandoned and decayed into an accumulation of ruins outside the medieval city. The only architectural elements to survive were the few temples that were transformed into churches, beginning in the 6th century, including S. Adriano, Ss. Cosma e Damiano, S. Maria Antiqua, the Oratorio dei Quaranta Martiri, and S. Lorenzo in Miranda. A few other structures were preserved and surrounded by fortified complexes belonging to the nobility. The Forum disappeared from historical memory, and the few literary attempts to reconstruct its ancient appearance (such as the *Mirabilia Urbis Romae,* the principal guide to the city during the Middle Ages) confused the buildings and capriciously mixed Christian and pagan traditions. During the Renaissance, when it was reduced to a grazing site, the Forum was plundered irremediably and utilized as a stone quarry for the rebuilding of the city. The new Rome of the popes destroyed the Rome of the Caesars precisely at a moment when the most cultivated Renaissance courts were harboring a passion for antiquity. The studies of German archaeologist Johann Joachim Winckelmann during the 18th century opened a new era of research, archeological excavations, and laws for the preservation of monuments, all of which have finally allowed the reconstruction of the area's millennial history. ⊠*Via dei Fori Imperiali and Piazza S. Maria Nova.*

Monastero di Tor de' Specchi

▦6 B1. The convent was founded in 1433 by Roman noblewoman Francesca de Ponziani (St. Frances of Rome), who established a congregation of Benedictine Oblates dedicated to charitable works (oblates dedicate themselves to service and take a vow of obedience from which they may withdraw at any time). The severe building encloses delightful cloisters and rooms, including the Cappella Vecchia, illuminated by Gothic windows, decorated with a fresco cycle (ca. 1468) with 25 scenes from the life of St. Frances, and covered with a fine 15th-century ceiling. Another space, perhaps designed as a refectory, has a green decorative scheme (ca. 1485) depicting the temptations of St. Frances. In 1596, in addition to the already existing **church of S. Maria de Curte**, a church consecrated to the **Ss. Annunziata** was erected. ⊠*Via della Tribuna di Tor de' Specchi 40.*

Oratorio di S. Giovanni in Oleo

▦8 D6. This small octagonal structure, perhaps a martyrium, was built in the 5th century on the site where the saint was thought to have suffered immersion in a cauldron of boiling oil, from which he emerged unharmed. Francesco Borromini, who designed an unusual coping for the circular drum, restored the building in 1658. The interior decoration (with *Scenes from the Life of St. John the Evangelist*) is dated 1716. ⊠*Via di Porta Latina.*

Orti Farnesiani
(Farnese Gardens)

▦6 C2–D2. The gardens were created by Cardinal Alessandro Farnese, nephew of Paul III, during the mid-16th century in an area of the Palatine rich in symbolic significance because it is tied to the mythical origins of Rome and to

③ Piazza del Campidoglio was created beginning in 1536 according to a design by Michelangelo, at the behest of Pope Paul III. The statue of Marcus Aurelius, at the center of the piazza, is a copy of the Roman original, now in the Musei Capitolini.

S. Francesca Romana ④, with its splendid five-story, 12th-century Romanesque bell tower, one of the most beautiful in the capital, framed by the ruins of the Roman Forum.

the memory of the emperors who had their opulent residences here. This nearly century-long project was begun by Il Vignola and completed by Carlo Rainaldi. An entrance in the Forum led through a series of ramps to the *Ninfeo della Pioggia* (a grotto) and the *Teatro del Fontanone,* then to an upper terrace with gardens and two aviaries built in the shape of arched pavilions with pagoda-style roofs. Little remains of the original gardens, the most beautiful on the Palatine; the present layout, with rectangular avenues and a variety of rare and exotic plants, is almost entirely the result of 19th-century projects. ⊠*Archaeological Zone of the Palatine.*

Palatino (Palatine)
▦6 C2–D2–D3. This is the hill where, according to tradition, Romulus founded Rome in the 8th century BC; here, too, near Romulus's hut, the first emperor, Augustus, constructed his house. His successors followed suit and built increasingly opulent dwellings. In time, the name of the hill, "palatium," became a term associated in all European languages with grand formal buildings. The shift of imperial power to Constantinople marked the beginning of the decline for the Palatine, although it continued to be, at irregular intervals, a location for sovereigns and popes. During the Byzantine domination, when the Dux (leader) of Rome resided here, Christian houses of worship were established over the ancient ruins. In the late 4th century, a space from Domitian's palace was occupied by an oratory dedicated to St. Caesarius, then converted to a monastery of Greek monks; S. Anastasia was founded during the same period. Subsequently S. Teodoro, S. Maria Antiqua, and the Monastery of S. Maria in Pallara were built; the latter was later dedicated to St. Sebastian. During the 11th and 12th centuries the hill was fortified and became the site of ferocious baronial struggles. In the Renaissance it was occupied by the principal patrician families, who covered it with villas and gardens, the most famous of which belonged to the Farnese (the Orti Farnesiani). Excavations and often vandalism were carried out during the 18th century; in the 19th century there began to be systematic archaeological research, which continues today. The archaeological area of the Palatine, in addition to containing an extraordinary group of masterpieces of ancient art, preserves a crude graffito that is of great importance to the history of Christian iconography: a crucified man with the head of a donkey, and a man at the foot of the cross with his arm raised and a Greek inscription that reads Alexamenos Worships His God. The author of the drawing was clearly making fun of a Christian. Dating from the first half of the 3rd century AD, this is one of the oldest representations of the Crucifixion. ⊠*Via S. Gregorio.*

Piazza del Campidoglio ③
▦6 B1. For centuries the Campidoglio was a center and symbol of power. First it was the stronghold of early Rome, then the location of prestigious public buildings, the mint, the state archives and, above all, the Temple of Jupiter, the greatest sanctuary in ancient Rome. It became the site of the most solemn public ceremonies, such as the investiture of the consuls and the celebration of military triumphs. Its sacred role endured through subsequent eras. Medieval German emperors came here to formally request the approval of the Roman people, and this is the site where the great poets were crowned with laurel. Beginning in the 12th century, the hill became the center of executive, judicial, and commercial power, and it was the principal site for government offices (the Senatori and Conservatori) and associations of artists and craftsmen. But the growing power of the papacy gradually did away with the municipal authorities centered on the Campidoglio and took over what had been the symbol of Rome's greatness, removing all trappings of civil power from the site. Paul III decided that the Campidoglio should become a site that symbolized the church's supremacy, and he turned the large-scale project over to Michelangelo. The artist came up with a theatrical solution—a trapezoidal terrace, with the senate building at the back, framed by two side palazzi, overlooking the city from a monumental staircase. The fulcrum of the piazza was the **equestrian statue of Marcus Aurelius,** a rare ancient bronze that escaped destruction because it was thought to be a portrait of Constantine, the first Christian emperor. This was the first monumental piazza in modern Rome, and the magnificent stage was the setting for a pause in the solemn papal processions from the Vatican to the Lateran, where the pope received homage from the Capitoline magistrates. Many churches, convents, and houses were built around the piazza and later demolished to make way for the construction of the monument to Vittorio Emanuele. The Campidoglio continues to be a place of power and memory of the ancient world. The senate building houses the offices of the municipal

administration, and the buildings on either side contain the **Musei Capitolini** (the Capitoline Museums), the oldest public art collection (which began with a donation from Sixtus IV in 1471) and one of the most magnificent in the world. ✉*Musei Capitolini, Piazza del Campidoglio,* ☎*06/671-03069.*

S. Anastasia

▦6 D2. The church was built at the foot of the Palatine in the 4th century, perhaps through the initiative of a sister of the emperor Constantine, who wanted to dedicate it to the venerated 3rd-century Roman martyr. Some of the saint's relics are in the church. During the Byzantine domination it became the official church of representatives of the Eastern empire who resided on the Palatine. After various renovations over the course of centuries, it was entirely rebuilt in the late 17th century, at the behest of Urban VIII, and the interior was redecorated in the early 18th century. ✉*Piazza S. Anastasia.*

S. Francesca Romana ④

▦6 C3. The church was built in the 9th century above the earlier Oratory of Ss. Pietro e Paolo, which in turn had been erected within the ancient Temple of Venus and Rome (2nd century AD). It was called S. Maria Nova to distinguish it from S. Maria Antiqua in the Roman Forum. The church was restored in the 12th century (the bell tower and beautiful apse mosaics depicting the Madonna and child with saints date from this phase) and was rebuilt once again in the 17th century. At the beginning of that century it took its present name, after the body of St. Frances of Rome was moved here from the Tor de' Specchi Convent. The sacristy contains a 5th-century icon with an image of the Virgin and some interesting paintings from the 16th to the 18th centuries. ✉*Piazza S. Francesca Romana 4.*

S. Giovanni a Porta Latina

▦8 D6. Built in the 5th century in the vicinity of the Oratory of S. Giovanni in Oleo, this church was renovated many times over the centuries, until the most recent restoration, which returned it to its Romanesque appearance. The interior, on a basilica plan, has an interesting painting cycle with *Scenes from the Old and New Testaments* dating from the 12th century. ✉*Via di Porta Latina 17.*

S. Gregorio Magno

▦6 E3. The church was built on the site of St. Gregory the Great's home, where the saint established a monastery in 575, dedicated to St. Andrew. The present exterior is the result of a 1629–1633 renovation ordered by Cardinal Scipione Borghese. The interior dates from the 18th century. The Salviati Chapel contains an ancient fresco of the Madonna and child, which, according to tradition, spoke to the saint. There is also a beautiful marble altar from the 15th century. At the back of the right nave is another prized altar, decorated with bas-reliefs depicting the so-called *30 Masses of St. Gregory.* Next to the church are three small chapels built in the early 17th century. The one in the center, dedicated to St. Andrew, has frescoes by Domenichino and Guido Reni (1608); the one on the right is the Oratory of St. Sylvia, mother of St. Gregory, and has a lively *Concert of Angels* by Guido Reni in the apse vault. The third chapel, dedicated to St. Barbara, has a large marble table from the 3rd century, said to be the one where an angel sat next to the poor to whom St. Gregory offered a meal. This legend, one of many connected to this extraordinary figure, is often represented in his iconography. ✉*Piazza S. Gregorio 1.*

S. Lorenzo in Miranda ⑤

▦6 C2. The ancient pagan temple of Antoninus and Faustina (AD 141) was transformed in the 7th century into a church, which preserved the solemn vestibule and six columns in front of the Baroque facade. It is dedicated to St. Laurence of Rome, one of the city's most venerated figures, perhaps because it was on this site that the trial took place that condemned him to martyrdom. The name "in Miranda" might derive from the Latin verb *mirari* (to admire), referring to the magnificent panorama of the Roman Forum that opened in front of the building. In 1429, Martin V gave the church to the Collegio degli Speziali (College of Chemists or Herbalists), now the Collegio Chimico Farmaceutico, which retains St. Laurence as its patron saint. The painting on the high altar, by Pietro da Cortona, depicts *The Martyrdom of St. Laurence* (1640). ✉*Via in Miranda 10.*

S. Maria Antiqua

▦6 C2. The church was installed in the 6th century in a room of a 1st-century AD building, perhaps part of the ancient imperial palace. It was called "Antiqua" in the 10th century, after a church erected over the temple of Venus and Rome

A

S. Maria in Aracoeli ⑥ has three naves divided by ancient columns made from different types of marble; (A) an ornate coffered wooden ceiling, and (B) a 13th-century brick facade.

The extraordinary Baroque altar in S. Maria in Campitelli's ⑦ was designed by Carlo Rainaldi (1667), who was also responsible for the overall design of the building; at the center, a priceless miraculous image of the Virgin.

⑥

⑦

became known as S. Maria Nova (S. Francesca Romana). Pontiffs from the East, who occupied the papacy for more than 150 years, lavished attention on this church, commissioning paintings for its walls many times over. The results are still visible in the exceptional layering of frescoes (at some points up to five superimposed one on top of another), which attest to the different styles in Roman art during the Byzantine period. These range from stiff frontal representations, similar to icons, such as a Virgin and child enthroned, to the right of the apse, to more fluid and naturalistic depictions, as in the fragmentary frescoes of the Annunciation, to the right of the apse (above the aforementioned Virgin) and on the southeast pier. At the time of Pope John VII (705–707), the building became the bishop's church of Rome and the center of Eastern-inspired piety in the city. The nearby **Oratorio dei Quaranta Martiri** (Oratory of the 40 Martyrs) is decorated with 8- and 9th-century frescoes of the torture of 40 soldiers put to death in Armenia because of their Christian faith during the persecutions of Diocletian. ✉*Largo Romolo e Remo 1.*

S. Maria in Aracoeli ⑥

▦**6 B1.** The church was erected in the 7th century at the highest point of the Capitoline Hill. It was a Benedictine abbey from the 10th century until the mid-13th century, when it was taken over by the Franciscans. The name of the church (which did not appear before the 14th century) recalls the legend that the emperor Augustus had an altar built here following the appearance of the Virgin and a prophecy announcing to him the birth of the Redeemer. The event is represented in a 12th-century altar in the left transept. During the late 13th century the church assumed its present form, and in 1348 the monumental stairway leading to the church was added as an offering to the Virgin for the end of the plague. The original austere atmosphere of the Franciscan church was altered over the centuries by the addition of an enormous quantity of ornaments, furnishings, and funerary monuments. The principal works include frescoes by Pinturicchio of *Scenes from the Life of St. Bernardine* (1486); Benozzo Gozzoli's *St. Anthony* (1454–1458); the *Tomb of Luca Savelli,* (ca. 1287), attributed to Arnolfo di Cambio; the tombstone of Giovanni Crivelli by Donatello (1432); and the 14th-century presbytery pulpits. As in all significant Roman churches dedicated to the Madonna, this one has a venerated Marian icon above the high altar; the painting dates from the 11th century. In a chapel next to the sacristy is a statue of the *Holy Child,* sculpted, according to legend, from wood from an olive tree in Gethsemane. The sculpture is an object of secular veneration because of its supposed miraculous powers, including the ability to heal the sick and resuscitate the dead. ✉*Piazza del Campidoglio 4.*

S. Maria in Campitelli ⑦

▦**5 B6.** The church was built in 1662–1667, on the site of an earlier church, to house an image of the Madonna to which the people attributed the miracle of the liberation of the city from the plague of 1656. Alexander VII entrusted Carlo Rainaldi with the design, and it is one of the architect's most successful projects. The facade with superimposed niches is enlivened by the skillful use of detached columns, and the interior has an original juxtaposition of a grand Greek-cross space and a narrower space with a dome and apse. The miraculous image of Mary on the high altar is a precious 11th-century work. ✉*Piazza Campitelli 9.*

S. Maria della Consolazione

▦**6 C1.** The church has its origins in the last wish expressed by a man condemned to death in 1385. On the site of his execution, beneath the nearby Tarpeian Rock, he asked that an image of the Madonna be placed, to console those who were sentenced to death. Later miracles attributed to this image made this a venerated site, and the church was built, then renovated starting in 1583 by Martino Longhi the Elder. Until 1936 the spacious edifice behind the church was occupied by the Ospedale della Consolazione, a hospital that specialized in trauma care, where physicians worked alongside benefactors and saints, including St. Luis Gonzaga, who died here in 1591 attending to victims of cholera. ✉*Piazza della Consolazione 84.*

S. Maria in Domnica

▦**6 F4.** This church is also known as S. Maria della Navicella, because of the presence of a small marble boat (*navicella*) in the piazza opposite, a 16th-century copy of an ancient ex-voto. Built in the 7th century on the site of a Roman barracks, the church and oratory constituted one of the first charitable institutions in the city dedicated to assisting the poor. It was rebuilt under Paschal I between 818 and 822 and restored during the 16th century, when the elegant exterior portico and wonderful inlay and gilded coffered ceiling were executed. The precious apse mosaics date from the time of Paschal I and are an important example of Roman art from the Carolingian period. The triumphal arch is dominated by the figure of Christ between two angels and the apostles, and the lower register

⑧

depicts Moses and Elijah. The vault of the apse has an image of the Virgin and child enthroned amid hosts of angels, with Paschal I kneeling and humbly touching her feet. ✉ *Piazza Navicella 10.*

S. Sebastiano al Palatino

▦6 D3. The entire eastern section of the Palatine (in the area of the churches of S. Sebastiano and S. Bonaventura) is occupied by a gigantic terraced area surmounted by the large temple of the god Elagabalus, who was identified with the sun. It was erected by the emperor of the same name (3rd century AD), who wanted to be worshiped as a god. The most sacred objects in Rome were assembled in this edifice, including the venerated Palladium, the ancient image of Pallas Athena from Troy. This explains the name of the church, **S. Maria in Pallara** (from the Palladium), erected in the Middle Ages in this area and later consecrated to St. Sebastian who, according to tradition, was martyred here. Mentioned in documents as far back as the 10th century, the church preserves some painting fragments from this era in the apse. The rest of the church was destroyed during the renovation ordered by Urban VIII in 1624. A short distance away, at 7 Via S. Bonaventura, is the church and monastery of **S. Bonaventura,** erected in 1625 by St. Bonaventure Grau, on the site of an ancient cistern of the Claudian aqueduct. ✉ *Via S. Bonaventura 1.*

S. Sisto Vecchio

▦8 C4. This ancient church (mentioned in the 4th century) is consecrated to Sixtus II, a pope and martyr killed during the persecutions of the emperor Valerian (258), along with many of his companions, including the deacon Laurence, to whom he is closely linked. In the 6th century Sixtus II's remains were moved to the church from the Catacombs of St. Calixtus. The church was rebuilt by Innocent III and in 1219 was given to St. Dominic de Guzmán, who established his first monastery in Rome here. The Romanesque bell tower dates from this period, as do some vestiges in the cloister and an interesting fresco cycle with *Scenes from the New Testament and the Apocrypha.* The entire complex was radically restructured in 1724–1730 by Benedict XIII. ✉ *Piazzale Numa Pompilio 8.*

S. Teodoro

▦6 C2. This church on a central plan was built around the mid-6th century, during a period of strong Byzantine influence in both art and religious orientation, confirmed by the dedication to St. Theodore of Euchaita, one of the most venerated Eastern martyrs, patron of soldiers and armed forces. The structure was entirely rebuilt by Pope Nicholas V (1453–1554), and the piazza opposite and the two-flight staircase are by Carlo Fontana (1703–1705). The apse mosaics of *The Redeemer with Sts. Peter, Paul, and Theodore* are from the original church. ✉ *Via di San Teodoro 7.*

S. Tommaso in Formis

▦6 E4. In 1207, Innocent III granted the ancient little church of S. Tommaso to St. John of Matha, who immediately installed the order he had founded in France, which was dedicated to the worship of the Trinity and to freeing slaves and prisoners. Near the church the Trinitarian fathers built a hospital, which prospered for two centuries, then fell into decline and was destroyed in 1925. The church, restored many times between the 16th and 18th centuries, has lost most of its medieval furnishings and structure. Of the Trinitarian monastic complex and hospital, part of the side facade remains, with a pointed arch door and a broad Romanesque entrance surmounted by a mosaic niche with a depiction of Jesus between two freed slaves. ✉ *Via S. Paolo della Croce 10.*

Ss. Cosma e Damiano ⑧

▦6 C2. The structure is the result of the unification of two buildings from the imperial period donated by King Theodoric to Pope Felix IV. The pontiff consecrated the buildings to Cosmas and Damian, two Eastern brothers who were physicians and martyrs, perhaps in opposition to the pagan cult of the Dioscuri, which had a temple nearby in the Roman Forum. The total renovation by Urban VIII (1632) saved the precious original mosaics in the apse, which depict Christ with Sts. Peter and Paul presenting the titular saints of the church, who hold their crowns of martyrdom, accompanied by St. Theodore of Euchaita and Felix IV. The grandeur of the figures, the balance of the composition, and the precise characterization are clear reminders of classical art inserted within a typically medieval transcendent atmosphere. Compositions with seven figures were enormously popular in Rome and perhaps had as their model the mosaic apse in S. Giovanni in Laterano, which no longer survives. ✉ *Via dei Fori Imperiali 1.*

The bowl-shaped apse vault of Ss. Cosma e Damiano ⑧. The unusual 6th- to 7th-century mosaic echoes a Roman compositional scheme with seven figures (Christ; Sts. Peter, Paul Cosma, Damian and Theodore; and Felix IV).

Piazza dei Ss. Giovanni e Paolo ⑨ is dominated by the brick mass of the church of the same name. The original structure is early Christian, and the superb bell tower is Romanesque. This is one of the quietest and most evocative corners in the Celio district.

⑨

⑩

Ss. Giovanni e Paolo ⑨

▦6 E4. The basilica has its origins in a titular church established in the house of the martyr brothers John and Paul, two Christian officials put to death during the papacy of Julian the Apostate (361–363) after they were discovered donating their wealth to poor Christians. The building was restored in the 12th century with the addition of a portico, a beautiful Romanesque bell tower (erected on the ruins of a Roman temple), and a monastery. In subsequent centuries the building underwent various renovations, and in 1952 the early Christian facade was restored. Excavations have uncovered a complex of 1st- to 5th-century buildings beneath the church, a noteworthy testament to early Christianity's existence within the pagan world. Some of the spaces have frescoes with mythological scenes, while others are decorated with Christian images, including the execution of three people, probably Crispus, Crispinianus, and Benedicta, companions of the titular saints. Next to the basilica is the 19th-century **Chapel of S. Paolo della Croce,** founder of the Passionist fathers (1694–1775), who have cared for the church since 1773. In addition to the three usual vows (poverty, chastity, and obedience), members of the order take a fourth vow to promote the devotion of Christ's Passion. ✉*Piazza dei Ss. Giovanni e Paolo 13.*

Ss. Luca e Martina ⑩

▦6 B2. During the 6th century a church was built here, dedicated to the martyr St. Martina (who lived in the 3rd century). The church was said to be "in three forums" because it is situated at the point where the Roman Forum meets the forums of Cesar and Augustus. Sixtus V gave the church to the Drawing Academy of St. Luke (1588), which had been established shortly before to offer apprenticeships and theoretical training to young artists. Restoration work directed by Pietro da Cortona, head of the academy, brought to light the bodies of several martyrs, including Martina. This led Urban VIII and his nephew, Cardinal Francesco Barberini, to finance construction of a grander building (the pope's coat of arms crowns the facade, and the heraldic bees of the Barberini appear throughout the church). Working for nearly 30 years (1635–1664), Pietro da Cortona created one of the most refined Baroque churches in Rome. In addition to a statue of the saint in a supine position by Niccolò Menghini (1635), there is a crypt, sumptuously decorated with marble and columns, and a gilded bronze altar above the tomb of St. Martina, another masterpiece by Pietro da Cortona. ✉*At the entrance to the Roman Forum.*

Ss. Quattro Coronati

▦6 D5. The dedication to four "crowned" saints, that is saints conferred with the crown of martyrdom, is somewhat complicated. One tradition speaks of four soldiers condemned for not having recognized the divinity of Asclepiades. These figures were later confused with four other Roman martyrs, Severus, Victorinus, Carpophorus, and Severian. This tale was then layered with a story of Dalmatian sculptors killed by Diocletian for refusing to sculpt a statue of that pagan god, with the result that this church is venerated by an association of stonecutters and marble workers. Erected in the 5th century, the church was transformed into a basilica by Leo IV (847–855), who was responsible for moving the remains of the martyred saints into the marble arches of the crypt. Between the 12th and 13th centuries a monastery and a charming cloister were added, and in 1246 the complex was transformed into a fortress, which often served as a refuge for pontiffs who did not feel safe in the Lateran. During this period the monastery chapel (the Oratory of St. Sylvester), reserved for private masses of the pope and curia, was decorated with a painting cycle depicting the legend of Sts. Sylvester and Constantine. The cycle was an outright papal manifesto that openly stated the pontiff's supremacy over the imperial power, embodied at that time in the extremely feared Holy Roman Emperor Frederick II . ✉*Piazza Ss. Quattro Coronati 20.*

10

Ripa, S. Saba, and Testaccio

In ancient times this area was populous, animated, and teeming with warehouses and commercial activity connected to the large river port. During the Middle Ages it became solitary and rural, scattered with abandoned ruins and isolated monastic settlements, and often afflicted by swampiness and malaria because of flooding of the Tiber. Urbanization did not come until the late 19th century, but construction tended to be respectful of the landscape and left open broad, unbuilt areas. In modern times, the district has developed various faces: an aristocratic, refined neighborhood on the Aventine; public buildings at the foot of the hill, near the river; and the working-class district of Testaccio.

Aventino

▦8 A1–A2. The solitude and silence that characterize this hill perpetuate its isolation, which dates from the most distant days of antiquity, and in fact the Aventine was not included within the urban boundaries until the 1st century AD. The district's archaeological legacy was in large part destroyed by post–World War II building development, but there are numerous vestiges of early Christian and medieval times. Some of the first and most significant early Christian places of worship were established here (S. Balbina, S. Prisca, S. Saba, S. Sabina), as well as monasteries and fortified settlements. Post-medieval architectural projects, such as the 18th-century compound of the Knights of Malta, by Giovanni Battista Piranesi, involved the modification and renovation of already existing buildings.

Casa dei Crescenzi

▦6 D1. The house of the Crescenzi, the most powerful Roman family from the 10th to the 12th century, was built between 1040 and 1065 to control the Tiber port that lay opposite. Like many of the fortresses built during the Middle Ages by the baronial class, the structure reutilized architectural elements from ancient monuments: the corbels with cherubs, the cornice, ceiling coffers with rosettes used as a window parapet. In addition to obvious practical and economic reasons, this recycling was dictated by a desire to "restore the ancient dignity of Rome," according to a long Latin inscription over the entrance arch. The building was used during the Middle Ages as the house of Pilate in the Easter Passion play along the Via Crucis, and the structure is also known by this name. ✉ *Via Petroselli 54.*

Cimetero degli Inglesi (English Cemetery)

▦8 D1. A source of fascination for many 19th-century Romantic artists, the Protestant or English cemetery is still extremely evocative. The cemetery was established in the 18th century for foreigners who were of other religious faiths and could not be buried in Catholic cemeteries. Set at the foot of the Pyramid of Gaius Cestius (the tomb of an eccentric 1st-century BC Roman, who wanted to emulate the pharaohs), it provides a solitary landscape of meadows, pines, and cypress trees that frames the tombs. Numerous famous figures are buried here, including poets John Keats and Percy Bysshe Shelley; painter Joseph Severn; and Antonio Gramsci, intellectual, co-founder of the Communist party in Italy, aetheist, and one of the few Italians buried here. ✉ *Via Caio Cestio.*

Complesso dell'Ordine dei Cavalieri di Malta (Compound of the Order of Knights of Malta) ②

▦5 F6. The Order of the Knights of Malta grew out of the Order of St. John of Jerusalem. Established in the 11th century, the Knights of Malta were a charitable rather than military organization, although their holdings on Rhodes and Malta created an effective defense against the Turkish threat. The compound's current appearance is the result of a radical restoration, ordered in 1764 by Cardinal G.B. Rezzonico (grand master of the order and nephew of Clement XIII) and entrusted to the period's most well known engraver, Giovanni Battista Piranesi. This was Piranesi's only architectural project, and it is a masterpiece of Neoclassical urban design. Recurrent motifs from the artist's prints are translated into stone: walls punctuated by obelisks, niches and trophies of arms alluding to the order's history, and the heraldic symbols of the Rezzonico family. Similar motifs appear on the facade of the adjacent church, **S. Maria del Priorato,** which appears to be made of fragments of ancient marbles. A peek through the keyhole of the door at number 3 in the piazza offers an beautiful framed view of the gigantic dome of S. Pietro. ✉ *Piazza Cavalieri di Malta 4.*

Isola Tiberina (Tiber Island) ①

▦5 C5–C6. Among the many legends that surround the island, the most famous refers to its boat-like shape, said to derive from the ship of Aesculapian, god of medicine, whom Romans invoked during a

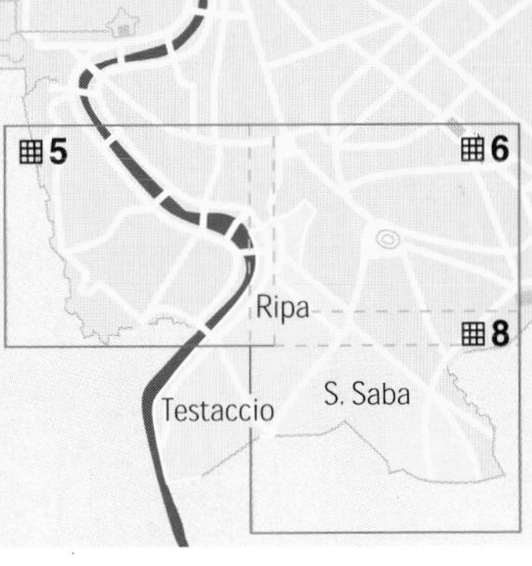

A shrine on the wall that encloses the Compound of the Order of the Knights of Malta, an exquisite Neoclassical project by Piranesi (1764–1766).

plague and to whom they dedicated a temple and hospital. From that time on the island was associated with healing. In 1584, the **Ospedale Fatebenefratelli** was built (and still stands in the piazza of the same name) by the Congregation of S. Giovanni di Dio. This group's members also were called "Fatebenefratelli" (literally "do good, brothers"), the phrase they would repeat when they asked for alms. The area was transformed into a leper asylum during the plague of 1656. The church of **S. Bartolomeo** (Piazza di S. Bartolomeo all'Isola) was built by the Holy Roman Emperor Otto II (10th century) on the ruins of the Temple of Aesculapian. The medieval well near the altar probably served as the old hospital font, said to have had extraordinary therapeutic properties. Often damaged by frequent floodings of the Tiber, the church was rebuilt in 1113 by Pope Paschal II, who gave the building one of the most harmonious Romanesque bell towers in Rome. The building was renovated in Baroque style in 1624. A porphyry basin beneath the high altar contains the remains of the apostle and martyr Bartholomew, who was famous for the miraculous healings he wrought during his work as an evangelist.

S. Alessio

▦5 F6. Dating from perhaps the 4th century and originally dedicated to St. Boniface, in the 10th century this church became a significant religious center for the Benedictines and a departure point for some of the most active evangelizers of the time, including St. Adalbert, bishop of Prague. Although totally renovated in the 18th century, the church preserves some significant medieval structures, which for the most part date from the rebuilding under Pope Honorius III (1217). These are five bell towers; the mosaic entrance that reutilizes ancient marble from the imperial period; the two small columns in the apse, which come from the 13th-century choir; and the Romanesque crypt, the only one of its type in Rome, which contains the remains of St. Thomas of Canterbury. In the left nave, an ornate 18th-century chapel reveals vestiges of a staircase associated with the legend of St. Alexius. He was a young, wealthy 4th-century Roman who converted to Christianity and departed for the East, where he lived an ascetic life. Returning to Rome after 17 years, he worked as a slave in his father's house without being recognized, sleeping in a space beneath the staircase. The legend provided a wealth of material for music, poetry, and art during the Middle Ages and the Baroque period, when a great many chapels, altars, and staircases were dedicated to the saint. ✉ *Piazza S. Alessio 23.*

S. Balbina

▦8 B3. According to tradition, St. Balbina, daughter of Quirinus, a Roman tribune, was killed with her father around the year 130 because they were both Christians. The church is first mentioned in a 6th-century document as Sanctae Balbinae, but its origins are older. Rebuilt many times, the church's current Romanesque appearance is the result of a radical restoration carried out in 1930. The high altar has a jasper urn containing the remains of the saint, her father, and St. Felicissimus. The sixth niche to the left has a fresco depicting the *Crucifixion of St. Peter* (12th century), perhaps connected to the legend that the chains of St. Peter were discovered by Balbina. A second legend relates how St. Balbina healed Pope Alexander I, who was also persecuted and imprisoned for his faith, by laying these same chains around his neck. For this reason Balbina is the patron saint of goiter patients. The most interesting work of art in the church is a marble relief with a *Crucifixion* dating from the 15th century (the fourth niche on the right). ✉ *Piazza S. Balbina 8.*

S. Cesareo de Appia

▦8 C5. Clement VIII, whose insignia are inscribed in the elegant gilded ceiling inside, rebuilt this church in the 16th century. It stands above a Roman house from the 2nd century AD, and a part of that building's black and white mosaic floor with sea scenes is still visible. The column in front of the building, like many others in Rome, indicated that this was a hospice-hospital for medieval pilgrims. ✉ *Via Porta S. Sebastiano.*

S. Eligio dei Ferrari
(St. Eligius of the Ironworkers)

▦6 C1. In 1453, Pope Nicholas V granted a small medieval church to the school of an assocation of iron artisans known as the Università dei Ferrari. The church was rebuilt and expanded in the following century, when it took on an exuberant Baroque appearance. St. Eligius was the patron saint of metal craftsmen, including goldsmiths, who left the university and the Confraternity of Ironworkers in 1509 and built their own church, S. Eligio degli Orefici. ✉ *Via S. Giovanni Decollato 9.*

S. Giorgio in Velabro

▦6 D1. "In Velabro" comes from the ancient name for the swampy depression between the Campidoglio and the Palatine, which was subject to recurring floods of the Tiber. The building was erected in the 5th–6th century in a Greek neighborhood and was

(A) The 18th-century Fontana del Tritone and, in the background, the facade and bell tower of S. Maria in Cosmedin ③.(B) The portico of the church contains the Bocca della Verità, a marble disk from the classical period, which is linked to a famous legend.

Detail of the decoration of a small, well-preserved sarcophagus in the 15th-century portico of S. Saba ④.

profoundly marked by Byzantine influences, which were also evident in other nearby churches (S. Anastasia, S. Maria in Cosmedin, S. Teodoro). The titular saint, St. George the Great, is a martyr from Cappadocia (a region in modern Turkey) who was venerated in the Middle Ages, particularly in the East, as a patron saint of soldiers and knights. A 20th-century restoration returned the church to its original Romanesque appearance, with a simple facade preceded by a portico and a basilica interior divided by recycled antique columns. ✉ *Via del Velabro 19.*

S. Giovanni Decollato
(St. John Beheaded)

▦**6 D1.** The church was erected beginning in the late 15th century by the Florentine Archconfraternity of S. Giovanni Decollato, or the Misericordia, which was established to assist victims of capital punishment. In 1540, the confraternity obtained the privilege of yearly freeing one person sentenced to death. The church's interior is completely frescoed by Tuscan Mannerist artists, as is the lovely oratory, which is decorated with scenes from the life of St. John the Baptist. The adjacent porticoed cloister, inspired by the Florentine Renaissance, was a burial place for the condemned who were put to death. The compound houses an archive and a museum related to the confraternity's activities. ✉ *Via S. Giovanni Decollato 22.*

S. Maria in Cosmedin ③

▦**6 D1.** The area in which the church stands, between the Velabrum and the Aventine, was inhabited by a populous Greek colony that was particularly important between the 7th and 9th centuries. Byzantium was politically supreme at that time, and there was an influx of refugees escaping to Rome from the iconoclast persecutions in the Byzantine Empire. The church has its origins in a lay charitable organization from the 6th century and was founded above the ancient Ara Massima of Hercules. It was rebuilt many times over the centuries, until a 19th-century project restored the Romanesque forms from the 12th century, the period its greatest splendor. The name derives from the Greek "kosmein" (to embellish), referring to the church's considerable decorative scheme, much of which was executed by mosaic artists. The sacristy preserves a mosaic on a gold ground that depicts the *Epiphany* (8th century) and was removed from the ancient basilica of S. Pietro. The church has another popular attraction: the ancient drain-cover with the face of a river god, located beneath the portico. It is called the **Bocca della Verità** (Mouth of Truth), because, according to legend, the hand of a liar, placed in the mouth opening, would be bitten. ✉ *Piazza Bocca della Verità 18.*

S. Omobono

▦**6 C1.** The 15th-century church of S. Salvatore in Portico (probably erected over a pagan edifice) was granted in 1575 to the Università dei Sarti, an association of tailors, who restored it and dedicated it to their patron saint, Homobonus of Cremona, a fabric merchant and miracle-worker. Near the church are the remains of a sacred area of exceptional archaeological importance, the two temples of Fortuna and Mater Matuta, discovered here in 1937. The temples were built by the Etruscan king Servius Tullius (579 BC–53 BC) and destroyed in the late 6th century when the republican regime was established, then rebuilt in the 4th century BC. Subsequent excavations have uncovered ancient materials from the Bronze Age (14th–13th century BC). ✉ *Vico Jugario*

S. Prisca

▦**8 B1-2.** Built between the 4th and 5th centuries, this church stands over a Roman residence that tradition identifies as the home of the young Prisca, daughter of Aquila and Priscilla, who offered hospitality to St. Peter and accompanied St. Paul on some of his missionary voyages. Prisca was baptized by Peter (the episode is depicted in the fine painting on the high altar). At the age of 13, she was condemned to be thrown to the lions and miraculously emerged unharmed, but was later decapitated. Numerous rebuilding projects have altered the early Christian appearance of the building, the most interesting part of which still stands underground. Archaeological excavations have revealed a sanctuary dedicated to the worship of the god Mithras and the Roman building that contained the original early Christian place of worship. ✉ *Via S. Prisca 11.*

S. Saba ④

▦**8 C2.** In the 7th century this was the site of a monastery dedicated to St. Sabbas , a leading Eastern monastic figure (AD 439–AD 532). The Eastern monks were replaced in the 10th century by the Benedictines of Montecassino, who were succeeded in the 13th century by the Cluniac monks, who completely renovated the church, embellishing it with Roman marbles. Two centuries later the church was taken over by the Cistercians. The elegant entrance is by

⑤

Giacomo, father of Cosma, whose name (cosmatesque) was taken for a famous dynasty of Roman marble-workers and mosaicists. The austere interior houses other works by these artists, most of which have been restored, including the floor, canopy, and episcopal throne. Above the latter is a dramatic 14th-century *Crucifixion.* ✉ *Piazza. G. L. Bernini 20.*

S. Sabina ⑤

▦5 F6. This church is an extraordinary example of a 5th-century Western Christian basilica, with original structure, furnishings, and decorations. It was founded in 425 by a priest, Peter of Illyria, during the papacy of Celestine I. Restored during the 8th and 9th centuries, it was granted by Honorius III to St. Dominic de Guzmán just after he approved the new Order of Dominicans (1216), to whom the church still belongs. Later additions during the Renaissance and Baroque eras were for the most part eliminated during the 20th century. The church contains precious elements that have been completely lost in other buildings, such as the magnificent colonnade in Greek marble, the schola cantorum (space for the choir), marble inlay of the side walls of the central nave, windows that make the interior so luminous, and the exceptional entrance with finely carved wooden doors. The doors depict *Scenes from the Old and New Testament,* which illustrate correspondences between Moses (the Law) and Christ (the Gospel). The fine original mosaics are less well preserved; certain fragments remain from the interior of the facade, which still has a monumental inscription, in perfect gold letters against a blue background, that celebrates the donor, Peter of Illyria, and Pope Celestine I. The two female figures to the sides of the inscription personify the church of the pagans ("ecclesia ex gentibus") and the church of the Jews ("ecclesia ex circumcisione"). Adjacent to the church is a convent, founded by St. Dominic de Guzmán, where St. Thomas Aquinas taught. ✉ *Piazza Pietro d'Illiria 1.*

Ss. Nereo e Achilleo

▦8 C4. The establishment of this place of worship (4th century), originally called "titulus fasciolae," is connected to St. Peter, who, according to legend, while escaping from prison lost a bandage (fasciola) he had used to bind a wound caused by his chains. The church took its current name from the two martyrs, Nereus and Achilleus, who were killed by Diocletian in the 3rd century and buried in the Domitilla Catacombs. Their remains and those of St. Flavia Domitilla are buried beneath the high altar. In 814, Pope Leo III ordered some restoration work and embellished the church with mosaics, traces of which remain in the triumphal arch (*The Transfiguration, The Annunciation, Madonna and Child*). The interior has 16th-century frescoes with scenes from the lives of the martyrs, a mosaic choir and episcopal throne, and a delicately ornamented marble candelabrum from the 15th century. ✉ *Viale delle Terme di Caracalla 28.*

Terme di Caracalla

▦8 C3–C4. The majestic ruins of the bath complex, opened by the emperor Caracalla in 217, were the most fascinating monument of the so-called Archaeological Walk, which was created between 1887 and 1914 to preserve and link within a single park the ancient remains between Piazza Venezia and the Appia Antica. This project was destroyed during the fascist regime by the transformation of the footpaths into traffic arteries. The gigantic bath complex included not only areas for bathing, but also gymnasiums, libraries, musical auditoriums, meeting rooms, gardens, and porticos. It was a place for both sports and cultural activity, and it offered Roman citizens an infinite variety of occasions for relaxation and amusement. Although well preserved, the Baths of Caracalla were originally much more magnificent, decorated with a profusion of statues, marbles, stuccowork, and mosaics. ✉ *Viale delle Terme di Caracalla 52.*

11

Esquilino, Castro Pretorio, Sallustiano, and Ludovisi

An ancient roman bas-relief from the Museo Nazionale Romano, one of Italy's major museum of antiquity.

① 

▦4 Ludovisi Sallustiano Castro Pretorio ▦6 ▦7 Esquilino

During the early imperial period, the Esquiline rione, which corresponded to the eastern part of the hill of the same name, had many public buildings, opulent villas, and a dense network of roads that are largely still in existence. During the 4th and 5th centuries, the villas were replaced by the basilicas of S. Croce in Gerusalemme and S. Maria Maggiore and some of the oldest Christian places of worship (S. Bibiana and S. Eusebio). Since the late 16th century, following Sixtus V's urban reorganization, the hill began to be repopulated with patrician villas. After 1870 these were demolished to make way for public buildings and the clerical class of the new state. The other three rioni developed in somewhat similar fashion, with a few notable examples of monumental structures from classical times (such as the Gardens of Sallust and the Barracks of the Praetorian Guard) and large 16th- to 18th-century patrician villas (including the magnificent Villa Ludovisi). Most of these were destroyed by late 19th-century development that created ministries, diplomatic buildings and missions, luxury hotels, and new street plans. After World War II, the area underwent further urban renewal, often of very high quality.

Anfiteatro Castrense

▦7 E4. This small amphitheater next to the basilica of S. Croce in Gerusalemme was part of the Sessorian Palace, an imperial building from the Severian period (3rd century AD), and owes its partial preservation to its inclusion in the Aurelian Walls. Next to the arch opened in the wall in modern times is the **Cappella di S. Maria del Buon Aiuto,** built by Sixtus IV in 1476 to house an image of the Virgin found on the site. The chapel is also known as S. Maria di Spazzolaria (*spazzola* means "brush" or "broom"), because of the of alms that were gathered here, even with a broom. ✉ *Piazza S. Croce in Gerusalemme 12.*

Arco di Sisto V

▦7 A2 . This is the only monument that officially bears the name of Pope Sixtus V, who worked tirelessly to transform the urban fabric of Rome (as well as the organization of the church). He built the Acquedotto Felice (the pope's name was Felice Peretti) and amid its arcades inserted one monumental arch with three barrel vaults of peperino and travertine, beneath which a road passed to the Baths of Diocletian. The aqueduct reutilized the water sources of an imperial aqueduct near Colonna and ended in the monumental Fountain of Moses in Piazza S. Bernardo. ✉ *Piazzale Sisto V.*

Casino dell'Aurora

▦4 B2. Along with a large palazzo, now incorporated into the United States Embassy, the Casino dell'Aurora is the only surviving structure from the 17th-century Villa Ludovisi, once considered one of the most beautiful villa-parks in the world. The villa was destroyed by postunification building speculation. The Casino is a 16th-century building, renovated by Cardinal Ludovisi in the mid-17th century on a cruciform plan, and altered again during the 19th-century. The building's name derives from the exceptional frescoes executed by Il Guercino in 1621. The depictions of *Aurora* in the vault and allegories of *Day* and *Night* in the side lunettes were decisive for the future of Baroque painting, anticipating by a decade the illusionism of Pietro da Cortona. ✉ *Via Aurora.*

Collegium Russicum

▦6 A6. The college was established (1928–1929) by Pius XI, during a period of religious persecution in the Soviet Union, to provide the clergy with suitable training to reestablish relationships with the Russian world. Annexed to the college is the 14th-century church **S. Antonio Abate,** now presided over by Russian Catholics of Byzantine Slavic rite. A lovely Romanesque entrance still stands, and the church's 18th-century interior has been adapted to the needs of the Eastern rite. ✉ *Via Carlo Alberto 2.*

Fontana del Mosè (Fountain of Moses)

▦4 D3. Opposite the church of S. Maria della Vittoria, this famous monument was designed by Domenico Fontana for Sixtus V as a showpiece of the Acqua Felice, the ancient Claudian aqueduct restored by the pontiff. The water from the Alban Hills was carried to the city's highest elevations. Sculptures on the fountain evoke the voyage of the Jews in the desert under the guidance of Moses, whose statue stands in the central niche. ✉ *Piazza S. Bernardo.*

Palazzo Massimo alle Terme, Museo Nazionale Romano ①

▦4 E4. Established in 1889 as the archaeological museum of Italy's

②

③

new capital city, this museum was first located in the complex made up of the Baths of Diocletian and the large cloister of S. Maria degli Angeli. The enormous quantity of materials, and the need to organize them more appropriately, made it necessary to find new exhibition spaces. The state acquired the Palazzo Massimo alle Terme and the Palazzo Altemps. A century after its birth, the Museo Nazionale Romano has been reorganized and modernized. Its collection of original documents illustrates the history and development of Rome in ancient times: art, public and private life, religion, economics, urban planning, and settlements outside the city. The museum's holdings are organized in four separate locations: Palazzo Altemps, Baths of Diocletian, Crypta Balbi, and Palazzo Massimo alle Terme. The latter was built in 1883–1887 by the Jesuit priest Massimiliano Massimo to house an educational institute on the grounds of the Pope Sixtus V's opulent Villa Peretti Montalto, which was built between 1576 and 1588 and later demolished to make way for the railway station. An enormous quantity of materials documents every aspect of Roman art, from the republican era to the time of Constantine. There are precious works of art from public buildings and the grand residences of the senatorial class, as well as original Greek sculptures imported to Rome in ancient times. ✉*Largo di Villa Peretti 1,* ☎*06/489–03500.*

Porta Maggiore

⊞**7 C4.** The majestic architecture of this doorway through the Aurelian Walls, with two barrel vaults flanked by niches, was formed from the arcades of two aqueducts from the Roman period (1st century AD). Opposite the entrance is the **Tomb of Eurysace,** a Roman baker from the Augustinian period (30 BC), who built one of the most unusual funerary monuments in Rome. The cylindrical architectural elements simulate the containers in which he mixed bread dough, and the bas-relief frieze illustrates in detail the various phases of bread making. Facing the piazza is the entrance to the **basilica of Porta Maggiore,** a subterranean sanctuary from the 1st century AD. The basilica's walls are entirely decorated in stucco with mythological scenes, masks, and various decorative motifs. The interpretation of the images is uncertain, but they perhaps depict the liberation of the soul from the weight of the body and its metamorphosis into a different life. ✉*Piazza di Porta Maggiore.*

S. Bernardo alle Terme ②

⊞**4 D3.** The church was built in 1598, in one of the corner circular halls of the Baths of Diocletian, by order of Caterina Nobili Sforza, niece of Julius III. It was dedicated to St. Bernard of Clairvaux, patron saint and founder of the Cistercians. The cylindrical construction is surmounted by a broad dome (72 feet in diameter) embellished with octagonal coffers that diminish in size toward the central opening, similar to that of the Pantheon. In 1647, a chapel in honor of St. Francis of Assisi was added. The various funerary monuments include one to the German painter Johann Friedrich Overbeck, founder of the Nazarene art movement, which had a certain success in Rome during the first half of the 19th century. ✉*Piazza S. Bernardo.*

S. Bibiana

⊞**7 B2.** Pope Simplicius (AD 468–AD 483) had this church built in honor of Roman St. Bibiana, who was martyred a century before. According to tradition, the remains of 10,000 Christian martyrs lie in a cemetery on the site, but this has no basis in fact. The church was restored by Honorius III (1224), then given a Baroque renovation (1624–1626) by the young Gian Lorenzo Bernini, who began his career as an architect with this project. Bernini created the lovely statue of the saint for the high altar. A precious alabaster basin from the 4th century is said to contain the remains of the titular saint and her mother and sister, who also were martyrs. Near the entrance is the column to which Bibiana is said to have been tied before being whipped to death. Until the 18th century the dust from this column and the mint that grew on the saint's tomb were used as a remedy against epilepsy. ✉*Via Giolitti 154.*

S. Croce in Gerusalemme ③

⊞**7 D4–E4.** The church was built on the site of the Sessorium (from the Latin *sedere,* "to stay"), the large imperial palace of Septimus Severus (3rd century), to which the Anfiteatro Castrense also belonged. (That amphitheater and the Coliseum are the only Roman amphitheaters still standing in Rome.) According to tradition the basilica was erected (AD 320) by Constantine to house the remains of the cross and other precious relics his mother, St. Helen, had brought back from Jerusalem. (The legend of the discovery of the true cross is illustrated in the late 15th-century fresco in the apse.) The

The vast dome of S. Bernardo alle Terme ② measures 72 feet in diameter. In the late 16th century, the church was created from one of the corner turrets of the ancient Baths of Diocletian

Behind the 19th-century Fontana delle Naiadi is the facade of S. Maria degli Angeli ④, carved from the most monumental spaces of the central element of the great Baths of Diocletian.

④

church was modified many times during the Middle Ages (when the tall Romanesque bell tower was erected), and then completely transformed under Benedict XIV (1743), who added the delightful facade that functions as a backdrop for the Strada Felice (now Via S. Croce in Gerusalemme). The interior, dominated by 12 colossal antique columns, has elaborate stuccowork and a mosaic floor. The Chapel of St. Helen is decorated with a magnificent Renaissance reproduction of a 5th-century mosaic. The so-called "Calvary" staircase leads to the Chapel of Relics, which contains fragments of the cross, a nail, two thorns from Christ's crown, a piece of the sponge that was offered to him, a fragment of the scroll that hung on the cross, and one of the 30 coins of Judas. Earth from Calvary lies beneath the floor. The basilica is emblematic of a new mentality and a new era for Christianity. It is deliberately and clearly separate from the imperial building, from which it is independent and at the same time dominates. This relationship would have been unthinkable prior to the reign of Constantine, when early Christian meeting places were simply placed within a secular architectural context. ⊠*Piazza S. Croce in Gerusalemme 12.*

S. Eusebio

▦**6 A6.** This is one of the oldest churches in Rome, and it is dedicated to the 4th-century Roman martyr who was a tireless opponent of Arianism. It seems that St. Eusebius of Bologna financed the construction (first mentioned in 474), and his remains lie beneath the altar. The facade is from the 18th century, and the interior preserves the Romanesque layout of the church rebuilt by Gregory IX (1238), with notable additions and embellishments from the 17th to the 20th centuries. The Celestines, a Benedictine order founded in 1264 by the hermit St. Peter Celestine (the future Celestine V), had charge over the church and monastery for some time. Dispersed by the French Revolution, the order survived in Italy until 1807. The Celestines had the lovely carved wooden choir built (1600) behind the high altar. The former monastery, now a barracks, still has a harmonious 16th-century cloister. ⊠*Piazza Vittorio Emanuele II 12/A .*

S. Isidoro

▦**4 C2.** Founded in 1622 by the Spanish Franciscans, this church is consecrated to St. Isidore (1070–1130), the patron saint of Madrid and of farm workers, who was canonized the same year the building was erected. In 1625, the building became a refuge for persecuted Irish Franciscans and is still the site of the Irish College. The church's most notable work is the Da Sylva Chapel, designed by Gian Lorenzo Bernini (1663). During the Napoleonic occupation, during which time the friars dispersed, the monastery became the home of the Nazarene painters, a group that revolved around the German artist Johann Friedrich Overbeck. Their name derived from the artists' "Nazarene-style," long hair and beards and from their communal and ascetic way of life. They proposed an anti-academic art, animated by strong religious sentiment and inspired by Christian medieval stories and legends. Their models were Giotto, Fra Angelico, and, most of all, Raphael and Dürer. ⊠*Via degli Artisti 41.*

S. Maria degli Angeli ④

▦**4 D4.** In answer to the appeals of a Sicilian priest who had had a vision of angels in the Baths of Diocletian, Pius IV decided to construct a church dedicated to the angels and the Christian martyrs who, according to legend, had built the baths. Michelangelo was entrusted with the design of the basilica, which occupies the most monumental spaces in the center of the baths. The pope granted the complex to the Carthusians, who constructed a monastery (probably also according to a design by Michelangelo). Michelangelo was respectful of the classical ruins, and even with his modifications and later interventions by Luigi Vanvitelli (1750), the building has admirably preserved its antique appearance, which is characterized by eight gigantic monolithic columns and three broad cruciform vaults. The transept and presbytery walls have large altarpieces, many of which come from S. Pietro. One chapel, one statue, and various paintings commemorate St. Bruno of Cologne (1035–1101), founder of the Carthusians, who stayed in Rome for two years as an advisor to Urban II. The ascetic and extremely rigorous life of the order is evoked by the small, austere cells of the **Certosa** (monastery) **of S. Maria degli Angeli,** which presents a clear contrast to the majestic antique structures and opulent basilica. A central element of the monastery was the large cloister (completed in 1565), enclosed by a portico of some hundred travertine columns. ⊠*Piazza della Repubblica.*

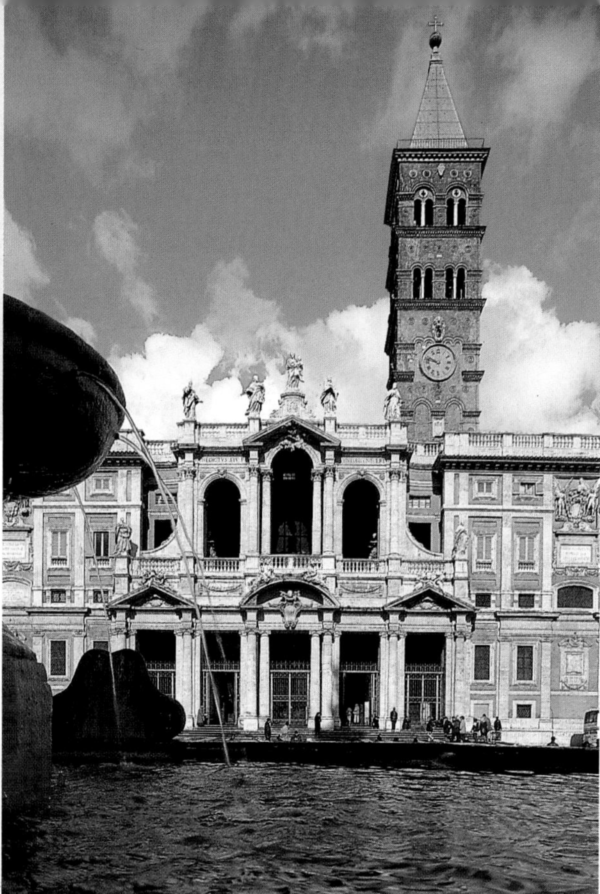

⑤ A large mid-18th-century portico, designed by Ferdinando Fuga, stands in front of the Baroque facade of the patriarchal basilica of S. Maria Maggiore. At the back of the basilica is a brick bell tower, the tallest in Rome, erected in 1377.

The Ecstasy of St. Teresa or, more correctly, *Teresa Transfixed by Love of God* (1646), the celebrated sculpture by Bernini, in S. Maria della Vittoria ⑦.

S. Maria della Concezione dei Cappuccini

▦**4 C2.** The church was built in 1626 for the Capuchin cardinal Antonio Barberini, brother of Urban VIII, in a suburban area dominated by the noble Barberini family. It houses works by Guido Reni, Domenichino, Caravaggio, and Pietro da Cortona, but it is best known for its unusual **Capuchin Cemetery,** installed in the subterranean chapels. The chapels are furnished in a macabre style that was particularly popular in Spain, with the skulls and bones of 4,000 Capuchin friars (a similar cemetery is located in the church of S. Maria dell'Orazione e Morte, on the Via Giulia, ☞ *77*). The skeletons were moved here from the old Capuchin monastery of S. Nicola de Portiis, now S. Croce e S. Bonaventura dei Lucchesi. ✉ *Via Veneto 27.*

S. Maria Maggiore ⑤

▦**4 F4.** The fourth of the patriarchal basilicas, this church was the centerpiece of Sixtus V's urban reconstruction (his Strada Felice led into the Piazza dell'Esquilino, behind the church). According to legend, the Madonna herself indicated to Pope Liberius (AD 352–AD 366) the site where he was to erect the church, with a miraculous snowfall on the peak of the Esquiline hill in August 356. For this reason, since the 11th century the church has also been known as S. Maria ad Nives, and every year, on the day of its founding, a high mass is celebrated, accompanied by a symbolic snowfall. In reality the basilica was erected by Sixtus III (AD 432–AD 440), immediately after the Council of Ephesus (431), which had proclaimed the dogma of Mary's virginity and maternity. The Marian cult, which is directly related to the birth of Jesus, expressed their beliefs in the mosaics of the triumphal arch and in relics from the Grotto of the Nativity in Bethlehem. The latter were brought to Rome in the 7th century and preserved in the oratory of the *presepio,* or crèche, beneath the Chapel of Sixtus V, which contains some nativity statues by Arnolfo di Cambio (1290). Despite innumerable interventions in later centuries (culminating in the 18th-century facade built by order of Benedict XIV), the grand layout of the original church is still visible, with three naves with 40 columns and magnificent mosaic decoration. Along the central nave, 36 panels illustrate *Scenes from the Old Testament,* which is styled in the Hellenistic-Roman tradition of continuous and realistic narration. The Byzantine-style mosaics of the triumphal arch illustrate episodes connected to Mary and the childhood of Christ and episodes that are not related in the Gospels and are therefore considered apocryphal. Above is an image inspired by the Apocalypse, with a bejeweled throne on which Christ will sit on Judgment Day. The apse mosaics, a masterpiece by Jacopo Torriti (1295), were created by order of Pope Nicholas IV. They depict *Scenes from the Life of the Virgin* and *The Coronation of Mary.* Two ornate side chapels are located in front of the high altar—the Sistine Chapel, conceived by Pope Sixtus V as his tomb and created by Domenico Fontana (1584–1587), and the Pauline Chapel, erected by Flaminio Ponzio for Pope Paul V Borghese (1611). The interior of the church is dominated not only by the mosaics, but also by the refined mosaic floor (12th century) and by the sumptuous coffered ceiling decorated with emblems of the client, Pope Alexander VI (1492–1503). It is said that the gilding was accomplished with the first gold brought from America. ✉ *Piazza S. Maria Maggiore.*

S. Maria della Vittoria ⑦

▦**4 C3.** The Discalced Carmelites chose this site, where there was an earlier chapel dedicated to St. Paul, to erect a monastery and church. In 1608, Carlo Maderno was entrusted with the project, which was financed by Cardinal Scipione Borghese. Maderno reproduced the general design of his earlier S. Andrea della Valle, and the facade by Giovanni Battista Soria makes the structure appear to be a

⑥ 

⑦ 

companion piece to the nearby church of S. Susanna. The church was reconsecrated to Mary after the victory of the Catholic imperial troops over the Lutherans near Prague, an event that was attributed to the prodigious influence of a painting of the Madonna and child carried into battle by a Carmelite friar. It later assumed an ornate Baroque appearance, thanks in part to the intervention of Gian Lorenzo Bernini in the Cornaro Chapel (1646). The famous *Ecstasy of St. Teresa,* one of the high points of this sculptor's art, portrays an expression of mystical agitation that involves both spirit and flesh. The words with which the saint (1515–1582) described the ecstatic experience in her *Libro de su vida* found an extraordinary interpreter in Bernini, who was able to combine spiritual tension and sensuality, two inseparable qualities of 17th-century devotion. ✉ *Via XX Settembre 17.*

Ss. Vito e Modesto ⑥

▦**6 A6.** In 1474 the church was rebuilt by Sixtus IV, on the site of an ancient place of worship. Changes made in subsequent centuries were eliminated for the most part by a 1973–1977 renovation that restored the 15th-century elements, such as the marble entrance and the two-mullioned Gothic-style windows of the facade. The interior houses two unusual altars in niches with Christ and the Virgin and, protected by a grate, the so-called "stone of iniquity." This was long believed to have been used for the martyrdom of many early Christians, but in reality it was a Roman funeral pillar. Next to the church is the **Arch of Gallienus,** with three barrel vaults, an Augustinian reconstruction of a door in the Servian Wall (Porta Esquilina) that was dedicated to Emperor Gallienus and his wife in AD 262. ✉ *Via Carlo Alberto 47.*

Terme di Diocleziano, Museo Nazionale Romano

▦**4 D4.** The largest bath complex in Rome (it could hold 3,000 people) was erected by Diocletian between AD 298 and AD 306. A colossal rectangular enclosure surrounded the central core, which had bath spaces and gymnasiums. The complex fell into ruins and, beginning in the 6th century, it was used to store grain and oil and for religious purposes. Under Pius IV (1561) a Carthusian monastery was installed; first Michelangelo (1561), then Luigi Vanvitelli (1749) contributed to the design and creation of the basilica of S. Maria degli Angeli. The best preserved structures in the ancient baths are those in the church: the two circular spaces in the corners of the enclosure (one has become S. Bernardo alle Terme) and the spaces adapted to house part of the collection of the Museo Nazionale Romano, namely the octagonal hall (planetarium) and the church of S. Isidoro in Formis. The archaeological materials exhibited here are organized according to large-scale themes: the establishment and early development of the city, artistic development of the republican era, arts and social classes, the history of the Latin language, and writing. ✉ *Via de Nicola 79,* ☏ *06/488–0530.*

12

Rome Outside the Walls

(1)

Bernini's *Apollo and Daphne* (1624), in the Galleria Borghese, depicts one of the metamorphosis described by the poet Ovid. Daphne, to escape Apollo's embrace, is transformed into a laurel plant.

The frescoes of the Catacombe di Priscilla (2) are some of the oldest examples of sacred painting tied to Christianity. They depict scenes from the Old and New Testament and images of life of the early Christian community.

The Aurelian Walls (3rd century AD) marked the outer limits of the city from medieval times until the 19th century. In republican and imperial times, the suburban stretches of the great consular roads that radiated out from Rome were marked by an uninterrupted series of tombs and villas. In late antiquity the landscape began to change, with the creation of sanctuaries commemorating martyrs, basilicas, and Christian cemeteries, which immediately became popular pilgrimage sites. In subsequent centuries, while pagan monuments decayed into ruins, the most important of these Christian complexes became distinct villages. In the 9th century, devastating Saracen invasions made it necessary to move the martyrs' remains to protected locations within the city walls, condemning most of the early Christian sites to decline and abandonment. The Roman countryside was transformed into a deserted area, frequently described by Romantic writers and dominated by a few basilicas along devotional routes (S. Lorenzo, S. Paolo, and S. Sebastiano). Beginning in the late 16th century, some ornate suburban residences were built (such as the Villa Giulia and the Villa Albani). In the 20th century this formerly deserted area has become for the most part a sea of cement.

Abbazia delle Tre Fontane (Abbey of the Three Fountains)

▦1 E3. This delightful complex on the Via Laurentina, surrounded by a eucalyptus grove, was built on the site of the apostle Paul's beheading. The name derives from the legend of three springs that gushed forth on the sites where Paul's head bounced, and where three churches were later built: **S. Paolo, Ss. Vincenzo e Anastasio,** and **S. Maria in Aracoeli.** Since 1868 the abbey has belonged to the Trappists, who reclaimed the area, which was then malaria-infested and abandoned. In the 7th century a monastery for Greek monks was established near the first church dedicated to the apostle (5th–6th century). The head of the martyr St. Anastasius the Persian was brought here, then the body of St. Vincent of Saragossa, the Spanish martyr who resisted atrocious tortures. Innocent II gave the monastery to the Cistercians (1138), who rebuilt it (it was their second monastery in Italy, after Chiaravalle) according to the aesthetic principles dictated by their founder and patron saint, St. Bernard of Clairvaux. The last changes were made in 1599, on the eve of the 1600 Holy Year, when the churches of S. Maria in Aracoeli and S. Paolo were renovated. The former (1582) received its name (Aracoeli means "altar of heaven") from a vision St. Bernard had on the site, of a ladder on which the souls in purgatory were ascending. This is also the site where legend has it 10,203 legionnaires and their general, Zeno, martyred under Diocletian, are buried. The Romanesque **Ss. Vincenzo e Anastasio** chuch, rebuilt with the nearby monastery of **S. Bernardo** (1221), preserves the austere monumentality of early Cistercian architecture. Seven altars contain the remains of both the titular martyrs and St. Zeno, as well as relics from the Holy Land. The monastery houses a fresco with a calendar of the months, a rare example of 14th-century secular painting. ✉ *Via delle Acque Salvie.*

Catacombe di Domitilla

▦1 D3. The most well known monument along the Via Ardeatina, the Catacombs of Domitilla are one of the two largest early Christian burial sites in Rome (along with the Catacombs of St. Callixtus). Established in the 3rd century around some pagan underground tombs, the catacombs developed on three levels over the next two centuries. The name derives from the owner of the property, Flavia Domitilla, a relative of the emperor Domitian who was exiled because of her Christian beliefs. The most important martyrs buried here were Nereus and Achilleus, Roman soldiers who, after having persecuted Christians, converted and suffered martyrdom under Diocletian. Over their tomb, Pope Siricius (384–399) had a large basilica built, and that edifice contains a depiction of the martyrdom of Achilleus carved into a column. In the 16th century the martyrs' remains were moved inside the walls, along with those of Domitilla, to the church that bears their name. Petronilla (depicted in a 4th-century fresco), a martyr presumed to be the daughter of St. Peter, was also buried in these catacombs. Her remains were moved to the Vatican in 757 by Pope Paul I, to fulfill a promise to Pepin, king of the Franks. Petronilla later became the patron saint of France, and her tomb was the coronation site for the Carolingian sovereigns. ✉ *Via Ardeatina 280.*

② 

Catacombe Ebraiche di Villa Torlonia (Jewish Catacombs of Villa Torlonia)

1 B4. In 1918 Jewish catacombs from the 3rd and 4th century were discovered in the park of the Villa Torlonia. They include two independent cemeteries, one of which has numerous inscriptions (mostly in Greek) with the names of the deceased. The other was probably more elaborate, judging from the presence of arched niches with paintings. ✉ *Via Nomentana.*

Catacombe dei Ss. Marcellino e Pietro

1 C5. Located along the ancient Via Labicana (now the Via Casilina), these catacombs were built during the 3rd century next to a pagan cemetery. They contain the remains of a great many martyrs, including Marcellinus and Peter, who died during the persecutions of Diocletian (304). Constantine built a monumental sanctuary dedicated to the martyrs that included a large basilica and mausoleum, both circular in format. Constantine's mother, St. Helen, was buried here, although the site was almost certainly originally meant for the emperor himself. The catacombs have an incomparable pictorial legacy, with more than 85 spaces frescoed with both Christian and pagan scenes, all well preserved and of a high artistic level. In 827 a shocking event—the plundering of the bodies of the titular saints, ordered by Einhard, Charlemagne's minister and biographer—condemned the complex to decay and abandonment. ✉ *Via Casilina 641.*

Catacombe di Priscilla ②

1 B3. The Christian cemetery takes its name from the Roman matron Priscilla, who, according to tradition, gave hospitality to the apostle Peter. It is one of the most important and popular pilgrimage sites, in part because of the presence of numerous papal tombs. Above the burial area, Pope Sylvester I (314–335) had a basilica built, which he then consecrated. Its present-day appearance is the result of a 1904–1907 renovation. The heart of the complex is the so-called *arenario,* originally a pozzolana quarry, which has always been considered one of the most ancient Roman catacomb sites (2nd–3rd century). It contains a great number of niches on which simple epitaphs of the deceased were painted in red. These are quite homogeneous, attesting to the egalitarian spirit that was typical of early Christianity, whereby social differences were ignored. One of the most important early Christian frescoes was discovered here, depicting a Madonna and child with a prophet. It dates from the years AD 230–AD 240, and is the oldest known image of the Virgin. ✉ *Via Salaria 430.*

Catacombe di S. Callisto

1 D4. The oldest and most important cemetery along the Via Appia is named for Callistus. He was the deacon to whom Pope Zephyrnus entrusted the administration of the church's first official cemetery. The area includes the tombs of many martyrs and popes, including Sixtus II, a venerated pontiff who was killed with his deacons during the persecution of 258. Nine 3rd-century pontiffs; popes Caius, Eusebius, and Cornelius; and the martyrs Calocerus, Parthenius, and Caecilia (whose remains were moved here in 821) are buried here. As Christianity spread, the catacombs grew to monumental size, and it became necessary to create easily accessible pathways for pilgrims, through a system of galleries and stairways leading from one sanctuary to another. ✉ *Via Appia Antica.*

Chiesa del Domine Quo Vadis

1 D3. Near the crossroads of the Via Appia and the Via Ardeatina is a little church, documented since the 9th century with the name S. Maria in Palmis. The current name, Domine Quo Vadis (Lord, where are you going?), refers to the well-known legend of the meeting between Christ and Peter, who was fleeing Rome to escape Nero's persecution. In answer to the apostle's question, Jesus replied, "I go to Rome to be crucified a second time," which led Peter to return to the city to face his martyrdom. The church's interior was renovated in the 17th century, and it houses a paving slab from the Via Appia, marked with footprints that the faithful have identified with those of Christ. ✉ *Via Appia Antica 51.*

Galleria Borghese ①

1 B3. The Borghese Gallery is located within the gardens of the Villa Borghese on the Pincian Hill. It was built for Cardinal Scipione Caffarelli Borghese (1579–1633), nephew of Paul V, to house his art collection. Cardinal Borghese had extraordinary artistic instincts and was motivated by an insatiable passion for the most prized works, which pushed him to steal Raphael's *Deposition* from the Baglioni Chapel in Perugia and to imprison Domenichino, who had refused to sell him a painting. But the cardinal was also greatly admired for his patronage of exceptional talents, including Bernini, Caravaggio, Guido Reni, and Rubens. In keeping with the cardinal's wishes, the building was designed to be a "theater of the universe." Its primary function as a center for art and culture was merged with the contemplation of nature, and the immense grounds contained vineyards, orchards, an aviary, a zoo, and rare exotic plants. The importance of both patron and his villa went well beyond the

exceptional quality of his collection of ancient and modern art. "His" artists inaugurated a new style, the Roman Baroque, which would be imitated throughout Europe. The villa and park were renovated between 1770 and 1800 by Marcantonio Borghese, who gave the interiors a rich Neoclassical decorative scheme, with paintings and stuccowork by well known artists from Italy and abroad. Shortly thereafter his son Camillo (1775–1832), husband of Marie-Paulette Bonaparte, Napoléon's sister, was forced to sell the emperor 344 pieces from his archaeological collection. The artworks are now housed in the Louvre. The Borghese Gallery's art collection, which was expanded over the centuries, is one of the best private collections in the world. It includes Cardinal Scipione's beloved ancient marbles and sculptures and paintings by Italian and foreign artists from the 16th throught the 20th century. Raphael's dramatic *Deposition,* Correggio's sensuous *Danae,* Canova's scandalous *Paolina Borghese,* and works by Caravaggio and Bernini are only the most popular pieces in this treasure trove of masterpieces. ✉ *Piazzale Scipione Borghese 5,* ☏ *06/854–8577.*

Mausoleo di S. Costanza ③

▦1 B4. This building is the burial site of Constantine's two daughters, Constantia (or Costanza) and Helena, neither of whom are saints. It is located near the large basilica of S. Agnese, where that saint is buried. The building was used as a baptistery, and it has been a church since 1254. The structure was thought to be a temple of Bacchus, because of the mosaics with harvest scenes, and it became a meeting place for artists in the 18th and 19th centuries. The solemn edifice on a central plan is covered with a dome resting on 12 pairs of granite columns. The interior of the central space is a corridor with barrel vaults covered in elegant mosaics with floral, geometric, and figurative motifs. The spherical vault once contained mosaics illustrating scenes from the Old and New Testaments, but these have completely vanished. The building houses a cast of the large porphyry sarcophagus of Costantia, the original of which is in the Vatican Museums. ✉ *Via Nomentana 349.*

Moschea (Mosque)

▦1 A3. This mosque and the adjacent Islamic cultural center were designed by Paolo Portoghesi and Vittorio Gigliotto (1984–1995). It is an eclectic building that combines rationalist and expressionist forms, reinterpreting the classical typology of the Islamic sanctuary according to the canons of postmodern architecture, of which Portoghesi is an active theoretician and practitioner. The large space is dominated by a series of piers and arches that support stepped domes. A museum and one of the largest Islamic libraries in Europe (40,000 volumes) are housed in the mosque complex. ✉ *Viale della Moschea,* ☏ *06/808–2167.*

Mura Aureliane (Aurelian Walls)

▦1 B2-B3-C2-C3-D3-C4. Faced with a growing threat of barbarian invasion, the emperor Aurelian (270–275) realized the need to provide Rome with a new enclosing wall, and he commissioned one to follow the outline of the hills and encompass preexisting edifices (such as the Castrense Amphitheater and the Pyramid of Caius Cestius). The wall was later fortified, rebuilt, and furnished with a new course of crenellated turrets. One of the best preserved sections contains the Porta Latina and the Porta Appia (now the **Porta S. Sebastiano**), the most monumental gateway in the entire complex. On the left pier are an image of the archangel Gabriel and a Latin inscription that recalls the 1327 victory of the Romans over the Angevins.

S. Agnese Fuori le Mura ④

▦1 B4. Near the tomb of the young martyr Agnes (the same saint to whom the church in Piazza Navona is dedicated) is a basilica erected by Constantine, then rebuilt by Honorius I (625–638). The Constantinian basilica (334–357), like others of that time (S. Lorenzo, S. Sebastiano, and Ss. Marcellino e Pietro), had an unusual circular plan, with side naves around the semicircular apse. Now only a few impressive ruins of the apse and the adjacent mausoleum wall remain. The basilica Honorius built, which has undergone numerous renovations, contains a notable apse mosaic that depicts the saint with the attributes of her martyrdom: fire and the sword. On the right is an image of a phoenix, symbol of immortality. The canopy above the high altar dates from a restoration from the time of Paul V (1614). It includes a statue of the saint by Nicolas Cordier (1605), who added a gilded bronze head, clothing, and hands to an antique alabaster torso. The nearby **Cimitero Maggiore Catacombs** (3rd–4th century) contains the remains of St. Emerentiana, thought to be the foster-sister of St. Agnes. The catacombs also have numerous paintings with biblical scenes and chairs carved into the tufa stone, perhaps used for funeral banquets. ✉ *Via Nomentana 349.*

S. Andrea

▦1 B3. Julius III ordered this church built in memory of his escape from prison during the sack of Rome in 1527. The design by Vignola (it was renovated in the 19th century) is cubic in form, with

(A) The tomb of S. Costantia ③, erected in the late 4th century.
(B) The interior, which is still tied to the style of Roman architecture, is embellished with mosaics of rare beauty, with fanciful naturalistic decorative schemes.

④ The interior of S. Agnese Fuori le Mura ④, with three naves divided by columns with beautiful Corinthian capitals. The apse contains a splendid Byzantine mosaic that depicts St. Agnes with popes Symmachus and Honorius.

an entrance with tympanum and a small elliptical dome, a new element in this architect's work. ✉ *Viale Tiziano.*

S. Lazzaro

▦**1 B2.** This Romanesque church, which takes its name from the surrounding district, stands at the foot of Monte Mario, below the Via Trionfale. It was built shortly after the year 1000 and originally was known as S. Maria Maddalena, which was also the name of a hospice for pilgrims. Via Trionfale was one of the roads traveled by pilgrims arriving from the north. After an asylum for lepers was established, the church was dedicated to Lazarus, the patron saint of lepers. The original Romanesque interior of the church is preserved, with three naves with recycled columns. A chapel is dedicated to St. Mary Magdalen, patron of vinedressers, who worked in the vicinity. ✉ *Via Trionfale.*

S. Lorenzo Fuori le Mura

▦**1 C4.** In AD 303, Constantine honored venerated Roman martyr St. Laurence of Rome by building a large basilica near the saint's tomb in the Cemetery of Cyriaca, on the Via Tiburtina. The basilica was flanked by the church of Pope Pelagius II (579–590), built directly over that martyr's tomb, which also contained the remains of the early martyr St. Stephen, brought from Byzantium. In subsequent centuries, while the Constantine basilica fell into ruin, the new church became the center of a fortified village, Laurentiopoli, which included two monasteries, churches, libraries, baths, and all the welfare structures necessary for aiding the poor and pilgrims. Pope Honorius III (1216–1227) is responsible for the present appearance of the basilica, which incorporated the Pelagian church into its presbytery. A tragic bombing in 1943 destroyed the portico, the facade, and much of the central nave, which were rebuilt with their original stones. The floor and the two pulpits of the central nave are precious examples of mosaic work from the time of Honorius. At the end of the nave is the dramatic presbytery, delimited by imposing columns that were taken from the underlying Pelagian basilica and which support an arched women's gallery. The episcopal throne (1254) and canopy (1148) are a fine examples of Romanesque marble work. The interior face of the triumphal arch contains a mosaic showing Christ enthroned between saints that comes from the church of Pelagius II. The cloister (late 12th century) is one of the few vestiges of medieval Laurentiopoli. ✉ *Piazzale del Verano.*

S. Pancrazio

▦**1 B2.** The basilica rises along the Via Aurelia, the ancient consular road that linked Rome to Etruria, Liguria, and Provence. It was also one of the principal arteries that passed through the Trastevere. The road began at the gateway of the same name, which in medieval times became Porta S. Pancrazio, in honor of the area's most venerated martyr. According to hagiographic tradition, Pancras came from Phrygia (Asia Minor) and died at age 15 in Rome during Diocletian's persecution (ca. 304). The young saint began to be venerated immediately after his death, particularly in his capacity as a protector of those accused of perjury. A cemetery grew up in the area around his tomb, and a small oratory later was transformed into a basilica by Pope Symmachus (498–514), who also ordered the construction of a hospice for pilgrims. The present basilica, built under Honorius I (625–638), was reconstructed in the 12th and again in the 17th century. ✉ *Piazza S. Pancrazio 5/D.*

S. Paolo Fuori le Mura ⑤

▦**1 D3.** The basilica dedicated to the apostle Paul rises above his tomb, a short distance from the site of his martyrdom (Abbey of the Three Fountains). In the Middle Ages this basilica, along with the Vatican, was the principal destination for pilgrims traveling to Rome. The basilica remained the largest in Rome until the construction of the new S. Pietro. Its history is an uninterrupted sequence of restorations, repairing damage from numerous earthquakes and fires, until the fire of 1823, which almost destroyed the original medieval structure. It was entirely rebuilt, following the ancient plan, and consecrated by

⑤ The ancient S. Paolo Fuori le Mura, one of the most hallowed sites in Christianity because St. Paul is so greatly venerated. The basilica was destroyed in the 19th century and rebuilt, hence its modern appearance.

Certain portions of the Via Appia ⑥ have a sublime appearance, with magnificent vegetation and vestiges of classical and early Christian antiquity. The consular road was laid out in 312 BC .

Pius IX in 1854. Constantine was responsible for the construction of the first, modest basilica. But popular veneration for St. Paul and his primary role in the conversion of the educated pagan classes resulted in a new, grander structure (375–423), the size of the present-day church. In the 8th century, a Benedictine monastery was added (this is the only of the four patriarchal basilicas still presided over by monks). Faced with the threat of Saracen invasions, John VIII (872–882) transformed the complex into a fortified citadel, which took the name of Giovannopoli, in honor of its founder. The bronze doors of the Porta Santa were made in Constantinople (1070) specifically for this building. Above the crypt, the high altar containing the tomb of the apostle is surmounted by an elegant Gothic canopy by Arnolfo di Cambio (1285), which miraculously survived the fire, as did the mosaics in the triumphal arch (5th century). The apse mosaics, executed for Honorius III by Venetian masters (ca. 1220), were heavily restored in the 19th century. The marble Easter candelabrum, nearly 20 feet tall, is decorated with scenes from the Passion and Resurrection. A masterpiece of 13th-century art, it was created by Pietro Vassalletto, who also designed the cloister, which, with its harmonious structure and decorative refinement, is one of the most beautiful in Rome. ✉ *Via Ostiense 186.*

S. Sebastiano

▦1 D4. This church stands in an area of the Via Appia called "ad catacumbas," from the Greek "katà kymbas," that is "near the hollow," perhaps referring to the pozzolana quarries that had contained first a pagan, then a Christian cemetery. The word catacombs was then extended to all the underground Christian burial places. This tomb area was well known throughout the Middle Ages, not only for the tomb of St. Sebastian, but also because of the tradition, perhaps legendary, that the remains of Sts. Peter and Paul were temporarily interred here. The first basilica, built by Constantine, was called Basilica Apostolorum, and it wasn't until the 9th century that it was consecrated to St. Sebastian, the Roman soldier shot to death by arrows during the persecution of Diocletian (298). The circular basilica that Constantine erected was rebuilt by order of Cardinal Scipione Borghese (1608). Above the tomb of St. Sebastian, the cardinal erected a new chapel, which contains a statue of the martyr made from a drawing by Gian Lorenzo Bernini. The Chapel of Relics contains what tradition holds is one of the arrows that pierced the saint and the column of his martyrdom. The cultural centerpiece of the catacombs is a porticoed courtyard where rites and funeral banquets in honor of Peter and Paul were held. The walls are covered with more than 600 examples Latin and Greek graffiti from the 3rd and 4th centuries, with invocations to the two apostles. The **Via delle Sette Chiese** ends nearby; this street, which leads out from S. Paolo Fuori le Mura, takes its name from the devotional route established by St. Philip Neri, which included visits to the four patriarchal basilicas and S. Lorenzo Fuori le Mura, S. Croce in Gerusalemme, and S. Sebastiano. ✉ *Via Appia Antica 136.*

S. Urbano

▦1 D4. This church, built in the 10th century, transformed an ancient Roman temple, probably constructed by Herodes Atticus (2nd century AD). A cultivated and wealthy Athenian and friend of the emperors Hadrian and Antoninus Pius, he had extensive landholdings in this area. The pagan building had a portico with four columns and brick walls. A 1634 addition resulted in the exterior walls between the columns and various interior restorations. Very little is known about the life and works of St. Urban. He was pope from 222 to 230 and, according to tradtion, was buried either in the Catacombs of St. Calixtus or in the Catacombs of Pretestato, near the church. ✉ *Vicolo S. Urbano*

Santuario della Madonna del Divino Amore

▦1 E5. This sanctuary was constructed in 1744 to house an image of the Madonna, considered miraculous, that had been removed from a tower of the nearby Castel di Leva. It immediately became a popular destination for pilgrims from the Roman countryside and the Castelli Romani. After the Allied troops disembarked in Anzio in 1944, the image was carried to safety in Rome, where Pius XII proclaimed it the protector of the city. ✉ *Via Ardeatina, Km 12.*

Via Appia ⑥

▦1 D3-D4-E4. The Appian Way was laid out in 312 BC by Appius Claudius Cieco, the Roman censor from whom the road takes its name. This famous road played a decisive role in the economic development of Rome, because it linked the city to southern Italy and thus to the rich trade from the eastern Mediterranean. Its initial segment traverses one of the most fascinating landscapes around the capital city, perhaps the only one that can evoke an image of the ancient outskirts of Rome, with its luxurious villas (which belonged to the Quintili, the Gordiani, and the Massenzio families) and tombs (the most famous and best preserved is that of Cecilia Metella). The road's reputation as a burial site continued with the rise of Christianity, when the first Christian cemeteries, S. Sebastiano and S. Callisto, emerged along its route.

6

⑦ The Villa Giulia was the result of a mid-16th-century competition among the talented architects Vasari, Ammannati, and Vignola. It is embellished with splendid decorations, such as the frescoes in its ambulatory. Its interior houses the Museo Nazionale Etrusco and contains pieces that have come from throughout Lazio (the exceptional *Sarcophagus of the Bride and Bridegroom* was found in Cerveteri).

Opposite:
The church of S. Francesca Romana amid the columns of the Forum.

Via Appia Pignatelli

⊞1 D4-E4. This road was completed in the 17th century as a link between the Via Appia Antica and the Via Appia Nuova. It is the site of the **Catacombs of Pretestato** (Pretestato's identity is unknown), which were developed within a pagan cemetery. The latter area was very likely set aside for members of the aristocracy, judging from the luxurious sarcophagi discovered here and the presence of an exceptionally large gallery, the so-called "spelunca magna" (large cave). According to tradition this is the burial site of Januarius (killed under Marcus Aurelius), Urban I, and the deacons Felicissimus and Agapitus, who were beheaded with Sixtus II in 258. Some burial chambers, particularly that of St. Januarius, have fine pictorial decorations. The **Jewish Catacombs of Vigna Randanini,** also on this road, are, along with the Villa Torlonia burial ground, the only Jewish cemeteries still in use in the city.

Via Ardeatina

⊞1 D3-D4-E4. The Via Ardeatina, the ancient artery that connected Rome to Ardea, emerges from the Aurelian Wall through the Porta Ardeatina and for quite some distance runs almost parallel to the Via Appia. The most famous and well preserved of its monuments are the **Catacombs of Domitilla** (Via Ardeatina 280), the most extensive in Rome. In 1991 the ruins of a circular basilica were discovered near the church of Domine Quo Vadis. Scholars have hypothesized that this may be the church built by Pope Mark in 336. Sources and old itineraries mention many other Christian structures along the Via Ardeatina, including the funerary basilicas of Pope Damasus I (366–384); the martyrs Mark, Marcellian, and St. Soter; and the sanctuary of the so-called "Greek Martyrs." Most of these can no longer be identified.

Via Salaria

⊞1 B3-A3. Perhaps the most ancient of the roads that led out from Rome, the Via Salaria takes its name from the exportation of salt from Rome to the hinterlands. Exiting from the Aurelian Walls, the road forked into the Salaria Vecchia, which soon become insignificant, and the Salaria Nuova, which roughly corresponded to the present road. Along the first section are various devotional stops mentioned in medieval itineraries: the **Catacombs of Bassilla**; the underground basilica of the martyr St. Hermes, built by Damasus in the 4th century and then replaced by a small oratory that housed a fresco with the oldest known image of St. Benedict; the **Catacombs of S. Panfilo** (Via Paisiello 24b), on the walls of which are numerous examples of graffiti by pilgrims. On the Salaria Nuova, in addition to the Catacombs of Priscilla, pilgrims visited the **Catacombs of S. Felicita** (Via Simeto 2), who, according to tradition, was the mother of seven sons martyred together because of their faith. She is the patron saint of women and mothers, and her blessing is invoked for the bendiction of children and the birth of sons. The small underground basilica contains an interesting 7th-century fresco. Farther along is the so-called **Cemetery of the Giordani** (at the corner of the Via Taro), known for the fine painting cycle with scenes from the Old and New Testaments (3rd–4th century).

Villa Albani Torlonia

⊞1 B3. During the Renaissance, palazzi were decorated with antique sculptures, but in the two subsequent centuries many buildings were erected specifically to house immense collections, such as the Villa Borghese in the 17th century and the Villa Albani in the 18th century. Cardinal Alessandro Albani, nephew of Pope Clement XI and the unrivaled collector in Rome during that period, built a grand museum-villa on the Via Salaria (1747–1767), where obelisks, sarcophagi, statues, and busts of emperors filled the rooms and dotted the park. Here Winckelmann, the cardinal's librarian, conducted his research, which became the basis of modern archaeological and art history. Much of the collection was moved to Paris by Napoléon, but in the subsequent century the Torlonia family restored the villa's splendor, filling it with works of exceptional value. ✉ *Via Salaria 92,* ☎ *06/686–1044*

Villa Giulia ⑦

⊞1 B3. The suburban villa (1551–1555) of Pope Julius III is a compendium of Mannerist architecture. Its many wings spread over terraces on different levels, with a juxtaposition of rectilinear and curvilinear elements, a dramatic succession of spaces along a longitudinal axis, and a close relationship between external and internal spaces. The theatrical loggia-enclosed grotto is the work of Ammannati and Vasari, and the severe, monumental facade is by Vignola. The building houses the **National Etruscan Museum,** which has a vast collection of sculptures, gold work, ceramics, bronzes, and other archaeological remains from Etruscan culture. ✉ *Piazzale di Villa Giulia 9,* ☎ *06/320–1951.*

ROME, THE YEAR 2000, AND THE CHRISTIAN JUBILEE

Rome, the year 2000 and the Christian Jubilee

The Rome Agency for Jubilee Preparations welcomes all visitors, tourists, and pilgrims to Rome to explore the city, to see its artistic treasures, and to participate in the celebration of the Jubilee and the passage to the year 2000.

This section offers visitors information on the projects that have been prepared for the year 2000, the calendar of major cultural events, and the official calendar of religious events prepared by the Holy See. An overview of the main Jubilee destinations and itineraries is also provided.

In addition to religious celebrations, a wide variety of cultural events will take place during the year 2000. Major art exhibitions and a rich program of theatrical and musical events will celebrate Rome's unparalleled artistic tradition from antiquity to today. The playbill for the year 2000 has something to offer the widest of audiences.

To prepare for this historic event, Rome and the Lazio Region have undertaken a major organizational effort. With funds provided by the Italian State, all the government departments involved have built new infrastructure, restored cultural heritage sites, and organized reception services. The private sector has also made a significant contribution to these preparations.

The Agency has a special role in the organization of events in the year 2000, including planning services, event management, and promoting cultural activities. The services that affect pilgrims and visitors most directly are the Jubilee volunteer activities and information services.

VOLUNTEER SERVICES

The Center for Jubilee Volunteers for Reception Activities, which is organized by the Central Committee of the Great Jubilee and the Rome Agency for Jubilee Preparations, is charged with recruiting, training, and organizing volunteers.

More than 50,000 volunteers have been recruited for the year 2000 to assist and inform pilgrims along the Jubilee itineraries and during celebrations, aid travelers with disabilities and children at places of worship, and monitor cultural heritage sites and parks.

The Center's office is open to all those who would like to help with reception activities and is located in Rome in Largo Santa Lucia Filippini 20, phone 06/678-9695.

INFORMATION

The Information Centers organized by the Agency offer computers and audiovisual rooms to provide information on reception services, the calendar of religious celebrations, and other events connected with the Jubilee year and the history and culture of the Jubilee.

The Centers are located at:

☞ the Museo del Risorgimento on Via di San Pietro in Carcere;
☞ the Auditorium on Via della Conciliazione;
☞ the Ala Mazzoniana of Termini railway station on Via Giolitti.

Additional information centers have been set up at train stations, airports, and the patriarchal basilicas in Rome; the main access routes into Rome; and at various sites around Lazio.

The Agency's Web site (www.romagiubileo.it) provides constantly updated information on services, cultural activities, special events, and other initiatives for the Jubilee and the start of the new millennium.

THE PILGRIMAGE TO ROME IN THE YEAR 2000

The Jubilees, or Holy Years, are normally called every 25 years. The great Jubilee of the year 2000 is the 26th ordinary Jubilee called in the past 700 years, although numerous "extraordinary" Jubilees have been decreed on special occasions outside the normal calendar. During a Jubilee year it is possible to obtain an indulgence (cancellation of punishments imposed for sins), which is why the year is known as a Year of Pardon. Over the years, the concept of forgiveness has been supplemented by many other spiritual and moral themes: conversion, reconciliation, solidarity, justice and service to others.

The Holy Year 2000 is the first to be celebrated simultaneously in Rome, Jerusalem, and all the churches of the world, making it a truly universal Jubilee.

In promoting the spiritual aspects of the event, Pope John Paul II set out the characteristics of the Jubilee pilgrimage to Rome in the *Bull of Indiction of the Great Jubilee of the Year 2000*:

"make a pious pilgrimage to one of the Patriarchal Basilicas, namely, the Basilica di S. Pietro in the Vatican, the Archbasilica of the Most Holy Savior at the Lateran (S. Giovanni in Laterano), the Basilica di S. Maria Maggiore and the Basilica di S. Paolo on the Ostian Way, and there take part devoutly in Holy Mass or another liturgical celebration; ... visit, as a group or individually, one of the four Patriarchal Basilicas and there spend some time in Eucharistic adoration and pious mediations, ending with the 'Our Father,' the profession of faith in any approved form, and prayer to the Blessed Virgin Mary. To the four Patriarchal Basilicas are added, on this special occasion of the Great Jubilee, the following further places, under the same conditions: the Basilica di S. Croce in Gerusalemme, the Basilica di S. Lorenzo in Campo Verano, the Santuario della Madonna del Divino Amore, and the Christian Catacombs."

The Main Jubilee Destinations

The main Jubilee destinations and itineraries have been defined by the agency in coordination with the Central Committee of the Great Jubilee of the Year 2000.

Numbers listed with each site refer to the map on pages 138–139.

PATRIARCHAL BASILICAS

Historically these are the main destinations of Jubilee pilgrimages. The majority of pilgrims will be visiting these sites during the great Jubilee of the year 2000.

1 S. Pietro
2 S. Paolo Fuori le Mura
3 S. Giovanni in Laterano
4 S. Maria Maggiore

WAY STATIONS

These comprise the churches near the patriarchal basilicas. They will serve as places for meditation, prayer, and preparation for the visit to the patriarchal basilica.

5 S. Lorenzo in Piscibus
6 S. Maria del Rosario in Prati
7 S. Maria in Traspontina
8 S. Monica
9 S. Spirito in Sassia
10 Abbazia delle Tre Fontane
11 Battistero Lateranense
12 S. Antonio da Padova a Via Merulana
13 S. Clemente al Laterano
14 S. Croce in Gerusalemme
15 S. Lorenzo in Palatio ad Sancta Sanctorum (Scala Santa)
16 SS. Quattro Coronati al Laterano
17 S. Prassede all'Esquilino
18 S. Pudenziana al Viminale
19 S. Antonio Abate all'Esquilino

CATACOMBS

The catacombs are sacred sites that date from the very origins of Christianity. In addition to their spiritual significance as burial sites of the martyrs and the first Christians, they are also one of the most important examples of subterranean architecture.

The main catacombs are:
20 S. Callisto

21 S. Sebastiano
22 Domitilla
23 Priscilla
24 S. Agnese
25 S. Pietro e Marcellino

PALEOCHRISTIAN BASILICAS

These basilicas are the first appearance of the church in public life, testifying to the growth and development of Christianity.

26 S. Agnese Fuori le Mura
27 S. Anastasia al Palatino
28 S. Balbina all'Aventino
29 S. Cecilia in Trastevere
30 S. Giovanni a Porta Latina
31 S. Lorenzo Fuori le Mura
32 S. Lorenzo in Damaso
33 S. Lorenzo in Lucina
34 S. Maria in Cosmedin
35 S. Maria in Domnica
36 S. Maria in Trastevere
37 S. Sabina all'Aventino

OTHER CHURCHES OR BASILICAS

Other destinations connected with the tradition of the Jubilee pilgrimage.

38 S. Agnese in Agone
39 S. Agostino in Campo Marzio
40 S. Andrea della Valle
41 S. Bartolomeo all'Isola
42 S. Crisogono
43 S. Giorgio in Velabro
44 S. Giovanni Battista dei Fiorentini
45 S. Ignazio di Loyola in Campo Marzio
46 S. Maria Ad Martyres (Pantheon)
47 S. Maria degli Angeli e dei Martiri
48 S. Maria del Popolo
49 S. Maria della Vittoria
50 S. Maria in Vallicella
51 S. Maria Sopra Minerva
52 S. Pietro in Montorio
53 S. Pietro in Vincoli a Colle Oppio
54 S. Stefano Rotondo al Celio
55 SS. XII Apostoli
56 SS. Cosma e Damiano in via Sacra
57 Ss. Giovanni e Paolo al Celio
58. SS. Nome di Gesù all'Argentina

NATIONAL CHURCHES

Traditional destinations where foreign pilgrims can participate in services given in their native language and receive spiritual, theological, and practical guidance.

59 **Argentina**—S. Maria Addolorata a Piazza B. Aires
60 **Armenia**—S. Nicola da Tolentino agli Orti Sallustiani
61 **Belgium**—S. Giuliano dei Fiamminghi
62 **Canada**—Nostra Signora del SS. Sacramento and SS. Martiri Canadesi
63 **Croatia**—S. Girolamo dei Croati a Ripetta
64 **Ethiopia**—S. Tommaso in Parione
65 **France**—S. Luigi dei Francesi in Campo Marzio
66 **Germany**—S. Maria dell'Anima
67 **Great Britain**—S. Silvestro in Capite
68 **Greece**—S. Atanasio
69 **Ireland**—S. Isidoro a Capo le Case
70 **Ireland**—S. Patrizio a Villa Ludovisi
71 **Lebanon**—S. Giovanni Marone
72 **Lithuania**—S. Casimiro a Via Appia Nuova
73 **Mexico and Latin America**—Nostra Signora di Guadalupe and S. Filippo Martire in Via Aurelia
74 **Poland**—S. Stanislao alle Botteghe Oscure
75 **Portugal**—S. Antonio in Campo Marzio
76 **Rumania**—S. Salvatore alle Coppelle
77 **Slovenia**—Collegio Sloveno
78 **Spain**—S. Maria in Monserrato degli Spagnoli
79 **Sweden**—S. Brigida a Campo de' Fiori
80 **Syria**—S. Maria in Campo Marzio
81 **Ukraine**—S. Giosafat al Gianicolo
82 **United States**—S. Susanna alle Terme di Diocleziano

OTHER PLACES OF DEVOTION

Sites that will host religious celebrations during the Jubilee.

83 Santuario del Divino Amore
84 Colosseo

The Main Jubilee Itineraries

The Jubilee itineraries indicated here are the oldest such routes and those that, in conformity with the desire of the popes to create a "holy city," are part of the devotional aspects of the Jubilee. Their total length is about 26 miles, and secondary itineraries add a further 15 miles, for a total of about 41 miles..

(*Use the list below as a key for the itineraries shown on the map)

S. Pietro–S. Paolo Fuori le Mura. Medieval devotional itinerary

S. Pietro–S. Maria del Popolo. Medieval devotional itinerary

S. Giovanni in Laterano–S. Maria Maggiore–S. Maria del Popolo. 16th-century devotional itinerary

S. Giovanni in Laterano– Colosseo–S. Maria del Popolo. 16th-century devotional itinerary

S. Pietro–S. Sebastiano Fuori le Mura. Devotional itinerary of the sites of the apostles

S. Pietro–S. Maria Maggiore. 16th–century devotional itinerary (in part)

S. Sebastiano Fuori le Mura–Santuario del Divino Amore. Modern devotional itinerary

S. Paolo Fuori le Mura–Abbazia delle Tre Fontane. Devotional itinerary at the site of St. Paul's martyrdom

The Tour of the Seven Churches was begun by St. Philip Neri around the middle of the 16th century. It included S. Pietro, S. Paolo Fuori le Mura, S. Sebastiano Fuori le Mura, S. Giovanni in Laterano, S. Croce in Gerusalemme, S. Lorenzo Fuori le Mura, and S. Maria Maggiore.

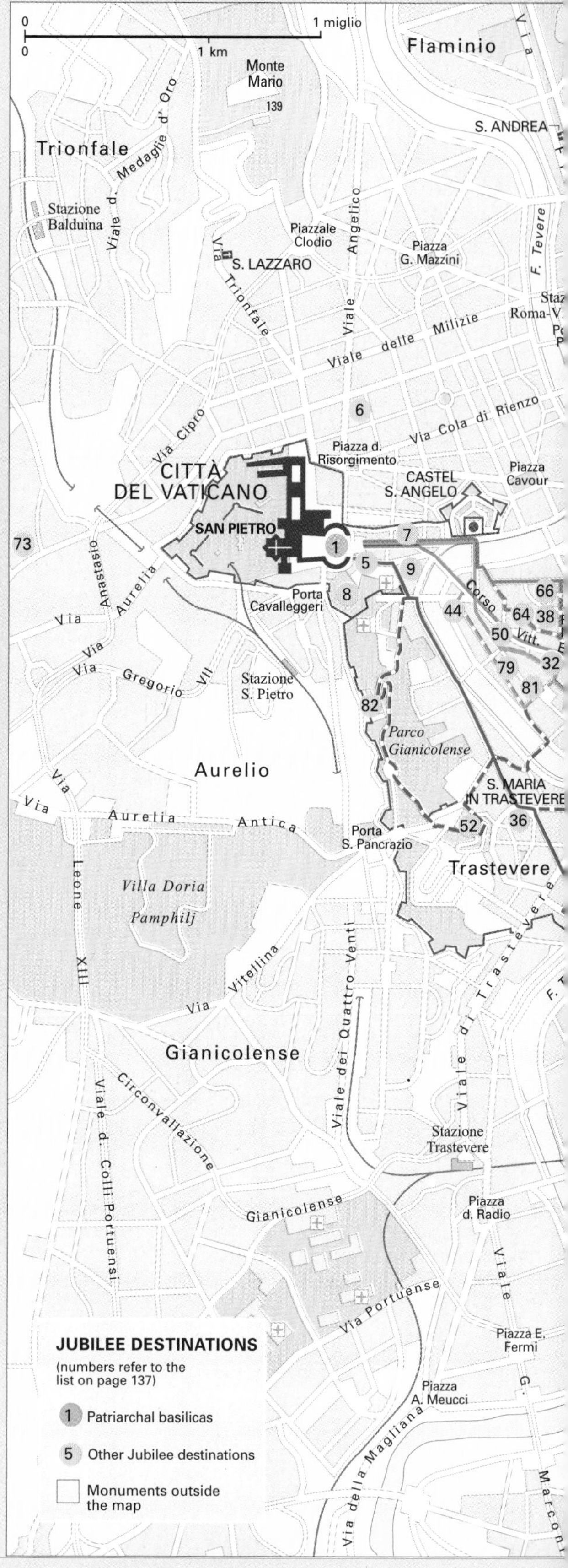

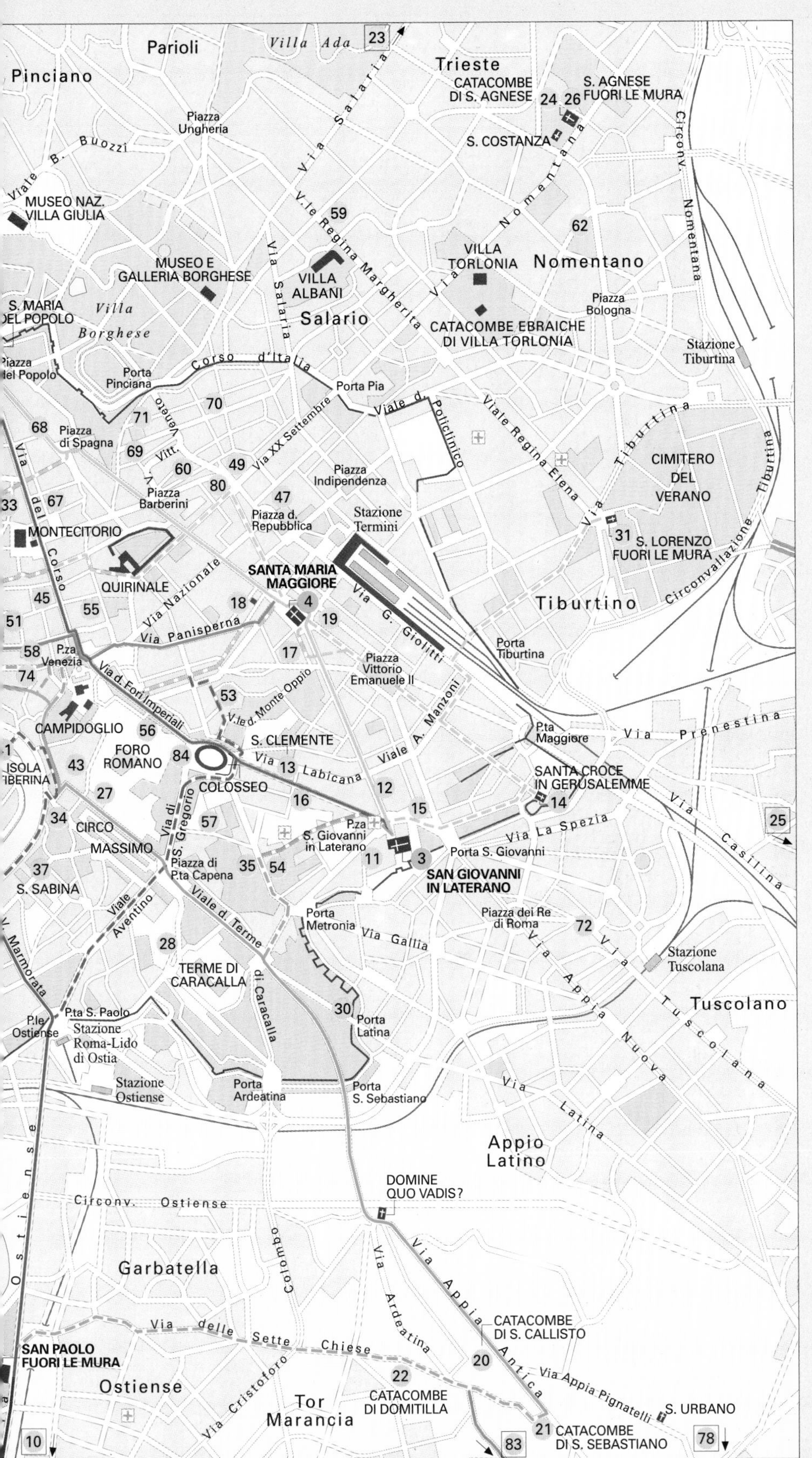

Parioli
Villa Ada
23
Trieste
Pinciano
CATACOMBE DI S. AGNESE
S. AGNESE FUORI LE MURA
24 26
Piazza Ungheria
Viale B. Buozzi
S. COSTANZA
Via Salaria
Via Nomentana
Circonv. Nomentana
MUSEO NAZ. VILLA GIULIA
59
62
MUSEO E GALLERIA BORGHESE
VILLA ALBANI
V.le Regina Margherita
VILLA TORLONIA
Nomentano
S. MARIA DEL POPOLO
Villa Borghese
Salario
Piazza Bologna
CATACOMBE EBRAICHE DI VILLA TORLONIA
Piazza del Popolo
Porta Pinciana
Corso d'Italia
Porta Pia
Stazione Tiburtina
70
Viale d. Policlinico
Viale Regina Elena
Via Tiburtina
68
Piazza di Spagna
71
Via XX Settembre
69
Via Vittorio Veneto
49
60
Piazza Indipendenza
CIMITERO DEL VERANO
Via del Corso
33
67
Piazza Barberini
80
47
Piazza d. Repubblica
Stazione Termini
31
S. LORENZO FUORI LE MURA
MONTECITORIO
Circonvallazione Tiburtina
QUIRINALE
Via Nazionale
SANTA MARIA MAGGIORE
45
55
18
4
Tiburtino
51
Via Panisperna
19
Via G. Giolitti
58
P.za Venezia
17
Porta Tiburtina
74
Via d. Fori Imperiali
Piazza Vittorio Emanuele II
53
V.le d. Monte Oppio
Viale A. Manzoni
CAMPIDOGLIO
56
P.ta Maggiore
Via Prenestina
S. CLEMENTE
FORO ROMANO
84
ISOLA TIBERINA
43
Via 13 Labicana
SANTA CROCE IN GERUSALEMME
COLOSSEO
27
12
14
Via di S. Gregorio
16
Via Casilina
25
15
34
CIRCO MASSIMO
57
P.za S. Giovanni in Laterano
Via La Spezia
11
3
Porta S. Giovanni
37
Piazza di P.ta Capena
35
54
S. SABINA
SAN GIOVANNI IN LATERANO
Viale d. Terme
Viale Aventino
Porta Metronia
Via Gallia
Piazza dei Re di Roma
72
V. Marmorata
28
Stazione Tuscolana
TERME DI CARACALLA
Via Appia Nuova
Via Tuscolana
Tuscolano
P.ta S. Paolo
30
Porta Latina
P.le Ostiense
Stazione Roma-Lido di Ostia
Via di Caracalla
Stazione Ostiense
Porta Ardeatina
Porta S. Sebastiano
Via Latina
Appio Latino
DOMINE QUO VADIS?
Circonv. Ostiense
Via Ostiense
Via Colombo
Garbatella
Via Ardeatina
Via Appia Antica
CATACOMBE DI S. CALLISTO
Via delle Sette Chiese
SAN PAOLO FUORI LE MURA
20
Via Appia Pignatelli
22
Ostiense
Via Cristoforo
Tor Marancia
CATACOMBE DI DOMITILLA
S. URBANO
21
CATACOMBE DI S. SEBASTIANO
10
83
78

Calendar of the Holy Year 2000

This is the official calendar of religious celebrations prepared by the Holy See. The Central Committee of the Great Jubilee of the Year 2000 graciously authorized the publication of the calendar here. Updates will be publicized on the Central Committee's official Web site (www.jubil2000.org).

December 1999[1]

24 Friday
Solemnity of the Birth of the Lord
Basilica di S. Pietro
Opening of the Holy Door
Mass at Midnight

25 Saturday
Solemnity of the Birth of the Lord
Basilica di S. Giovanni in Laterano and S. Maria Maggiore
Opening of the Holy Door
Mass during the day
Basilica di S. Pietro
Urbi et Orbi Blessing
Holy Land
Opening of the Jubilee
Local Churches
Opening of the Jubilee

31 Friday
Basilica di S. Pietro
Prayer vigil for the passage to the year 2000

January 2000

1 Saturday
Solemnity of Mary, Mother of God
Basilica di S. Pietro
Holy Mass
World Day of Peace

2 Sunday
Second Sunday after Christmas
Basilica di S. Pietro
Day for Children

6 Thursday
Solemnity of the Epiphany of the Lord
Basilica di S. Pietro
Holy Mass
Episcopal Ordinations

9 Sunday
Feast of the Baptism of the Lord
Holy Mass
Celebration of the sacrament of Baptism for children

18 Tuesday
Beginning of the Week of Prayer for Christian Unity[2]
Basilica di S. Paolo Fuori le Mura
Opening of the Holy Door
Ecumenical celebration

25 Tuesday
Feast of the Conversion of St. Paul
Basilica di S. Paolo Fuori le Mura
Ecumenical celebration for the conclusion of the Week of Prayer for Christian Unity

28 Friday
Memorial of St. Ephrem
Basilica di S. Cecilia in Trastevere
Divine Liturgy in the East Syrian Rite (Malabarese)

February 2000

2 Wednesday
Feast of the Presentation of the Lord
Basilica di S. Pietro
Liturgy of light and Holy Mass
Jubilee of Consecrated Life

9 Wednesday
Memorial of St. Maron
Basilica di S. Maria Maggiore
Divine Liturgy in the Syro-Antiochene Rite (Maronite)

11 Friday
Memorial of Our Lady of Lourdes
Basilica di S. Pietro
Holy Mass
Celebration of the Sacrament of the Anointing of the Sick
Jubilee of the sick and health-care workers

18 Friday
Memorial of Blessed John (Beato Angelico)
Basilica di S. Pietro
Jubilee of artists

20 Sunday
Jubilee of permanent deacons

22 Tuesday
Solemnity of the Chair of St. Peter Apostle
Basilica di S. Pietro
Holy Mass
Jubilee of the Roman Curia

25 Friday–27 Sunday
Study convention on the implementation of the Second Vatican Ecumenical Council

March 2000

5 Sunday
Ninth Sunday in Ordinary Time
Basilica di S. Pietro
Beatification of Martyrs

8 Wednesday
Ash Wednesday
Penitential procession from the *Basilica di S. Sabina to the Circus Maximus*
Holy Mass and imposition of ashes
Request for pardon[3]

9 Thursday
Basilica di S. Paolo Fuori le Mura
Eucharistic Adoration

10 Friday
Basilica di S. Giovanni in Laterano
Way of the Cross and penitential celebration

11 Saturday
Basilica di S. Maria Maggiore
Recitation of the Rosary

12 Sunday
First Sunday of Lent[4]
Basilica di S. Giovanni in Laterano
Rite of Election and the enrolment of the names of the catechumens

16 Thursday
Basilica di S. Paolo Fuori le Mura
Eucharistic Adoration

17 Friday
Basilica di S. Giovanni in Laterano
Way of the Cross and penitential celebration

18 Saturday
Basilica di S. Maria Maggiore
Recitation of the Rosary

19 Sunday
Second Sunday of Lent
Basilica di S. Maria degli Angeli
East Syrian Rite (Malabarese)
Basilica di S. Giovanni in Laterano
First scrutiny of catechumens

20 Monday
Solemnity of S. Joseph, husband of the Blessed Virgin Mary
Jubilee of craftsmen

23 Thursday
Basilica di S. Paolo Fuori le Mura
Eucharistic Adoration

24 Friday
Basilica di S. Giovanni in Laterano
Way of the Cross and penitential celebration

25 Saturday
Solemnity of the Annunciation of the Lord
Nazareth Basilica of the Annunciation
Liturgical celebration linked with the Basilica di S. Maria Maggiore and the world's major Marian shrines to underscore the dignity of women in the light of Mary's mission (*Mulieris dignitatem*)

26 Sunday
Third Sunday of Lent
Basilica di S. Giovanni in Laterano
Second scrutiny of catechumens

30 Thursday
Basilica di S. Paolo Fuori le Mura
Eucharistic Adoration

31 Friday
Basilica di S. Giovanni in Laterano
Way of the Cross and penitential celebration

April 2000

1 Saturday
Basilica di S. Maria Maggiore
Recitation of the Rosary

2 Sunday
Fourth Sunday of Lent
Basilica di S. Giovanni in Laterano
Third scrutiny of catechumens

6 Thursday
Basilica di S. Paolo Fuori le Mura
Eucharistic Adoration

7 Friday
Basilica di S. Giovanni in Laterano
Way of the Cross and penitential celebration

8 Saturday
Basilica di S. Maria Maggiore
Recitation of the Rosary

9 Sunday
Fifth Sunday of Lent
Basilica di S. Pietro
Beatification of Confessors
Basilica di S. Giovanni in Laterano
Rite of giving the Creed and the Lord's Prayer to the catechumens

13 Thursday
Basilica di S. Paolo Fuori le Mura
Eucharistic Adoration

14 Friday
Basilica di S. Giovanni in Laterano
Way of the Cross and penitential celebration

15 Saturday
Basilica of S. Maria Maggiore
Recitation of the Rosary

Holy Week

16 Sunday
Palm Sunday of the Lord's Passion
Piazza S. Pietro
Commemoration of the Lord's entry into Jerusalem and Holy Mass

18 Tuesday
Tuesday of Holy Week
In the Major Basilicas
Communal celebration of the sacrament of Penance with individual absolution

20 Thursday
Holy Thursday
Basilica di S. Pietro
Chrism Mass
Basilica of St. John Lateran
Mass of the Lord's Supper

21 Friday
Good Friday
Basilica di S. Pietro
Celebration of the Lord's Passion
Colosseum
Solemn Way of the Cross

23 Sunday
Easter Sunday—the Resurrection of the Lord
Basilica di S. Pietro
Easter Vigil of the Holy Night: Service of Light, Liturgy of the Word, Baptismal Liturgy (Celebration of the Rite of Christian Initiation of Adults), Eucharistic Liturgy
Mass during the Day
Urbi et Orbi Blessing

30 Sunday
Second Sunday of Easter
Basilica di S. Pancrazio
Mass for newly baptized adults

May 2000

1 Monday
Memorial of St. Joseph the Worker
Holy Mass
Jubilee of workers

6 Saturday
Basilica di S. Maria Maggiore
Recitation of the Rosary

7 Sunday
Third Sunday of Easter
Colosseo
Ecumenical service for the "new martyrs"

13 Saturday
Basilica di S. Maria Maggiore
Recitation of the Rosary
Piazza S. Pietro

14 Sunday
Fourth Sunday of Easter
Basilica di S. Pietro
Holy Mass
Priestly Ordinations
World Day of Prayer for Vocations

18 Thursday
80th Birthday of the Holy Father
Piazza S. Pietro
Holy Mass
Jubilee of clergy

20 Saturday
Basilica di S. Maria Maggiore
Recitation of the Rosary

25 Thursday
Jubilee of scientists

26 Friday
Basilica di S. Maria degli Angeli
Divine Liturgy in the Alexandrian-Ethiopian Rite
(Feast of Mary Covenant of Mercy)

27 Saturday
Basilica di S. Maria Maggiore
Recitation of the Rosary

28 Sunday
Sixth Sunday of Easter
Holy Mass
Jubilee of the Diocese of Rome

31 Wednesday
Vigil of the Solemnity of the Ascension of the Lord
Basilica di S. Pietro
First Vespers of the Solemnity

June 2000

1 Thursday
Solemnity of the Ascension of the Lord
Basilica di S. Pietro
Holy Mass

2 Friday
Jubilee of migrants and itinerants

4 Sunday
Seventh Sunday of Easter
Holy Mass
Day of Social Communications
Jubilee of journalists

10 Saturday
Vigil of the Solemnity of Pentecost
Piazza S. Pietro
Solemn Vigil of Pentecost

11 Sunday
Solemnity of Pentecost
Basilica di S. Pietro
Day of Prayer for collaboration among the different religions[5]

18 Sunday
Solemnity of the Holy Trinity
Basilica di S. Giovanni in Laterano
Celebration of the opening of the International Eucharistic Congress

22 Thursday
Solemnity of the Body and Blood of Christ
Basilica di S. Giovanni in Laterano
Eucharistic procession

25 Sunday
Closing of the International Eucharistic Congress

29 Thursday
Solemnity of the Apostles Peter and Paul
Basilica di S. Pietro
Holy Mass and imposition of the pallium on Metropolitan Archbishops

July 2000

2 Sunday
13th Sunday in Ordinary Time
Station Mass of the Jubilee

9 Sunday
14th Sunday in Ordinary Time
Jubilee celebration in the prisons

16 Sunday
15th Sunday in Ordinary Time
Station Mass of the Jubilee

23 Sunday
16th Sunday in Ordinary Time
Station Mass of the Jubilee

30 Sunday
17th Sunday in Ordinary Time
Station Mass of the Jubilee

August 2000

5 Saturday
Vigil of the Feast of the Transfiguration of the Lord
Basilica di S. Maria Maggiore
Prayer vigil[6]

6 Sunday
Feast of the Transfiguration of the Lord
Basilica di S. Paolo Fuori le Mura
Second Vespers of the Feast

14 Monday
Vigil of the Solemnity of the Assumption of the Blessed Virgin Mary
Basilica di S. Maria Maggiore
Incense Rite of the Coptic Liturgy

15 Tuesday
Solemnity of the Assumption of the Blessed Virgin Mary
Opening of the 15th World Youth Day

19 Saturday–20 Sunday
20th Sunday in Ordinary Time
Prayer Vigil and Holy Mass
Conclusion of the 15th World Youth Day
Jubilee of youth

27 Sunday
21st Sunday in Ordinary Time
Station Mass of the Jubilee

September 2000

3 Sunday
22nd Sunday in Ordinary Time
Basilica di S. Pietro
Beatification of Confessors

8 Friday
Feast of the Birth of the Blessed Virgin Mary
Solemn Celebration to recall the birth of the Mother of the Lord in relation to the birth of our Savior Jesus Christ

10 Sunday
23rd Sunday in Ordinary Time
Basilica di S. Pietro
Holy Mass
Jubilee of university teachers

14 Thursday
Feast of the Exaltation of the Holy Cross
From the *Basilica di Santa Croce in Gerusalemme* to the *Basilica di S. Giovanni in Laterano*
Stational Procession
Basilica di S. Giovanni in Laterano
Vespers in the Armenian Rite and the Rite of Antasdan

15 Friday
Opening of the International Marian-Mariological Congress
Jubilee of Pontifical Representatives

17 Sunday
24th Sunday in Ordinary Time
Jubilee of senior citizens

24 Sunday
25th Sunday in Ordinary Time
Holy Mass
Conclusion of the International Marian-Mariological Congress

October 2000

1 Sunday
26th Sunday in Ordinary Time
Piazza S. Pietro
Canonization

3 Tuesday
Day for Jewish-Christian Dialogue

7 Saturday
Memorial of Our Lady of the Rosary
Recitation of the Rosary and torchlight procession

8 Sunday
27th Sunday in Ordinary Time
Basilica di S. Pietro
Holy Mass
Jubilee of Bishops on the occasion of the 10th Ordinary General Assembly of the Synod of Bishops
Act of dedicating the new millennium to the protection of Mary

14 Saturday–15 Sunday
Third Worldwide Meeting of the Holy Father with Families

15 Sunday
28th Sunday in Ordinary Time
Piazza S. Pietro
Holy Mass
Celebration of the Sacrament of Matrimony
Jubilee of families

20 Friday–22 Sunday
International Missionary-Missiological Congress

21 Saturday
Basilica di S. Maria Maggiore
Celebration of the Rosary

22 Sunday
29th Sunday in Ordinary Time
Basilica di S. Pietro
Holy Mass
World Mission Day

28 Saturday
Basilica di S. Maria Maggiore
Recitation of the Rosary

29 Sunday
30th Sunday in Ordinary Time
Olympic Stadium
Holy Mass
Jubilee of athletes

31 Tuesday
Vigil of the Solemnity of All Saints
Basilica di S. Pietro
First Vespers of the Solemnity

November 2000

1 Wednesday
Solemnity of All Saints
Basilica di S. Pietro
Holy Mass

2 Thursday
Commemoration of All the Faithful Departed

4 Saturday
Celebration in the Ambrosian Rite

5 Sunday
31st Sunday in Ordinary Time
Holy Mass
Jubilee of those involved in public life

12 Sunday
32nd Sunday in Ordinary Time
Holy Mass
Day of thanks for the gifts of creation
Jubilee of the agricultural world

19 Sunday
33rd Sunday in Ordinary Time
Basilica di S. Pietro
Holy Mass
Jubilee of the military and the police

21 Tuesday
Feast of the Presentation of the Blessed Virgin Mary
Basilica di S. Maria in Trastevere
Divine Liturgy in the Syro-Antiochene Rite (Syrian and Malankarese)

24 Friday
Opening of the World Congress for the Apostolate of the Laity

26 Sunday
Solemnity of Christ the King
Basilica di S. Pietro
Holy Mass
Conclusion of the World Congress for the Apostolate of the Laity

December 2000[7]

2 Saturday
Vigil of the First Sunday of Advent
Basilica di S. Pietro
First Vespers of Sunday

3 Sunday
First Sunday of Advent
Basilica di S. Paolo Fuori le Mura
Holy Mass
Basilica di S. Pietro
Holy Mass
Jubilee of the disabled

8 Friday
Solemnity of the Immaculate Conception of the Blessed Virgin Mary
Basilica di S. Maria Maggiore
Akathistos Hymn

10 Sunday
Second Sunday of Advent
Basilica di S. Giovanni in Laterano
Holy Mass

16 Saturday
Basilica di S. Maria Maggiore
Celebration in the Mozarabic Rite

17 Sunday
Third Sunday of Advent
Basilica di S. Paolo Fuori le Mura
Holy Mass
Jubilee of the entertainment world

24 Sunday
Solemnity of the Birth of Our Lord
Basilica di S. Pietro
Midnight Mass

25 Monday
Solemnity of the Birth of Our Lord
Basilica di S. Pietro
Mass during the day
"Urbi et Orbi" Blessing

31 Sunday
Basilica di S. Pietro
Prayer Vigil for the passage to the new millennium[8]

January 2001

1 Monday
Solemnity of Mary Mother of God
Basilica di S. Pietro
Holy Mass
World Day of Peace

5 Friday
Vigil of the Solemnity of the Epiphany of the Lord
Basilica di S. Giovanni in Laterano, S. Maria Maggiore, and S. Paolo Fuori le Mura
Holy Mass
Closing of the Holy Door[9]
Holy Land
Closing of the Jubilee
Local Churches
Closing of the Jubilee

6 Saturday
Solemnity of the Epiphany of the Lord
Basilica di S. Pietro
Closing of the Holy Door

NOTES

(1) Material will also be prepared for the local churches for the season of Advent, for the ceremony of opening of the Holy Door, and for the prayer vigil for the passage to the year 2000.

(2) During the week ecumenical celebrations will take place in the basilicas and churches of Rome, presided over by representatives of the Christian denominations. Material will also be prepared for the local churches.

(3) The church "cannot cross the threshold of the new millennium without encouraging her children to purify themselves through repentance of past errors and instances of infidelity, inconsistency, and slowness to act" (Tertio millennio adveniente, *n. 33; cf. also ibid., nn. 34–36).*

(4) For the season of Lent, material will also be prepared for the local churches.

(5) Material will also be prepared for the local churches.

(6) In response to the request of the Patriarch of Constantinople, Bartholomew I.

(7) Material will be prepared for the local churches for the season of Advent.

(8) Material will also be prepared for the local churches.

(9) Material will also be prepared for the local churches for the closure of the Holy Door.

Rome Above and Below

New excavations, museums, and architecture for the city in the year 2000

"For 364 days of the year you can be completely detached from Rome as a city, live there without seeing it or, worse, suffer through it. But then, wrapped up in your troubles in the back of a taxi stopped at a traffic light, a familiar street suddenly appears in a play of color and light that you had never seen before ... and you feel that a magical connection has been formed, a feeling of peace that melts away your tension ... it gives you another sense of time, of life, of yourself." Thus Federico Fellini described the moments in which the "ancient charm" of the city would strike him and touch his heart. So many Romans and foreigners, pilgrims, artists, and harried tourists have felt the same sensation, one that you never forget once you have experienced it.

This is a special season for that "ancient charm." Above all, the city is preparing itself to host the extraordinary human and religious event of the Jubilee, an occasion through which an ancient and deep spirit will transmit a strengthened sense of its universality. An event that will introduce millions of pilgrims and visitors to the splendor of the Rome of the great basilicas, while the more curious will be able to rediscover the multitude of less-evident traces of a religious history, details that will sharpen their memories of the event and enhance the emotion of the experience.

The Forums, the Coliseum, the Oppian Hill *History Uncovered*

The excavations at the Imperial Forums are the most extensive ongoing archaeological works in the world. Following the recent excavations at the Forum of Nerva, in the next few years some 37,660 square feet of the Forum of Caesar, 59,180 square feet of the Forum of Peace, and 64,560 square feet of the Forum of Trajan will be brought into the light of day. The last is perhaps the most majestic, built on the orders of the emperor after his conquest of the Dacians and inaugurated in AD 112. The recovery effort will create a giant open-air museum stretching from the Coliseum to the Capitoline Hill and the Markets of Trajan, where a Museo dei Fori will be established, devoted principally to Roman architecture from the imperial period. The entire area is accessible along the Via Sacra itinerary, which runs past the Temple of Vesta and the Roman Curia.

The Coliseum is also due to receive an upgrade for the Jubilee: an internal elevator will facilitate access, and the arcades, tunnels, and the floor of the Coliseum arena will be open. By the year 2002 the entire monument will be accessible to the public, from the underground chambers (which will host museum exhibits) to the balcony of the attic.

Across the road from the Coliseum, the Oppian Hill area is an inexhaustible source of new discoveries: Nero's Domus Aurea, a vast residence with more than 500 rooms, was built over by Trajan and is undergoing a complex restoration. During recent excavations, the "fresco of the painted city" was discovered under the Trajan library, depicting a fascinating turreted city. The work's subject and size (about 110 square feet) make it one of the most important archaeological discoveries in years.

The Great Capitoline Hill *A Hill Regained*

The Great Capitoline Hill project promoted by the city government is restoring the Capitoline Hill to its ancient central role. Once completed, the hill will be the focal point for a "city of archaeology and art," and it will stretch from the Circus of Flaminius and the Theater of Marcellus to the Imperial Forums and the Parco della Via Appia. Following the restoration of the palazzi designed by Michelangelo, the entire museum complex, comprising the Tabularium, the Palazzo Senatorio, and the Casina dei Pierleoni, will be refurbished. The Pinacoteca Capitolina will also be restored and improved. The entire hill will be enclosed, turning it into an oasis in the center of the modern city and a wonderful cultural attraction with breathtaking views.

In the year 2000 the exhibition area will be supplemented with a new space designed by architect Carlo Aymonino, to be constructed in the Giardino Romano of the Palazzo dei Conservatori and the adjacent Giardino Caffarelli. The hall, covered by a 17-foot transparent roof, will be the final home of the original statue of Marcus Aurelius. A glass wall will open to the garden and another wall will serve as a background to the decorations of the pediment of the Temple of Apollo Sosiano. To its right will be placed the reconstruction of the cella of the temple, recovered thanks to the intelligent use of existing remains.

Crypta Balbi, built on the ancient theater erected in 13 BC by Lucius Cornelius Balbus and not far from the Capitoline Hill (between Via Caetani and Via delle Botteghe Oscure), will also be restored. It is one of the few examples of archaeological excavations of a medieval site in Rome. The restored spaces will house an exhibit on the history of the site and of medieval Rome between the 5th and 9th centuries.

Via Appia, Via Latina
The Southern Reaches

The area to the south of the Coliseum extends all the way to the slopes of the Colli Romani and is home to one of the world's largest archaeological sites. This is a countryside unique in its extraordinary balance of history and environment. The leading minds of the city fought a long and courageous battle to defend the area, and now we are seeing the fruits of their efforts.

For the year 2000 the Appia Antica will finally be healed of the terrible wound inflicted by the construction of Rome's Ring Road during the 1950s and 1970s. Two 14,000-foot tunnels will banish the cars that divide the queen of Roman roads, and the area will be replanted and repaved. It will form the largest pedestrian area in Europe, extending from the Circus of Maxentius to the Mausoleo di Cecilia Metella in a continuous itinerary alternating between countryside and ancient, often monumental, ruins. The restoration will bring the Parco della Caffarella together with the Appia Antica as its axis, creating a single space of unmatched archaeological and naturalistic value, with a total area of more than 49,400 acres punctuated by Roman tombs, catacombs, aqueducts, and sacred sites against the background of the Roman hinterland.

The archaeological oasis will include the Parco delle Tombe di Via Latina, a vast necropolis with perfectly preserved frescoes and stuccowork. The park comprises the tombs of the Barberini, the Pancrazi, and the Valeri, along with related structures (tabernae, terrace with nymph, fountain) and the paleochristian church dedicated to St. Stephen. The Sepolcreto degli Scipioni will also be reopened, and the Museo delle Mura Aureliane at Porta San Sebastiano will be refurbished. An upgrade is also in store for the famous Villa of the Quintili, the extraordinary residence of the two consuls (and brothers) that has furnished statuary to museums around the world. The spectacular terraced structure of the complex offers a view of the surrounding countryside. Recent excavations have uncovered marvelously preserved thermal baths.

S. Pietro
A "Factory" at Work

A delicate, scientific cleaning job has been performed at S. Pietro to restore the original brilliant splendor of the Maderno facade and the statues of the attic level. The job began with careful preliminary studies and has been carried out with sophisticated techniques. Execution of the works has been supervised by the Fabbrica di San Pietro (the "factory" of St. Peter's), whose plans for restoring the massive wall called for cleaning the travertine, followed by stuccoing and replacement of missing pieces and a final surface treatment.

The surface is enormous: some 753,200 square feet. After a long study, a low-pressure (no more than 0.4 atm) water-based cleaning technique, using a stream of water mixed with travertine powder (a soft abrasive), was adopeted. The subsequent stuccoing has been particularly challenging, because some stuccowork had to be replaced completely, and other areas had to be repaired. Particularly difficult was stuccowork done in 1985-1986 that had turned gray and cracked into a dense network of lines across the surface, problems that were revealed in a complex photogrammetric analysis by ENI.

The Fabbrica has also been at work in the atrium of the basilica to restore the stuccowork and in the Vatican necropolis in the area around St. Peter's Tomb under the altar of the Confessione and the great baldacchino of Bernini: a place of unequaled emotion and faith.

Palazzo Braschi
The Past Finds a Home

The year 2000 will see the return of Rome's museum. After being closed to the public for 10 years, the Museo di Roma will finally reopen, with its varied collection of iconography, ceramics, sculptures, medieval lapidary, and furnishings, all housed in one of the last great palazzi in the city center, Palazzo Braschi. The Braschi family and Pope Pius VI spared no expense in its construction towards the end of the 18th century, and they are the subject of an exhibition that is temporarily interrupting the restoration works.

The restoration of the palazzo, which in addition to the Museo di Roma also houses the Gabinetto delle Stampe and the Archivio Fotografico Comunale, will be carried out in two stages. The first stage will conclude with the inauguration of the exhibition, while the inventory and reorganization of the vast collection of material will continue. A permanent exhibit on the pomp and circumstance of city life between the 16th and 19th centuries will be created. Temporary exhibits on a range of themes will gradually bring the entire collection to the public eye.

The building's location—between Piazza Navona, where the traditional entry door will be reopened, Piazza di San Pantaleo, and Piazza Pasquino—makes it an ideal place for a museum visit to the city. The addition of a multimedia system for consulting documents and works will raise the museum to the international standards represented by the Musée Carnavalet in Paris and the Victoria & Albert Museum in London.

The Great Museums

The Ancient Goes to Court

The Museo Nazionale Romano opened several new buildings—the Renaissance-era Palazzo Altemps, which holds the statuary of the great collections of the nobility, and the Museo di Palazzo Massimo, which offers a view of the Imperial Age through statues, mosaics, and above all the extraordinary frescoes from the villas of the emperors—that completed its integrated system, but the comprehensive refurbishing was capped by the definitive relocation of museum headquarters at the Baths of Diocletian, which had been the original nucleus since 1889. The new epigraphical section in the former masterpiece hall has been completed, and the public will be readmitted to the section on the pre- and protohistory of Rome. The large chapel by Michelangelo will be reopened after meticulous restoration work.

The Galleria Nazionale d'Arte Antica will be housed in more appropriate quarters after the full recovery of Palazzo Barberini, a masterpiece of Roman Baroque architecture constructed by Pope Urban VIII. The extensive restoration involved the facade, the furnishings, the gallery spaces, and the Princess Carolina Apartments. Other rooms are now being restored and will be used for international exhibitions. A modern reception center will direct visitors to all museums, which hold works dating from the Renaissance through the 18th century.

Beloved by Romans and one of the most popular destinations among tourists—thanks in part to its strategic location—Castel Sant' Angelo, with its roughly 2000 years of history, is already a museum. For the Jubilee, its numerous collections will be reorganized and a visitor orientation and assistance service will be created to make visits easier and more enjoyable.

The Scuderie Papali

Exhibitions in the Stables

Built between 1722 and 1732, the Scuderie Papali (Papal Stables), together with the Palazzo del Quirinale and the Palazzo della Consulta, mark the broad space of Piazza del Quirinale, an example of the perfect melding of buildings of different eras and styles into an integrated whole.

As part of the major events planned for the year 2000, the Presidency of the Italian Republic has granted the City of Rome the use of the Scuderie for cultural activities related to the Jubilee celebrations. The city has in turn entrusted management of the space to the Rome Agency for Jubilee Preparations, which plans to use it as a center for temporary exhibitions. To ensure the complete accessibility of the building, the Soprintendenza per i Beni Ambientali e Architettonici (the Department of the Preservation of Architectural and Environmental Landmarks) has begun restoration and restructuring works designed by architect Gae Aulenti.

The Scuderie abut the wall enclosing the Colonna garden and are built on the site of the Roman Temple of Serapis. The original design for the complex was prepared by Roman architect Alessandro Specchi (1668–1729), on a commission from Pope Innocent XIII. Clement XII completed the work, assigning the job to Florentine architect Ferdinando Fuga (1699–1781), who was also responsible for the Palazzo della Consulta. The building kept its original function until 1938, when it was turned into a garage. The restoration will recover a building with an excellent location, making available more than 32,280 square feet of exhibition space of unparalleled value to the city.

Villa Borghese

Museum Park

Cardinal Scipione Borghese transformed 200 acres of former vineyard outside the city walls into a villa, which is today experiencing a renaissance. The plan for the comprehensive restoration and reorganization of Villa Borghese and its many treasures is already producing results. The public will for the first time be able to visit the Casino del Graziano, a delightful 16th-century villino previously used as a storehouse, with frescoes by students of Domenichino and Reni. But this is only one part of the project, which is also slated to restore the villa's entire treasure of green spaces, monuments, sculptures, fountains, and decorative niches.

The rebirth is completed by the recent reopening of the Galleria Borghese in the heart of the villa, after years of restoration work that has returned the splendors of the collection to the admiring gaze of the public. This extraordinary mixture of park, nature, and art in the center of the city is joined by two more major attractions: the Galleria Nazionale d'Arte Moderna e Contemporanea and the Museo Nazionale Etrusco in Villa Giulia.

At Villa Giulia, the museum's permanent collection is being expanded in the splendid Renaissance building commissioned by Pope Julius III, with a new wing devoted to the pre-Italic civilization of the Falisci. Work is also under way on a radical refurbishment involving the expansion of exhibition space in nearby Villa Poniatowski, which can be visited by way of a connecting passage running alongside the park of Villa Strohl-Fern.

Near Villa Borghese is the Hendrik Christian Andersen Museum, the home, museum, and studio of the American sculptor and painter born in Bergen, Norway, in 1872. Andersen lived in Rome from 1896 until his death in 1940. The neo-Renaissance building, erected in the 1920s, is being restored and contains the artist's sculptures, paintings, and drawings for his utopian design for a "Global City."

The Centrale Montemartini is home to some of the masterpieces of the Capitoline Museums, including the sculptures. Their stay at the former electric plant, inaugurated by King Vittorio Emanuele III in 1912, was supposed to have been temporary, but the juxtaposition of ancient statuary and industrial archaeology was an immediate hit with the public.

The Galleria Comunale d'Arte Moderna has found its own home in another monument of old industrial Rome, on the premises of the former Birreria Peroni, which was designed in a Liberty-inspired style by architect Giovannoni between 1902 and 1922. The large complex covers more than 172,160 square feet. Not only will the site have temporary and permanent exhibits, it will also become a fully operational center for cultural production for the visual arts, similar to other such initiatives around the world. The permanent collection of works by the masters of Italian contemporary art at Villa Glori, the city's first open-air art park, will be expanded.

Finally, the 387,360 square feet of the former Montello barracks, a short distance from the Città della Musica, will be the site of the new Centro per le Arti Contemporanee, based on the design by architect Zaha Hadid, winner of the international competition. The center, which will be a full-fledged community for the promotion of today's languages of expression, will house contemporary art dating from 1960 on. It will also host temporary exhibits and will have sections devoted to architecture, multimedia, and the visual arts.

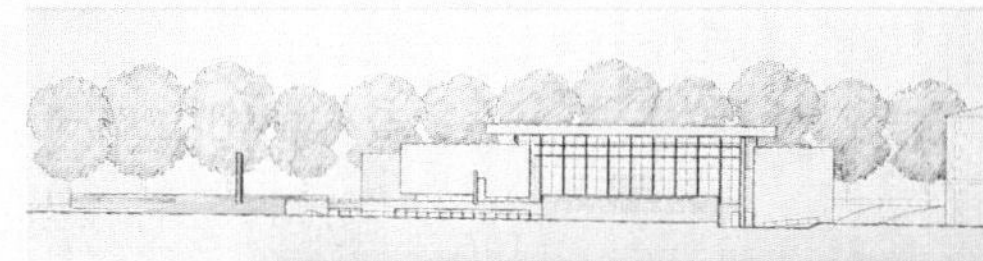

RICHARD MEIER

Richard Meier, the Pritzker Prize winner in 1984, is the creative force behind the design of the church at Tor Tre Teste, one of the works symbolizing the Jubilee of the year 2000.

The design, shown in the model at right embodies the theme of welcome and dialogue. Three large shells close one of the sides.

Meier is also responsible for the refurbishment of the Ara Pacis of Augustus, the altar celebrating the triumph of the Pax Romana. The glassed-in structure dating from 1939 will be removed and replaced by a museum that will give the monument the visibility and accessibility it deserves. In the drawing above, the view from the east.

RENZO PIANO

For Rome, the creation of the Città della Musica in the Flaminio quarter of the city marks the end of a 60-year gap, from the demolition of the old concert hall at the Mausoleo di Augusto. The three separate halls of the new complex were conceived by Renzo Piano as three enormous beetles. At left, a model of the complex and, below, a sectional view of one of the halls.

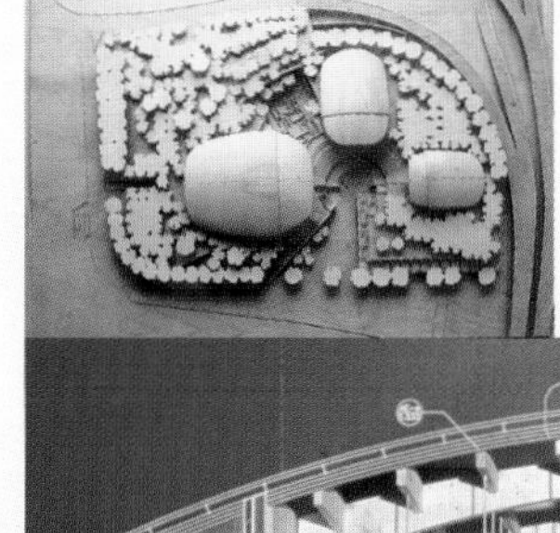

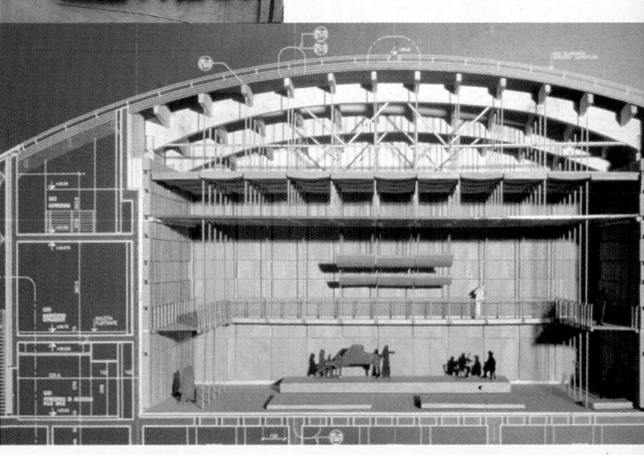

The Jubilee and Culture

A program of some of the events planned for the year 2000 in Rome. The complete and updated program of the cultural events is available at the Agency's Web site (www.romagiubileo.it).

Exhibitions

Pilgrims and Jubilees in the Middle Ages: Medieval Pilgrimages to St. Peter's Tomb (350–1350)
October 1999–February 2000
The pilgrimage seen as a journey of faith and an encounter between different peoples and cultures.
Museo Nazionale di Palazzo Venezia (the Saloni Monumentali and the Barbo Apartment)
✉*Via del Plebiscito 118*
☏*06/841–2312*

Francesco Borromini Architect 1599–1667: Structure and Metamorphosis
December 1999–February 2000
The complete work of Francesco Borromini: drawings (those preserved at the Albertina and never before exhibited), casts, relief models, medals, portraits, a scientific seminar, an international conference, guided tours and Borromini itineraries.
Palazzo delle Esposizioni
✉*Via Nazionale 194*
☏*06/474–5903*

Impressionists and the Avant-garde
December 1999–June 2000
Masterpieces of Impressionist and Post-Impressionist painting from the Hermitage Museum in St. Petersburg. The exhibit presents some 100 paintings by 25 great artists from between 1870 and 1920, tracing the development of art over the period from Monet to Léger.
Scuderie Papali
✉*Via XXIV Maggio 16*
☏*06/678–6648.*

Roma: Universalitas Imperii
Throughout the Jubilee year.
The dislocation of the various ethnic groups that were absorbed into Roman society is conveyed through itineraries designed around monuments, archaeological sites, and subterranean areas, many of which are little known to the general public.
Circuito dei Musei Archeologici Romani (Roman archeological museums).

Villa Medici, the Dream of a Cardinal
November 1999–March 2000
Following the restoration of Villa Medici, the French Academy will present the most important works from the collection of Cardinal Ferdinando de' Medici, one of the greatest art patrons and collectors of the 16th century.
Villa Medici
✉*Viale Trinità dei Monti 1/A*
☏*06/676–11*

Cassiano dal Pozzo (1588–1657): Artistic Culture and Scientific Experimentation in the Rome of the Barberinis
December 1999–February 2000
Palazzo Barberini (Cardinal Francesco Library)
✉*Via delle Quattro Fontane 13*
☏*06/482–4184*

Roy Lichtenstein
December 1999–April 2000
Works and sketches by the great U.S. artist, recently deceased. With the contribution of the Estate of Roy Lichtenstein.
Chiostro del Bramante
✉*Via Arco della Pace 5*
☏*06/688–09035*

Islamic Art in Lazio
December 1999–March 2000
An exhibition divided in two sections: sacred vestments and Oriental fabrics: a meeting of Christianity and the Islamic world; and elements of Oriental art in Christian iconography.
Palazzo Brancaccio, Museo Nazionale d'Arte Orientale
✉*Via Merulana 248*
☏*06/487–4415*

Capogrossi: The Centenary of His Birth
January 2000
Sixty paintings by the Roman artist born in 1900.
Galleria Nazionale d'Arte Moderna
✉*Viale delle Belle Arti 131*
☏*06/322–981*

The Braschi Family and Palazzo Braschi
January–March 2000
To celebrate the restoration and reorganization of the museum, an exhibition will pay homage to the Braschi family, reconstructing its history and its role in politics and commissioning artwork in the last decade of the 18th century.
Palazzo Braschi
✉*Piazza di San Pantaleo 10*
☏*06/688–02713*

Goya
February–April 2000
Palazzo Barberini (the salone Pietro da Cortona)
✉*Via delle Quattro Fontane 13*
☏*06/481–4591*

Yemen: The Queen of Sheba
March 2000
Palazzo Ruspoli
✉*Via del Corso 418*
☏*06/687–4704*

Modern and Ancient Rome in the 17th Century as Seen by a Contemporary: Giovan Pietro Bellori
March–June 2000
An overview of the figurative arts in 17th-century Rome described by a unique contemporary observer: Giovan Pietro Bellori, archaeologist, historiographer, and driving force behind major artistic events and important archaeological discoveries. In connection with a related exhibition in Bologna.
Palazzo delle Esposizioni
✉*Via Nazionale 194*
☏*06/474–5903*

The Year 1300: The First Jubilee. Boniface VIII and His Times
March–July 2000
Artworks produced in Rome at the end of the 13th century by Giotto, Arnolfo, Cavallini, Torriti. Exhibitions, seminars, music, theater, itineraries, and art, with links to satellite exhibits and events.
Museo Nazionale di Palazzo Venezia (the saloni monumentali and the Barbo Apartment)
✉*Via del Plebiscito 118*
☏*06/841–2312*

Meetings: Contacts and Exchanges Between Cultures
March–December 2000
Everyday objects as evidence of the vital circulation of cultural

experience.
Museo Preistorico e Etnografico Luigi Pigorini
✉ *Piazza Marconi 14*
☎ *06/549–52238*

Roman Fraternitas

September–December 2000
Museo Nazionale di Palazzo Venezia (the Saloni Monumentali and the Barbo Apartment)
✉ *Via del Plebiscito 118*
☎ *06/841–2312*

The Road and the Holy City: Music and Art in Interreligious Dialogue

Throughout the Jubilee year.
Exhibitions, musical events and an international conference at dates throughout the Jubilee year on the theme "Pilgrimage and the Holy City" viewed in the light of the five major religions: Christianity, Judaism, Islam, Hinduism and Buddhism.
S. Andrea al Quirinale and the Pontifical Gregorian University

Arts and Music

April 2000
A critical assessment of the relationship between two disciplines that have been closely linked throughout the 20th century: music and the figurative arts. The exhibition will be housed in the new premises of the Galleria Comunale d'Arte Moderna e Contemporanea (Municipal Gallery of Modern and Contemporary Art).
Ex stabilimento Birra Peroni (the former Peroni Brewery)
✉ *Via Cagliari 29*
☎ *06/474–2848*

Christiana Loca

April 2000
The conclusion of a series of conferences that began in 1998 and will continue in 1999. An exhibit on ancient Christianity: the integration of Christianity within the city with objects, relief models, and charts.
The vaults of the Basilica di S. Maria Maggiore

Paris Expo 1900: The Universal Exposition of 1900 in Paris

May–July 2000
Paintings, posters, prints, photographs, illustrated books, magazines, souvenir objects, postcards, and official programs from the spectacular Exposition of the Belle Epoque.
Area Domus
✉ *Via del Pozzetto 124*
☎ *06/442–37261*

Views of Rome

May 2000
Calcografia
✉ *Via della Stamperia 6*
☎ *06/699–801*

City, Garden, Memory

May–August 2000
A series of exhibitions inaugurated in 1998 and devoted to contemporary art. The works of the leading artistic figures weave a dialogue with the ancient against the background of Villa Medici and its gardens.
Villa Medici
✉ *Viale Trinità dei Monti 1/A*
☎ *06/676–11*

"Exodus": Photographs by Sebastião Salgado

June–September 2000
The photographs, presented in Rome in their world premiere, tell the story of the large and dramatic migrations over the five continents.
Scuderie Papali
✉ *Via XXIV Maggio 16*
☎ *06/678–6648*

Art in Italy: The Test of Modernity

November 2000–January 2001
A critical assessment of modernity in art, captured between the end of the 19th century and the early years of the 20th century.
Galleria Nazionale d'Arte Moderna e Contemporanea
✉ *Viale delle Belle Arti 131*
☎ *06/322–981*

The Light of the Spirit in 20th-Century Art

July–October 2000
The concept of the sacred in modern art viewed through the works of the main artistic figures of the century, from Picasso to Matisse, Malevich, Mondrian, Brancusi, and Boccioni, as well as contemporary artists such as Kounellis, Serra, Judd, and others.
Palazzo delle Esposizioni
✉ *Via Nazionale 194*
☎ *06/474–5903*

Botticelli and The Divine Comedy

September–December 2000
Drawings on parchment by Sandro Botticelli illustrating the cantos of the *Divine Comedy.* The works are preserved at the Vatican's Apostolic Library and in the collections of the Staatliche Museen Preussischer Kulturbesitz in Berlin.
Scuderie Papali
✉ *Via XXIV Maggio 16*
☎ *06/678–6648*

St. Caecilia: The Myth of Music Between the Sacred and the Profane

October 2000–January 2001
Palazzo Barberini (Cardinal Francesco Library)
✉ *Via delle Quattro Fontane 13*
☎ *06/481–4591*

Cleopatra

October 2000
Organized in collaboration with the British Museum and the National Gallery in Washington. The first complete exhibition on the historical figure of Cleopatra, queen of Egypt, enemy of the Romans, and arbiter of the destiny of the ancient world.
Palazzo Ruspoli
✉ *Via del Corso 418*
☎ *06/687–4704.*

The Hidden God

October–December 2000
Collection of 17th-century French religious masterpieces by Poussin, Champagne, Le Nain, and others, accompanied by a conference and musical events.
Villa Medici
✉ *Viale Trinità dei Monti 1/A*
☎ *06/676–11*

Christian Rome

October 2000
The closing archaeological exhibit of the year 2000, tracing the transition from classical Roman art under the influence of Christian Rome from the 3rd century to the end of the 4th century. The show provides complete documentation of all forms of art in Rome: painting, sculpture, minor arts, and monuments. The exhibit will feature special itineraries.
Palazzo delle Esposizioni
✉ *Via Nazionale 194*
☎ *06/474–5903*

Jerico: Ten Thousands Years of History in Palestine
November 2000
Museo Nazionale di Castel Sant'Angelo
✉ *Lungotevere Castello 1*
☎ *06/681–911*

The 20th Century
December 2000
An exhibit of some 180 paintings and sculptures from the most important schools of 20th-century Italian art.
Scuderie Papali
✉ *Via XXIV Maggio 16*
☎ *06/678–6648*

The Beaux-Arts Tradition
Dates to be determined
An exploration of American artistic circles at the close of the nineteenth century, assessing the impact of classical culture on artists such as Augustus St. Gaudens, John La Farge, Charles Follen McKim and many others.
American Academy in Rome
✉ *Via A. Masina 5*
☎ *06/584–6425*

Music and Theater

The start of the musical season of the Jubilee year is dominated by two major events: Mozart's *Coronation Mass,* directed by Riccardo Muti in S. Pietro on Christmas Eve 1999, and the inauguration of the Città della Musica with a concert directed by Myung-Whun Chung. The soloists are Cecilia Bartoli, Natalie Dessay, Martha Argerich, and Maximilian Vengerov.

Throughout the year the entire city and much of the region of Lazio will host a continous series of musical events, both in traditional settings for music and in churches, squares, abbeys, and archaeological sites that fill the area.

The **Accademia di Santa Cecilia** has dedicated a special concert season to the Holy Year, distinguished by the rediscovery of the great Italian tradition of sacred music.

The Easter Festival will be a special occasion for sacred music, with the revival of the ancient tradition of music in churches and oratories as accompaniment for all the rites of Easter week.

In *Orfeo ed Euridice* by Gluck, *Mosè* by Rossini (in the original French edition), and *Parsifal* by Wagner, the three composers tackle the themes of rebirth and redemption. This is the poetic motif that runs through the program of the **Teatro dell'Opera di Roma** in the year 2000, offering a musical reflection on the theme of the sacred without neglecting the traditional repertory, which will highlight Puccini's *Tosca* and Bellini's *Norma.*

A multitude of other musical and theatrical events has been planned. The most important include the twice daily concerts in the Benedictine church of S. Anselmo all'Aventino and the Festival of the Sacred, organized by the Fondazione Romaeuropa, with music and dance from around the world.

The **Teatro di Roma** has organized a series of productions for the Jubilee to addresses the spiritual and social issues facing us in the new millennium. The special Jubilee season opens in January with the Raffaello Sanzio group's production of *Genesi, from the Museum of Sleep* by Romeo Castellucci, with an original score by Scott Gibbons. It continues in the spring with *La seconda vita di Francesco d'Assisi*
by José Saramango, directed by Marco Baliani.

The year 2000 will also see a new itinerant production of Luca Ronconi's *Laudari medioevali,* Raffaele Viviani's *I Dieci Comandamenti,* Giorgio Barberio Corsetti's *Graal,* and many other events, including Pina Bausch's special Jubilee production, *Ein Stück.*

During the summer, Teatro Argentina will put on *Sette Spettacoli per un Nuovo Teatro Italiano e per il 2000,* seven new productions selected in a public competition that seek to create a new theatrical idiom.

The calendar of events is not devoted solely to sacred music, but also includes many other initiatives ranging from modern music to theater and dance: from the Festa Italiana with traditional dance and music at the Teatro Sistina, to the European Music Festival in all the piazzas of the city, to the Autumn Festival, organized by ETI (the Italian Theater Council), with concerts and international avant-garde theater productions.

This section of the guide has been prepared by the Agenzia Romana per la Preparazione del Giubileo (Rome Agency for Jubilee Preparations). The Agency is a publicly owned limited company. Its task is to provide technical and organizational support to the government bodies in charge of supplying the services needed by visitors during the Jubilee. Its shareholders are the City of Rome, the Province of Rome, Lazio Region, the Rome Chamber of Commerce, the Ministry of the Treasury (through the Deposits and Loans Fund), the City of Florence, and the City of Naples.

Piazza Adriana 12, 00193 Rome
Phone ++39/06/681–671
Web site: www.romagiubileo.it
e-mail: agenzia@romagiubileo.it

Artists in Rome
Index
Rome Atlas

The Contarelli Chapel, in the church of S. Luigi dei Francesi, with St. Matthew and the Angel *and the* Calling of Matthew, *by Caravaggio*

Artists in Rome

From time immemorial, Rome, the capital of Christianity, has been the center of artistic activity, more than any other city in Europe. Artists of extraordinary talent and fame created works that punctuate the landscape of the Eternal City. The pages that follow present some of the most celebrated architects, painters, and sculptors in Rome, who gave most to the city and are mentioned most frequently in the pages of Holy Rome. *A series of concise biographies will acquaint readers with the artists who have shaped the face of Rome over the centuries.*

Alessandro Algardi

Sculptor (1595–1654)

Algardi's apprenticeship with Ludovico Carracci in Bologna and his restoration work of ancient stuccos for Cardinal Ludovisi in Rome (1625) were fundamental parts of his training. While sensitive to the poetics of Bernini and the paintings of Pietro da Cortona, he was inspired by classical ideals of composure and compositional balance. Significant works include his stucco statues of *St. John the Evangelist* and the *Magdalen* for S. Silvestro al Quirinale (1628–1629); *St. Philip and the Angel,* for S. Maria in Vallicella (1640); and the monumental projects undertaken during the papcy of Innocent X Pamphilj (*Monument to Leo XI* and a marble altarpiece depicting *The Meeting of Attila and Pope Leo,* both in S. Pietro). He also executed numerous significant portraits: *Olimpia Pamphilj,* now in the Galleria Doria Pamphilj, and *Garzia Mellini,* in S. Maria del Popolo.

Arnolfo di Cambio ①

Sculptor and architect (1245–1302)

Influenced by the Gothic style, Arnolfo di Cambio harmoniously merged three-dimensional decoration and architecture. After working as an assistant to Nicola Pisano in Siena, he went to Rome in 1277 to work for Charles of Anjou. There he came under new influences, including classical and late antique sculpture and the French Gothic style, with its elegant linear quality. In two large baldachins, in S. Paolo Fuori le Mura (1285) and S. Cecilia in Trastevere (1293), he created original architectural schemes that merge with the sculpted portions. Although his works in Rome are signed (a votive chapel of S. Boniface VIII in the old S. Pietro in the Vatican, 1301; a bronze statue of St. Peter in the Vatican basilica, ☞ *photograph above*), they are most likely from his workshop. It is probable that he also participated in the alterations to S. Maria in Aracoeli (1280–1285).

Gian Lorenzo Bernini ③

Architect, sculptor, and set designer (1598–1680)

Bernini was the dominant figure in Baroque Rome. His career as an architect began with the election of Pope Urban VIII (1623) and reached its apex during the papacy of Alexander VII. In the basilica of S. Pietro he created the bronze baldachin with spiral columns (☞ *photograph at right*), the throne of St. Peter (1657–1666), the Scala Regia, and the final layout of the elliptical piazza (beginning in 1656). He designed fountains (the Fontana del Tritone in Piazza Barberini, the Fontana dei Fiumi in Piazza Navona), churches (S. Andrea al Quirinale), and palaces (Palazzo Montecitorio and Palazzo Barberini). His most memorable sculptures include *The Ecstasy of St. Teresa* in S. Maria della Vittoria (1644–1652), *Blessed Ludovica Albertoni* in S. Francesco a Ripa, and the marble groups of *Apollo and Daphne, Aeneas and Anchises,* and *David* in the Galleria Borghese.

Francesco Borromini ②

(Francesco Castelli) Architect (1599–1667)

A brilliant figure in the architectural world of Baroque Rome, Borromini spent some years in Milan before going, at the end of 1619, to the capital, where he remained for the rest of his life. He began his activity working as a stonecutter in S. Pietro. He then went to work for Bernini and became his principal assistant. His first independent project was the construction of the cloister (☞ *photograph above*), monastery, and church for S. Carlo alle Quattro Fontane (1638–1641). Here, as in his later works in Rome (the oratory and monastery of the Filippini, S. Ivo alla Sapienza, the renovation of the interior of S. Giovanni in Laterano, S. Agnese, the facade of the Collegio di Propaganda Fide), he experimented with novel spatial inventions (elliptical plans, undulating surfaces, theatrical arrangement of light sources, decorative abundance).

Bramante

(Donato di Pascuccio di Antonio) Architect and painter (1444–1514)

Bramante arrived in Rome after the fall of the Sforza family in Milan (1499). In the Eternal City, he designed the cloister of S. Maria della Pace (1500) and the circular tempietto of S. Pietro in Montorio (begun in 1502). The latter was the first great mid-Renaissance monument, and its elements, taken from ancient architecture, make it a symbol of universal harmony. When Julius II ascended to the papacy (1503), Bramante found an ideal client. He was involved in the

3
OVES
ΣΥ
BO

④ 

⑤ 

⑥ 

renovation projects for the Holy See, where he designed the Belvedere courtyard, which links the palace and villa of Innocent VIII. It is articulated on three levels and culminates in a large semicircular piazza. He proposed a central plan for S. Pietro surmounted by a vast dome, a scheme favored by humanist culture. The building was begun, but the death of the pope put an end to the project.

Caravaggio ④

(Michelangelo Merisi) Painter
(1571–1610)

Caravaggio grew up in Lombardy, and during his early years in Rome (1592–1593), he painted predominantly still lifes. Cardinal Francesco Maria del Monte, his first powerful patron in Rome, gave him lodgings in his palace and entrusted him with the fresco decoration of his laboratory (Casino Ludovisi). His genre scenes (*The Card Players*, 1595) and his early religious subjects for private use (*Rest on the Flight into Egypt*, 1595) date from this period. Thanks to the cardinal's patronage, he decorated the Contarelli Chapel in S. Luigi dei Francesi (1599–1602, ☞ *151*). There, in *The Calling of Matthew* (☞ *see detail above*) and *The Martyrdom of Matthew*, everyday reality invades a grand sacred scene for the first time. The dramatic use of light and the somewhat unseemly realism of the subjects is accentuated in works such as the *Conversion of Paul* (S. Maria del Popolo), the *Deposition* (Vatican Pinacoteca), and the *Madonna of the Pilgrims* (S. Agostino).

Annibale and Agostino Carracci

Painters
(1560–1609 and 1557–1602)

In 1582 brothers Agostino and Annibale Carracci founded the Accademia dei Desiderosi in Bologna (later renamed Accademia degli Incamminati), where the art of the Renaissance was evoked in works with simple tones and figures with faces and stances that were both natural and idealized. From 1595 onward, Annibale was in Rome, working for Odoardo Farnese. Agostino asked his brother to decorate the Farnese Gallery (1597), but disagreements between the two led Agostino to leave the city. In his work, Annibale returned to Renaissance forms and proposed a new concept of landscape, which became the central element of his compositions (*Flight into Egypt*, c. 1604, in the chapel of the Palazzo Aldobrandini).

Giacomo della Porta ⑤

Architect and sculptor (1533–1602)

A student of Vignola and follower of Michelangelo, Giacomo della Porta created a substantial body of work that helped to solidify those great Renaissance architects' concepts (the two-story church facade, the palazzo) into definitive building types. He continued Michelangelo's Campidoglio project (Palazzo dei Conservatori; Palazzo Senatorio, ☞ *see photograph above*), and he succeeded Vignola as architect of the Chiesa del Gesù in Rome, designing its facade (1573–1584). He became the architect of S. Pietro, where he completed Michelangelo's facade overlooking the garden and constructed the smaller domes and the great dome. He also designed the Oratory of the Crucifix (1568) and the nave of S. Giovanni dei Fiorentini (1582–1592).

Domenichino ⑦

(Domenico Zampieri) Painter
(1581–1641)

A student of Ludovico Carracci in Bologna, Domenichino arrived in Rome and entered the circle of Annibale Carracci, collaborating with him on the Farnese Gallery. Using Carracci as a model, he developed a formula for classicism that is characterized by precision of drawing and compositional balance. The classical ideal did not prevent him from looking at reality, which he maintained as an essential point of reference. In S. Luigi dei Francesi, his *Scenes from the Life of St. Caecilia* (1614, ☞ *see detail at right*) represent the culmination of his style. He painted his *Last Communion of St. Jerome* (1614, Vatican Pinacoteca) and *Diana and Nymphs Hunting* (Galleria Borghese) during the second decade of the century. His frescoes for S. Andrea della Valle are noteworthy, although they fail to achieve the triumphant Baroque vision expressed in the dome by Lanfranco, his contemporary.

Carlo Fontana ⑥

Architect (1634–1714)

Carlo Fontana settled in Rome in 1655. He began his activity as an assistant to Pietro da Cortona, Rainaldi, and Bernini, for whom he worked for 10 years. He executed numerous projects, including S. Margherita in Trastevere, S. Biagio in Campitelli, the concave facade of S. Marcello al Corso (1683, ☞ *see photograph above*), and the Ospizio Apostolico in S. Michele a Ripa Grande, in collaboration with Ferdinando Fuga. He designed numerous chapels for churches in Rome, including the Cybo Chapel in S. Maria del Popolo (1683–1687), as well as the baptismal font in S. Pietro (1692–1698). He restored and in large part rebuilt the church of SS. Apostoli (1702) and completed Palazzo Montecitorio by Bernini, from whom he had inherited the position of papal architect. Over time he became the undisputed leading architect in Rome and was considered the person most responsible for the classicizing academic style into which the Baroque declined.

7

Domenico Fontana
Architect (1543–1607)

Architect to Sixtus V, he designed and saw to completion the urban redesign of Rome, with the opening of the Via Sistina and the streets that run from S. Maria Maggiore to S. Giovanni in Laterano, S. Croce in Gerusalemme, and S. Lorenzo. Fontana is also known for the erection of the obelisk in Piazza S. Pietro and for various engineering and hydraulic projects. His masterpiece is the Palazzo Lateranense (1586), followed by the SS. Sacramento Chapel in S. Maria Maggiore, which has a central plan. Little remains of his Ospizio dei Cento Preti, a building commissioned by the pope in 1587. He designed the original Salone Sistino in the Vatican Library (1587–1589), which contains opulent late-16th-century frescoes.

Ferdinando Fuga ⑧
Architect (1699–1782)

A Florentine by birth, Fuga created all his principal projects in Rome. Chosen by Clement XII and then by Benedict XIV to be architect of the papal palaces, he completed the Quirinal Palace, adding the Segretario delle Cifre building and a new wing, the "manica lunga." His works in Rome reveal a passage from a personal vocabulary adhering to Baroque parameters to forms more closely tied to classicism. These projects include the Palazzo della Consulta (1732–1737), the facade for S. Maria Maggiore (1741–1743, ☞*see photograph above*), and alterations to the Palazzo Corsini, formerly the Riario (1736). In the latter project, his sophisticated late-Baroque language achieves its most elegant results. His other works include the churches of S. Maria dell'Orazione e Morte (1733–1737) and S. Apollinare.

Carlo Maderno ⑨
Architect (1556–1629)

In 1588 Maderno settled in Rome and became an assistant to his uncle, Domenico Fontana. In 1603 he was appointed architect of S. Pietro; that same year he completed the facade for the church of S. Susanna (☞*see photograph above*), a revolutionary design that broke with the then current Mannerist style and announced the Baroque. S. Susanna and the majestic dome of S. Andrea della Valle are considered his masterpieces, although he is better known for his work on S. Pietro. During the papacy of Paul V, he won a competition to complete the basilica. He elongated Michelangelo's centralized plan and built the facade (1612). Other noteworthy projects include the remarkable dome for S. Giovanni dei Fiorentini (1519), the Palazzo Mattei, and the Palazzo Barberini (built almost entirely after his death, by Bernini).

Michelangelo Buonarroti ⑩
Architect, sculptor, painter, and poet (1475–1564)

Michelangelo left his indelible mark during each of his sojourns in Rome. He sculpted the *Pietà* (☞*see detail atbove*) and, for the tomb of Julius II, *the Rebel Slave,* the *Dying Slave,* and the *Moses* (1513–1516). Between 1508 and 1512 he painted a magnificent fresco cycle for the Sistine Chapel, with powerful figures of Prophets, Sybils, and Nudes and scenes from Genesis. Clement VII commissioned him to add a fresco of the *Last Judgment* (1537–1541), which would become a turning point in the artistic development of the Western world. He is responsible for the urban plan of the Piazza del Campidoglio (1546–1547) and the church of S. Maria degli Angeli, and the construction of the apse portion of S. Pietro (1547), with its majestic dome.

Pietro da Cortona
(Pietro Berrettini) Painter and architect (1596–1669)

The official artist of the papal court, Pietro da Cortona is second only to Bernini in the history of the Roman Baroque. He arrived in Rome in 1613 and was a follower of both the classicism of Annibale Carracci and the pictorial freedom of Rubens. The warm, gilded images of his large-scale frescoes convey his great inventiveness and talent: *Triumph of Divine Providence* (1633–1639) on the ceiling of the great hall of the Palazzo Barberini, *Story of Aeneas* (1647) in the Palazzo Pamphilj, frescoes for the dome and nave of the Chiesa Nuova. His first important building, the church of Ss. Luca e Martina, is considered the first great Baroque church; his use of concave and convex forms in the facade of S. Maria della Pace can also be classified as Baroque. His facade for S. Maria in Via Lata exhibits a gradual elimination of Mannerist elements and an acceptance of those elements typical of Roman monumentality.

Pinturicchio ⑪
(Bernardino di Betto) Painter (1454–1513)

Pinturicchio worked in close proximity to Verrocchio's circle. He later worked autonomously in Rome, Perugia, Spoleto and Orvieto. In Rome, he collaborated with Perugino on the decoration of the Sistine Chapel (1481–1483) for Sixtus IV. His most challenging undertaking was the decoration of the Borgia Apartment (1492–1494, ☞*see detail of* Resurrection *at right*)). His other projects in Rome are the Bufalini Chapel in the church of the Aracoeli and S. Maria del Popolo (Chapel of S. Girolamo, 1488; Chapel of S. Caterina, 1489; Cybo Chapel).

(11)

(12)

(13)

Raphael Sanzio (12)
Painter and architect (1483–1520)
Raphael was brought to Rome by Julius II in 1508, to work with Perugino, Sodoma, Bramantino, and others on the decoration of the Vatican *Stanze* (1509–1514). During this period, he painted the *Triumph of Galatea* fresco for Agostino Chigi, in the loggia of the Farnesina (☞ *see detail above*), and the Sybil frescoes for the Chigi Chapel in S. Maria della Pace. He also devoted his energies to architecture. His first building was S. Eligio degli Orefici (1509, rebuilt in the early 17th century). In 1517, as Superintendent of Antiquities, he demonstrated his interests in his design for the Villa Madama, which had a circular courtyard and numerous rooms with apses and niches, inspired by Roman baths. He was named papal architect in 1514, a post previously held by Bramante; in this capacity he designed a variation on Bramante's plan for S. Pietro. Raphael's Chigi Chapel in S. Maria del Popolo (1512–1513), on a central plan, was finished by Bernini.

Carlo Rainaldi
Architect (1611–1691)
A dominant figure in Rome's late 17th-century architecture, Rainaldi developed his own majestic manner, notable for its theatrical qualities and for the mix of Mannerist and Baroque elements employed by his great contemporaries (particularly Bernini). With his father, he began S. Agnese in Agone, on a Greek cross plan, but the project was taken away from him the following year and turned over to Borromini. Carlo Rainaldi's principal projects are all in Rome: S. Maria in Campitelli; the facade of S. Andrea della Valle; the exterior of the apse and tribune of S. Maria Maggiore; S. Maria in Montesanto and S. Maria dei Miracoli, the twin churches in Piazza del Popolo that connect Via del Babuino, Via del Corso, and Via Ripetta, the three principal streets that radiate out toward the center of the city.

Guido Reni
Painter (1575–1642)
Bolognese painter Guido Reni was a champion of classicism. A student of Ludovico Carracci, he often worked in the papal city, where he was influenced by the work of both Raphael and Caravaggio. His *Crucifixion of St. Peter* (1604), painted for the church of S. Paolo alle Tre Fontane and now in the Vatican Pinacoteca, follows Caravaggio's style. Fulfilling prestigious commissions, he frescoed the Sala delle Nozze Aldobrandini, the Sala delle Dame in the Vatican (1608–1609), and S. Gregorio al Celio. He also decorated the Chapel of the Annunciata on the Quirinale. His greatest work in Rome is the fresco *Aurora*, in the Casino of the Palazzo Pallavicini Rospigliosi (c. 1612–1614).

Jacopo Sansovino
(Jacopo d'Antonio Tatti) Sculptor and architect (1486-1570)
A Florentine who worked predominantly as a sculptor, Sansovino arrived in Rome in 1506. His first works in the city bear the sign of competition with Michelangelo, and after a bitter conflict with him, he drew upon classical precursors to an even greater degree. In 1519 he won a competition for the design of the church of S. Giovanni dei Fiorentini, but his initial design with a central plan was soon abandoned. During the 1527 sack of Rome he fled to Venice, where he remained until his death. His works in Rome include a statue of *St. James* in S. Maria Monserrato and the *Madonna and Child* (1521) in S. Agostino, a much-loved devotional effigy. The church of S. Marcello al Corso also bears signs of his contribution.

Sangallo the Younger (13)
(Antonio Giamberti da Sangallo)
Architect (1484–1546)
From 1503 onward, Sangallo the Younger worked in Rome, where, after the death of Raphael, he became the principal architect of the high Renaissance for two decades. He trained with his uncles (he was the nephew of Antonio da Sangallo the Elder and Giuliano da Sangallo) and worked as a designer for the architects Bramante and Peruzzi. In 1516 he assisted Raphael, who was working in S. Pietro reinforcing Bramante's walls. Various palazzi have been attributed to him, particularly the Palazzo Baldassini (1520) and the Palazzo del Banco di S. Spirito (1521– 1524). His masterpiece is the Palazzo Farnese (begun in 1534, completed by Michelangelo in 1546), the most monumental of the Renaissance palaces (☞ *see photograph above*).

Vignola
(Jacopo Barozzi) Architect and author (1507–1573)
In the mid-16th century this Bolognese artist moved to Rome, where he became the favored architect of the Farnese family. He worked within civil architecture circles, both in the capital and in various towns in Lazio (the suburban residence of Julius II, the Villa Giulia, and the Palazzo Farnese in Caprarola), but his religious buildings are his most successful. The tempietto of S. Andrea was the first example of sacred architecture on an oval plan, a scheme that was widely taken up by Baroque architects. He repeated this plan in his design for S. Anna dei Palafrenieri (1555). In his Chiesa del Gesù, he conceived an architectural model that became the prototype for Counter-Reformation churches.

Index

Principal entries in text appear in ***boldface****. References to the Rome Atlas are preceded by* ⊞ *(for example* ⊞1 C2 *indicates map 1, grid coordinates C2)*

A

B

C

D

E

F

N

O

P

Rome Atlas

Main thoroughfare.

Street with steps and arcade.

Railway.

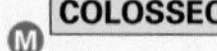

Subway/Underground stop.

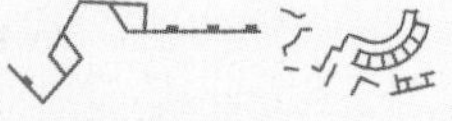

Walls and archeological sites.

Important landmark.

Palace or public building; hospital; developed area.

Church. Synagogue.

Park or garden.

Cemetery.

Scale 1:7500 (1 cm = 75 m)

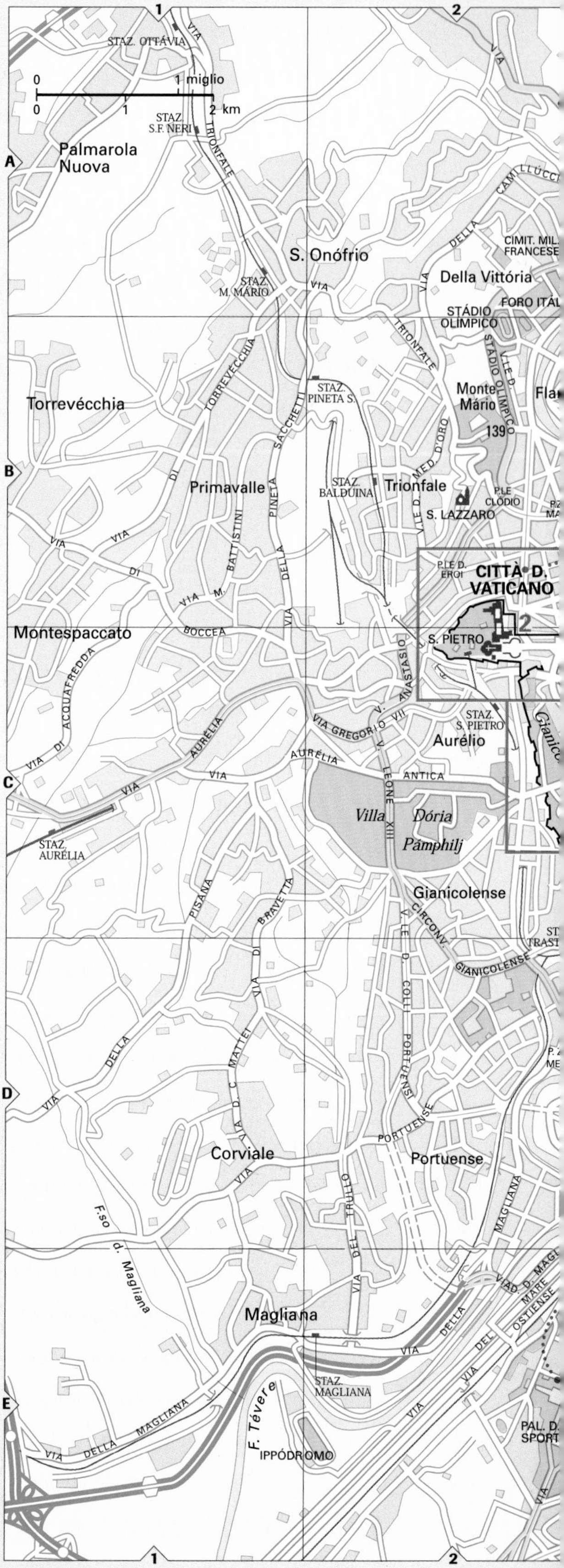

Palmarola Nuova
S. Onófrio
Della Vittória
Torrevécchia
Monte Mário
Primavalle
Trionfale
S. LAZZARO
CITTÀ D. VATICANO
S. PIETRO
Montespaccato
Aurélio
Villa Dória Pamphilj
Gianicolense
Corviale
Portuense
Magliana
IPPÓDROMO

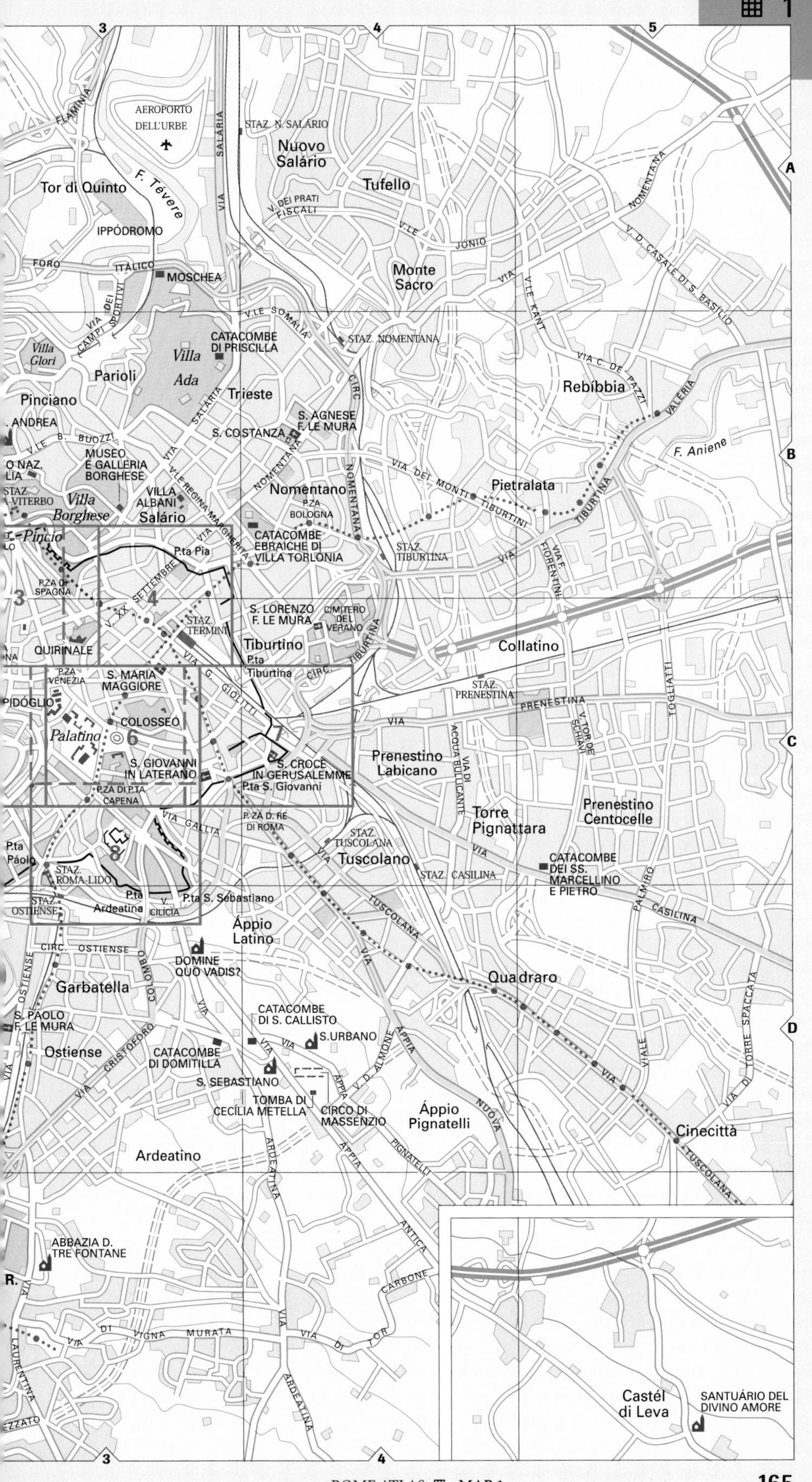
AEROPORTO DELL'URBE
FLAMINIA
SALARIA
STAZ. N. SALÁRIO
Nuovo Salário
Tufello
Tor di Quinto
F. Tévere
IPPÓDROMO
V. DEI PRATI FISCALI
V.LE JÓNIO
NOMENTANA
V. D. CASALE DI S. BASILIO
FORO ITALICO
MOSCHEA
Monte Sacro
V.LE KANT
V.LE SOMÁLIA
VIA DEI CAMPI SPORTIVI
Villa Glori
CATACOMBE DI PRISCILLA
Villa Ada
STAZ. NOMENTANA
Parioli
Trieste
VIA C. DE PAZZI
Rebíbbia
VALERIA
Pinciano
S. AGNESE F. LE MURA
S. COSTANZA
F. Aniene
MUSEO E GALLERIA BORGHESE
VILLA ALBANI
Salário
Villa Borghese
Nomentano
VIA DEI MONTI TIBURTINI
Pietralata
TIBURTINA
P.ZA BOLOGNA
CATACOMBE EBRAICHE DI VILLA TORLONIA
Pincio
P.ta Pia
STAZ. TIBURTINA
VIA F. FIORENTINI
P.ZA DI SPAGNA
V. XX SETTEMBRE
S. LORENZO F. LE MURA
CIMITERO DEL VERANO
STAZ. TERMINI
Tiburtino
Collatino
QUIRINALE
P.ta Tiburtina
P.ZA VENEZIA
S. MARIA MAGGIORE
VIA G. GIOLITTI
STAZ. PRENESTINA
PRENESTINA
TOGLIATTI
COLOSSEO
Palatino
V. TOR DE SCHIAVI
S. GIOVANNI IN LATERANO
S. CROCE IN GERUSALEMME
P.ta S. Giovanni
Prenestino Labicano
VIA ACQUA BULLICANTE
P.ZA DI P.TA CAPENA
VIA GALLIA
P. ZA D. RE DI ROMA
Torre Pignattara
Prenestino Centocelle
STAZ. TUSCOLANA
Tuscolano
STAZ. CASILINA
CATACOMBE DEI SS. MARCELLINO E PIETRO
STAZ. ROMA-LIDO
STAZ. OSTIENSE
P.ta Ardeatina
V. CILICIA
P.ta S. Sebastiano
PALMIRO
CASILINA
Áppio Latino
CIRC. OSTIENSE
DOMINE QUO VADIS?
COLOMBO
Garbatella
Quadraro
VIA TUSCOLANA
CATACOMBE DI S. CALLISTO
S.URBANO
S. PAOLO F. LE MURA
Ostiense
VIA CRISTOFORO
CATACOMBE DI DOMITILLA
VIA APPIA NUOVA
V. D. ALMONE
VIALE
V. DI TORRE SPACCATA
S. SEBASTIANO
TOMBA DI CECÍLIA METELLA
CIRCO DI MASSÉNZIO
Áppio Pignatelli
PIGNATELLI
Cinecittà
Ardeatino
ARDEATINA
APPIA ANTICA
ABBAZIA D. TRE FONTANE
CARBONE
VIA DI VIGNA MURATA
VIA DI TOR
LAURENTINA
Castél di Leva
SANTUÁRIO DEL DIVINO AMORE

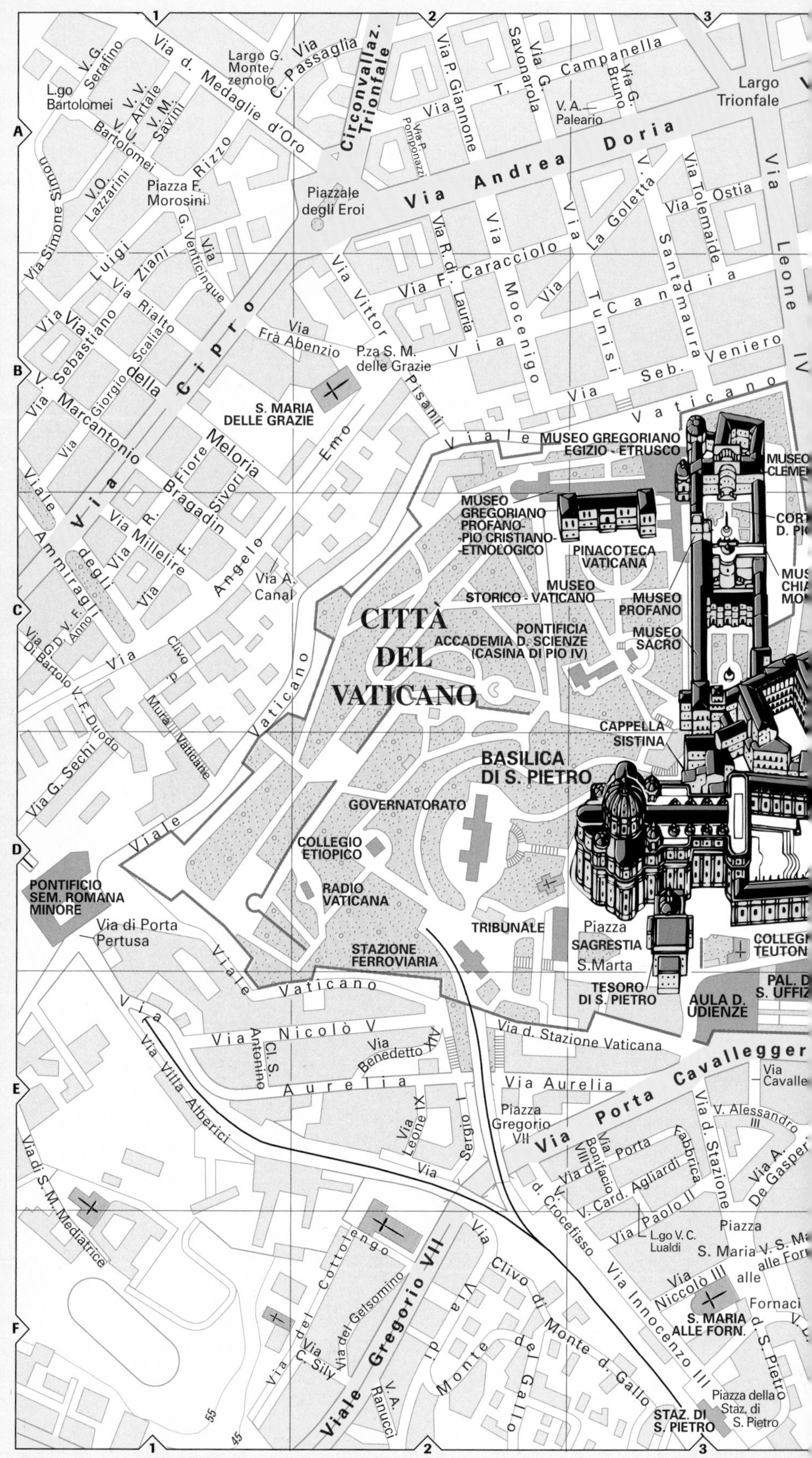

CITTÀ DEL VATICANO
S. MARIA DELLE GRAZIE
MUSEO GREGORIANO EGIZIO - ETRUSCO
MUSEO GREGORIANO PROFANO-PIO CRISTIANO-ETNOLOGICO
PINACOTECA VATICANA
MUSEO STORICO - VATICANO
MUSEO PROFANO
MUSEO SACRO
PONTIFICIA ACCADEMIA D. SCIENZE (CASINA DI PIO IV)
CAPPELLA SISTINA
BASILICA DI S. PIETRO
GOVERNATORATO
COLLEGIO ETIOPICO
RADIO VATICANA
TRIBUNALE
STAZIONE FERROVIARIA
Piazza S.Marta
SAGRESTIA
TESORO DI S. PIETRO
AULA D. UDIENZE
PONTIFICIO SEM. ROMANA MINORE
S. MARIA ALLE FORN.
STAZ. DI S. PIETRO
Piazza della Staz. di S. Pietro
Via Andrea Doria
Via Cipro
Viale Vaticano
Via Aurelia
Via Porta Cavalleggeri
Viale Gregorio VII
Circonvallaz. Trionfale
Largo Trionfale
Piazzale degli Eroi
Piazza F. Morosini
Via d. Medaglie d'Oro
Via Candia
Via Leone IV
Via Sebastiano Veniero
Via d. Stazione Vaticana
Via Innocenzo III
Clivo di Monte d. Gallo
Via Nicolò V
Via Leone XIII
Piazza Gregorio VII

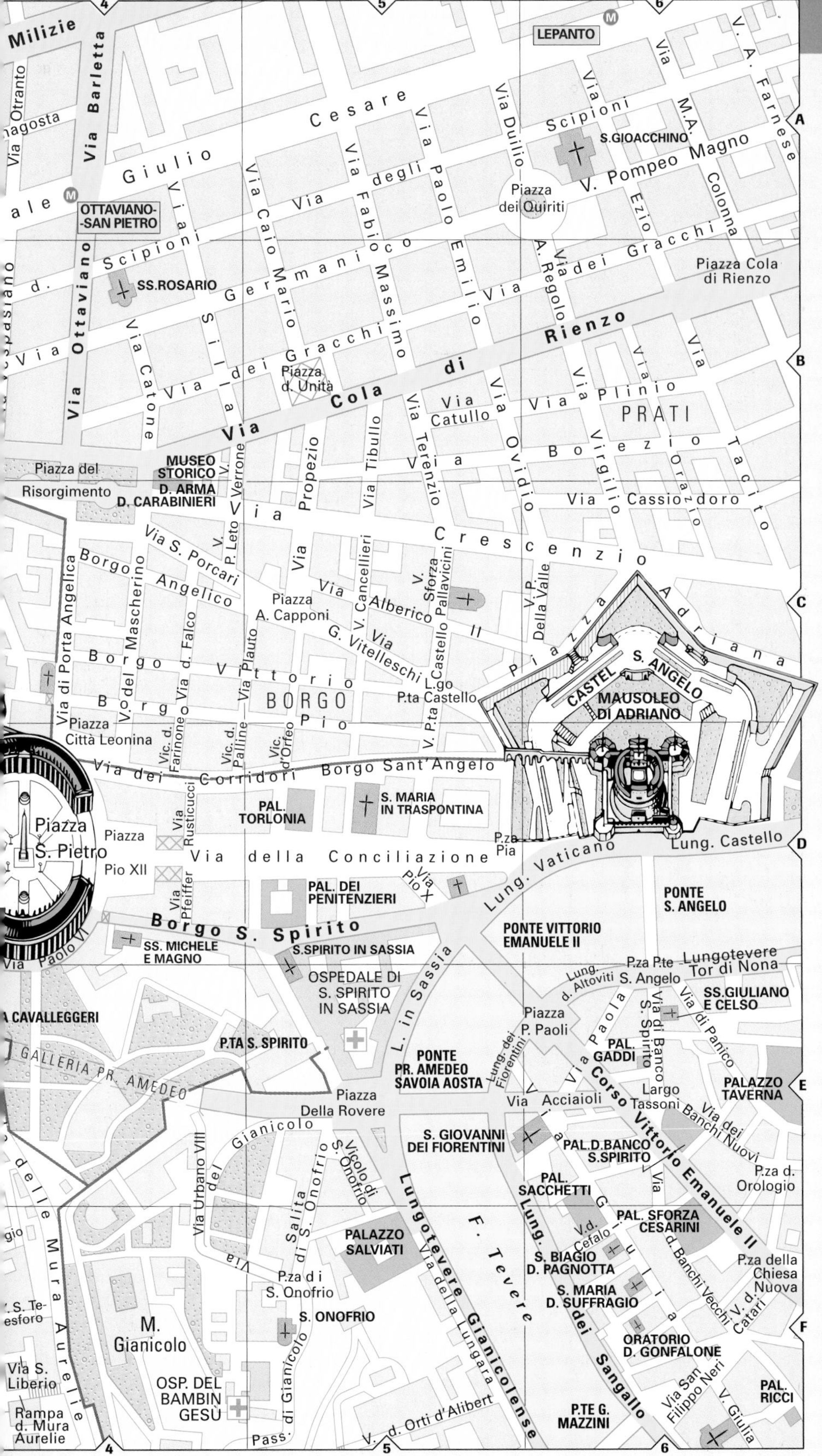

LEPANTO
OTTAVIANO-SAN PIETRO
S.GIOACCHINO
SS.ROSARIO
Piazza dei Quiriti
Piazza Cola di Rienzo
Via Cola di Rienzo
Piazza d. Unità
PRATI
Piazza del Risorgimento
MUSEO STORICO D. ARMA D. CARABINIERI
Via Crescenzio
Piazza A. Capponi
BORGO
L.go P.ta Castello
CASTEL S. ANGELO
MAUSOLEO DI ADRIANO
Piazza Adriana
Piazza Città Leonina
Via dei Corridori
Borgo Sant'Angelo
Piazza S. Pietro
Piazza Pio XII
PAL. TORLONIA
S. MARIA IN TRASPONTINA
Via della Conciliazione
P.za Pia
Lung. Vaticano
Lung. Castello
PAL. DEI PENITENZIERI
PONTE S. ANGELO
Borgo S. Spirito
SS. MICHELE E MAGNO
S.SPIRITO IN SASSIA
PONTE VITTORIO EMANUELE II
OSPEDALE DI S. SPIRITO IN SASSIA
Lungotevere Tor di Nona
SS.GIULIANO E CELSO
CAVALLEGGERI
P.TA S. SPIRITO
GALLERIA PR. AMEDEO
PONTE PR. AMEDEO SAVOIA AOSTA
Piazza P. Paoli
PAL. GADDI
PALAZZO TAVERNA
Piazza Della Rovere
Corso Vittorio Emanuele II
S. GIOVANNI DEI FIORENTINI
PAL.D.BANCO S.SPIRITO
PAL. SACCHETTI
P.za d. Orologio
PALAZZO SALVIATI
PAL. SFORZA CESARINI
S. BIAGIO D. PAGNOTTA
P.za della Chiesa Nuova
S. MARIA D. SUFFRAGIO
F. Tevere
Lungotevere Gianicolense
Lung. dei Sangallo
P.za d i S. Onofrio
S. ONOFRIO
M. Gianicolo
ORATORIO D. GONFALONE
OSP. DEL BAMBIN GESÙ
PAL. RICCI
P.TE G. MAZZINI
Via della Lungara
V. d. Orti d'Alibert
Via S. Liberio
Rampa d. Mura Aurelie
Via delle Mura Aurelie

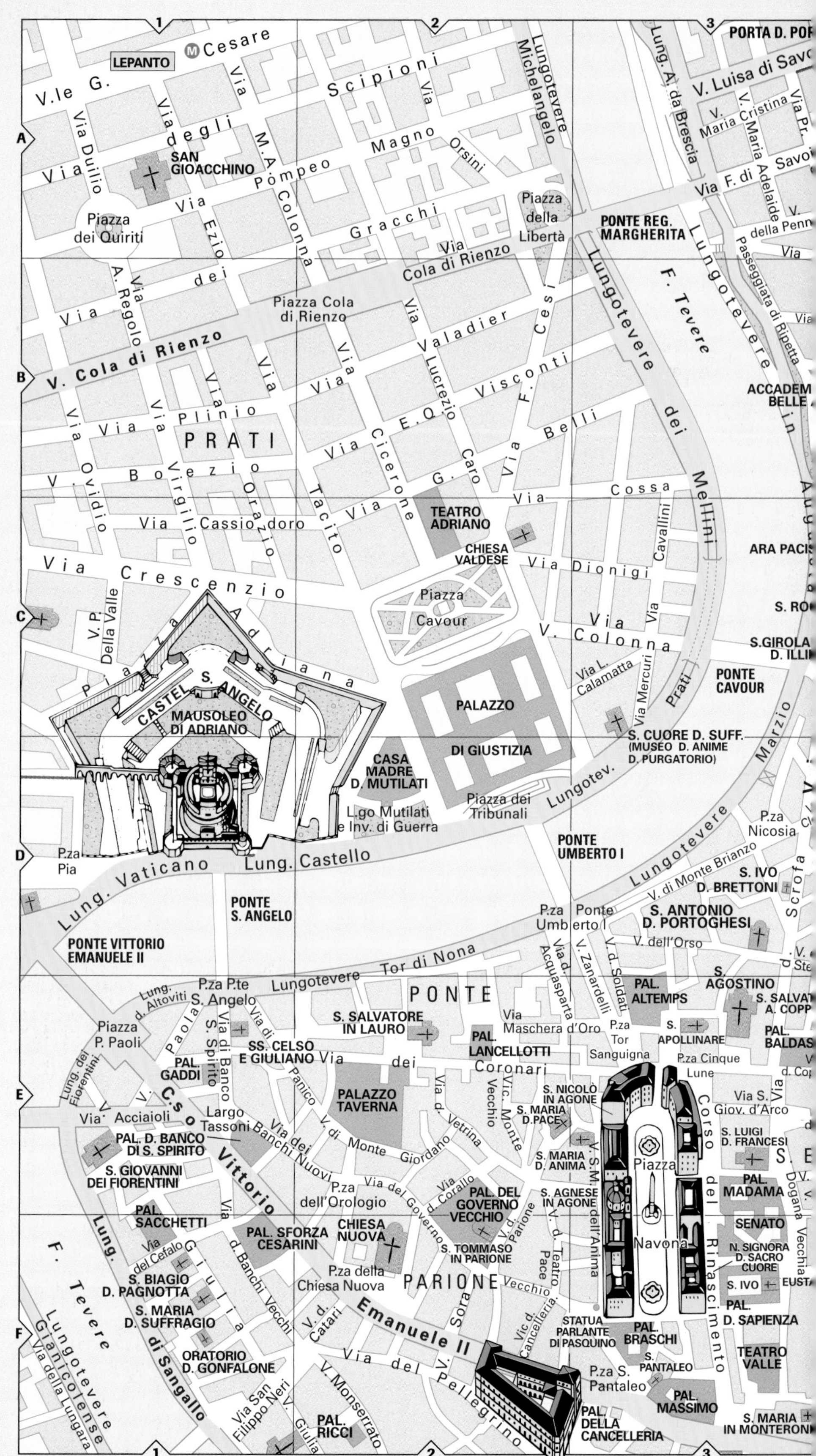
LEPANTO
Cesare
V.le G.
Via degli Scipioni
Via Duilio
SAN GIOACCHINO
Via Pompeo Magno
Via M.A. Colonna
Via Orsini
Lungotevere Michelangelo
Lung. A. da Brescia
PORTA D. POP
V. Luisa di Savoia
V. Maria Cristina
V. Maria Adelaide
Via F. di Savoia
Piazza dei Quiriti
Via Ezio
Via Gracchi
Piazza della Libertà
PONTE REG. MARGHERITA
V. della Penna
Passeggiata di Ripetta
Via Cola di Rienzo
Via dei
Via A. Regolo
Piazza Cola di Rienzo
F. Tevere
Lungotevere
V. Cola di Rienzo
Via Valadier
Via F. Cesi
Via Visconti
Lungotevere dei Mellini
ACCADEM BELLE
Via Plinio
PRATI
Via Lucrezio
Via E.Q.
Via Belli
Via Cicerone
V. Ovidio
Via Bo ezio
Via Virgilio
Via Orazio
Via Tacito
Via G. Caro
Via Cossa
TEATRO ADRIANO
Via Cassiodoro
CHIESA VALDESE
Via Cavallini
ARA PACIS
Via Crescenzio
Via Dionigi
Piazza Cavour
V. Colonna
S. ROC
V.P. Della Valle
Piazza Adriana
S.GIROLA D. ILLI
CASTEL S. ANGELO
MAUSOLEO DI ADRIANO
PALAZZO DI GIUSTIZIA
Via L. Calamatta
Via Mercuri
Prati
PONTE CAVOUR
S. CUORE D. SUFF. (MUSEO D. ANIME D. PURGATORIO)
CASA MADRE D. MUTILATI
Lungotev.
Marzio
Piazza dei Tribunali
L.go Mutilati e Inv. di Guerra
P.za Nicosia
P.za Pia
Lung. Vaticano
Lung. Castello
PONTE UMBERTO I
Lungotevere
V. di Monte Brianzo
S. IVO D. BRETTONI
Scrofa
PONTE S. ANGELO
P.za Umberto I
Ponte Umberto I
S. ANTONIO D. PORTOGHESI
V. dell'Orso
PONTE VITTORIO EMANUELE II
Via d. Acquasparta
V. Zanardelli
V. d. Soldati
Lungotevere Tor di Nona
Lung. d. Altoviti
P.za P.te S. Angelo
PONTE
PAL. ALTEMPS
S. AGOSTINO
S. SALVAT A. COPP
Piazza P. Paoli
Paola
Via S. Spirito
Via di Banco
S. SALVATORE IN LAURO
Via Maschera d'Oro
P.za Tor Sanguigna
S. APOLLINARE
PAL. BALDAS
PAL. GADDI
SS. CELSO E GIULIANO
Via dei Coronari
PAL. LANCELLOTTI
P.za Cinque Lune
Lung. dei Fiorentini
Via di Panico
PALAZZO TAVERNA
Via d. Vetrina
Vic. Vecchio
Vic. Monte
S. NICOLÒ IN AGONE
S. MARIA D.PACE
Via S. Giov. d'Arco
Corso del Rinascimento
Via Acciaioli
Largo Tassoni
Via dei Banchi Nuovi
V. di Monte Giordano
C.so Vittorio
PAL. D. BANCO DI S. SPIRITO
S. LUIGI D. FRANCESI
S. MARIA D. ANIMA
V. S.M. dell'Anima
Piazza Navona
S. GIOVANNI DEI FIORENTINI
P.za dell'Orologio
Via del Governo Vecchio
Via d. Corallo
PAL. DEL GOVERNO VECCHIO
S. AGNESE IN AGONE
PAL. MADAMA
Dogana Vecchia
PAL. SACCHETTI
PAL. SFORZA CESARINI
CHIESA NUOVA
V. d. Parione
V. d. Teatro Pace
SENATO
Via del Cefalo
Via d. Banchi Vecchi
S. TOMMASO IN PARIONE
N. SIGNORA D. SACRO CUORE
Lung. F. Tevere
S. BIAGIO D. PAGNOTTA
Giulia
P.za della Chiesa Nuova
PARIONE
Vecchio
S. IVO
EUSTA
S. MARIA D. SUFFRAGIO
V. d. Catari
Sora
Vic. d. Cancelleria
STATUA PARLANTE DI PASQUINO
PAL. BRASCHI
PAL. D. SAPIENZA
Lungotevere Gianicolense
Via della Lungara
ORATORIO D. GONFALONE
Emanuele II
Via del Pellegrino
S. PANTALEO
TEATRO VALLE
Via di Sangallo
P.za S. Pantaleo
PAL. MASSIMO
Via San Filippo Neri
V. Giulia
V. Monserrato
PAL. RICCI
PAL. DELLA CANCELLERIA
S. MARIA IN MONTERONI

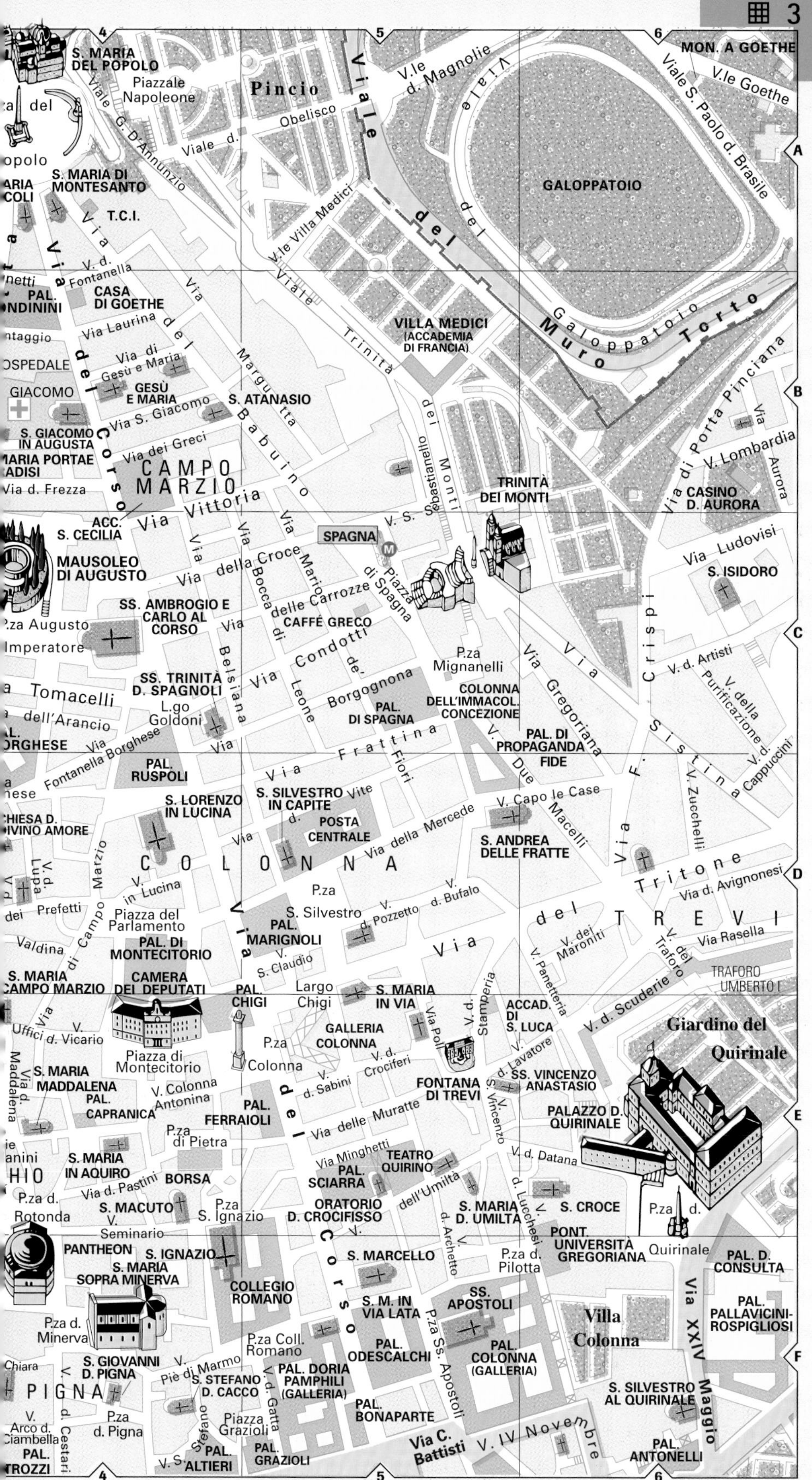
S. MARIA DEL POPOLO
Piazzale Napoleone
Pincio
Viale del Muro Torto
GALOPPATOIO
MON. A GOETHE
VILLA MEDICI (ACCADEMIA DI FRANCIA)
TRINITÀ DEI MONTI
SPAGNA
MAUSOLEO DI AUGUSTO
CAMPO MARZIO
COLONNA
TREVI
S. ISIDORO
CASINO D. AURORA
Via Vittoria
Via Condotti
Via del Corso
Via del Babuino
Via Sistina
Via del Tritone
FONTANA DI TREVI
PAL. DI MONTECITORIO
CAMERA DEI DEPUTATI
PAL. CHIGI
GALLERIA COLONNA
Piazza Colonna
PANTHEON
S. IGNAZIO
S. MARIA SOPRA MINERVA
COLLEGIO ROMANO
PAL. DORIA PAMPHILI (GALLERIA)
PAL. COLONNA (GALLERIA)
SS. APOSTOLI
PALAZZO D. QUIRINALE
Giardino del Quirinale
Villa Colonna
PAL. D. CONSULTA
PAL. PALLAVICINI-ROSPIGLIOSI
Via XXIV Maggio
V. IV Novembre
Via C. Battisti
PAL. BONAPARTE
PONT. UNIVERSITÀ GREGORIANA
S. ANDREA DELLE FRATTE
PAL. DI PROPAGANDA FIDE
COLONNA DELL'IMMACOL. CONCEZIONE
PAL. DI SPAGNA
CAFFÈ GRECO
S. SILVESTRO IN CAPITE
POSTA CENTRALE
S. LORENZO IN LUCINA
PAL. RUSPOLI
Piazza di Spagna
TRAFORO UMBERTO I

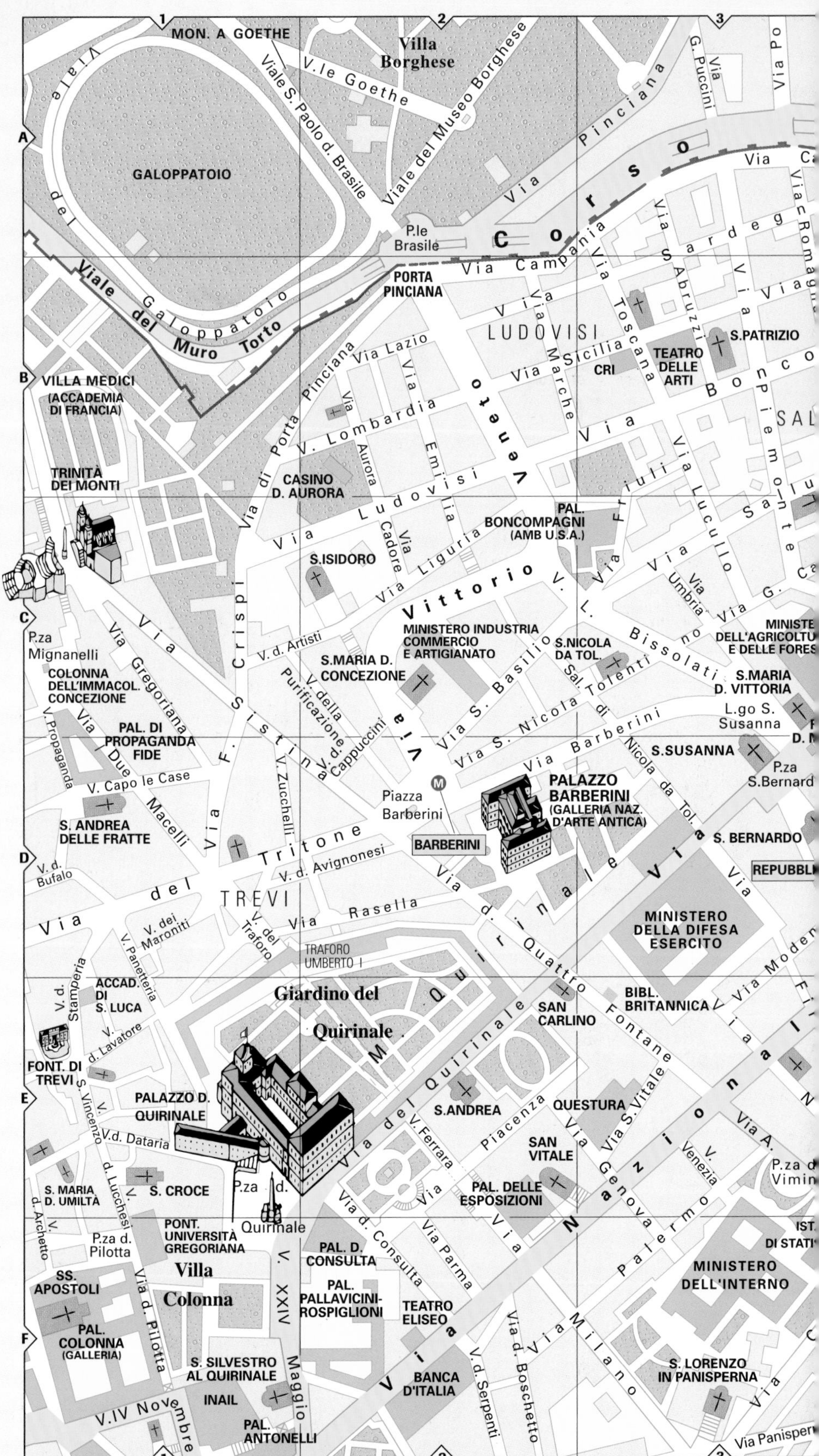

MON. A GOETHE
Villa Borghese
V.le Goethe
Viale S. Paolo d. Brasile
Viale del Museo Borghese
GALOPPATOIO
P.le Brasile
Corso
Via Pinciana
Viale del Muro Torto
Viale Galoppatoio
PORTA PINCIANA
Via Campania
LUDOVISI
VILLA MEDICI (ACCADEMIA DI FRANCIA)
TRINITÀ DEI MONTI
CASINO D. AURORA
Via Veneto
Via Lombardia
Via Ludovisi
PAL. BONCOMPAGNI (AMB U.S.A.)
S.ISIDORO
Vittorio
S.PATRIZIO
TEATRO DELLE ARTI
CRI
P.za Mignanelli
COLONNA DELL'IMMACOL. CONCEZIONE
PAL. DI PROPAGANDA FIDE
MINISTERO INDUSTRIA COMMERCIO E ARTIGIANATO
S.MARIA D. CONCEZIONE
S.NICOLA DA TOL.
S.MARIA D. VITTORIA
L.go S. Susanna
S.SUSANNA
P.za S.Bernardo
S. ANDREA DELLE FRATTE
Piazza Barberini
BARBERINI
PALAZZO BARBERINI (GALLERIA NAZ. D'ARTE ANTICA)
S. BERNARDO
REPUBBL
Via del Tritone
TREVI
Via Rasella
TRAFORO UMBERTO I
MINISTERO DELLA DIFESA ESERCITO
ACCAD. DI S. LUCA
Giardino del Quirinale
SAN CARLINO
BIBL. BRITANNICA
FONT. DI TREVI
PALAZZO D. QUIRINALE
S.ANDREA
QUESTURA
SAN VITALE
Via Nazionale
S. MARIA D. UMILTÀ
S. CROCE
P.za d. Quirinale
PAL. DELLE ESPOSIZIONI
PONT. UNIVERSITÀ GREGORIANA
P.za d. Pilotta
SS. APOSTOLI
Villa Colonna
PAL. D. CONSULTA
PAL. PALLAVICINI-ROSPIGLIONI
TEATRO ELISEO
MINISTERO DELL'INTERNO
PAL. COLONNA (GALLERIA)
S. SILVESTRO AL QUIRINALE
INAIL
BANCA D'ITALIA
PAL. ANTONELLI
S. LORENZO IN PANISPERNA
V.IV Novembre
Via Milano
Via Panisperna

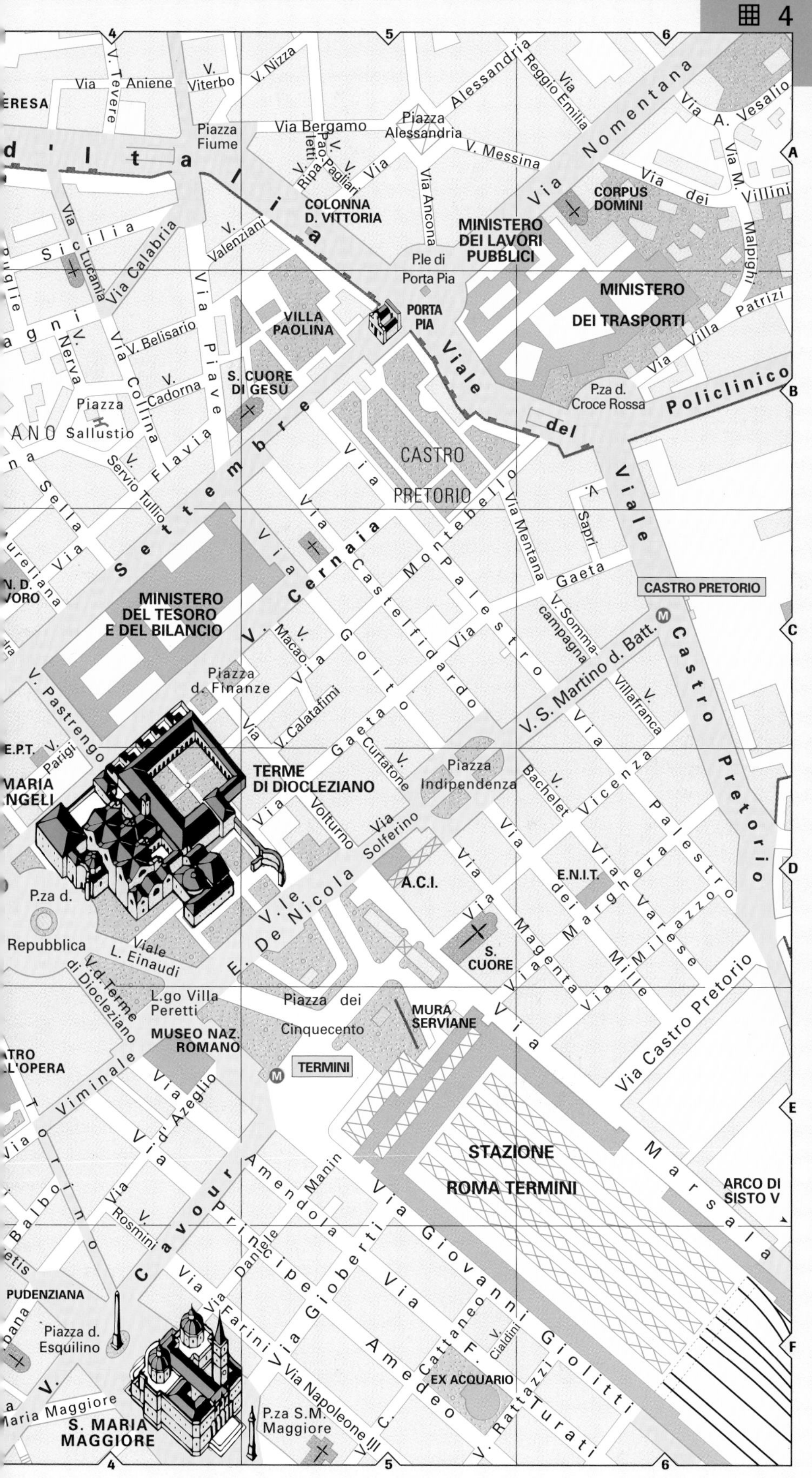

PORTA PIA
VILLA PAOLINA
COLONNA D. VITTORIA
MINISTERO DEI LAVORI PUBBLICI
CORPUS DOMINI
MINISTERO DEI TRASPORTI
S. CUORE DI GESÙ
CASTRO PRETORIO
MINISTERO DEL TESORO E DEL BILANCIO
TERME DI DIOCLEZIANO
A.C.I.
E.N.I.T.
S. CUORE
MURA SERVIANE
MUSEO NAZ. ROMANO
TERMINI
STAZIONE ROMA TERMINI
ARCO DI SISTO V
EX ACQUARIO
PUDENZIANA
S. MARIA MAGGIORE
Piazza Fiume
Piazza Alessandria
P.le di Porta Pia
P.za d. Croce Rossa
Piazza Sallustio
Piazza d. Finanze
Piazza Indipendenza
P.za d. Repubblica
Piazza dei Cinquecento
L.go Villa Peretti
Piazza d. Esquilino
P.za S.M. Maggiore
Via Nomentana
Viale del Policlinico
Viale Castro Pretorio
Via XX Settembre
Via Cernaia
Via Goito
Via Palestro
Via Montebello
Via Castelfidardo
Via Volturno
Via Solferino
Via Vicenza
Via Marsala
Via Giovanni Giolitti
Via Principe Amedeo
Via Cavour
Via Viminale
Via Torino
Via Gioberti
Via Farini
Via Napoleone III
Via Castro Pretorio
Via Magenta
Via Milazzo
Via Varese
Via dei Mille
Via Gaeta
Via Mentana
Via Piave
Via Collina
Via Flavia
Via Sicilia
Via Calabria
Via Alessandria
Via Bergamo
Via Messina
Via Ancona
Viale L. Einaudi
V. Pastrengo
V.le E. De Nicola
Via Amendola
Via Manin
Via d'Azeglio
Via dei Villini
Via M. Malpighi
Via A. Vesalio
Via Villa Patrizi
CASTRO PRETORIO

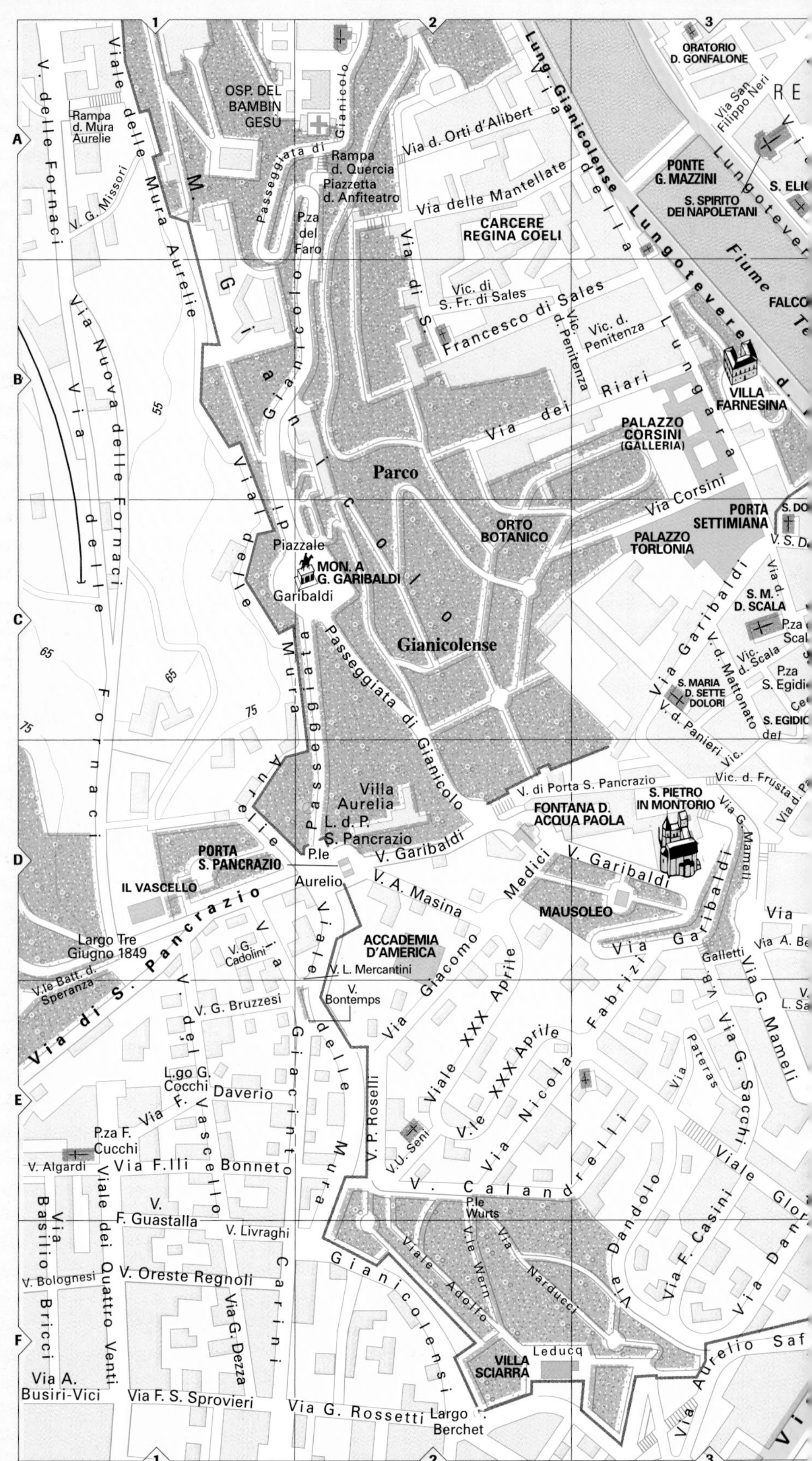
OSP. DEL BAMBIN GESU
Rampa d. Mura Aurelie
Viale delle Mura Aurelie
V. delle Fornaci
V. G. Missori
Passeggiata di Gianicolo
Rampa d. Quercia
Piazzetta d. Anfiteatro
P.za del Faro
Via d. Orti d'Alibert
Via delle Mantellate
CARCERE REGINA COELI
Lung. Gianicolense
Via della Lungara
ORATORIO D. GONFALONE
Via San Filippo Neri
PONTE G. MAZZINI
S. SPIRITO DEI NAPOLETANI
S. ELI
Lungotevere
Fiume Tevere
FALCO
Via di S. Francesco di Sales
Vic. di S. Fr. di Sales
Vic. d. Penitenza
Vic. d. Penitenza
Via dei Riari
VILLA FARNESINA
PALAZZO CORSINI (GALLERIA)
Via Corsini
PORTA SETTIMIANA
S. DO
V. S. D.
PALAZZO TORLONIA
ORTO BOTANICO
Parco Gianicolense
Via Nuova delle Fornaci
Via delle Fornaci
Via Gianicolo
Viale delle Mura Aurelie
Piazzale Garibaldi
MON. A G. GARIBALDI
Passeggiata di Gianicolo
Passeggiata
S. M. D. SCALA
P.za d. Scala
Vic. d. Scala
Via Garibaldi
V. d. Mattonato
P.za S. Egidio
S. MARIA D. SETTE DOLORI
S. EGIDIO
V. d. Panieri
Vic. d. Frusta
Vic.
V. di Porta S. Pancrazio
S. PIETRO IN MONTORIO
Via G. Mameli
FONTANA D. ACQUA PAOLA
Villa Aurelia
L. d. P. S. Pancrazio
P.le Aurelio
V. Garibaldi
PORTA S. PANCRAZIO
IL VASCELLO
V. A. Masina
Medici
MAUSOLEO
Via Garibaldi
Via A. Be
Galletti
Largo Tre Giugno 1849
Via di S. Pancrazio
V.le Batt. d. Speranza
V. G. Cadolini
Viale delle Mura Gianicolensi
ACCADEMIA D'AMERICA
V. L. Mercantini
V. Bontemps
Via Giacomo
Viale XXX Aprile
V. G. Bruzzesi
Via del Vascello
Via Giacinto Carini
V.le XXX Aprile
Via Nicola Fabrizi
Via Pateras
Via G. Sacchi
Via G. Mameli
V. L. Sa
L.go G. Cocchi
Via F. Daverio
V. P. Roselli
V.U. Seni
P.za F. Cucchi
V. Algardi
Via F.lli Bonnet
Viale dei Quattro Venti
V. F. Guastalla
V. Livraghi
V. Calandrelli
P.le Wurts
V.le Wern
Via Narducci
Viale Adolfo
Via Dandolo
Via F. Casini
Viale Glori
Via Dan
Via Basilio Bricci
V. Bolognesi
V. Oreste Regnoli
Via G. Dezza
Gianicolensi
VILLA SCIARRA
Leducq
Via Aurelio Saffi
Via A. Busiri-Vici
Via F. S. Sprovieri
Via G. Rossetti
Largo G. Berchet
55
65
65
75
75
A
B
C
D
E
F
1
2
3

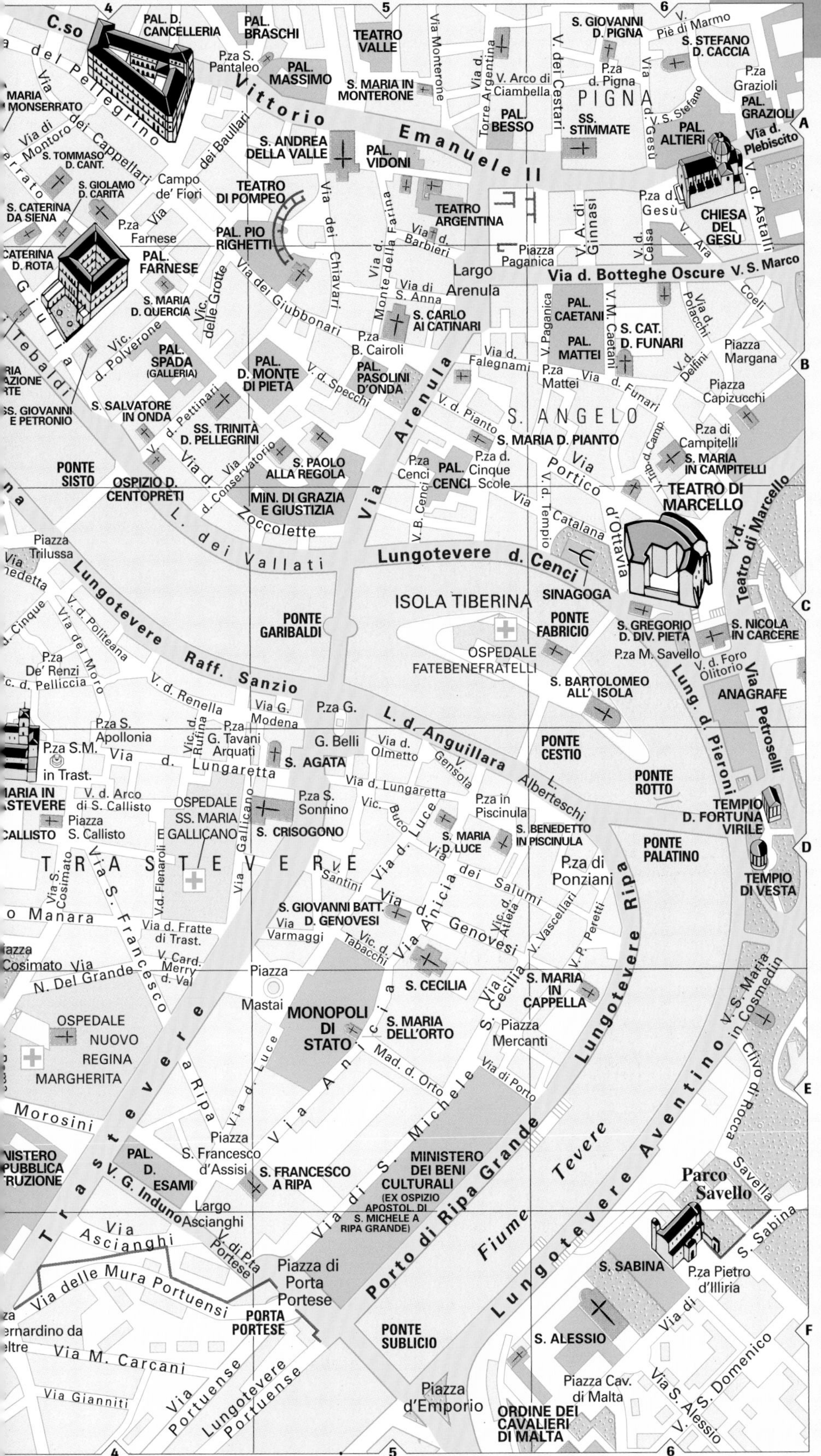

4
5
6
A
B
C
D
E
F
C.so Vittorio Emanuele II
PAL. D. CANCELLERIA
PAL. BRASCHI
TEATRO VALLE
Via Monterone
S. GIOVANNI D. PIGNA
V. Piè di Marmo
S. STEFANO D. CACCIA
Via del Pellegrino
P.za S. Pantaleo
PAL. MASSIMO
S. MARIA IN MONTERONE
Via d. Torre Argentina
V. Arco di Ciambella
V. dei Cestari
P.za d. Pigna
PIGNA
Via d. Gesù
P.za Grazioli
PAL. GRAZIOLI
MARIA MONSERRATO
Via dei Cappellari
Via di Montoro
V.S. Stefano
PAL. ALTIERI
Via d. Plebiscito
PAL. BESSO
SS. STIMMATE
S. ANDREA DELLA VALLE
PAL. VIDONI
Via dei Baullari
S. TOMMASO D. CANT.
S. GIOLAMO D. CARITA
Campo de' Fiori
TEATRO DI POMPEO
Via dei Chiavari
TEATRO ARGENTINA
V. A. di Ginnasi
P.za d. Gesù
CHIESA DEL GESÙ
V. d. Astalli
S. CATERINA DA SIENA
P.za Farnese
PAL. PIO RIGHETTI
Via d. Monte della Farina
Via d. Barbieri
Piazza Paganica
V. d. Celsa
V. Ara Coeli
CATERINA D. ROTA
PAL. FARNESE
Via dei Giubbonari
Largo Arenula
Via d. Botteghe Oscure
V. S. Marco
Via Giulia
S. MARIA D. QUERCIA
Vic. delle Grotte
Via di S. Anna
S. CARLO AI CATINARI
V. Paganica
PAL. CAETANI
V.M. Caetani
S. CAT. D. FUNARI
Via d. Polacchi
Via Tebaldi
Vic. d. Polverone
PAL. SPADA (GALLERIA)
PAL. D. MONTE DI PIETÀ
P.za B. Cairoli
PAL. PASOLINI D'ONDA
Via d. Falegnami
PAL. MATTEI
P.za Mattei
Via d. Funari
V. d. Delfini
Piazza Margana
Piazza Capizucchi
V. d. Specchi
SS. GIOVANNI E PETRONIO
S. SALVATORE IN ONDA
Via d. Pettinari
SS. TRINITÀ D. PELLEGRINI
Via Arenula
V. d. Pianto
S. ANGELO
S. MARIA D. PIANTO
P.za di Campitelli
S. MARIA IN CAMPITELLI
PONTE SISTO
OSPIZIO D. CENTOPRETI
Via d. Conservatorio
S. PAOLO ALLA REGOLA
MIN. DI GRAZIA E GIUSTIZIA
P.za Cenci
PAL. CENCI
P.za d. Cinque Scole
Via Portico d'Ottavia
TEATRO DI MARCELLO
V. d. Teatro di Marcello
Via d. Zoccolette
V. B. Cenci
V. d. Tempio
Via Catalana
Piazza Trilussa
L. dei Vallati
Lungotevere d. Cenci
SINAGOGA
ISOLA TIBERINA
PONTE GARIBALDI
PONTE FABRICIO
S. GREGORIO D. DIV. PIETÀ
S. NICOLA IN CARCERE
Lungotevere Raff. Sanzio
OSPEDALE FATEBENEFRATELLI
P.za M. Savello
V. d. Foro Olitorio
Via Petroselli
V. d. Politeana
Via del Moro
P.za De' Renzi
V. d. Renella
S. BARTOLOMEO ALL' ISOLA
ANAGRAFE
Lung. d. Pierleoni
P.za S. Apollonia
Via G. Modena
P.za G. G. Belli
L. d. Anguillara
Vic. d. Rufina
P.za G. Tavani Arquati
P.za S.M. in Trast.
Via d. Lungaretta
S. AGATA
Via d. Olmetto
V. Gensola
L. Alberteschi
PONTE CESTIO
PONTE ROTTO
MARIA IN TRASTEVERE
V. d. Arco di S. Callisto
OSPEDALE SS. MARIA E GALLICANO
P.za S. Sonnino
Via d. Lungaretta
P.za in Piscinula
TEMPIO D. FORTUNA VIRILE
Piazza S. Callisto
S. CRISOGONO
Vic. Buco
Via d. Luce
S. MARIA D. LUCE
S. BENEDETTO IN PISCINULA
PONTE PALATINO
TRASTEVERE
Via S. Cosimato
V.d. Flenaroli
Via dei Salumi
P.za di Ponziani
TEMPIO DI VESTA
Via S. Francesco
V. Santini
Via Ripa
Via Manara
S. GIOVANNI BATT. D. GENOVESI
Via Anicia
Via d. Genovesi
Vic. d. Atleta
V. Vascellari
V. P. Peretti
Via d. Fratte di Trast.
Via Varmaggi
Vic. d. Tabacchi
Piazza Cosimato
Via N. Del Grande
V. Card. Merry d. Val
Piazza Mastai
S. CECILIA
Via Cecilia
S. MARIA IN CAPPELLA
Lungotevere Ripa
V. S. Maria in Cosmedin
OSPEDALE NUOVO REGINA MARGHERITA
MONOPOLI DI STATO
S. MARIA DELL'ORTO
Piazza Mercanti
Mad. d. Orto
Via di Porto
Clivo di Rocca Savella
Via Morosini
Viale Trastevere
Via d. Luce
Via a Ripa
Via S. Michele
Lungotevere Aventino
Piazza S. Francesco d'Assisi
PAL. D. ESAMI
S. FRANCESCO A RIPA
MINISTERO DEI BENI CULTURALI (EX OSPIZIO APOSTOL. DI S. MICHELE A RIPA GRANDE)
Porto di Ripa Grande
Fiume Tevere
Parco Savello
V. G. Induno
Largo Ascianghi
Via Ascianghi
V. di Pta Portese
Via di S. Sabina
Via delle Mura Portuensi
Piazza di Porta Portese
S. SABINA
P.za Pietro d'Illiria
PORTA PORTESE
PONTE SUBLICIO
S. ALESSIO
Via M. Carcani
Via Portuense
Lungotevere Portuense
Piazza d'Emporio
Piazza Cav. di Malta
Via S. Alessio
V. S. Domenico
Via Giannitti
ORDINE DEI CAVALIERI DI MALTA

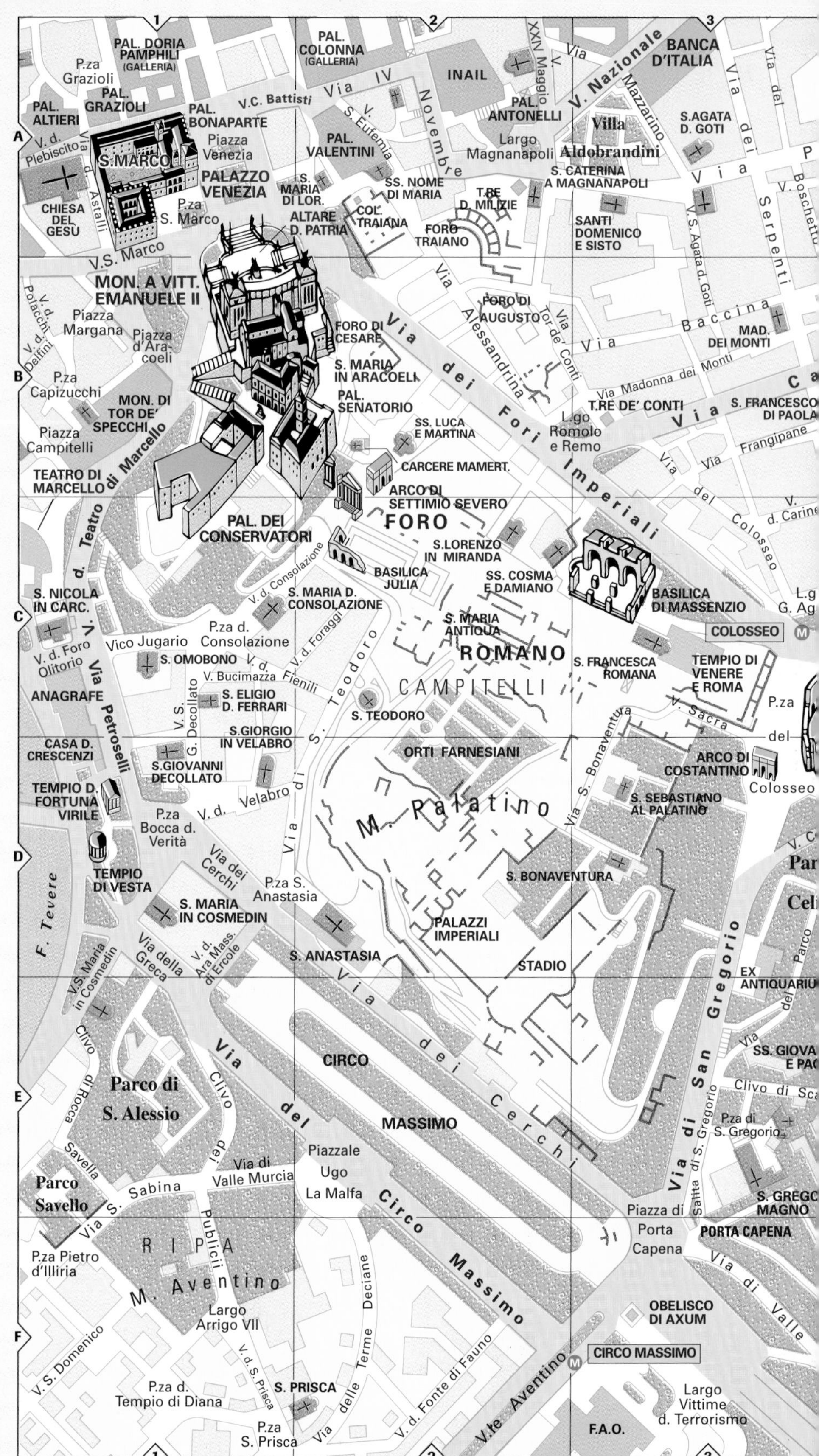
PAL. DORIA PAMPHILI (GALLERIA)
PAL. COLONNA (GALLERIA)
BANCA D'ITALIA
INAIL
P.za Grazioli
PAL. GRAZIOLI
PAL. ALTIERI
PAL. BONAPARTE
PAL. ANTONELLI
Villa Aldobrandini
S.AGATA D. GOTI
S.MARCO
Piazza Venezia
PAL. VALENTINI
Largo Magnanapoli
PALAZZO VENEZIA
S. CATERINA A MAGNANAPOLI
CHIESA DEL GESÙ
P.za S. Marco
S. MARIA DI LOR.
SS. NOME DI MARIA
T.RE D. MILIZIE
ALTARE D. PATRIA
COL. TRAIANA
FORO TRAIANO
SANTI DOMENICO E SISTO
MON. A VITT. EMANUELE II
FORO DI AUGUSTO
Piazza Margana
Piazza d'Ara-coeli
FORO DI CESARE
MAD. DEI MONTI
S. MARIA IN ARACOELI
PAL. SENATORIO
P.za Capizzucchi
MON. DI TOR DE' SPECCHI
T.RE DE' CONTI
S. FRANCESCO DI PAOLA
SS. LUCA E MARTINA
L.go Romolo e Remo
Piazza Campitelli
CARCERE MAMERT.
TEATRO DI MARCELLO
ARCO DI SETTIMIO SEVERO
FORO
PAL. DEI CONSERVATORI
S.LORENZO IN MIRANDA
BASILICA JULIA
SS. COSMA E DAMIANO
BASILICA DI MASSENZIO
S. NICOLA IN CARC.
S. MARIA D. CONSOLAZIONE
S. MARIA ANTIQUA
COLOSSEO
P.za d. Consolazione
ROMANO
Vico Jugario
S. OMOBONO
S. FRANCESCA ROMANA
TEMPIO DI VENERE E ROMA
ANAGRAFE
CAMPITELLI
S. ELIGIO D. FERRARI
S. TEODORO
S.GIORGIO IN VELABRO
CASA D. CRESCENZI
ORTI FARNESIANI
ARCO DI COSTANTINO
S.GIOVANNI DECOLLATO
Colosseo
TEMPIO D. FORTUNA VIRILE
S. SEBASTIANO AL PALATINO
M. Palatino
P.za Bocca d. Verità
TEMPIO DI VESTA
S. BONAVENTURA
P.za S. Anastasia
S. MARIA IN COSMEDIN
PALAZZI IMPERIALI
S. ANASTASIA
STADIO
EX ANTIQUARIU
F. Tevere
CIRCO
SS. GIOVA E PA
Parco di S. Alessio
MASSIMO
P.za di S. Gregorio
Piazzale Ugo La Malfa
Parco Savello
S. GREGO MAGNO
Piazza di Porta Capena
PORTA CAPENA
RIPA
P.za Pietro d'Illiria
M. Aventino
Largo Arrigo VII
OBELISCO DI AXUM
CIRCO MASSIMO
S. PRISCA
P.za d. Tempio di Diana
Largo Vittime d. Terrorismo
P.za S. Prisca
F.A.O.
Via dei Fori Imperiali
Via del Circo Massimo
Via dei Cerchi
Via di San Gregorio
V.le Aventino
Via del Teatro di Marcello
Via Petroselli
V. Nazionale
Via IV Novembre
A B C D E F
1 2 3

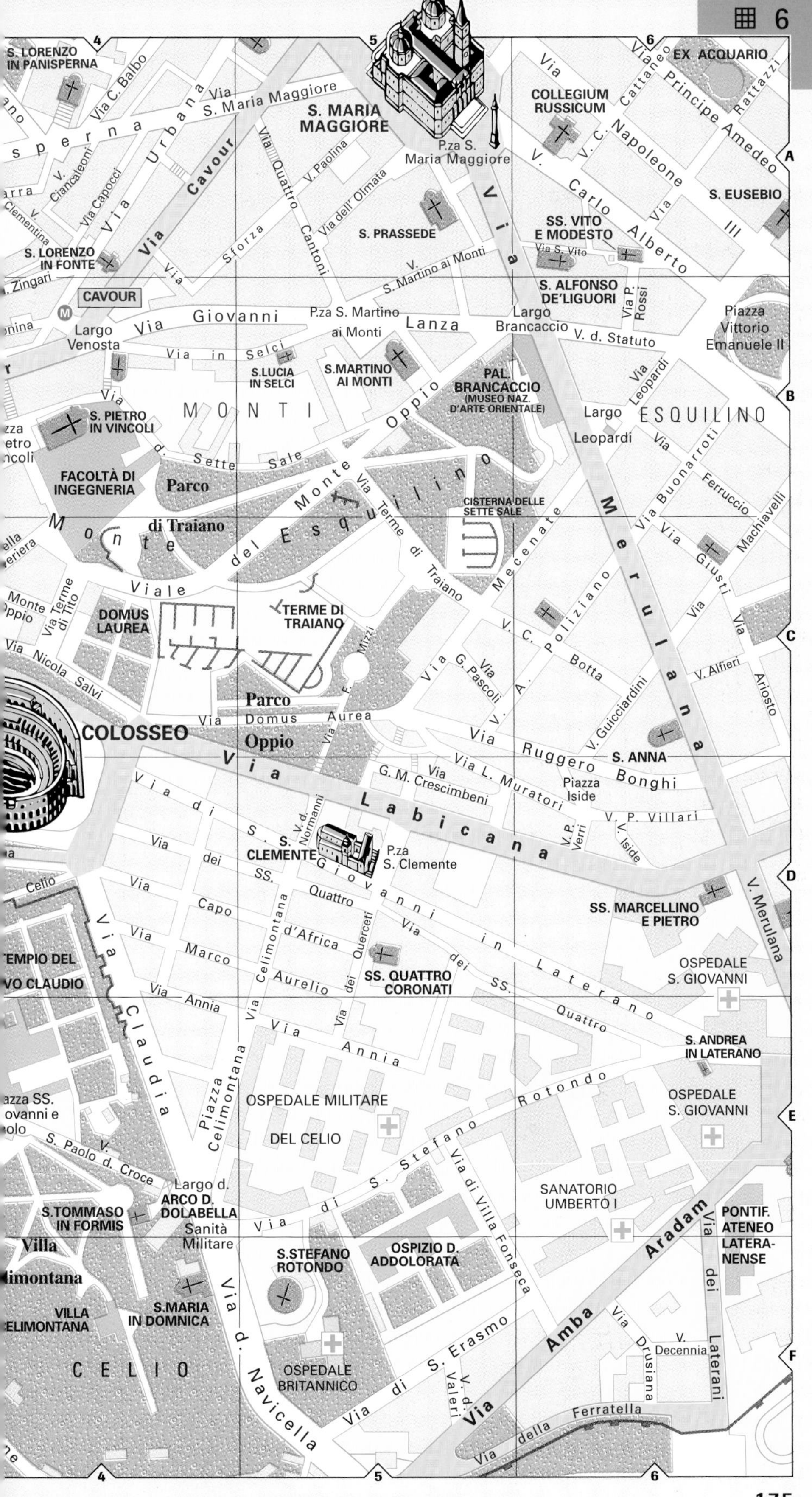
S. MARIA MAGGIORE
P.za S. Maria Maggiore
S. LORENZO IN PANISPERNA
COLLEGIUM RUSSICUM
EX ACQUARIO
S. PRASSEDE
SS. VITO E MODESTO
S. EUSEBIO
S. LORENZO IN FONTE
CAVOUR
S. ALFONSO DE'LIGUORI
P.za S. Martino ai Monti
Largo Brancaccio
Piazza Vittorio Emanuele II
Largo Venosta
S.LUCIA IN SELCI
S.MARTINO AI MONTI
PAL. BRANCACCIO (MUSEO NAZ. D'ARTE ORIENTALE)
Largo Leopardi
S. PIETRO IN VINCOLI
MONTI
ESQUILINO
FACOLTÀ DI INGEGNERIA
Parco di Traiano
CISTERNA DELLE SETTE SALE
DOMUS LAUREA
TERME DI TRAIANO
Parco Domus Oppio
COLOSSEO
S. ANNA
Piazza Iside
S. CLEMENTE
P.za S. Clemente
SS. MARCELLINO E PIETRO
OSPEDALE S. GIOVANNI
SS. QUATTRO CORONATI
S. ANDREA IN LATERANO
OSPEDALE MILITARE DEL CELIO
Piazza Celimontana
SANATORIO UMBERTO I
Largo d. ARCO D. DOLABELLA
S.TOMMASO IN FORMIS
Sanità Militare
PONTIF. ATENEO LATERANENSE
Villa Celimontana
S.STEFANO ROTONDO
OSPIZIO D. ADDOLORATA
VILLA CELIMONTANA
S.MARIA IN DOMNICA
CELIO
OSPEDALE BRITANNICO
Via Cavour
Via Merulana
Via Labicana
Via Giovanni Lanza
Via Carlo Alberto
Via Amba Aradam
Via Claudia
Via d. Navicella
Viale del Monte Oppio
Via di S. Stefano Rotondo
Via di S. Giovanni in Laterano
Via della Ferratella

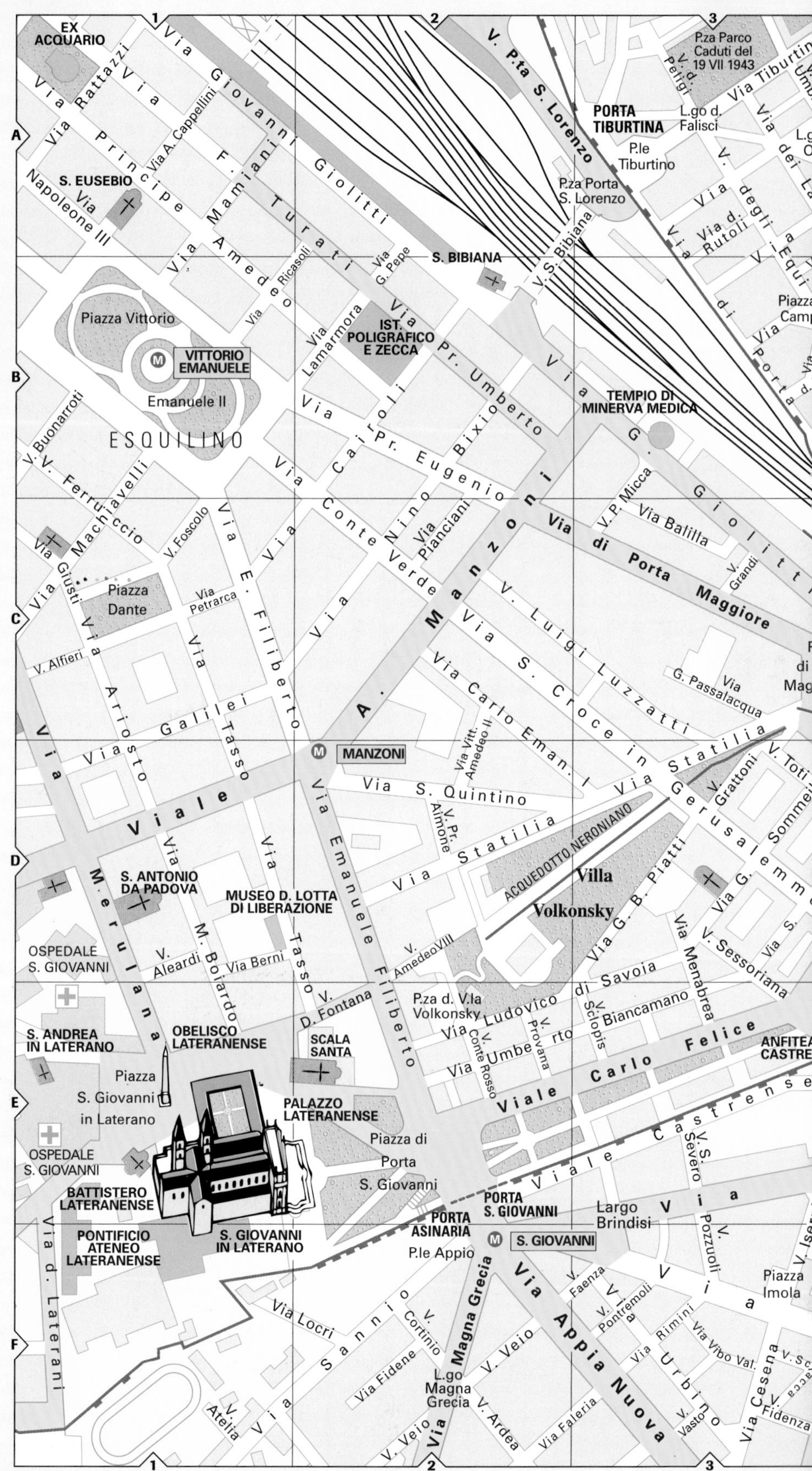

EX ACQUARIO
PORTA TIBURTINA
S. EUSEBIO
S. BIBIANA
IST. POLIGRAFICO E ZECCA
VITTORIO EMANUELE
Piazza Vittorio Emanuele II
ESQUILINO
TEMPIO DI MINERVA MEDICA
Piazza Dante
MANZONI
S. ANTONIO DA PADOVA
MUSEO D. LOTTA DI LIBERAZIONE
Villa Volkonsky
ACQUEDOTTO NERONIANO
OSPEDALE S. GIOVANNI
S. ANDREA IN LATERANO
OBELISCO LATERANENSE
SCALA SANTA
PALAZZO LATERANENSE
Piazza S. Giovanni in Laterano
Piazza di Porta S. Giovanni
BATTISTERO LATERANENSE
PONTIFICIO ATENEO LATERANENSE
S. GIOVANNI IN LATERANO
PORTA ASINARIA
PORTA S. GIOVANNI
S. GIOVANNI
ANFITEATRO CASTRENSE
Largo Brindisi
P.le Appio
L.go Magna Grecia
Piazza Imola
Via Giovanni Giolitti
Via Principe Amedeo
Via F. Turati
Via Pr. Umberto
Via Merulana
Viale Manzoni
Via A. Manzoni
Via Emanuele Filiberto
Via di Porta Maggiore
Via S. Croce in Gerusalemme
Viale Carlo Felice
Viale Castrense
Via Appia Nuova
Via Magna Grecia
Via Sannio
Via Statilia
Via Carlo Eman. I
Via Conte Verde
Via Cairoli
Via Nino Bixio
Via Ludovico di Savoia
Via Umberto Biancamano
Via d. Laterani
V. Pta S. Lorenzo

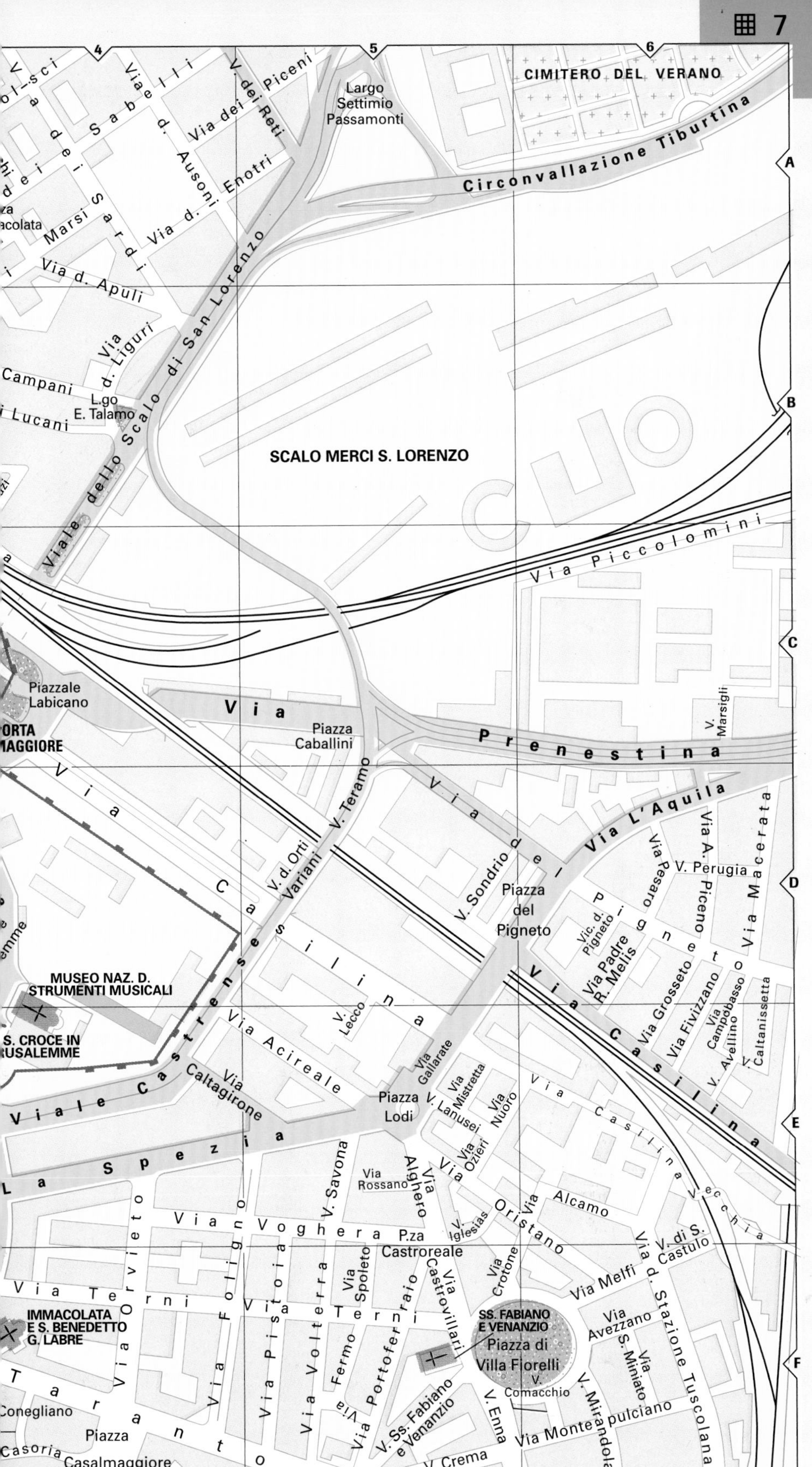
CIMITERO DEL VERANO
Largo Settimio Passamonti
Circonvallazione Tiburtina
Via dei Piceni
V. dei Reti
Via d. Enotri
Via d. Ausoni
Viale d. Sabelli
Via dei Sardi
Via d. Marsi
Via d. Apuli
Via d. Liguri
Campani
L.go E. Talamo
Lucani
Viale dello Scalo di San Lorenzo
SCALO MERCI S. LORENZO
Via Piccolomini
Piazzale Labicano
PORTA MAGGIORE
Via Prenestina
Piazza Caballini
V. Marsigli
V. Teramo
Via del Pigneto
Via L'Aquila
V. Sondrio
Piazza del Pigneto
Via Pesaro
V. Perugia
Via A. Piceno
Via Macerata
Vic. d. Pigneto
Via Padre R. Melis
Via Grosseto
Via Fivizzano
Via Campobasso
V. Caltanissetta
V. Avellino
Via Casilina
V. d. Orti Variani
MUSEO NAZ. D. STRUMENTI MUSICALI
S. CROCE IN GERUSALEMME
Viale Castrense
V. Lecco
Via Acireale
Via Caltagirone
Via La Spezia
Via Gallarate
Via Mistretta
Via Nuoro
Piazza Lodi
V. Lanusei
Via Ozieri
Via Casilina Vecchia
Via Alghero
Via Rossano
V. Savona
Via Oristano
Via Alcamo
V. Iglesias
Via Voghera
P.za Castroreale
Via Orvieto
Via Foligno
Via Pistoia
Via Volterra
Via Spoleto
Via Portoferraio
Via Castrovillari
Via Crotone
Via Melfi
Via d. Stazione Tuscolana
V. di S. Castulo
Via Terni
IMMACOLATA E S. BENEDETTO G. LABRE
SS. FABIANO E VENANZIO
Piazza di Villa Fiorelli
V. Comacchio
Via Avezzano
Via S. Miniato
V. Mirandola
Via Fermo
Via Ss. Fabiano e Venanzio
V. Enna
Via Montepulciano
V. Crema
Via Taranto
Conegliano
Piazza Casalmaggiore
Casoria
Via Sardi
A
B
C
D
E
F
4
5
6

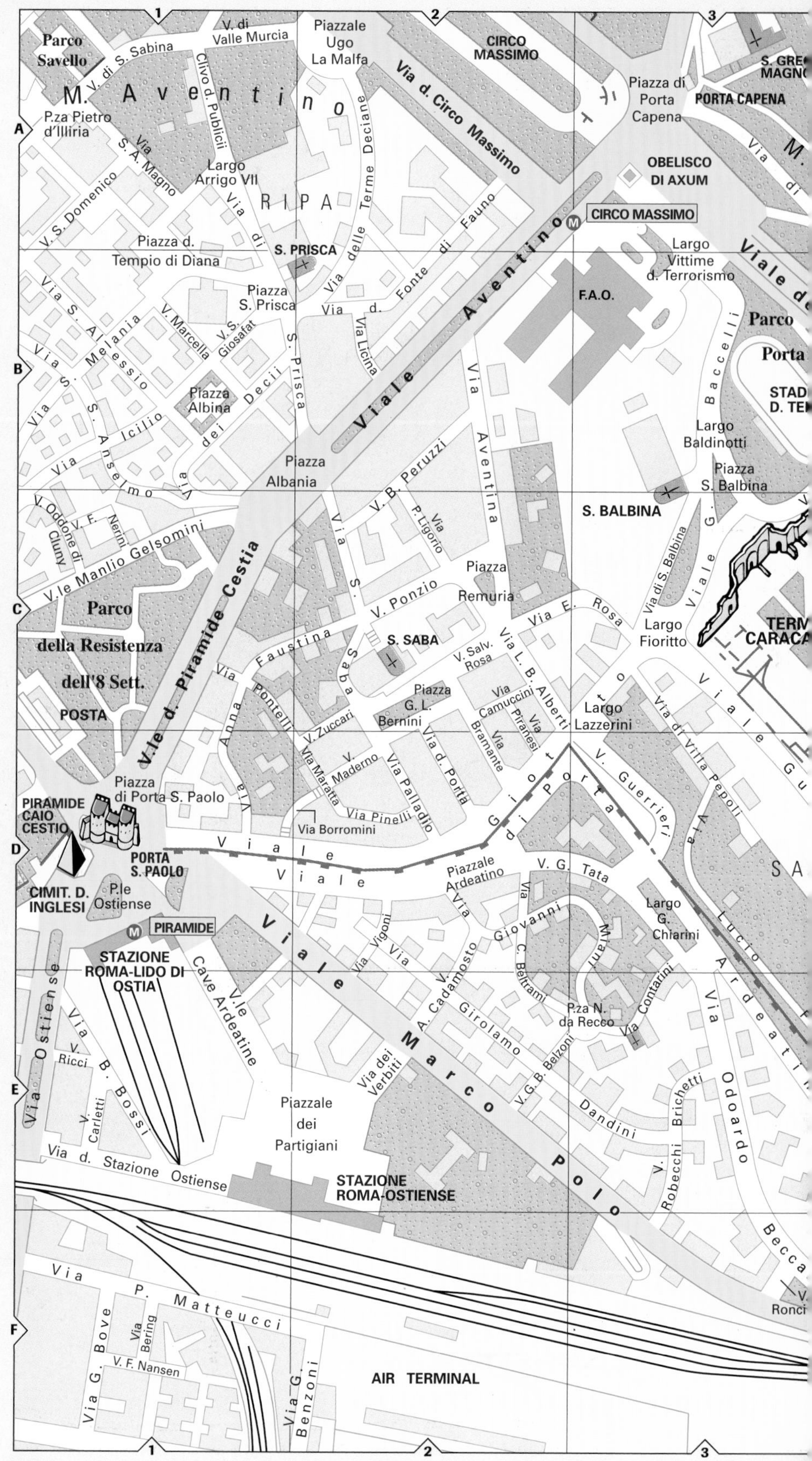
Parco Savello
M. Aventino
RIPA
CIRCO MASSIMO
Piazzale Ugo La Malfa
Via d. Circo Massimo
Piazza di Porta Capena
PORTA CAPENA
OBELISCO DI AXUM
CIRCO MASSIMO
S. PRISCA
Viale Aventino
F.A.O.
Largo Vittime d. Terrorismo
Parco Porta
S. BALBINA
Piazza Albania
Piazza Albina
Piazza S. Prisca
Piazza d. Tempio di Diana
Largo Arrigo VII
P.za Pietro d'Illiria
Parco della Resistenza dell'8 Sett.
POSTA
V.le d. Piramide Cestia
S. SABA
Piazza Remuria
Piazza G. L. Bernini
Largo Fioritto
Largo Lazzerini
TERM CARACA
Piazza di Porta S. Paolo
PIRAMIDE CAIO CESTIO
PORTA S. PAOLO
CIMIT. D. INGLESI
P.le Ostiense
PIRAMIDE
STAZIONE ROMA-LIDO DI OSTIA
Viale Marco Polo
Piazzale Ardeatino
Largo G. Chiarini
P.za N. da Recco
Piazzale dei Partigiani
STAZIONE ROMA-OSTIENSE
Via d. Stazione Ostiense
Via P. Matteucci
AIR TERMINAL
Via Ostiense
Via Odoardo
Largo Baldinotti
Piazza S. Balbina
Viale Giotto
Viale di Porta Ardeatina
Via Guerrieri
Via Giovanni Miani
Via Girolamo Dandini
V. Robecchi Brichetti
Via Ardeatina
V.le Cave Ardeatine

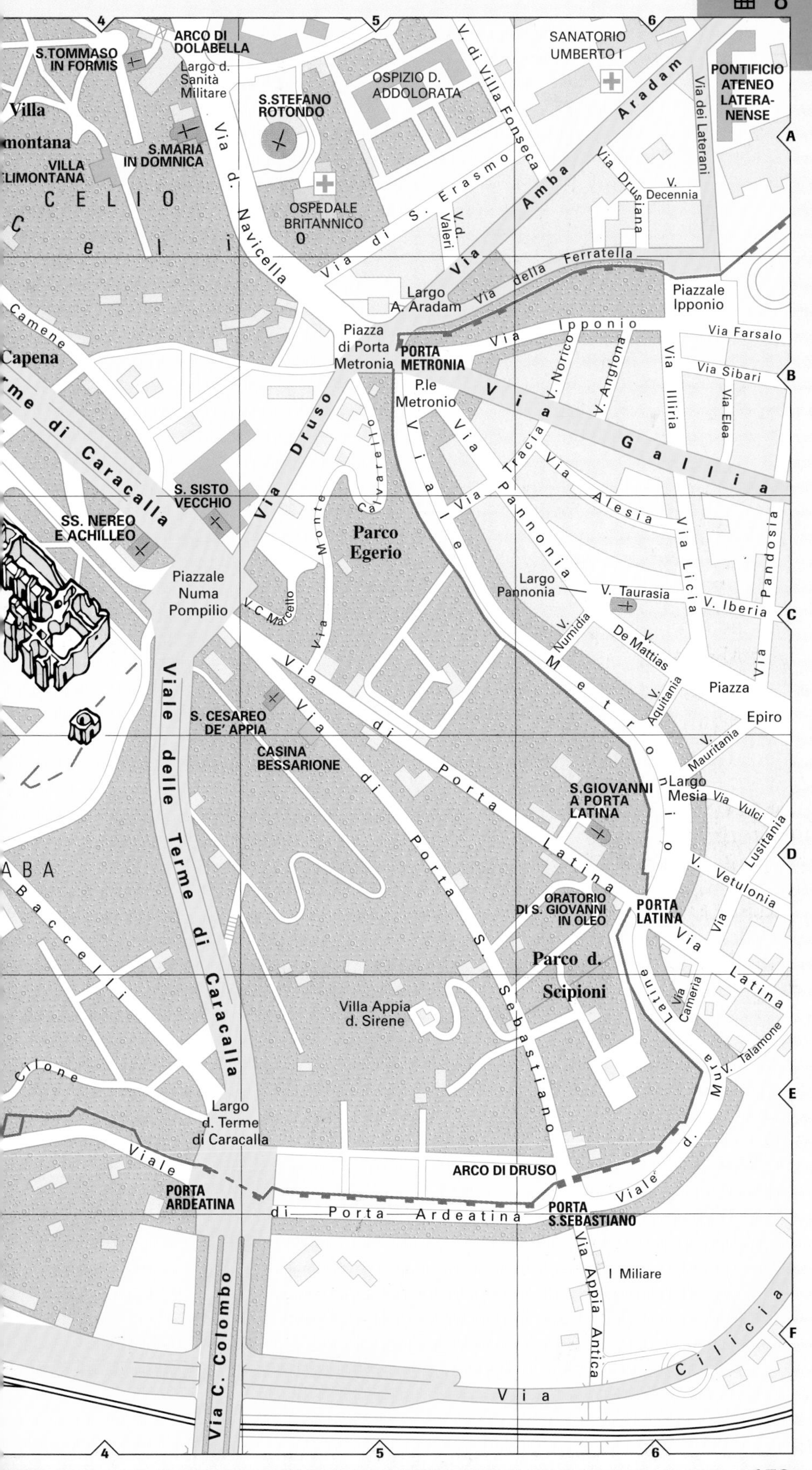
ARCO DI DOLABELLA
S.TOMMASO IN FORMIS
Largo d. Sanità Militare
Villa
montana
VILLA
CELIMONTANA
S.MARIA IN DOMNICA
S.STEFANO ROTONDO
OSPIZIO D. ADDOLORATA
SANATORIO UMBERTO I
PONTIFICIO ATENEO LATERANENSE
Via dei Laterani
Via Amba Aradam
V. di Villa Fonseca
Via d. Navicella
OSPEDALE BRITANNICO
Via di S. Erasmo
V.d. Valeri
Via Drusiana
V. Decennia
CELIO
Via della Ferratella
Piazzale Ipponio
Largo A. Aradam
Piazza di Porta Metronia
PORTA METRONIA
P.le Metronio
Via Ipponio
Via Farsalo
Via Sibari
Via Illiria
Via Elea
V. Norico
V. Anglona
Via Gallia
Camene
Capena
Terme di Caracalla
Via Druso
S. SISTO VECCHIO
SS. NEREO E ACHILLEO
Via Monte Calvarello
Parco Egerio
Viale Metronio
Via Tracia
Via Pannonia
Via Alesia
Via Licia
Via Pandosia
Largo Pannonia
V. Taurasia
V. Iberia
Piazzale Numa Pompilio
V.C Marcello
V. Numidia
V. De Mattias
V. Aquitania
Piazza Epiro
V. Mauritania
Largo Mesia
Via Vulci
Lusitania
Via di Porta Latina
Via di Porta S. Sebastiano
Viale delle Terme di Caracalla
S. CESAREO DE' APPIA
CASINA BESSARIONE
S.GIOVANNI A PORTA LATINA
ORATORIO DI S. GIOVANNI IN OLEO
PORTA LATINA
V. Vetulonia
Via Latina
Parco d. Scipioni
Via Cameria
Villa Appia d. Sirene
V. Talamone
Mura Latine
ABA
Baccelli
Cilone
Largo d. Terme di Caracalla
Viale di Porta Ardeatina
PORTA ARDEATINA
ARCO DI DRUSO
PORTA S.SEBASTIANO
Viale d. Mura
Via Appia Antica
I Miliare
Via C. Colombo
Via Cilicia
A
B
C
D
E
F
4
5
6

PHOTO CREDITS

The churches of S. Andrea al Quirinale, S. Ignazio, S. Maria sopra Minerva, S. Maria della Scala, S. Prassede, S. Pudenziana, S. Sabina, S. Silvestro in Capite, Ss. Cosma e Damiano, Ss. Giovanni e Paolo are owned by the Fondo Edifici di Culto, which is administered by the Department of Interior's Central Office for Religious Affairs. We thank the F.E.C. for providing the necessary permits.

Rome Agency for Jubilee Preparations: 136, 137, 146 right, 148 left (by kind permission of the magazine *Capitolium*)

Marco Anelli (by kind permission of Fabbrica di San Pietro in Vaticano): 145 left

Photographic Archive of the Touring Club Italino: 12, 24 d, 26 top, 30, 32 bottom left, 36 left, 43 top, 43 center, 46–47, 58 left, 58 right, 80 right

Olivo Barbieri from *San Pietro in Vaticano. Emozioni nel tempo*, TCI 1998 (by kind permission of Fabbrica di San Pietro in Vaticano): 5, 22, 28 bottom, 152 left, 153, 156 right

Giancarlo Costa: 34 top, 35 top, 37 top, 38 top, 39 top, 42 bottom, 44 center, 45 top

Aralodo De Luca: 26 bottom left, 26 bottom right, 95, 128, 129, 157 center

Double's: 40, 43 bottom left, 46, 47 bottom

Fototeca Storica Nazionale: 44 right

Il Dagherrotipo: Stefano Chieppa 23 bottom, 35 bottom; Stefano Occhibelli 68 left, 68 right; Giovanni Rinaldi 18 top, 146 left

Marka: Vito Arcomanno 19 bottom, 48; U.P.P.A. 48

Scala: 13, 14 left, 15 top, 16 left, 17, 20 top, 20 bottom, 21 right, 21 bottom, 24 left, 27, 28 left, 33 top, 33 bottom, 41 top, 41 bottom left, 41 bottom right, 42 left, 43 bottom right, 44 left, 45 bottom, 47 top, 57 left, 57 right, 63 right, 64, 85 right, 92 left, 127 right, 130 left, 131, 154 left, 155, 157 left, 157 right

Antonio Sferlazzo: 12 bottom, 38 bottom left, 38 bottom right, 39 bottom, 49, 54 left, 71 left, 72 left

Sime: Johanna Huber 15 bottom, 31, 53, 54 right, 55, 56, 67 right, 74, 92 right, 108 left, 130 right, 132, 133, 134 right; Giovanni Simeone 2–3, 52, 70 left, 70 right, 94, 110, 111, 121 left, 123, 144

Luca Sorrentino (by kind permission of the magazine *Capitolium*): 145 right